Open Innovation and Startups

This book comprehensively discusses the cooperation of corporations with startups in the context of accelerator programs. It focuses on recognizing how open innovation can catalyze startups' development and success, and benefit corporations through access to new business models, innovative products, services and technologies developed outside the R&D departments of large organizations.

This book presents a variety of collaboration models, motivations, barriers and potential for collaboration, offering readers a wealth of theoretical and practical knowledge based on the author's research and experience in managing startup acceleration programs for multinational corporations. Readers will gain insight into the challenges and critical aspects of startup accelerator programs via a detailed analysis of open innovation theory and collaboration strategies. Based on literature and empirical research, the author offers practical guidance on how corporations should prepare and conduct acceleration activities to maximize the potential of innovation from startups and increase the chances of success.

Open Innovation and Startups will appeal to scholars and researchers in the fields of innovation studies, entrepreneurship and organizational studies.

Michał Bańka is a leader in the Polish startup capital investment market and researcher of open innovation, organizational innovation, organizational structures, startup ecosystems, new venture opportunities and organization–environment relations. He is one of Poland's most renowned experts in cooperation between startups, venture capital funds and corporations. He is the founder and manager of a startup accelerator called Accelpoint. His firm services a portfolio of international corporations like AXA, Santander, Orange and PKO BP. Having received a Doctorate degree in economic sciences, specializing in business management, from the Warsaw University of Technology, Michal is currently an Assistant Professor and the Head of Division in the Faculty of Mechanical and Industrial Engineering. He is also a visiting scholar at the Stanford University School of Engineering.

Routledge Open Business and Economics

Routledge Open Business and Economics provides a platform for the open access publication of monographs and edited collections across the full breadth of these disciplines including accounting, finance, management, marketing and political economy. Reflecting our commitment to supporting open access publishing, this series provides a key repository for academic research in business and economics.

Books in the series are published via the Gold Open Access model and are therefore available for free download and re-use according to the terms of Creative Commons licence. They can be accessed via the Routledge and Taylor & Francis website, as well as third party discovery sites such as the Directory of OAPEN Library, Open Access Books, PMC Bookshelf and Google Books.

Note that the other Business and Economics series at Routledge also all accept open access books for publication.

Sensitivity Analysis for Business, Technology, and Policymaking
Made Easy with Simulation Decomposition (SimDec)
Edited by Mariia Kozlova and Julian Scott Yeomans

Corporate Social Responsibility and the Supply Chain
CSR Collaboration with Suppliers
Monika Jedynak

Blockchain Technology in Project Finance
A Legal and Practical Model for Financing Mega-Investments
Witold Srokosz, Paweł Lenio and Grzegorz Sobiecki

Open Innovation and Startups
Michał Bańka

For more information about this series, please visit: https://www.routledge.com/Routledge-Open-Business-and-Economics/book-series/ROBE

Open Innovation and Startups

Michał Bańka

Routledge
Taylor & Francis Group
LONDON AND NEW YORK

First published 2025
by Routledge
4 Park Square, Milton Park, Abingdon, Oxon OX14 4RN

and by Routledge
605 Third Avenue, New York, NY 10158

Routledge is an imprint of the Taylor & Francis Group, an informa business

The publication of the book was subsidised by the Warsaw University of Technology.

British Library Cataloguing-in-Publication Data
A catalogue record for this book is available from the British Library

ISBN: 978-1-032-88920-7 (hbk)
ISBN: 978-1-032-88922-1 (pbk)
ISBN: 978-1-003-54036-6 (ebk)

DOI: 10.4324/9781003540366

Typeset in Sabon
by codeMantra

To my loving wife, children, and entire family

Contents

Figures

Tables

Introduction

In the face of fiercer hyper competition present in many sectors of the economy, dynamic technological growth and the ensuing convergence of industries, it is becoming a more and more comprehensive challenge for businesses to maintain and hone their competitive edge. In this context the concept of open innovation has gained importance and is becoming one of the fundamental terms used in the broadly conceived theory of management. Its scope encompasses new cooperation models, in particular between large organizations (corporations) and recently formed innovative firms (startups) that have unique technological and business solutions. The core assumption underlying this concept is that businesses should not restrict themselves solely to internal research and development (R&D) activities, but should actively search for innovation by collaborating with external partners. That is also why global corporations are more and more frequently positioning cooperation with startups as part of their innovation and growth strategies. The array of this cooperation ranges from loose and informal relations to substantially more compulsory and intensive forms of cooperation.[1]

Even though the managers of large organizations emphasize the availability of funding for innovative and technologically advanced projects, one cannot, however, disregard the overall reduction in available funds and the pressure placed on corporate finance across the value chain. In current business conditions companies are curtailing their experiments with solutions that do not afford grounds for deriving benefits. Focusing on targeted efforts that engender great opportunities for rolling out innovation and maximizing earnings is therefore crucial. At the same time, it is a challenge when managing organizations in the context of value creation, cost effectiveness and rapid adaptation to evolving market conditions. This situation also contributes to higher competition among startups for whom a business partnership with a corporation may determine whether they survive and develop. Corporations that cooperate with startups gain access to innovative products, services and technologies. At the same time, they mitigate financial risk without incurring hefty investment expenditures related to their development as part of their

DOI: 10.4324/9781003540366-1

own R&D activities. In this context the cooperation between corporations and startups has donned a new dimension where both parties strive to attain synergies and reciprocal benefits while attenuating investment risk and the risk of incurring financial losses.

Acceleration programs for startups that foster interactions between the startup community – their innovative products, services and technologies – and corporations constitute a new research area in the field of management. This issue, originally theoretical in nature, is taking on a significant practical dimension. The effectiveness of inter-organizational cooperation is crucial for the adaptation and implementation of the innovative solutions offered by startups within the structures of large entities, their partners and clients. Accordingly, this monograph responds to the growing need for taking a scientific approach to these acceleration programs involving startups and corporations alike in light of open innovation theory. It forms a summary of the Author's body of work who has actively contributed to developing a startup ecosystem in Poland since 2008. His efforts have entailed setting up and managing programs and financial instruments to facilitate the development of startups, seed investments and venture capital. They have focused on supporting the business environment, including higher places of learning, clusters, venture capital/seed capital funds, business angel networks, startup accelerators, loan, surety and guarantee funds and the Warsaw Stock Exchange.

The research problem addressed by this monograph concentrates on analyzing inter-organizational cooperation between corporations and startups in acceleration programs. This monograph's major objective is to systematize and expand knowledge regarding inter-organizational cooperation between corporations and startups in acceleration programs from the vantage point of open innovation theory. This knowledge will be expanded in three crucial areas

1 Specifying how inter-organizational cooperation between startups and corporations in acceleration programs is perceived and analyzing its importance to both parties.
2 Setting goals for cooperation between startups and corporations and the difficulties and challenges encountered accompanied by an analysis of the extent to which the parties achieve their goals in acceleration programs.
3 Identifying the key attributes (predictors) characterizing startups that potentially enhance their chances for successful inter-organizational cooperation in acceleration programs.

Table 0.1 depicts the scope of the problem area and the research goals.

This monograph employs the following research methods:

- review of literature available in the Web of Science and Scopus spanning the years from 2003 to 2022 (up to the end of December) conducted in accordance with the PRISMA methodology (Preferred Reporting Items for Systematic Reviews and Meta-Analyses),

Table 0.1 Scope of the problem area and research goals

Chapter	*Scope of the problem area*	*Research goals*
Chapter 1	Open innovations in the inter-organizational cooperation between corporations and start-ups	1 Defining and explaining the core terms in open and closed innovations. 2 Comparing open and closed innovation along with an analysis of innovation processes. 3 Researching the role of cooperation in the open innovation model, in particular, identifying an organization's motives for undertaking cooperation with external partners while researching the network dimension in approaching cooperation. 4 Discussing prospective obstacles in inter-organizational cooperation under the open innovation model. 5 Researching the potential for cooperation between start-ups and corporations in the open innovation model, including their cooperation strategy. 6 Characterizing the cooperation models between corporations and start-ups in terms of the goals, principles and financial needs. 7 Comprehending how innovation processes are shaped in market models for attracting start-ups to corporations.
Chapter 2	Analyzing the diverse aspects of operations, the models for start-up accelerators, their structures, programs, activities and inter-organizational cooperation at the post-acceleration stage	1 Defining the term and essence of start-up accelerators. 2 Discussing the acceleration program framework encountered. 3 Discussing the operational models for accelerators and start-up acceleration programs. 4 Defining the sources and strategies for funding start-up accelerators. 5 Presenting the phases in the operation of an acceleration program involving corporations. 6 Discussing the forms of inter-organizational cooperation between corporations and start-ups at the post- acceleration stage.
Chapter 3	Research methodology	1 Conducting a thorough review of literature. 2 Defining the research gap. 3 Discussing the applied research approach. 4 Portraying a characterization of the research groups.

(*Continued*)

Table 0.1 (Continued)

Chapter	*Scope of the problem area*	*Research goals*
Chapter 4	Diagnosis and importance of the inter-organizational cooperation between start-ups and corporations in acceleration programs	1 Specifying the essence of start-ups establishing cooperation with corporations while confirming the existence of impediments to achieving that. 2 Specifying the importance of corporations establishing cooperation with start-ups. 3 Specifying the importance of acceleration programs to assist in establishing cooperation between start-ups and corporations. 4 Specifying the importance of acceleration programs to support the implementation of start-ups' solutions in corporations. 5 Verifying whether the participation of start-ups and large organizations in acceleration programs engenders greater benefit than the expenditures incurred to establish and maintain their cooperation.
Chapter 5	The objectives of corporations and start-ups as part of inter-organizational cooperation within acceleration programs, the encountered difficulties and challenges accompanied by an analysis of the degree to which their goals are attained.	1 Specifying the importance of the goals for establishing cooperation guiding start-ups and corporations as part of acceleration programs. 2 Specifying the importance of the difficulties encountered by corporations and start-ups during their cooperation in acceleration programs. 3 Specifying the importance of the challenges encountered by corporations and start-ups when they participate in acceleration programs. 4 Researching whether the assumed goals of cooperation are achieved by the parties as a result of participating in acceleration programs.
Chapter 6	The attributes of start-ups that may potentially contribute to the success of inter-organizational cooperation.	Identifying the key attributes (predictors) characterizing start-ups that may potentially enhance their chances for successful inter-organizational cooperation in acceleration programs as part of six blocks of variables 1 cooperation with a corporation; 2 actions taken and cooperation established; 3 evaluation of the goals of cooperation with a corporation; 4 evaluation of readiness for cooperation with a corporation; 5 founding members' demographic variables; 6 start-up's demographic variables.

Source: Proprietary material.

- analysis of the database of the National Science Center in Cracow with an eye to R&D projects involving startups and accelerators,
- field observations (direct and overt) of startup acceleration programs involving corporations and the results of that cooperation presented at the end of a given round of the acceleration program during demo day. Importantly, the field observations lasted several years to eliminate the impact exerted by irrational enthusiasm for the phenomena under investigation.

For the purpose of precisely investigating this research topic and focusing on the key issues from the vantage point of the business entities taking part in acceleration programs the author administered direct interviews with the representatives of the startups, accelerators and corporations. They pertained to inter-organizational cooperation between businesses as part of the acceleration programs. As a result thereof, a proprietary research tool was developed and subsequently CAWI research was administered among representatives of the startups and corporations. The obtained findings form the basis for some of the meditations in this monograph.

This monograph consists of two major parts. The first part concentrates on theoretical, explanatory and conceptual meditations that are characterized by their reciprocal penetration and the comprehensiveness of the approach. This part forms the theoretical foundation for the overall work and is indispensable to comprehend the topic of managing contemporary organizations in terms of inter-organizational cooperation between corporations, startups and startup accelerators in light of open innovation theory. The second part concentrates on presenting the findings of empirical research. On top of presenting the detailed findings, this part also includes generalized conclusions and their implications for the theory and practice of management. Figure 0.1 schematically depicts the research process and its stages. This illustration facilitates comprehension of the research approach employed and the phases of the undertaken analysis.

The **first chapter** of the monograph conducts a thorough analysis and comparison of two innovation models – open and closed – with consideration given to their characterizations and innovation processes in the context of the operation of businesses. The primary purpose was to provide the reader with an in-depth comprehension of the key differences between these models and build the theoretical basis for further analysis of inter-organizational cooperation between startups and corporations. This chapter depicts in detail the motivations that incline large organizations to get involved in cooperation with external entities. It also identifies the prospective obstacles in their cooperation. Various cooperation models between corporations and startups were discussed, including competitions, hackathons, internet platforms, venture building, strategic partnerships, cooperation with R&D departments, incubators, corporate accelerators, corporate venture capital funds and the acquisition of startups. An analysis of the variety of goals, rules of operation and financial needs related to the foregoing cooperation models has also been presented, which is of crucial significance to gain a

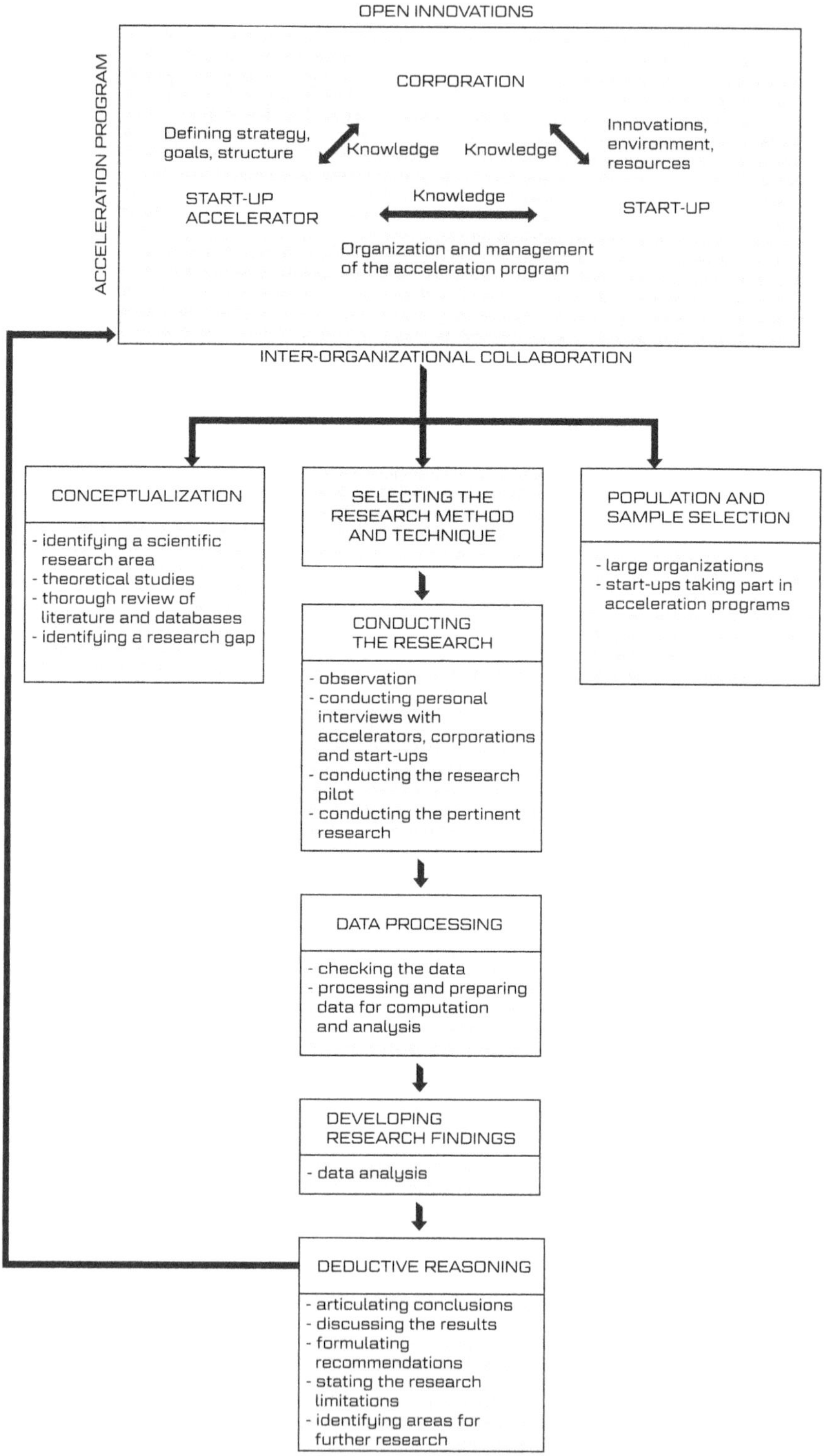

Figure 0.1 Course of the research process

Source: Proprietary material.

grasp of the impact they exert on the effectiveness of inter-organizational cooperation and on innovation processes as part of the open innovation model. The considerations in the **second chapter** are focused on analyzing the key aspects of the frameworks for startup accelerators that form a significant supplement to the issues raised in the first chapter. Kicking off with cooperation between corporations and independent external accelerators, we move from the model for setting up a startup accelerator within a corporation to the model for cooperation between a corporate accelerator and an external startup accelerator separate from a large organization. This analysis pertained to the attributes, advantages and challenges these models have while taking into account the various types of accelerators such as equity accelerators, non-equity accelerators and accelerators operating in a performance-base and hybrid model. In addition, the three major types of acceleration programs were depicted: general and industry-related programs with subject-matter paths. Each one of them features its own unique approach to inter-organizational cooperation and concentration on corporations' needs. The second key aspect for the considerations in this chapter was the discussion of the various procedures for organizing acceleration programs such as on-site, virtual and mixed programs along with their unique pros and cons and the ensuing implications. Special attention was paid to the proprietary analysis of the stages in an acceleration program involving corporations. This analysis spanned stages such as planning, recruiting startups to join a program, preparing for tests and testing solutions in a corporate environment. The subject of inter-organizational cooperation was also taken up following the formal completion of an acceleration program by analyzing possibilities such as equity investments, R&D cooperation, business partnerships and technology licensing. These meditations portray the complexity and dynamism of open innovations in terms of cooperation between corporations and startups. Choosing the right model and acceleration program for attaining effective inter-organizational cooperation takes on special meaning. **Chapter 3** depicts a methodological approach to defining the research gap and the grounds for research regarding inter-organizational cooperation between corporations and startups in acceleration programs. The key element in these considerations was the systematic literature review completed using the PRISMA methodology based on an analysis of two scientific databases: Web of Science and Scopus. A review of the scientific articles in the BazEkon database was conducted and the database containing the grant programs administered by the National Science Center in Cracow was vetted. This stage made it possible not just to identify the current research gap but also to demarcate the avenues for further research work. This chapter ends with a characterization of the two subject groups (startups and large organizations), forming the basis for further detailed analysis of their mutual interactions in the context of inter-organizational cooperation. **Chapter 4** presents findings of empirical research on the analysis into how inter-organizational cooperation in acceleration programs is perceived. Five research topics were investigated to gain an understanding of the interactions between the parties in terms of the importance of establishing cooperation, the importance and significance of acceleration programs and the evaluation of whether the benefits flowing from participating in acceleration programs outweigh the investments incurred by the parties. This purpose was achieved through detailed research from the vantage point of startups and corporations to gain a versatile picture of the impact acceleration programs exert on these two groups. **Chapter 5** expands on the findings of the empirical research presented in the previous chapter. The findings highlighted the significance of acceleration programs, especially when it comes to rolling out innovation and the fact that the benefits ensuing from the established cooperation surpass the expenditures incurred to establish and sustain it. For that reason, this chapter focuses on an in-depth analysis of inter-organizational cooperation between startups and corporations giving consideration to various aspects such as goals, difficulties and the related challenges. An evaluation was subsequently conducted on the extent to which the two parties achieve their intended goals for cooperation as a result of their participation in acceleration programs. **Chapter 6**, the final chapter, deals with identifying the attributes that are characteristic of startups that may contribute to successful cooperation. It is important to be cognizant of these attributes (predictors) on account of their eventual impact on enhancing the effectiveness of cooperation, including the greater opportunities for the parties to attain their intended goals relating to inter-organizational cooperation. Identifying predictors may also accrue other benefits, such as mitigating the risk of unsuccessful cooperation, optimizing the resources provided by accelerators and corporations and growing the value of the acceleration programs pursued by attracting the attention of other startups, corporations and investors. This knowledge will enable corporations and accelerators to select program participants more accurately and will potentially augment the chances for implementing innovation in the community of large organizations. In turn, it will give startups an edge in better preparing themselves to engage in cooperation and curtail possible losses while in some circumstances contributing to higher survival rates.

The **conclusion** contains a composite summary of the key conclusions presented in the previous parts of the monograph. This book explores and does a deep dive to analyze the multi-faceted area of open innovation while focusing on the dynamic and multi-dimensional collaboration between corporations and startups in acceleration programs. The monograph thereby forms a significant contribution to developing literature on the subject matter. Enriches the discussion on the role of open innovation in terms of inter-organizational cooperation between large organizations and startups in acceleration programs.

Note

1 Skala, A. (2018). *Startupy. Wyzwanie dla zarządzania i edukacji przedsiębiorczości*. Kraków: Wydawnictwo edu-Libri.

1 Open innovations

Theoretical and practical treatment of startup acceleration programs

This chapter focuses on two fundamental approaches to innovation in businesses: open and closed. The fundamental concepts of these models were presented while highlighting their unique characteristics and significance in terms of companies' operational strategies. The differences between open and closed innovation were analyzed in detail while paying attention to their processes, management and impact on the operation of organizations in respect of innovation. The processes under investigation were depicted in detail, as were their three types: inbound, outbound and coupled, and the impact they exert on developing and implementing innovation. The later part of the chapter concentrates on the role of an organization's cooperation with other market participants in an open innovation model, while examining a corporation's motivation to get involved in such cooperation and the obstacles to forging inter-organizational partnerships. The growing significance of startups in open innovation, including the strategies for attracting them to corporations and various models of cooperation were also discussed, such as competitions, hackathons, internet platforms, venture building, strategic partnerships, cooperation with research and development (R&D) departments, corporate incubators, corporate accelerators, corporate venture capital (CVC) funds and acquisitions. In terms of the foregoing cooperation models, how the development phases of startups can affect the application of selected models and how innovation processes are shaped in these models were analyzed.

1.1 Concept and essence of open and closed innovations

The term "open innovation" was formally defined and introduced into academic discourse by H.W. Chesbrough. It constitutes a counterweight to the closed innovation approach. Open innovation involves the utilization of ideas, projects and solutions generated inside the company as well as outside the company. It also entails blending internal and external paths and processes for rolling up innovation on the market. This paradigm assumes that firms not only have the ability but also the obligation to incorporate internal and external projects, as well as commercialization paths, into their

DOI: 10.4324/9781003540366-2

own innovation processes.[1,2] Accordingly, open innovations are also linked to not only the target inbound flow of knowledge but also the outbound flow, which contributes to accelerating the creation of innovation, shorter times for marketing new products and services and tweaking the functioning of processes inside organizations. The open approach indicates that businesses should take advantage of solutions originating in their surroundings, and in justified instances seen from the vantage point of corporate development and generating profits, they should also enable other entities to take advantage of their resources and solutions, which they themselves are not fully tapping into at a given moment in time.

In turn, the closed approach to innovation is characterized by having an R&D department in a large organization that is considered to be a key factor contributing to its competitiveness. In this model innovations are related to endeavoring to retaining the greatest degree of control over the innovation process and protecting intellectual property, which is supposed to guarantee a high level of innovation in the solutions construed using in-house resources. The approach to developing internal R&D departments and conducting long-term research programs led to the formation of closed vertical models of innovation processes in which the corporate exerted a dominant impact and in principle ran the process independently. The organization's approach to "closed innovation" was characterized by uncertainty to other available solutions on the market in the context, for instance, of limited trust to the quality and value of the solutions delivered by third parties, or actions of other market participants. That is why the initiated development, financing and commercialization of products, services and technology took place as part of in-house tangible and intangible resources and within the bounds of the organization.[3] The closed model of innovation processes calls for internal control of the process. The generated ideas and projects go through the innovation funnel and are subject to internal evaluations during the course of work on their development. The ones that make it through the selection process and subsequently into internal development can ultimately enter the organization's distribution channel network and be offered to end-users or partners cooperating with a corporation. Figure 1.1 presents a model illustrating closed innovations.

At present, innovation is perceived by businesses as a key indicator of organizational survival and growth. Market growth requires corporations to create radical landmark innovations that are frequently accomplished in partnership with external entities.[4] Landmark innovations are characterized, among other things, by material growth in existing functionalities, significant enhancement of cost effectiveness and higher economic risks and capabilities.[5] However, radical innovation is hard for large corporations to achieve,[6] while possible obstacles for its introduction can be related for instance to the industry in which they operate or the culture of innovation inherent in an organization. The architecture of contemporary business has become complicated and therefore the development of new technologies, methods of

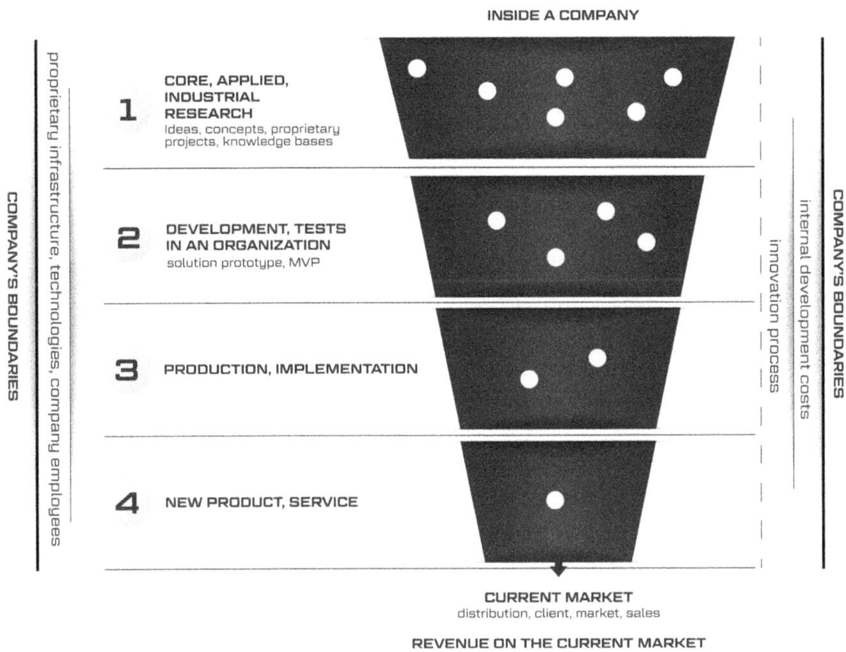

Figure 1.1 Closed innovation model.

Source: Proprietary material based on Chesbrough (2003).

management and the global reach of the Internet have not only accelerated the pace of rolling out innovation but also altered their form and how they are perceived by end-users.[7] At a time when the paradigm for closed innovation has ceased to comport with the current conditions for the operation of businesses on the global market, the need has emerged for altering the approach and being receptive to the open innovation model. Thus, the major underlying causes for switching from a closed innovation model to an open innovation model are as follows[8]:

1 the development of new technologies, especially information and communication technologies and the frequent need to blend different technologies for the purpose of pursuing an innovative process;
2 inexpensive and immediate access to enormous quantities of data, storage space, greater computing capacity, new distribution channels and above all direct access to consumers at any time[9];
3 the advent of new mechanisms and forms of organization and cooperation between businesses, for example, startup accelerators;
4 shortening of the product life cycle, and the high costs of running R&D work;
5 rising mobility on the labor market.

Table 1.1 Selected approach for the open innovation term

Author/year	*Approach*
Chesbrough (2003)	Open innovation means that a business can and should tap into both internal and external projects and ideas in its processes, as well as internal and external paths for rolling innovation out on the market.
Gassmann and Enkel (2004)	Open innovation means an organization is open to innovation and knowledge coming from the outside world. Cooperation with partners, clients and suppliers is important for the purpose of rolling innovation out on the market faster than the competition.
Laursen and Salter (2006)[10]	An organization's openness to innovation is understood to mean the number of external sources of innovative activity in a business. The greater this number, the greater the openness of a business.
West and Gallagher (2006)[11]	Open innovation is considered to entail the actions of a business focused on vetting its own internal and external sources of innovation for the purpose of creating opportunities for the creation of innovation while engaging the resources and paths that are available in an organization.
Dittrich and Duysters (2007)[12]	Open innovation means a firm is open when the innovation development paths lead one to traverse the surpassable bounds of an organization. The entities operating in an organization's surroundings also initiate projects and ideas. In addition, an organization fosters the ability for other market entities to work and utilize the research it has conducted.
Perkman and Walsh (2007)[13]	Open innovation is assumed to be a result ensuing from the cooperation of partners, consortium partners and inter-organizational networks as opposed to just the work of a single organization.
Lichtenthaler (2008)[14]	Open innovation relies on the efficient management of technological undertakings (procurement, operation, sales) run internally and externally in an innovation process.
Chesbrough and Bogers (2014)[15]	Open innovation is a distributed innovation process based on the target management of the flow of knowledge from outside a firm and also from a business to transcend its external boundaries, or in both directions. The flow of knowledge can be for a fee or free of charge according to the strategy adopted and the organization's business model.

Source: Proprietary material based on Gianiodis et al. (2010); Lewandowska (2018).

Various definitions of open innovation can be found in scientific literature. Table 1.1 compiles some of the selected definitions.

Therefore, the key assumption in the approach to open innovation is cooperation among businesses in the market environment, where the development of new products and services calls for varied approaches.[16] To meet the challenges of the contemporary market businesses search for new value creation models that engage market participants in the innovation generation process.[17] This is related to the reciprocal taking of action in driving innovation and making tangible and intangible resources available to the participants in the process. The mere establishment of cooperation is the outcome of circumstances and signals flowing into an organization from other market participants. This calls for corporations to be open to change and poised to undertake the risk of cooperation with entities that frequently are not previous market partners. Undertaking cooperation calls not only for employing more and more sophisticated tools and technologies, but above all for tweaking strategies relating to the approach used by corporations thus far to innovation processes, including the skill of managing such cooperation by its management team.[18] Firms operating in an open innovation model are perceived by the market as the ones that are more open to change. When electing to cooperate with entities operating outside the bounds of a business, an organization is guided by its desire to gain access to new solutions on the market, curtail the risks and capital expenditures related to R&D work, for example, involved with maintaining its own research infrastructure, and endeavoring to reach scale. We can treat the following as belonging to this group of entities: technology transfer centers, research centers, startup accelerators.

As one may observe, the cooperation undertaken has ever greater significance in the operating strategies of businesses as it is more and more difficult to attain success, or retain their market position when acting alone.[19] This is related to technological progress and the capacity to absorb it, changes in the product and service offering for end users, and the number of entities participating in the process of creating innovation and delivering value, which are interconnected by inter-organizational bonds.[20] The mere growth in the significance of cooperation among various entities is currently deemed to be one of the most important developmental trends in the contemporary value creation mechanisms.[21]

Since open innovation is connected to enhancing trust in projects and solutions originating from outside an organization and the varying approach to possible forms and methods of their subsequent commercialization, including the penetration of new markets, the issue of trust should therefore be examined in a multi-dimensional approach.[22, 23] This approach should reference not just credibility and reliability, but also competences, predictability and openness. It is worth observing that trust is important since it constitutes an organizational resource[24] and it defines the readiness to accept another party[25] while it additionally motivates entities to cooperate and brings them closer to one another while stimulating innovative behavior and fosters opportunities for diminishing transactions costs.[26] However, it must be pointed out that excessive trust may exert an adverse impact on innovation processes, as Francis Bidault and Alessio Castello demonstrated in their research. In their opinion, the dearth of in-depth discussion on the projects being undertaken and the effort to accept them quickly may also lead to negative consequences

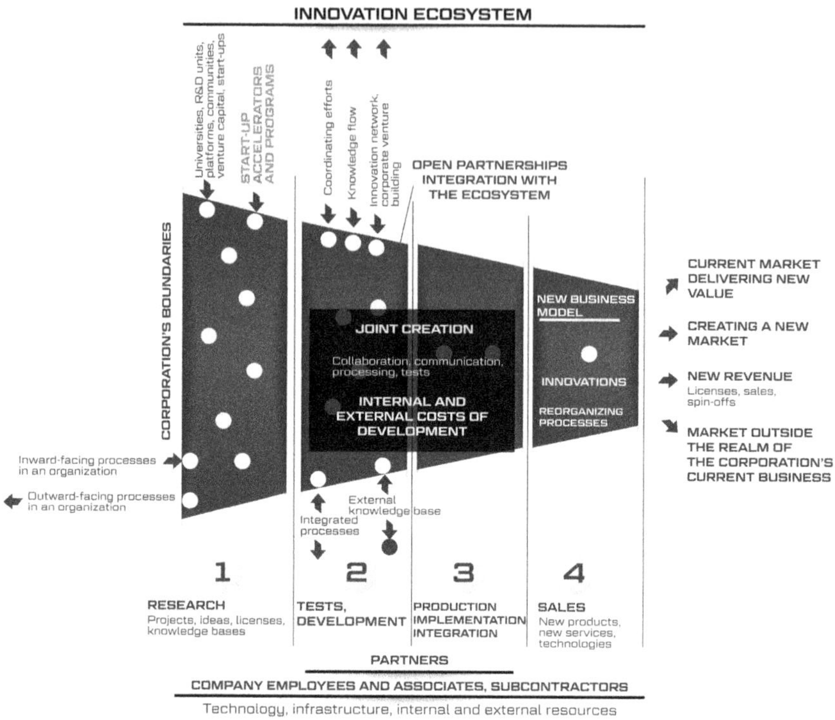

Figure 1.2 Open innovation model.

Source: Author's own work based on Chesbrough (2003).

in the innovation process.[27] The level of trust between cooperating organizations frequently ensues from the level of trust of their employees, knowledge pertaining to their partners and their credibility, while the latter is also a reflection of the trust present in society.[28] It is also important that trust in the context of open innovation creates conditions that are conducive to effective learning processes, an organization's internal and external integration, enhancing productivity, innovation and introducing change. It fosters investments and the proper allocation of resources while strengthening managerial decisions. At the same time, one must remember that trust changes depending on needs, expectations, attitudes, professional experience and the information an organization receives and management styles.[29]

The consequence of abandoning the traditional perception of the boundary of a business in connection with the bidirectional penetration of intellectual property, projects, technologies, solutions and associates between an organization and its surroundings is the vertical disintegration of innovation processes. Figure 1.2 depicts a model illustrating open innovation.

In his research, Chesbrough observed that many promising projects ultimately fail to achieve the intended results where open innovation requires continuous development in an organization, skillful management of knowledge transfer processes, sourcing and selecting projects, a suitable approach to various forms of commercialization, intellectual property protection, properly shaping a firm's relationships with its surroundings, especially its partners and consortium members working on innovation or the ones in its possession.

In his opinion, partners should not be relegated solely to the role of supplying an idea or project, but should take part in reaping the benefits. For that reason, an organization should build lasting relationships with its partners who should participate in the entire process, including its commercialization and the diffusion of the solution formed as a result of their cooperation. Moreover, when managing the open innovation model, one should pay attention to ensuring suitable mechanisms for tracking the progress made in the projects under execution. Attention should also be paid to vetting the projects submitted to an organization to determine their utility and capacity for future absorption. When many organizational cells or partners are involved, it may be difficult to maintain their understanding of the innovation process and their approach to it on equal footing. Another challenge in management is ensuring work is not duplicated when it may have been done previously in an organization, or outside an organization by one of its cooperating partners.

1.2 Differences in the approach to open and closed innovations

Table 1.2 presents the differences between an organization's approach to the closed innovation process and the open innovation approach.[30]

The research conducted by T. Saebi and N.J. Foss[31] is also noteworthy. They drew attention to the necessity of an organization adapting to open innovation. Adaptation should entail the introduction of change with suitable lead time in the organization's pre-existing procedures, management culture, motivation system and organizational structure so that a business is capable to the greatest possible degree of utilizing innovations ensuing from different sources for the purpose of value creation in a firm, for example, using databases of patents, publications and reports from other entities operating in the business's environment.[32] Engaging external partners in the innovation process requires a business to alter its approach to the work done by organizational cells. In particular, this applies to the ones that work on innovation and cooperate with entities in a corporation's market environment. Frequently, the scope of tasks of such a business unit within an organization operating in an open innovation model is expanded to include the role of innovation broker. The very method of looking for innovation is determined by the environment in which a firm operates,[33] where organizations should not base their activities solely one source, but rather on several sources. By doing so, they enhance their chances of augmenting the effectiveness of their innovation activity.[34] As has been observed, large organizations can conduct innovative activity on their own and purchase innovation from external entities or rely on merging internal and external activity. Measuring costs and revenue is helpful in the management

Table 1.2 Attributes and principles in force in open and closed innovation with an eye to selected parameters

Parameters	*Attributes and rules*	
	Closed innovation	*Open innovations*
Personnel/ people	Striving to employ and retain highly qualified staff.	Striving to cooperate with the best possible experts hailing from different entities. Not all of the experts and associates are hired on a permanent basis in the organization.
Conducting R&D work and the findings thereof	The discovery and development processes and the ensuing results take place inside the organization. To obtain benefits the business makes discoveries on its own and at the same time reaps the benefits they produce. The business finances R&D work using its own resources. The time and resources for R&D work are defined. The risk of failure resides solely with the business.	The findings of research originating from cooperation with external partners are just as valuable as the findings that are made inside the organization. A business does not have to be the author of research to be able to extract and reap benefit from it. Research can be conducted outside an organization in consortiums or partnerships or with the co-participation of other market entities. The solutions formed evolve due to changing technology, market demand and the operation of the partners. Work is not strictly dependent on time and resources but on the progress made, the engaged partners, market needs, the results of the tests conducted and their chances of attaining commercial success. The risk of failure is shared by the consortium participants, partners.
Moment for releasing an innovation on the market	The race to be first. The company that is the first one to roll out a solution (product or service) on the market becomes the leader.	Having a robust business model is more important that striving to be the first player on the market that rolled out the innovation.
The number of solutions on which the business is working and market success	The number of projects and ideas speaks to the strength of an organization and its market success. It also evidences market leadership.	The ultimate utilization and ability to align projects and innovation from inside and outside to an organization's business model is what matters. The integration of prospective sources of innovation with a firm's resources and potential is observed.

(*Continued*)

Table 1.2 (Continued)

Parameters	*Attributes and rules*	
	Closed innovation	*Open innovations*
Intellectual property rights	Intellectual property protection is an organization's priority. Focusing efforts on limiting the ability of other market entities to reap benefit. Compiling intellectual property for the purposes solely of proprietary projects run inside a business.	Providing access to intellectual property, knowledge and infrastructure to entities operating in an organization's inner and outer surroundings. Option to purchase intellectual property from the market. Openness to innovation is not identical to a business abandoning intellectual property protection, where it is important to enable the engaged parties to reap benefit in line with the concluded agreements.

Source: Proprietary material on the following basis: Chesbrough (2003); Skrzypek and Sagan (2018).

team making the decision to select the model of cooperation. Figure 1.3 depicts the analysis of cost and revenue mix.

It is also worth highlighting that the emergent intellectual property, for example, in the form of patents, is considered to be a certain type of asset that may be treated not just as contributing to value creation in an organization, a potential source of new revenue in a company (external sales), but also an asset that can be used to alter the business model functioning in an organization. As one may observe a company's business model may be changed not only as a result of the creation of intellectual property but also as the result of its purchase from outside a company. Under this approach the business operates on the market as an active seller or buyer. This marks a major difference to closed innovation in which intellectual property management is grasped as the value employed solely for an organization's own needs (including projects), which is subsequently subject to protection through copyrights, patents and industrial designs.[35]

1.3 Processes in an open innovation model

Gassmann and Enkel defined three innovation processes that are characteristic for the open innovation model. The basis for distinguishing them is the direction of the flow of innovation[36]:

1 Open inbound innovation (or *outside-in*). In this model the process of innovation flow from outside the firm into the organization is prevalent, making for instance technology and the products of existing startups available and useful to a corporation.

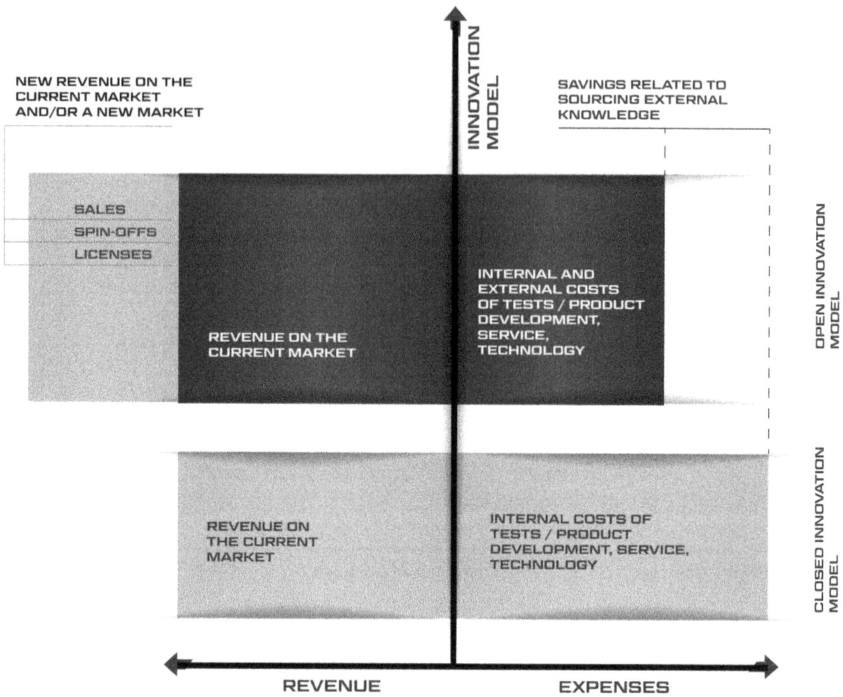

Figure 1.3 Revenue and cost mix in open and closed innovation models.

Source: Proprietary material based on Chesbrough (2006); Lewandowska (2018).

2 Open outbound innovation (or *inside-out*). In this model the process of innovation flow from the business to the outside world is prevalent.
3 Coupled open innovation. The innovation flow takes place through cooperation between businesses as part of business networks at various stages of an innovation process.

Figure 1.4 depicts the foregoing operation of innovation processes in an open model.

In the open innovation model businesses employ various approaches to these three processes. This approach is largely determined by the adopted strategy and the business model in existence in an organization. Business model is a structure defining the mutual links between different departments of a business that specify how the organization interacts with its surroundings, including its clients, partners and suppliers.

The model precisely states how a company cooperates with these entities for the purpose of value creation while simultaneously indicating the mechanisms that enable a company to seize value effectively. The business model clarifies how a business pursues the innovation process, while cooperating with external partners and to what extent it gets involved in these interactions

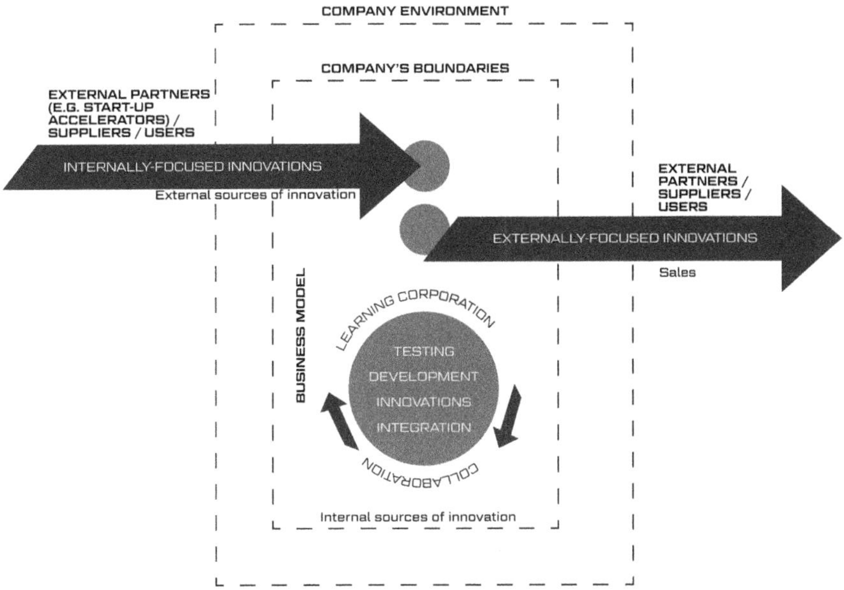

Figure 1.4 Innovation process model in open innovations.

Source: Proprietary material on the basis of Gassman and Enkel (2004).

to generate value for its clients and obtain benefit for its own organization.[37] Hence collaboration signifies the mutual influence taking place between the organizations in which an exchange is taking place, for instance, of information[38] or resources, while the participating entities demonstrate commitment, and this attitude is mutual.[39] It is noteworthy that under this approach one should not anticipate symmetrical engagement or exchange as market entities differ in terms of their potential, goals and contribution made to cooperation.[40] The business model properly selected for the operation of a given business is considered to be a major determinant of a company's market success.[41] The defined strategy and adopted business model form an arrangement of cohesive assumptions and mutually dependent actions whose purpose is to achieve specified goals. This corresponds with the assumption that businesses react to the changes transpiring in their environment. It is the decision of a business on whether a given technology will be distilled inside its organization or secured through purchase or cooperation with external partners.[42] Chesbrough articulated six attributes characterizing the business model including the following[43]:

1 the value proposition offered on the market (to a group or a group of clients) by a business;
2 market segments and a company's revenue sources;
3 evaluation of the level of a company's earnings and costs;

4 value chain structure;
5 adopted competitiveness strategy;
6 position of a business in its network involving suppliers and clients.

1.3.1 *Inbound process*

This process entails obtaining knowledge, technologies and innovative projects by a company for a fee or free of charge, and then in some instances their further development and improvement for the purposes of the actions being undertaken. Under this approach, a company sources knowledge and innovation through licensing, patents, cooperation with businesses holding innovative solutions, technologies, by acquiring an entity or an organized part thereof, tapping into the knowledge flowing from partners, suppliers, non-governmental organizations, clients and end users free of charge. In the inbound process, emphasis is placed on forging partnerships and associations with other organizations, companies, research entities, etc. for the purpose of gaining access to the resources of these entities. It is also done to glean knowledge, ideas, projects and technologies from outside a company's bounds. Here, they may be sourced for a fee or free of charge. It is worth observing that effectively blending external sources of knowledge with an organization's internal resources, including its intellectual capital may constitute an organization's competitive advantage on the market. The possibility of having cooperating entities and end users be incorporated in the innovation process is one of the benefits of employing the inbound process. The risks related to the failure of innovation are also limited on account of the early inclusion of partners, suppliers and clients in the process.

1.3.2 *Outbound process*

An outbound process involves the engagement of entities functioning in an organization's surroundings to commercialize the solutions that were worked out inside a corporation and that are not currently used or that do not fit the adopted growth strategy (e.g., not very valuable, impossible to employ in the firm). This process is related to the transfer of an organization's knowledge, technology and intellectual capital outside the boundaries of a business. This is possible thanks to the licensing of technology, the sales of patents or discoveries and having the firm set up special-purpose vehicles. A licensing agreement may curtail the rights to dispose of its subject matter (e.g., a limited license) or grant the full rights for an entity to take advantage of it to the same extent as the licensor (referred to as a full license).[44] The purpose of transferring assets outside the bounds of a company in the outbound process is to reap business benefits by marketing new products and services that are currently not within the scope of interest of a business, that do not comport with the adopted business model and that would not receive a chance of development or commercialization within a large organization under the adopted innovation model. This process is in a certain sense connected to open inbound innovation as the operation of a company that is focused on sourcing knowledge and technology from the outside world generates an opposite trend in the operation of another organization. Here, it is noticeable on the market that the interest of entrepreneurs in extending licenses is relatively minor. This is linked to the management of a corporation being more inclined to source knowledge internally than opening up to outbound activities. Managers start with the assumption that disclosing too much knowledge outside the company may in the future entail a potential weakening of their firm's market position and lead to diminishing its competitive edge.[45]

1.3.3 *Coupled process*

The final process to be discussed in the open innovation model is based on the former two (inbound and outbound). It is predicated on an organization forming formal and informal networks, strategic alliances, cooperation with organizations, agents for innovation (e.g., startup accelerators) at various stages of the innovation process.[46] As part of the coupled process participants reciprocally share knowledge, shared learning is achieved, the resources of the entities are harnessed (including resources that may be rare, that do not have substitutes and that at the same time are complementary with the ones a participant has). The entities render the services required to develop an innovative product or service and they also share the benefits stemming from the crafted solution according to a concluded contract. Therefore, innovations under this approach are the outcome of actions based on knowledge and the cooperation established between organizations. These actions rest on the practical application of existing or newly created information, knowledge and technology. It should be observed that knowledge is gained through cognitive efforts. Thus, newly created knowledge is difficult to transfer outright so that it could immediately fulfill the assumptions in an organization because learning is required, the introduction of suitable mechanisms inside an organization is also frequently required and a suitable path for its integration must be procured.[47] The flow of knowledge, services, access to resources and the future split of earnings are defined in the concluded cooperation agreement, and in particular the relations between the entities, the distinct nature of the project undertaken by the parties and the limitations related thereto. Through their cooperation in a coupled process the parties share risk, incur lower financial and non-financial outlays and extract benefits from synergy.[48]

1.4 Cooperation in an open innovation model

One of the foundations for securing and strategically developing innovation in corporations is having an effective mechanism for the purpose of scanning the expansive market environment of a business to search for signals of a possible opportunity or need to make a change in how the organization functions. The sources of these signals may come not just from academic communities, current clients, suppliers, trade events and entrepreneurs but also startup accelerators, which are playing an increasingly more pronounced role on the market[49] and startups themselves as they are dealing with innovations and new technologies on a daily basis.[50] The signals concerning the need for corporations to search for and roll out innovation may assume the nature of ephemeral impulses or be continuous and related to the following blocks: customer behavior, globalization and competition, policy and regulations, technologies and investments, environmental factors and intra-organizational factors.[51] Figure 1.5 depicts these blocks.

By monitoring these blocks, compiling and analyzing incoming signals businesses can not only stay abreast of new solutions appearing on the market but also respond correctly to the threats on the horizon for the products they currently offer on the market. In that way, they have a change of assuming the role of an entity that can alter the rules of a game before the competition does that. However, not all companies perceive the signals pertaining to prospective threats and opportunities on a timely basis or interpret them properly. On account of their size some companies think that they have an advantage on the market regardless of the changes transpiring in their environment. This is a faulty approach and marks the beginning of trouble as the pace and scope of change transpiring in the environment demand that organizations constantly respond to change, including alignment of their business model to the prevailing conditions. Another unfavorable behavior

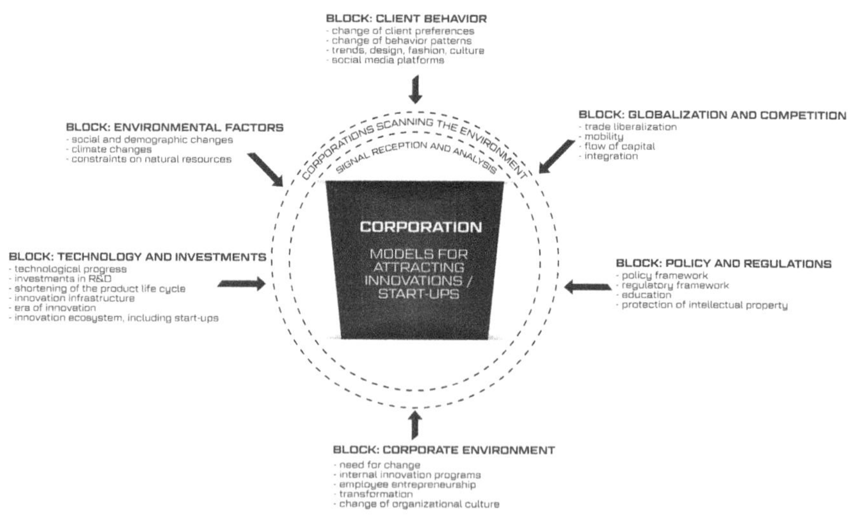

Figure 1.5 Blocks of factors affecting the search for and implementation of innovation by corporations.

Source: Proprietary material.

seen among businesses is the conservative approach to change related to treating the solution offered to date on the market as its core business and generating profits as this allowed the organization to gain its market leadership position. Unfortunately, such a myopic approach means that another company may emerge in a corporation's surroundings with a competitive innovative solution that will cause the current leader to surrender its market position. The skill of capturing the signals and instigating change in the innovative process forms the basis for sustaining and growing the competitiveness of large organizations. Approximately one-third of the businesses on the list of the top 500 companies disappear on average every ten years as they are displaced by other organizations.[52] Sourcing or creating innovation forms the basis for building a competitive edge in companies, especially those operating in sectors subject to rapid change (e.g., technology).[53] Cooperating in the process of creating and commercializing innovation is a multi-phase process in which the engaged partners must make many decisions, thereby affecting their ultimate market success or failure. Many factors contributing to the prospective failure of cooperation may be identified, such as[54]:

1 lack of alignment in terms of complementary resources;
2 lack of alignment in terms of cultural compliance in decision-making processes;
3 lack of trust among participants;
4 improper approach to the method of coordinating cooperation, or managing conflict and change;
5 lack of the capacity to adapt the exchange processes between entities,
6 unpredictability of the changes transpiring in the environment of the cooperating organizations, for example, legal and environmental and the pandemic.

In that way the decisions related to innovation processes and the actions undertaken in this process, in order to accrue the expected results in the form of future implementations and commercialization should be examined not only in tactical categories but also strategic categories by the organization's management.[55] When a company introduces an innovation on the market it engenders new opportunities whose desired outcome is value growth, business development, establishment of new markets or new applications (utility). At present, the challenge for an organization's management is not just the concentration of effort on value creation while harnessing its own resources and the innovation process while applying new technologies, but above all the skill of intercepting solutions available on the market and pursuing the suitable instruments related thereto. In conjunction with that, cooperation is not grasped solely in an internal context as the formation and management of teams within the organization and its resources, but also more broadly above all as a model for cooperation between businesses or organizations focused on the emergence of innovation or its transfer to corporations for the purpose of integration, implementation and discounting.

The benefits from cooperation hinge not only on the type of established cooperation and the form thereof but also on the prevailing culture of innovation and the technical and technological level of the cooperating companies. As they search for innovation and work to develop and commercialize it, businesses enter into cooperation with entities operating outside such an organization.[56] This cooperation is grasped as an economic and organizational phenomenon bound by the relationships that transpire between the entities endeavoring in this same period to execute goals that are not mutually exclusive. The multiple entities engaged in this activity mean that the various participants can strive to achieve their intended goals in a varying manner.[57] The instigation of cooperation frequently ensues from limited resources and from the needs a business is unable to satisfy as it operates unilaterally.[58] The major motive for undertaking cooperation is to maximize the pursuit of the goal defined by the companies.[59] Maximization is conditional upon the resource-related potential of companies, their adopted strategy, business model, the culture of innovation in an organization (based on the will to implement innovation, the freedom to implement, legal and procedural determinants, the capability and skill of implementing it and the actions taken), the organization of the external surroundings, the partners sourced for cooperation (selection of partners and projects), trust,[60] realistic clear goals, effective communication, culture of work and sharing resources.[61, 62] Four groups of factors contributing to the ultimate success of cooperation have been distinguished,[63] that is, technological factors, behavioral factors, financial factors and process-related factors. The process of cooperation undertaken by parties creates an opportunity for companies to secure the ability to cooperate and develop innovation processes.[64] Cooperation partners may be entities that are dependent on one another, for example, within a corporate group or legally distinct from one another.

1.5 Motives for organizations to cooperate in an open innovation model

The undertaking of cooperation by organizations is associated with an approach determining the ability to build, protect and strengthen competitive position. In the activities of companies the notion of cooperation refers to the context of multiple aspects and multiple dimensions, for example, in the innovation process, in the creation of products and services and in organizational or marketing activities.[65] Cooperating companies pursue the goals of the interested parties that simultaneously stem from their interests and that at the same time form their principal motivation for joining to engage in cooperation.[66] Motives are subject to change over time due to the modification of the prevailing conditions on the market, the change in the operating strategy and business model.[67] The motives for cooperation in innovation are divided into ones that directly pertain to the innovation process (e.g., increasing the scale and productivity of the R&D work being done, limiting own costs, creating value[68]) and that are indirectly related to it (access to new markets, interception of innovation, opening up to new clients and users of the solutions under design[69,70]). John Hagedoorn divided the motives for cooperation in innovation into three groups[71]:

1 Motives stemming from the fundamental and applied research and the general characterization of the technological processes associated with the comprehensiveness of new technologies and the changes transpiring on the market, including the desire to curtail the risk of failure in the projects undertaken.[72]
2 Motives concerning the conduct of the innovation process related to the desire to source new resources and knowledge for a business from the partners participating in the process of creating innovation as well as jointly combining efforts and the synergy achieved thanks to that, economies of scale, shortening the time of executing and testing solutions and providing for influence over the intellectual property protection process.[73]
3 Motives related to access to new markets and looking for market opportunities: undertaking cooperation as part of innovation processes affords the opportunity of increasing the number of products and services offered by a firm on the market while also creating opportunities to gain access to new market segments and technologies.[74]

For the purposes of this monograph the following approach has been chosen to define the term of cooperation, which means a method of acting that leads to the joint attainment of goals that are mutually not at odds with one another. In turn, the entities themselves elect to cooperate because they are motived by the greater probability of achieving benefits than in the case of acting alone.[75,76] In addition, during the course of cooperation, they establish various relationships and forms of influence in line with the concluded contracts and formal and informal agreements. The exchange of information, services, resources and work transpiring between the parties is mutual, while the actions undertaken in the innovation process are cohesive, coordinated and agreed upon by the partners.[77] The actions taken span R&D work, as well as financial and commercial expenditures for the purpose of bringing about the creation/development of innovation.[78] The success of cooperation hinges on the skill of molding and managing relationships and on the parties providing for the following[79]:

1 suitable communication in all their joint activities (seamless flow of information, sharing knowledge and information);
2 quality of cooperation (each party benefits);
3 credibility in cooperation (trust in the mutually undertaken efforts);

4 investment in cooperation (time, financial means, human resources, infrastructure and own back office);
5 sustainability and continuity (long-term approach to cooperation).

That is also why it is important for the cooperation between the entities to be organized so that the processes related to innovation are interrelated through a set of interdependencies[80] focused on sourcing and selecting projects, developing and vetting them in a real or test environment and commercializing them.

1.6 Network approach to cooperation in open innovations

Since a substantial portion of the knowledge, technologies and innovative solutions are outside the organization, it is critical to reach the organization. Firms are compelled to search for it to transcend the conventially perceived boundaries of an organization that are growing more and more fuzzy. The bidirectional flow of intellectual property, knowledge, projects and experts in connection with the creation of new space, that is, the cooperation network is observable. This network is a set of dependencies (relationships) between businesses and other entities. The linkages between parties may be formal or informal. Mutual interactions take place between entities.[81] This approach features the constant search, investigation and usage of the various chances innovation and work on innovation in cooperation with other market participants afford. In addition, it features the integration of external sources of innovation with the internal resources in an organization. It also features the engagement of partners (e.g., startup accelerators) to intermediate, cooperate while creating innovation or integrate it within the structure of a business.

The development of information and telecommunication and information and communication technologies and as a result the growing degree to which society and economies are bound by a network has precipitated a situation in which the operational activity of businesses is more and more frequently run in the internet and as part of network forms of business cooperation in which entities are working to achieve a joint goal.[82,83]

To be able to develop businesses should focus the activities they undertake on cooperating with their surroundings to be able to run joint ventures.[84] The success of cooperation depends on innovation, openness to undertake joint projects, limiting opportunistic behavior and the suitable management of the cooperation process. That is also why the paradigm for open innovation has become a new network-based source of competitive edge. In the value creation process firms make changes in their efforts and elect to switch from a traditional approach to the value chain – understood as a series of actions taken during the development of a product or service that are related to one another within a logical entirety in such a way so as to obtain added value – to a value network.[85] Thanks to the duly selected bonds of cooperation, if one is speaking of the number and quality of partners, the time horizon, the areas of cooperation being undertaken within the scope of innovation, the forms and rules for defining it, it is possible for corporations to obtain better outcomes for the adopted operating model.[86] Accordingly, value as part of cooperation arises as an effect of tapping into the resources to be found not only within the bounds of a business but also of tapping into the surroundings of a business and the established agreements with entities that are frequently independent albeit connected to one another through network-based relationships. Thereby the value of many of the products and services being created at present is the sum total of the partial added values in the network process of their creation by the partners cooperating with one another as part of a network.[87] This approach also calls for procuring a suitable level of flexibility in the organizational structure of a business.[88] The cohesiveness of the network is procured by mechanisms such as reciprocity, reputation and efficacy in achieving goals, among others.[89] This is vital having regard for an organization's susceptibility to the changes transpiring within in connection with testing and introducing new products and services as well as adapting to innovation processes within its pre-existing structure.[90] The flexibility and at the same time the sustainability of an organizational structure are a desirable attribute required for the functioning of contemporary organizations operating in an open innovation model. A structure should ensure the pursuit of goals while making it possible for the organization to operate without interruption and while also giving it the ability to adapt to the evolving conditions outside the organization. Such an approach makes it possible to implement change quickly and seamlessly and adapt a solution to the new determinants in connection with the innovations rolled out in an organization as part of cooperation with the market environment.

From the perspective of the resource-based approach in strategic management, the significance of cooperation as part of a cooperation network is related to enhancing competitiveness in connection with holding strategic resources or having access to them.[91] Cooperation allows one to enhance the level of this edge as it provides access to additional resources in the form of resources belonging not just to the members of a network but also to the resources of the network itself.[92, 93] Importantly, differences in the technical or technological level of the parties may affect the benefits ensuing from the undertaken cooperation.[94] It is accepted that cooperating businesses should have knowledge about the pending process of cooperation on innovation; however, this knowledge should differ so that this exchange can accrue benefits to the engaged parties. Thus, businesses should strive to a situation in which equilibrium stemming from the existing cognitive distance prevails as it produces more effective outcomes in the open innovation model while simultaneously controlling distance, which may weaken the reciprocal understanding of innovation processes.[95] This distance is customarily determined by the position taken in the innovation process and its impact on the emergence and implementation of the target solutions on the market.

1.7 Obstacles to cooperation in open innovations

Obstacles to establishing cooperation between entities may usually pertain to cultural, organizational and industrial aspects.[96] In addition, the high costs of conducting innovative activity, competitive pressure and budget-related limitations are deemed to be a major obstacle.[97, 98] Additionally, the concerns associated with delays in the supply of products and services and the failure to uphold the conditions of an executed agreement and the concern related to amendments to the contractual clauses, the lack of mutual trust, the lack of information or its limited flow may be included among the frequent obstacles to establishing cooperation between businesses.[99] Other obstacles that are encountered are the negative historical experiences associated with cooperation, the potential risk of future competition arising as a result of the established cooperation, legal obstacles and the less than conducive environment for firms to operate.[100,101]

Having regard for the cooperation of businesses as part of the open innovation model, one may not disregard the limitations stemming from that, not the least of them being the amount of capital expenditures made by businesses to perform R&D work, or the higher degree of co-dependency of cooperating entities and thereby the potentially high cost of a possible change of partner or the adopted rules for cooperation.[102] Factors impeding partnerships with startups on the side of corporations are frequently not just insufficient flexibility but also the organizational rigidity and excessive focus on procedural issues.[103] Mature businesses with complicated and well-established structures encounter difficulties when it comes to stimulating innovation. Protracted decision-making processes, the lack of engagement and support on the part of the management of a business and corporate inertia are a major factor impeding the perception of potential when establishing partnerships.

Obstacles to cooperation between corporations and startups

Despite the growing awareness of the benefits flowing from partnership with startups, corporations also perceive a host of obstacles to cooperating with startups, which means that this cooperation frequently does not come to fruition, or that it fails to produce the intended outcomes. Researchers point to the current inseparable contradictions in the decision-making process and the appearance of intense emotional reactions on the part of the management of a corporation and a startup in reference to the actions taken.[104] Corporations and startups differ from one another in terms of their culture of operation on many planes. Even discrepancies that apparently seem to be minor may lead to major impediments to cooperation and generate communication and organizational errors between a corporation and a startup. Smaller inconsistencies can accumulate, and as a result they may lead to failure in cooperation on innovation.[105] Other research pertaining to obstacles to cooperation has also indicated problems related to communication and relationships, cultural challenges related to the philosophy of operation between cooperating entities and the suitable designation and enforcement of tasks in the undertaken cooperation process between the corporation and the startup.[106] Despite the objective benefits cooperation produces, these obstacles are perceptible to startups in the process of inter-organizational cooperation. They focus on the differences in the method of functioning in connection with the divergent velocity in realizing innovation processes.[107] For startups the rigid framework for the functioning of large businesses may represent a hefty challenge. The frequent problem of not having mechanisms for cooperation, the hierarchical structure and the long, non-transparent decision-making processes.[108] Other works regarding obstacles to cooperation point out the challenges pertaining to cultural and procedural obstacles[109] as well as strategic obstacles[110] and how each party is poised for integration.[111]

The obstacles outlined above most frequently stem from the differences in how startups and corporations function. Startups are poised to engage in creative and direct activity while mature businesses are dominated by a multitude of procedures and decision-making processes that engender differences in their approach to cooperation. One of the more important business values for startups entails independence, dynamism and the freedom to make decisions, which is frequently just the opposite of corporate reality. Thus, establishing business relationships that are beneficial to both parties requires understanding the mutual motivations and limitations. Therefore, the parties' grasp of the existing obstacles that affect their cooperation is significant when it comes to successful cooperation in an open innovation model.

1.8 Potential offered by startups and their solutions in an open innovation model

Startups are defined in a multitude of ways. One of the more prevalent definitions indicates that a startup is a temporary organization that is searching for a recurring and scalable business model[112] that is endeavoring to create new solutions.[113] In turn, E. Ries defines a startup as an "institution established to create a new product or service in extremely uncertain conditions".[114] In her work Agnieszka Skala has portrayed the understanding of the term startup based on the ten most frequently quoted articles based on data from the Web of Science Core Collection (Table 1.3).

By analyzing the foregoing definitions one may assume that a startup is a new business, customarily a technology business that is at an early stage of development. Its strong link to innovation is a startup's characteristic attribute. In addition, startups frequently market new products or services that have the potential to become a breakthrough in their industries. Startups extract benefits from the overall economic development stemming from globalization and digitalization.[115]

In contrast to traditional small firms, startups as a rule endeavor to achieve fast and substantial growth and scaling up their operations despite

Table 1.3 The understanding of the term "startup" in the ten most frequently quoted articles on the "startup" subject matter according to the Web of Science Core Collection

No	*Published since 2010*	*Published since 2013 with the word "start-up" in the title*	
1	Ostrom and others [2010] • Beginning company	Mollick [2014]: • Commercial cultural or artistic undertaking	Blank [2013]: • Temporary organization looking for a scalable business model
2	Mollick [2014]: • Commercial cultural or artistic undertaking	Schlaegel, Koenig [2014]: • Beginning company	Román, Congregado, Millán [2013]: • New undertaking
3	Liñán, Rodrigez-Cohard, Rueda-Cantuche [2011] • New firm	Blank [2013]: • Temporary organization looking for a scalable business model	Cassar [2014]: • New undertaking
4	Schlaegel, Koenig [2014] • Beginning company	Kautonen, Gelderen, Fink [2015]: • New firm	Conti, Thursby, Rothaermel [2013]: • High-tech industry firm
5	Cumming, Schmidt, Walz [2010]: • Firm co-funded by VC	Cavusgil, Knight [2015]: • Young firm	Semrau, Werner [2014]: • New firm
6	Blank [2013]: • Temporary organization looking for a scalable business model	Klotz and others [2014] • new firm	Harms [2015]: • Undertaking built according to the lean start-up methodology
7	Townsend, Busenitz, Arthurs [2010]: • New undertaking	Audretsch [2014]: • New firm built on knowledge	Criaco and others [2014]: • Technology company formed at a university
8	Ceccagnoli and others [2012]: • Small independent software companies	Liñán, Fayolle [2015]: • New firm	Hyytinen, Pajarinen and Rouvinen [2015]: • New firm
9	Kautonen, Gelderen, Fink [2015]: • New firm	Coad and others [2013] • New firm	Guerrero, Urbano [2014]: • Company formed at a university
10	Liñán, Rodrigez-Cohard, Rueda-Cantuche [2011] • New firm	Hoogendoorn, Oosterbeek and Van Praag [2013]: • New firm	Pe'er, Keil [2013] • New firm

Source: Skala (2018).

having limited resources. That is also why the business models of startups are designed so as to facilitate the rapid scaling up of their products and services for larger markets, frequently thanks to the usage of modern technologies. Startups are characterized by their less formalized structure than traditional businesses while their employees and associates are customarily strongly engaged and motivated to achieve success. This stems from their culture of entrepreneurship, flexibility and capability of adapting to the constantly evolving market conditions and continuous technological progress.[116] The short period of operating on the market stems from risk and uncertainty. Many startups do not survive their first year of operation due to financial troubles, market competition or ineffective business models. Moreover, on top of their own funds startups readily rely on external financing, for example, venture capital, business angels and startup accelerators to accelerate their development and scaling up.[117] Frequently, the selection of the form of external financing by a startup drives the future success of the business, the securing and retention of its position on a competitive market and its further development.[118] The culture of work in new companies is based on creativity and openness. Thanks to that it is possible to experiment and make rapid decisions on undertaking the execution of projects in the conducted operations. Figure 1.6 depicts the key attributes that are characteristic of startups.

Within the context of open innovation startups are not just a source of new technologies and ideas, they are also critical players in the cooperation networks that are formed. Their role as pioneers in the application of new technologies and services and the implementation of new business models makes them valuable partners for large organizations when it comes to developing and rolling out forward-looking solutions. Startups are constantly looking for their operational path on the market, their sustainable and profitable business model. Startups can introduce their innovations in larger systems through cooperation, partnerships and licensing, thereby contributing to the development and diffusion of new technologies and solutions on the market. This cooperation frequently encompasses not just the exchange of

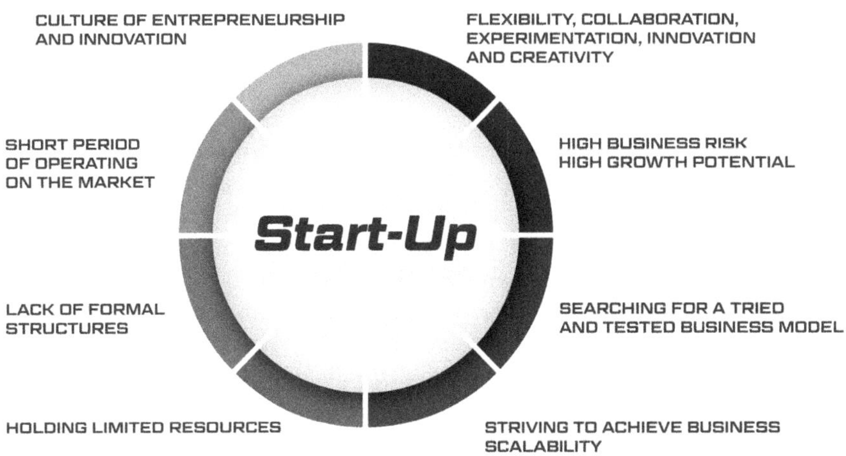

Figure 1.6 Characteristic attributes of startups.

Source: Proprietary material.

technology but also sharing knowledge, skills and experience, which makes it possible to use resources better and shorten the time needed to roll out innovation on the market. In addition, interactions with corporations and access to their client databases, infrastructure and experts, sales channels and financing afford startups support within the scope of the pending work on an innovative solution. These resources are crucial for the growth and development of startups, enabling them not just to commercialize their innovations but also to improve and adapt them to the market's evolving needs. Thanks to that startups cannot just survive on the competitive market but also become important players in their industries.[119]

1.9 Potential for cooperation between corporations and startups in open innovations

The decisions made by managers referencing innovations under design involve large question marks. Extensive uncertainty accompanies them, and forecasting is becoming more and more complicated. An organization's effective approach to innovation processes calls for analyses that make it possible to understand the nature, essence and character of phenomena and the processes transpiring on the market, as well as identifying the opportunities and threats ensuing from the established cooperation network. Large organizations take actions as part of a specific business model to assuage the needs known to them of a specific market segment. This calls for them to find a method of adding an element characteristic of startups – namely, searching. The topic of corporations searching for technologies and innovative solutions stems largely from the open innovation concept which is becoming more universal. As has been indicated this model assumes the utilization, among other things, of the flow of knowledge between external entities and the organization, whereby it becomes possible to source knowledge and innovation from various sources, which drives the pro-innovation policy espoused by large corporations. On the other hand, the suppliers of these solutions in the form of startups have the ability to take advantage of the value afforded by a large organization, for example, infrastructure, market access, client network.[120] For that reason corporations are aware that to maintain their competitive position on the market and effectively and successfully pursue innovation processes, they must append external partners,[121] also from the startup ecosystem treating them as a source of innovation and integration with an organization's internal processes.[122] Many corporations rest their approach to innovation on three pillars: corporate entrepreneurship; cultivating strategic partnerships; and various models of cooperation with startups.[123] By combining their strengths, knowledge and resources synergy is achieved forming added value for the participants involved in a cooperation network.

As has been observed, development and competing on the market are associated with the necessity of efficiently sourcing innovation. For that reason, corporations should have the ability to identify, attract and cooperate with an ever greater number of startups than till now as the startup ecosystem is getting bigger and more distributed. In addition, large organizations must also be aware of their value offering for prospective startups. In a certain sense other market participants such as venture capital funds interested in innovative solutions are becoming competitors of corporations as they see they representing potential investment opportunities. The startups operating on the market in many instances gain an edge in innovation over large businesses thanks to the difference stemming from their agility in management, their approach to risk in conducting R&D activity, their lean organizational structure and their drive to grow quickly. Such businesses do not customarily have suitable resources and sales channels, nor do they frequently have the capacity to harness economies of scale on account of operating on small markets and having access to a limited number of end users. To market innovative solutions and technologies startups must look for partnerships directly with large organizations or indirectly through entities functioning on the market such as startup accelerators. In turn, corporations holding a suitable back office and resources frequently lack knowledge regarding the appearance of new technologies and solutions on the market that would enable them to create or adopt solutions and subsequently sell innovative products and services on markets. Figure 1.7 depicts the attributes characterizing the strengths and weaknesses of startups and corporations in the inter-organizational cooperation model.

The parties' open approach to designing and implementing innovation seems to be a necessary prerequisite for the development of startups and corporations alike as part of the undertaken organizational cooperation. The engaged parties perceive value in their mutual relations and the benefits ensuing from such cooperation. The main reason is that the appearing breakthrough technologies bring totally new value propositions to the market that

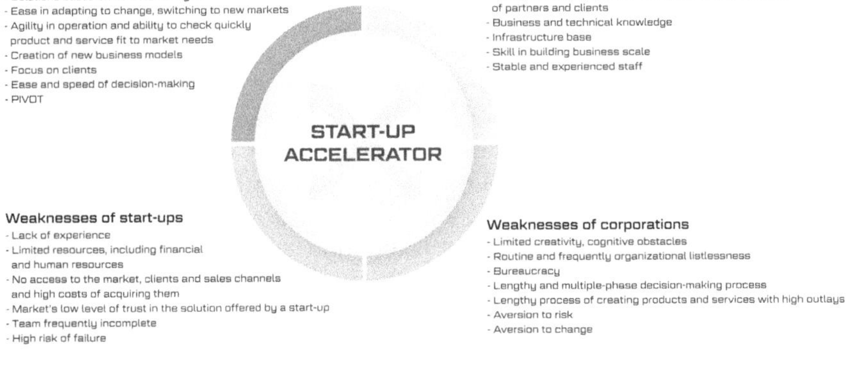

Figure 1.7 Strengths and weaknesses of startups and corporations in a collaboration model.

Source: Proprietary material.

did not previously exist.[124] Therefore, in the cooperation model, it is important to define properly the roles and thereby identify the entity that will play the role of organizer and manager of the innovation process as part of the established inter-organizational cooperation. The model established by large businesses for attracting startups in the form of a CVC fund is more and more frequently being supplanted by models, which in some instances appear to be better aligned to the situation and seem to be able to overcome the cooperation gap between new companies and corporations better.[125] For that reason over the last several years the actions not just of corporations, which aim to establish cooperation with startups have been noticeably visible on the market but also of the participants of the startup ecosystem themselves even if just through the operation of corporate startup accelerators whose task is to bring together new innovative companies and their solutions with large organizations.

From the vantage point of the author's experience, and also based on the findings of available research, it is worth noting that despite the attempts undertaken by corporations to take advantage of the complementary products offered by startups, the results obtained have frequently fallen short of the expectations held in the process undertaken by the parties. The divide between the corporate and startup method of working, resources, differences in the culture of innovation and characteristics places genuine challenges on bringing the two parties together to work jointly on developing innovation and integrating solutions in the environment of large organizations and further implementation and diffusion.

1.10 Strategies for cooperation between corporations and startups

The corporate strategy for cooperating with startups is a corporation's action plan in terms of cooperating with new innovative companies and the startup ecosystem. This is the method whereby a large organization identifies, shapes and manages relationships with startups to achieve specified strategic goals, especially in terms of attracting innovation from outside the bounds of an organization. Frequently, large organizations face a dilemma between protecting their current sources of revenue and implementing external innovative projects that may be important for the survival of a corporation.[126] This is a classic dilemma between exploration and exploitation that require different organizational forms in terms of culture, strategy and leadership.[127] The approach to the strategy for cooperation takes into account relationships with different participants in the ecosystem such as startups, incubators, startup accelerators, investors, research institutions, social networks.[128] The key components for a corporate strategy to cooperate with startups entail the following:

1 **Identifying goals and benefits.** A corporation should have clearly defined goals, including the business goals and benefits it intends to achieve through

cooperation with startups. This may for instance entail technological innovation, new product development, access to new markets, enhancing an organization's flexibility or optimizing internal processes. It is important for the entire organization, including the teams responsible for cooperation with new companies to be familiar with these goals. The key elements of this process are as follows:

identifying the areas in which cooperation with startups is the most desirable. These areas may vary, for example, scope of technology development, reorganization of processes, expansion onto new markets;

identifying the areas in which the innovations of startups may contribute to a corporation gaining a competitive edge in the form of strengthening its product offering, enhancing operational processes or tweaking its business model for instance;

specifying the benefits which a corporation expects of its cooperation with startups in connection with the execution of goals. For example, this may entail gaining new clients, access to new technologies, augmenting the culture of innovation, growing market share, improving relations with clients;

analyzing the activity of the competition whereby the corporation is able to design its own unique approach to cooperating with startups and their innovations.

2 **Uninterrupted analysis of the startup ecosystem.** A corporation should be up-to-date with the structure and dynamics of the local and global startup ecosystem. It should be aware of the linkages that exist with other markets and what the prospects for growth are. It is worth identifying technological innovations, business models and social changes that may exert an impact on the industry in which the corporation operates. Identification and analysis can pertain to startups in different phases of growth, accelerators, incubators, venture capital funds, universities, trade organizations and other entities supporting the development of startups. It is worth constantly running activities involving the assessment of prospective partners, technologies, industrial trends so as to be able to select the most suitable partners for inter-organizational cooperation. This will make it possible to glean knowledge first-hand and cultivate relationships with the market, which may facilitate later cooperation when implementing innovations in the open innovation model.
3 **Definition of cooperation models.** Cooperation models are grasped as different types of frameworks and structures that demarcate the way in which a company collaborates with startups. A corporation's strategy should take into account the various cooperation models with startups such as acceleration programs, equity investments, acquisitions, joint R&D projects, business partnerships, etc.
4 **Selection of suitable startups.** Effectively identifying and selecting startups that are consistent with the goals and strategy of a corporation exert a significant impact on the final chances for attaining inter-organizational cooperation. A corporation's activities should be focused on analyzing and

picking those startups that are aligned to the greatest degree to the goals of that corporation and may accrue not just added value to the organization but also mutual benefits to the parties. Therefore, it is crucial to align the selection of startups to the strategy adopted by a corporation, and regularly update and adapt the evaluation criteria depending on evolving goals, business needs and changes in an organization's business environment.

5 **Monitoring and adaptation of strategy.** The adopted strategy for cooperating with startups should be monitored in terms of the progress in pursuing inter-organizational cooperation. Based on the obtained results and the experience gained, the strategy should be aligned to the market reality. Accordingly, monitoring and adapting strategy are iterative. This enables a corporation to respond effectively to changes, communicate with partners and improve cooperation with startups.[129] This will enable corporations to sustain strategic compatibility and achieve the intended goals in the long-run.

It is noteworthy that cooperation between corporations and startups should be flexible and open to change. The dynamics involved in the operation of the startup ecosystem may require an organization's current strategy to be adjusted to the situation prevailing in its surroundings. What is crucial is maintaining balance between tapping into the innovative potential of startups and achieving the business goals of corporations. Establishing cooperation with startups is therefore perceived as a major source of innovation for large corporations.

1.11 Cooperation models with startups and attracting innovation to corporations

In recent years the expansion of new initiatives, models and programs through which corporations are getting involved with startups has been observed. The growing number of available programs for corporations (inbound programs) is creating more opportunities for large organizations to consider this as a form of operation in the open innovation model. These programs are adapted in such a way so as to enable corporations to cooperate with a greater number of startups and their innovative solutions.[130] One may distinguish several models for attracting innovation to a corporate in the strategy for cooperation, which Figure 1.8 depicts. It is important that these models are not mutually exclusive and may be run by corporations in parallel. These models differ not only in terms of their scope, scale, expenditures and goals but also in terms of the challenges the management faces. They serve different purposes and as a rule there are no contradictions between them.[131] In addition, each one of the models described below offers its own distinct mechanisms for sourcing innovation and consequently for generating value for a corporation. The management of a corporation, depending on

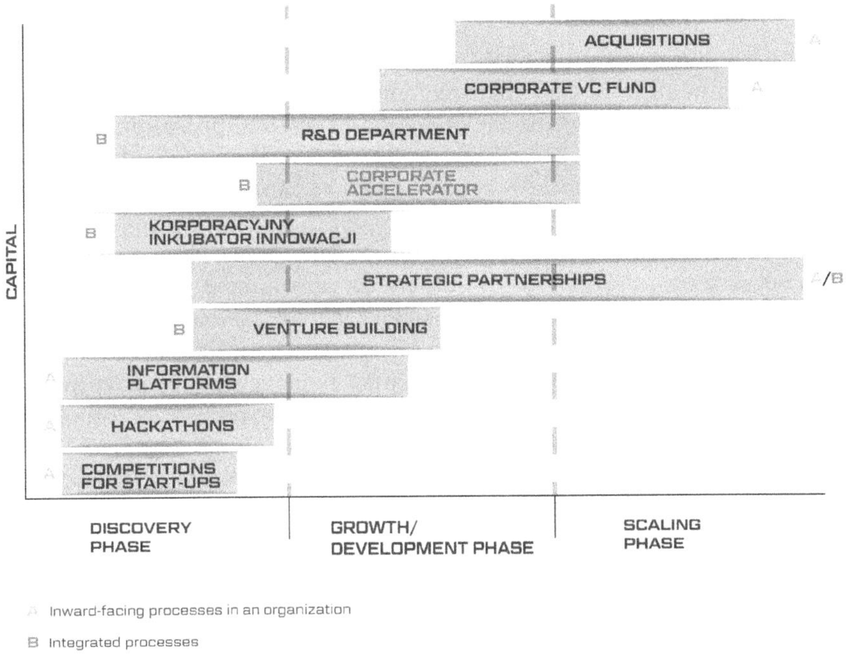

Figure 1.8 Models to attract innovation to corporations.

Source: Proprietary material.

the model selected, should remember that time is needed to attain the desired outcomes in each one of these models. One should remember that a newly launched program for startups in the first period of operation generates primarily costs as even rapidly developing young businesses need time to work out their solutions in cooperation with the organization's business units and grow sufficiently such that they have any impact whatsoever on the financial statements of corporations.

As one may see in Figure 1.8, the models for attracting innovation are suitably dedicated to a specific phase of development of a startup. Some models flourish with startups that are in the initial phase of development and are just working on their solution (e.g., the hackathon model). In turn, when it comes to startups that are actively operating on the market and selling a solution on international markets, a CVC fund model may be more attractive for them than a hackathon. What is also important is that each one of these models calls for corporations to provide financing, and in some instances adapt their structure and provide infrastructural resources. In keeping with the presented models one may observe a certain regularity entailing the following, that the higher a given model is on the scale, the greater the capital requirements. The models indicated in Figure 1.8 rely on different goals, principles, characteristics and financial requirements that are briefly described below.

1.11.1 Model 1. Competitions for startups

- **Goals:** contests aim to identify those innovative startups that have ideas, solutions or technologies that may enrich the offering of a corporation or contribute to enhancing the operation of internal processes. By organizing competitions corporations can identify novel solutions that portend market and technological potential and that can be implemented in the organization in the future.
- **Rules:** corporations announce competitions with specific challenges or topics in which startups proffer their solutions. As part of the announced competition corporations receive applications that may be examined by the organization's employees. The jury customarily evaluates the submissions in terms of their originality, innovativeness, market potential and compliance with the competition's designated criteria. After selecting projects, a corporation may propose prizes to the victorious teams of the startups. These prizes may assume the form of a proposal to continue working together, financing or some other support contemplated by the clauses in the competition's rules and regulations. A competition may be a one-off event, or a regular event.
- **Characterization:** competitions are open to solutions from different industries and they help corporations identify potential market innovations. In addition, they are a prime opportunity to promulgate innovation by incentivizing startups to design original solutions for the challenges defined by corporations. It is worth noting that by taking part in a competition startups promote their solutions and gain an opportunity to augment their recognition on the market. Competitions for startups require a relatively small amount of financial expenditure needed to organize and promote them. Concurrently, a corporation should remember to provide a financial prize or other benefits for the victors.

1.11.2 Model 2. Hackathons

- **Goals:** are organized so that startup teams can quickly develop new solutions, prototypes or test ideas with an eye to the needs of corporations. This is also an opportunity for corporations to identify talented programmers, designers and engineers who can accrue value to the organization.
- **Rules:** a hackathon is a programming marathon during which teams focus on developing for a specific goal.[132] The participants of a hackathon work in groups on problems or challenges designated by a corporation, for example, writing a specific fragment of code or solving a specific problem.[133] They endeavor to create operational prototypes or applications in a very short period, that is, most frequently within 48 hours that correspond to a specific challenge. By organizing a hackathon, a corporation may search for ideas for new products and services or search for solutions to identified problems in the organization. Sometimes, during a hackathon corporations promulgate their own technological solutions based on which the teams are supposed to create solutions.

- **Characterization:** hackathons are conducive to the development of innovation and inter-organizational cooperation, and may also form a starting point for further cooperation and supporting the development of innovation from outside the bounds of an organization. In principle, hackathons promote intense and creative cooperation among their participants. Participants represent different areas of knowledge that enable them to look at a challenge in a multi-dimensional manner and apply an interdisciplinary approach to innovation. On account of time limitation hackathons compel participants to take risk, which is conducive to generating innovative solutions. Organizing a hackathon, just like in the competition model, requires less financial means; however, a corporation must provide capital to organize an event, prizes, infrastructure and possibly financing for the best projects selected during an event.

1.11.3 Model 3. Internet platforms

- **Goals:** the fundamental goal is to create a virtual space in which startups can present their innovations, products or services, or, less frequently, have the ability to a limited extent to test a solution using the technology supplied by a corporation.[134] In turn, for corporations internet platforms are a tool to identify and attract startups, and in some instances to be treated as a method of reaping profits by selling a startup's solution through a platform to other market participants.
- **Rules:** corporations create internet platforms that operate as a virtual place where startups can create profiles, describe their solutions, present the solution offered on the market and lay out their accomplishments to-date. Platforms frequently facilitate interactions between startups and representatives of corporations, enabling the exchange of information, plan meetings, present products and assess prospective benefits.
- **Characterization:** internet platforms act as virtual showrooms where startups can demonstrate their technologies, products and services. Platforms provide access to information thanks to the functionality of freely scrolling through the profiles of startups and their offerings. Importantly, an internet platform affords the ability for parties to manage their relationships. Corporations can track the progress of projects and analyze their potential. They also create an opportunity to launch talks regarding possible cooperation with the business units of large organizations. In the event an organization has its own tools, for example, for business partners in the form of a procurement or auction platform, then one can consider whether the possibility exists of adopting it to administering a virtual space for cooperating with startups. Creating and maintaining an internet platform for startups require on one hand financial means for technological development, marketing, technical support and staff salaries, and on the other hand, in the event of making the decision to cooperate, this requires providing resources for future cooperation.

1.11.4 Model 4. Venture Building

- **Goals:** the goal of venture building is for a corporation to build a business from the idea/minimum viable product (MVP) stage to scaling it up in cooperation with a partner. Thus, the fundamental goal is to create and develop new daughter companies that operate as businesses and whose core task is development and accelerated commercialization of new projects, technologies or products, customarily in the environment of a corporation.
- **Rules:** building a solution from scratch creates an active field to work not only on the part of the organization but also on the part of the startup team. Corporations become a company's co-shareholders. These businesses are usually separate from the firm's main structure. Their separation creates the possibility for the team to operate in a more independent and flexible manner without placing a burden at the same time on the main corporation. Newly formed businesses may be managed by specialized teams that exert control over the process of creating a product or service. Venture building allows for the creation of new innovative products or services that may be marketed as new brands. Corporations invest capital and resources in these companies and supply industrial knowledge, mentoring and operational support.
- **Characterization:** venture building is an approach that is characterized by a corporation establishing a relationship for the purpose of creating a solution that is aligned to the needs of a large organization from the very beginning.

This approach is characterized by concentration on creating innovation as an integral part of the innovation development strategy in a corporation. The venture building model engages a corporation in project-related activities and the formation of new startups, which is related to the requisite capital investments in developing these businesses and their infrastructure.

1.11.5 Model 5. Strategic partnerships with startups

- **Goals:** strategic partnerships are a model in which corporations establish relationships with startups for the purpose of achieving mutual benefits. The principal goal is to utilize complementary competences (knowledge, skills) and resources and the parties' potential to achieve specific business goals, supply innovative solutions to the market, create innovative solutions and strengthen competitiveness.
- **Rules:** corporations and startups enter into contracts and agreements that define the scope of cooperation and the parties' rights and duties. Cooperation may encompass the joint development of products, sharing resources, access to clients, knowledge transfer, technology integration and distribution of services. The established partnership may be short-term related to

a specific undertaking or long-term spanning many years of cooperation. Through negotiations the parties jointly specify their goals and expectations related to inter-organizational cooperation.
- **Characterization:** strategic partnerships create an opportunity for the parties to harness their unique competences and resources in a way that accrues mutual benefits.

Partnerships may lead to jointly developing and implementing new products and services that may combine unique attributes, resources and the capabilities of market partners. Through partnerships parties can tap into synergy, which may lead to augmenting the value and competitive position of corporations and startups on the market. Strategic partnerships may take time and a higher capital commitment.

1.11.6 Model 6. Corporate innovation incubator

- **Goals:** a corporate innovation incubator is a model in which dedicated structures are created to support startups and develop innovative projects that will ultimately be useful for large organizations. The primary goal of a corporate incubator is to source and support startups and project teams to enable them to develop innovative projects, not just at the level of products and services but also as part of internal processes and organizational culture.[135] The technological development of a corporation is considered to be the primary purpose of running a corporate incubator.[136]
- **Rules:** the incubators established by corporations, which are in principle dependent on them, offer office space to work, knowledge, capital sometimes as well as the other infrastructural resources of large organizations for beginning teams or startups.[137] Just as in the case of other activities related to sourcing innovation for a corporation, similarly in this case one should provide for the process of picking and selecting projects for incubation and formalize cooperation by entering into the appropriate contract related to participation in an incubation program. The participants of an incubation program have access provided to a contact network, knowledge and experts who shorten the founders' learning process through the advisory services provided in the initial phase of creating their businesses.[138] In contrast to a corporate accelerator, incubation does not involve very intense work in a very short period. The incubation-related activities of the team or startup may sometimes last as long as one to two years while the incubator team forms a liaison between program participants and the business units of a corporation and the mentors and experts.
- **Characterization:** corporate incubators customarily offer support to startups that are in the initial phase of development, that is, the idea or prototype phase. They rarely have their first client.[139] In turn, the incubated solution itself requires the support of the corporation in terms of further business development, operating strategy, designing and developing

technology with an eye to its future application in a large organization. The representatives of an incubator may organize training sessions or workshops, provide mentoring grasped as providing the ability to learn through experience and having more seasoned persons offer assistance and support in conquering problems,[140] networking partners and supply other resources that are indispensable in an incubation program, for example, in the form of access to office space, an R&D center, laboratories.[141] Providing suitable mentors poised to cooperate is a big challenge for organizations and is important for properly preparing a product or service for future cooperation. The operation of an incubator is also focused on actively looking for startup solutions on the market that potentially dovetail with a corporation's business. It is worth noting that employees of corporations interested in creating and developing new innovative projects can also avail themselves of the support provided by a corporate incubator. In that manner innovation incubators also serve the purpose of developing the culture of innovation within a corporation. They create a space that promotes openness to new ideas, gives a chance to experiment and cooperate actively with corporate departments and externally as part of inter-organizational cooperation. Corporate incubators need financial means to maintain and develop the incubator, provide infrastructure and possibly financial support for the incubated startups.

1.11.7 Model 7. Corporate startup accelerator

- **Goals:** the primary goal of a corporate startup accelerator and its acceleration program is to support startups in enabling them to develop innovative projects, not just at the level of products and services but also as part of internal processes and organizational culture and securing those projects that are ultimately attractive to the business units of large organizations.[142]
- **Rules:** corporations may organize their own acceleration programs as part of a defined unit within an organization. A program lasts for a specified time that is customarily no longer than six months. Such a program involves extending intensive support for selected startups. It is focused on preparing and testing a product, service or technology on the infrastructure of a corporation or in its environment.
- **Characterization:** for startups participating in a corporate acceleration program is an opportunity to refine their solution, test it and build relationships with industrial leaders, and it is also an opportunity to enter the market. In turn, for corporations it is chiefly an opportunity to gain access to innovations (scouting) and technologies and talents coming from outside the bounds of a large organization, while ultimately it is a chance to enhance an organization's competitiveness and innovativeness.[143] Corporate accelerators serve as a means to mitigate risk in highly innovative projects. Corporate startup accelerators require the provision of capital for tasks related to recruiting startups, offering support, mentoring, tests,

investments and other services contemplated by an acceleration program. What is important is that in this model a corporation, in the event a decision is made following the completion of acceleration to implement a solution in its environment, should furnish funds for the implementation of the innovation at the post-acceleration stage.

1.11.8 Model 8. Cooperation between startups and the R&D department

- **Goals**: the model for attracting startups to corporations through the operation of a dedicated unit within a corporation whose purpose is not just to conduct its own research in keeping with the organization's needs but also to be open to cooperation with external entities, including startups. The purpose of cooperation is to pursue joint R&D projects, conduct experiments and develop new technologies.
- **Rules**: the R&D department conducts searches on the market for prospective partners for cooperation in innovation; it possibly connects with startups that direct inquiries to the research department of a corporation requesting cooperation. A contract is entered into between the parties to govern the terms and conditions of R&D cooperation. The goals, scope of activity, work schedule and responsibility for various tasks and possibly the rights to the work done, including the concept for the further commercialization of the solution, for example, in the corporation's environment and the future split of profits are specified. Then the parties execute the R&D project while sharing knowledge, experience and resources. The R&D department plays the lead role in the process. Pursuant to the concluded agreement, after completing the project the parties can implement the findings obtained during their work in their products, services or processes. This increases their chances of enhancing their competitiveness and adopting to the rapid changes transpiring on the market.
- **Characterization**: cooperation with the R&D department of a corporation is an effective method of inter-organizational cooperation. It entails combining the resources and competences of a corporation with the means and skills startups have at their disposal. Cooperation is conducive to the coupled approach to innovation by blending the complementary resources, knowledge and experience of different entities. It is worth noting that the parties to cooperation share not just their resources but also the risk associated with the research, which is beneficial to corporations and startups alike. In conjunction with running an R&D department a corporation should not only secure funds for operating activity, staff, procurement and maintenance of infrastructural facilities but also procure funding for cooperation as part of the joint projects pursued with external partners, including startups. Such cooperation will require capital for joint research, conducting experiments and the investments needed for further research work in connection with proceeding through the *Technology Readiness Level.*

1.11.9 *Model 9. Corporate venture capital fund*

- **Goals:** the goals of CVC funds may vary depending on the strategy of the organization that elects to set up such an instrument. In principle, a CVC fund is a type of investment fund that operates as part of a large corporation or on its behalf and whose fundamental task is to explore new markets and invest in startups whose technologies and solutions may produce added value for the corporation through commercialization or assistance in altering the organization's business model and growing the organization's asset value, also by generating a financial return on the portfolio of investments made by the fund. CVC funds are rewarded on the basis of their performance by shareholders in the same way as a corporation's other activities.[144] What is important is for the corporate fund to conduct its business in such a way so as to be capable of competing on the market with other venture capital funds.
- **Rules:** CVC funds analyze startups and their solutions, primarily evaluating their growth potential, innovativeness, management team, pure investment risk and above all the impact they can exert on enhancing synergy between the environment of the corporation and the solution offered by the startup. It is worth remembering that just as in the case of other models, it is also true that funds provide not just capital but they can also provide strategic advisory services to startups. Funds can second a representative to a startup's supervisory board or management board to give them the ability to influence the strategic decisions being made.
- **Characterization:** an investment made by a CVC fund in a startup undertaking is an opportunity to give it access to new technologies, innovative solutions for the purpose of developing or improving its own products and services.

According to H. Chesbrough,[145] a CVC fund is a corporation's investment in innovations from outside and organization that it can commercialize. Accordingly, CVC funds cooperate with the business units of a large organization to ensure the maximum benefit to both parties and ultimately to integrate the investment made in a startup with the corporation's strategic goals.[146]

In addition, corporations set up these types of funds as a way to expand their footprint on the new technologies market and also to mark their presence in the startup ecosystem. CVC funds are ordinarily entities whose sole investor is a corporation. That is also why corporate funds frequently invest financial means in startups on behalf of large organizations. A CVC may have an unlimited term of existence if it is set up within the structures of a corporation. Maintaining a fund's structure entails risks and benefits spread over time.[147] The functioning of a corporate fund requires the organization to furnish extensive capital expenditures, in many instances as much as several hundred million Euro to conduct due diligence and make investments in startups. That is why few corporations can allow themselves to launch such a model to attract startups. A corporate fund's investments are pegged to the corporation's operating strategy. One should have in mind that on the market one can run into two types of corporate funds, that is, funds established as part of the organizational structure or funds managed by an external entity that is usually independent of the corporation. In the case of a fund managed by an external entity, the corporation's ability to influence the investment decisions made is clearly less pronounced that in the case of a CVC established as part of the organizational structure. A fund managed in this manner may make decisions contrary to the will of a corporation. In turn, one drawback of this solution is that it may be treated as an external entity since it is not directly entrenched in the organizational structure. Consequently, it may have impeded access to the resources and back office of a large organization. The diminished will of a corporation's business units to get involved in the projects of such a fund may also be noticeable in this event. In turn, for a corporate fund entrenched in the structure it may be a challenge to determine operating efficiency and the decision-making pace, which is slower than in the event of an externally managed corporate fund.

1.11.10 Model 10. Acquisitions of startups

- **Goals:** the model for a corporation to acquire startups involves a corporation acquiring startups to expand its own portfolio of products, services and technologies offered on the market. The fundamental goals of this model are as follows: gaining access to new technologies, talents and markets or streamlining a corporation's existing processes through integration of the solutions of startups with the environment of a large organization.
- **Rules:** a corporation conducts activities on the market to identify solutions that dovetail with its growth strategy.[148] Subsequently, the entire equity stake or a majority equity stake is acquired. The acquisition process is predicated on assessing a startup's potential, its technology, team and synergies with the corporation. After completion of an acquisition the corporation kicks off the process of full integration with its structure.
- **Characterization:** corporations treat the startup acquisition model as a method of rapidly gaining access to advanced technologies and solutions that may be difficult to create with their own resources or very time-consuming. In some instances, corporations allow the acquired startups to operate as independent entities that retain their autonomy and organizational culture. Acquiring startups allows corporations to enlarge their own product or service offering while also attracting new clients. This also gives a corporation the possibility of extending its activities to new market areas or to appear on new markets. Acquiring startups and their breakthrough solutions and technologies creates an opportunity for a corporation to play an active role in shaping the future of the industry in which it operates. Integrating with startups also accelerates a corporation's ability to create new products and solutions and adapt more rapidly to changes

on the market. The market acquisition model requires substantial capital associated with the acquisition of a startup. Furthermore, just like in a CVC fund it may prove to be necessary for an organization to secure funds for integration, additional development of the offered technology, product or service or expand the acquired solution on a new market.

1.12 Models for attracting startups and the phases for startup development

The models for attracting startups identified above in this chapter are duly applicable, depending on the strategy adopted by a corporation and its needs, to firms in a specific phase of growth. Three stages of a startup's development are distinguished in accordance with the division encountered in the scientific literature:

a **idea/MVP stage** – means startups in an early stage of development that have an idea for a product or service, or have an MVP;
b **growth stage** – startups already have a developed product or service, and they usually also have their first paying clients and specific revenue. They are in the phase of active development and concentrating on intense growth;
c **scale up stage** – startups in this phase have attained considerable market success. They have a well-established position on the market, they have a client database and they generate substantial revenue. Their goal is to scale up operations and penetrate new markets.

Each one of the foregoing three growth stages of a startup is characterized by its unique goals, actions, challenges and financial capabilities. Accordingly, Table 1.4 depicts how startups evolve from their initial concept to full scale up and what crucial aspects are perceptible for each one of the growth phases.

It is therefore important to adjust the model to the specific situation in which a large organization finds itself. Table 1.5 depicts which models for attracting startups are suitable for each one of these types of startups ("Yes") and which ones may be in principle unsuitable ("No"). The tabular list below may help corporations adapt their strategies for attracting startups to meet their current needs and objectives giving consideration to the phase of development of innovative firms.

For startups in the idea/MVP phase competitions, hackathons, internet platforms, corporate R&D department, corporate incubator and venture building are more suitable because these models make it possible to put forward concepts and early MVPs and work somehow from the very outset on a solution. For instance, a competition for startups makes it possible to present an idea to a corporation while hackathons make it possible to create prototypes quickly and experiment with ideas.

Table 1.4 Development phases of startups: goals, activities, success indicators and challenges

Phase	*Major goals*	*Key activities*	*Success indicators*	*Challenges*
Idea/MVP stage	• Formulating the MVP • Verifying the concept for the idea on the market	• Researching the market, collecting users' opinions • Prototyping and testing • Building a team	• Validating the idea • Interest of clients in the MVP developed	• Limited financing • Verifying the idea • No clients
Growth stage	• Customer acquisition • Product development • Securing stable sources of revenue	• Marketing and sales • Product adaptation and optimization • Compiling the team	• Growing the number of solution users • Product development • First revenue turning into stable revenue	• Market competition • Managing the organization's growth and enlarging team
Scale up stage	• Market expansion • Growing scale of operations	• Optimizing processes • Marketing at scale • Expansion onto international markets	• Recognition and market share • Stable growth • Expansion of the infrastructure	• Managing a large scale of operations • International competition • Logistics challenges

Source: Proprietary material.

Table 1.5 List of models for attracting startups depending on their development phase

Model for attracting start-ups	*Start-up in the idea/MVP phase*	*Start-up in the growth phase*	*Start-up in the scaling phase*
Competitions	Yes	Yes	No
Hackathons	Yes	No	No
Internet platforms	Yes	Yes	Yes
Venture Building	Yes	Yes	No
Strategic Partnerships	No	Yes	Yes
Corporate Incubator	Yes	No	No
Corporate Accelerator	No	Yes	Yes
R&D Department	Yes	Yes	Yes
Corporate VC Fund	No	Yes	Yes
Market Acquisition Mechanism	No	Yes	Yes

Source: Proprietary material.

In turn, for startups in the growth phase the vast majority of models is suitable with the caveat that those models are more preferred that are focused on the need for obtaining support and development for a solution that in principle already exists. A corporation supports startups with its resources to develop their activities and helps them achieve the subsequent growth stages for their product and service, especially those that are looking for compliance, a fit with the corporation and merging it with its clients and partners, for example, through the corporate accelerator operation model.

In turn, for startups in the scaling up phase the most suitable models are the ones that involve support in market expansion to a greater degree. Startups that are prominent, have a market share, and offer a fully vetted solution tested on a sizable client group are highly sought after. Those actions are preferable that support scaling up, for example, in the form of a strategic partnership model.

1.13 Innovation processes in the models for attracting startups to corporations

The models for attracting startups to corporations presented above differ from one another in terms of their goals, rules and above all their approach to innovation processes. These processes may take the direction of inbound innovation to a corporation just as occurs with the following models: competitions, hackathons, internet platforms, CVC funds and acquisitions of startups. In the case of strategic partnership models, venture building, cooperation with the R&D department, a corporate incubator and a corporate accelerator, a coupled process is applied. This is the combination of an inbound process while on the other hand it requires the undertaking of joint efforts in respect of the submitted solution, for example, to refine and test it. Table 1.6 presents the subordination of innovation processes to the various models and is accompanied by a detailed analysis.

This chapter provides a comprehensive analysis of the various aspects associated with open and closed innovations and inter-organizational cooperation between corporations and startups. This will facilitate the comprehension of the key attributes of both approaches. It focuses on a detailed discussion of the theoretical and practical aspects of cooperation, providing readers with insight into the major issues and various approaches to the topic of how large organizations establish relations with innovative companies (startups). This will support further analyses and discussions pertaining to inter-organizational cooperation while emphasizing the role of cooperation and the motives organizations espouse when establishing partnerships with startups. An analysis of the network approach in the approach to cooperation has been conducted.

Table 1.6 Innovation processes in cooperation models between corporations and startups

No	*Model*	*Process type*	*Process description*
1	Competitions for start-ups	Inbound process in a corporation	This process entails forwarding the project submissions filed by start-ups into responses to the competition announced by a corporation. A corporation may select winners, but only after the decision to implement can it begin work on integrating the start-up's solution with the organization.
2	Hackathons	Inbound process in a corporation	Innovation processes are more concentrated on a solution to the challenge announced by a corporation, as opposed to integrating a project inside an organization from the outset.
3	Internet platforms	Inbound process in a corporation	This process pertains more to the technical and organizational side in connection with the requirement to maintain the platform and manage the projects put forward by start-ups.
4	Venture Building with the participation of a start-up	Coupled process	In this process the corporation actively participates in creating and developing the innovation. This process calls for profound cooperation and integrating the start-up team with the business unit of a large organization.
5	Strategic partnerships with start-ups	Coupled process	This process may encompass jointly developing solutions, developing products and services, sharing knowledge, distributing the product on the market and selling it jointly.
6	Corporate innovation incubator	Coupled process	This process involves cooperation and developing the ideas of start-ups in partnership with a corporation. The work is most frequently conducted using the organization's infrastructure and its resources.
7	Corporate start-up accelerator	Coupled process	This process concentrates on intensive cooperation between a cooperation and a start-up in conjunction with the need of aligning and testing the solution offered by a start-up. The tests are conducted as part of the process in the corporation's production or test environment.

(*Continued*)

Table 1.6 (Continued)

No	*Model*	*Process type*	*Process description*
8	Cooperation between start-ups and the R&D department	Coupled process	This process pertains to cooperation between corporations and start-ups in the field of running joint R&D work. This process may involve joint research, developing projects and technology, testing and experimenting.
9	Corporate venture capital fund	Inbound process in a corporation/ coupled process	This means a capital investment in a start-up. Through the partial link to the corporate fund the start-up has an easier path to reaching the corporation and its resources and as a result collaboration on developing the product or service.
10	Acquisitions of start-ups	Inbound process in a corporation	After acquiring a start-up, a corporation may continue to develop the product, service or technology within its own structure as part of its own resources. The organization may also take the decision to cease the activities of the acquired start-up and, for instance, transfer its human resources and know-how to the larger organization. This then becomes an internal process for the corporation.

Source: Proprietary material.

This chapter also contains an analysis of the innovation processes in the open innovation model while discussing the prospective obstacles that may hinder the development and implementation of innovative solutions in corporations. The most frequent models for cooperation between corporations and startups have also been characterized. This forms the theoretical grounds for in-depth consideration of the cooperation model as part of acceleration programs. Innovation processes were analyzed within the context of cooperation between large organizations and startups, which is crucial to grasp the benefits and challenges associated with various models for attracting innovation to corporations, including their suitability to the various growth phases of startups.

In that manner this chapter provides a comprehensive look at the theoretical and practical aspects of implementing innovation and inter-organizational cooperation within the context of open innovations. It provides valuable conclusions not just for scientists but also for the representatives of corporations and startups that strive to establish effective cooperation as they operate on the market.

Notes

1 Skrzypek, E., & Skrzypek, A. (2019). Uwarunkowania i konsekwencje innowacyjności organizacji w gospodarce współdzielenia. In M. Cisek (Ed.), *Innowacje i cyfryzacja gospodarki* (pp. 25–44) Siedlce: Wydawnictwo Uniwersytetu Przyrodniczo-Humanistycznego w Siedlcach.
2 Sopińska, A., & Dziurski, P. (2018). *Otwarte innowacje: perspektywa współpracy i zarządzania wiedzą*. Warszawa: Oficyna Wydawnicza SGH.
3 Katz, R., & Allen, T. J. (1985). Organizational issues in the introduction of new technologies. In *The management of productivity and technology in manufacturing* (pp. 275–300). Boston, MA: Springer.
4 Madjar, N., Greenberg, E., & Chen, Z. (2011). Factors for radical creativity, incremental creativity, and routine, noncreative performance. *Journal of Applied Psychology*, *96*, 730–743.
5 Vahs, D., & Brem, A. (2015). *Innovationsmanagement: Von der Idee zur erfolgreichen Vermarktung*. Stuttgart: Schäffer-Poeschel.
6 Christenson, C. (1997). *The innovator's dilemma*. Cambridge, MA: Harvard Business School Press.
7 Lyytinen, K., Yoo, Y., & Boland Jr, R. J. (2016). Digital product innovation within four classes of innovation networks. *Information Systems Journal*, *26*(1), 47–75.
8 Sopińska, A., & Mierzejewska, W. (2017). *Otwarte innowacje produktowe realizowane przez przedsiębiorstwa działające w Polsce: podejście zasobowe* (p. 37). Warszawa: Oficyna Wydawnicza SGH.
9 Richter, N., Jackson, P., & Schildhauer, T. (2018). Outsourcing creativity: An abductive study of open innovation using corporate accelerators. *Creativity and Innovation Management*, *27*(1), 69–78.
10 Laursen, K., & Salter, A. (2006), Open for innovation: the role of openness in explaining innovation performance among U.K. manufacturing firms. *Strategy Management Journal*, *27*, 131–150. https://doi.org/10.1002/smj.507
11 West, J., & Gallagher, S. (2006) Challenges of Open Innovation: The Paradox of Firm Investment in Open-Source Software. *R&D Management*, *36*, 319–331. https://doi.org/10.1111/j.1467-9310.2006.00436.x
12 Dittrich, K., & Duysters, G. (2007). Networking as a Means to Strategy Change: The Case of Open Innovation in Mobile Telephony. *Journal of Product Innovation Management*, *24*, 510–521. https://doi.org/10.1111/j.1540-5885.2007.00268.x
13 Perkmann, M., & Walsh, K. (2007). University-industry relationships and open innovation: Towards a research agenda. *International Journal of Management Reviews*, *9*(4), 259–280. https://doi.org/10.1111/j.1468-2370.2007.00225.x
14 Lichtenthaler, U. (2008). Open Innovation in Practice: An Analysis of Strategic Approaches to Technology Transactions. *IEEE Transactions on Engineering Management*, *55*, 148–157. https://doi.org/10.1109/TEM.2007.912932
15 Chesbrough, H., & Bogers, M. (2014) Explicating Open Innovation: Clarifying an Emerging Paradigm for Understanding Innovation. In: Chesbrough, H., Vanhaverbeke, W., & West, J., (Eds.), *Open innovation: New frontiers and applications* (pp. 3–28), Oxford: Oxford University Press. https://doi.org/10.1093/acprof:oso/9780199682461.003.0001
16 Urbaniec, M., & Żur, A. (2021). Business model innovation in corporate entrepreneurship: Exploratory insights from in-house accelerators. *International Entrepreneurship and Management Journal*, *17*(2), 865–888.
17 Dyduch, W. (2021). Tworzenie i przechwytywanie wartości w przedsiębiorstwach w Polsce: ocena podejmowanych działań, identyfikacja kluczowych zmiennych oraz ich wpływ na efektywność. *Przegląd Organizacji*, *6*, 7–16.

18 Krzakiewicz, K., & Cyfert, S. (2020). *Podstawy zarządzania organizacjami*. Poznań: Wydawnictwo UEP.
19 Von Hippel, E. (2005). Democratizing innovation: The evolving phenomenon of user innovation. *Journal für Betriebswirtschaft*, *55*, 63–78.
20 Czakon, W. (2014). Zarządzanie międzyorganizacyjne jako kompetencja przedsiębiorstwa. In A. K. Koźmiński & D. Latusek-Jurczak (Ed.), *Relacje międzyorganizacyjne w naukach o zarządzaniu* (pp. 186–217). Warszawa: Wolters Kluwer SA.
21 Koźmiński, A. K., & Latusek-Jurczak, D. (2014). *Relacje międzyorganizacyjne w naukach o zarządzaniu*. Warszawa: Wolters Kluwer SA.
22 Svensson, G. (2004). Vulnerability in business relationships: The gap between dependence and trust. *Journal of Business & Industrial Marketing*, *19*(7), 469–483.
23 Ganesan, S., & Hess, R. (1997). Dimensions and levels of trust: Implications for commitment to a relationship. *Marketing Letters*, *8*(4), 439–448.
24 Gambetta, D. (2000). Can we trust trust. *Trust: Making and Breaking Cooperative Relations*, *13*, 213–237.
25 Mayer, R. C., Davis, J. H., & Schoorman, F. D. (1995). An integrative model of organizational trust. *Academy of Management Review*, *20*(3), 709–734.
26 Brito, C., & Costa e Silva, S. (2009). When trust becomes the fourth. *The Marketing Review*, *9*(4), 289–299.
27 Bidault, F., & Castello, A. (2010). Why too much trust is death to innovation. *MIT Sloan Management Review*, *51*(4), 33.
28 Danik, L. (2009). Zaufanie na rynku instytucjonalnym. In H. Brdulak, E. Duliniec, & T. Gołębiowski (red.), *Partnerstwo przedsiębiorstw jako czynnik ograniczania ryzyka działalności gospodarczej* (pp. 25–36). Warszawa: Oficyna Wydawnicza SGH.
29 Bugdol, M. (2010). *Wymiary i problemy zarządzania organizacją opartą na zaufaniu* (p. 7). Kraków: Wydawnictwo Uniwersytetu Jagiellońskiego.
30 Chesbrough, H. W. (2003). *Open innovation: The new imperative for creating and profiting from technology*. Boston: Harvard Business Press.
31 Saebi, T., & Foss, N. J. (2015). Business models for open innovation: Matching heterogeneous open innovation strategies with business model dimensions. *European Management Journal*, *33*(3), 201–213.
32 Almeida, P., & Kogut, B. (1999). Localization of knowledge and the mobility of engineers in regional networks. *Management Science*, *45*(7), 905–917.
33 Dahl, M. S., & Pedersen, C. Ø. (2004). Knowledge flows through informal contacts in industrial clusters: Myth or reality? *Research Policy*, *33*(10), 1673–1686.
34 Tether, B. S., & Tajar, A. (2008). The organisational-cooperation mode of innovation and its prominence amongst European service firms. *Research Policy*, *37*(4), 720–739.
35 Dahlander, L., & Gann, D. M. (2010). How open is innovation? *Research Policy*, *39*(6), 699–709.
36 Gassmann, O., & Enkel, E. (2005). Open innovation Forschung. In M. Weissenberger-Eib (Ed.), *Gestaltung von Innovationssystemen* (pp. 289–308). Kassel: Cactus Group Verlag.
37 Zott, C., & Amit, R. (2010). Business model design: An activity system perspective. *Long Range Planning*, *43*(2–3), 216–226.
38 Klimas, P. (2012). Operacjonalizacja bliskości organizacyjnej. *Prace Naukowe Uniwersytetu Ekonomicznego we Wrocławiu*, *260*, 195–205.
39 Czakon, W. (2005). Istota relacji sieciowych przedsiębiorstwa. *Przegląd Organizacji*, *9*, 10–13.
40 Jap, S. D. (2001). "Pie sharing" in complex collaboration contexts. *Journal of Marketing Research*, *38*(1), 86–99.

41 Peters, C., Blohm, I., & Leimeister, J. M. (2015). Anatomy of successful business models for complex services: Insights from the telemedicine field. *Journal of Management Information Systems*, *32*(3), 75–104.
42 Dudzik, T., Gołębiowski, T., Lewandowska, M., & Witek-Hajduk, M. (2008). *Modele biznesu polskich przedsiębiorstw* (p. 57). Warszawa: Oficyna Wydawnicza SGH.
43 Chesbrough, H. (2010). Business model innovation: Opportunities and barriers. *Long Range Planning*, *43*(2–3), 354–363.
44 Szewc, A., Zioło, K., & Grzesiczak, M. (2011). *Umowy jako prawne narzędzie transferu innowacji*. Warszawa: Polska Agencja Rozwoju Przedsiębiorczości.
45 Fosfuri, A. (2006). The licensing dilemma: Understanding the determinants of the rate of technology licensing. *Strategic Management Journal*, *27*(12), 1141–1158.
46 Baloh, P., Jha, S., & Awazu, Y. (2008). Building strategic partnerships for managing innovation outsourcing. *Strategic Outsourcing: An International Journal*, *1*(2), 100–121.
47 Podręcznik Oslo (2020). *Zalecenia dotyczące pozyskiwania, prezentowania i wykorzystywania danych z zakresu innowacji* (p. 50). Warszawa: Pomiar działalności naukowo-technicznej i innowacyjnej, GUS.
48 Roszkowska-Menkes, M. (2015). *Otwarte innowacje: w poszukiwaniu równowagi* (p. 125). Warszawa: Oficyna Wydawnicza SG.
49 Kanbach, D. K., & Stubner, S. (2016). In-house accelerators as recent form of startup engagement: The what, the why, and the how. *Journal of Applied Business Research (JABR)*, *32*(6), 1761–1776.
50 Kohler, T. (2016). Corporate accelerators: Building bridges between corporations and startups. *Business Horizons*, *59*(3), 347–357.
51 Markides, C. (2006). Disruptive innovation: In need of better theory. *Journal of Product Innovation Management*, *23*(1), 19–25.
52 Jelonek A., & Moczała D. (2020). *Metody I techniki projektowania innowacji*. Warszawa: Polskie Wydawnictwo Ekonomiczne.
53 Krzakiewicz, K., & Cyfert, S. (2019). Strategic orientations of the organization-entrepreneurial, market and organizational learning. *Management*, *23*(1), 7–19.
54 Kale, P., Dyer, J. H., & Singh, H. (2002). Alliance capability, stock market response, and long-term alliance success: The role of the alliance function. *Strategic Management Journal*, *23*(8), 747–767.
55 Gwarda-Gruszczyńska, E. (2013). *Modele procesu komercjalizacji nowych technologii w przedsiębiorstwach. Uwarunkowania wyboru-kluczowe obszary decyzji* (pp. 10–11). Łódź: Wydawnictwo Uniwersytetu Łódzkiego.
56 Dyduch, W. (2019). Entrepreneurial strategy stimulating value creation: Conceptual findings and some empirical tests. *Entrepreneurial Business and Economics Review*, *7*(3), 65–82.
57 Klimas, P. (2014). *Sieci innowacji: implikacje bliskości organizacyjnej*. Katowice: Prace Naukowe/Uniwersytet Ekonomiczny w Katowicach.
58 Gierszewska, G., & Romanowska, M. (2003). *Analiza strategiczna przedsiębiorstwa* (p. 169). Warszawa: PWE.
59 Stępień, B. (2011). *Międzynarodowa kooperacja gospodarcza z polskiej perspektywy* (p. 15). Polskie Wydawnictwo Ekonomiczne.
60 Brito, C., & Costa e Silva, S. (2009). When trust becomes the fourth. *The Marketing Review*, *9*(4), 289–299.
61 De Wit, B. (2007). *Meyer r. Synteza strategii*. Warszawa: PWE.
62 Danik, L., & Żukowska, J. (2011). Czynniki wpływające na sukces kooperacji polskich przedsiębiorstw w innowacjach (w przekroju branżowym). Prace

Naukowe Uniwersytetu Ekonomicznego we Wrocławiu. *Problemy regionalizmu i globalizacji*, *221*, 123–136.
63 Nowak, D. (2012). *Zarządzanie międzyorganizacyjnymi relacjami kooperacyjnymi w przedsiębiorstwach przemysłowych*. Poznań: Wydawnictwo Uniwersytetu Ekonomicznego w Poznaniu.
64 Van Beers, C., & Zand, F. (2014). R&D cooperation, partner diversity, and innovation performance: An empirical analysis. *Journal of Product Innovation Management*, *31*(2), 292–312.
65 Donaldson, B., & O'toole, T. (2007). *Strategic market relationships: From strategy to implementation*. New Jersey: John Wiley & Sons.
66 Tuusjärvi, E., & Möller, K. (2009). Multiplicity of norms in intercompany cooperation. *Journal of Business & Industrial Marketing*, *24*(7), 519–528.
67 Nooteboom, B. (1999). Innovation and inter-firm linkages: New implications for policy. *Research Policy*, 28(8), 793–805.
68 Khanna, T., Gulati, R., & Nohria, N. (1998). The dynamics of learning alliances: Competition, cooperation, and relative scope. *Strategic Management Journal*, *19*(3), 193–210.
69 Sakakibara, M. (1997). Heterogeneity of firm capabilities and cooperative research and development: An empirical examination of motives. *Strategic Management Journal*, *18*(S1), 143–164.
70 Katz, M. L. (1995). Joint ventures as a means of assembling complementary inputs. In Kalyan Chatterjee & Barbara Gray (Eds.), *International joint ventures: Economic and organizational perspectives* (pp. 5–22). Dordrecht: Springer.
71 Hagedoorn, J. (1993). Understanding the rationale of strategic technology partnering: Interorganizational modes of cooperation and sectoral differences. *Strategic Management Journal*, *14*(5), 371–385.
72 Rutkowski, I. P. (2007). *Rozwój nowego produktu: metody i uwarunkowania*. Warszawa: Polskie Wydawnictwo Ekonomiczne.
73 Liebeskind, J. P., Oliver, A. L., Zucker, L., & Brewer, M. (1996). Social networks, learning, and flexibility: Sourcing scientific knowledge in new biotechnology firms. *Organization Science*, *7*(4), 428–443.
74 Powell, W. W. (1987). Hybrid organizational arrangements: New form or transitional development? *California Management Review*, *30*(1), 67–87.
75 Tidström, A. (2006). *Conflicts when competitors cooperate: Exploring elements of conflicts from a business network perspective* (p. 13). Helsinki: Swedish School of Economics and Business Administration.
76 Gulati, R. (1998). Alliances and networks. *Strategic Management Journal*, *19*(4), 293–317.
77 Czakon, W. (2007). *Dynamika więzi międzyorganizacyjnych przedsiębiorstwa* (p. 35). Katowice: Prace Naukow. Akademia Ekonomiczna w Katowicach.
78 Adamik, A. (2012). Partnerzy, formy i obszary współpracy małych i średnich przedsiębiorstw w regionie i ich efektywność. In A. Adamik (Ed.), *Współpraca małych i średnich przedsiębiorstw w regionie. Budowanie konkurencyjności firm i regionu* (p. 252), Warszawa: Difin.
79 Wilding, R., & Humphries, A. S. (2006). Understanding collaborative supply chain relationships through the application of the Williamson organisational failure framework. *International Journal of Physical Distribution & Logistics Management*, *36*(4), 308–329.
80 Fajczak-Kowalska, A. (2012). Wpływ współpracy partnerskiej firm na funkcjonowanie łańcucha dostaw. *Studia Ekonomiczne Regionu Łódzkiego*, *1*, 113.
81 Duczkowska-Piasecka, M. (2012). *Model biznesu w zarządzaniu przedsiębiorstwem*. Warszawa: Oficyna Wydawnicza SGH.
82 Barczak, B. J. (2012). Źródła efektów synergicznych w sieciach organizacyjnych. In R. Borowiecki & T. Rojek (Ed.), *Współpraca międzyorganizacyjna*

w działalności przedsiębiorstw: klastry, alianse, sieci (pp. 1–187), Kraków: Fundacja Uniwersytetu Ekonomicznego.

83 Thorelli, H. B. (1986). Networks: Between markets and hierarchies. *Strategic Management Journal*, *7*(1), 37–51.

84 Latusek-Jurczak, D. (2014). Sieci międzyorganizacyjne jako struktury współpracy – podstawowe pojęcia analityczne. In A. K. Koźmiński & D. Latusek-Jurczak (Ed.), *Relacje międzyorganizacyjne w naukach o zarządzaniu, wyd. Relacje międzyorganizacyjne w naukach o zarządzaniu* (pp. 23–45), Warszawa: Wolters Kluwer SA.

85 Porter, M. E. (2006). *Przewaga konkurencyjna: Osiąganie i utrzymywanie lepszych wyników*. Helion.

86 Zakrzewska-Bielawska, A., & Adamik, A. (2013). Organizacja w sieciach współpracy-od prostych do złożonych form współpracy międzyorganizacyjnej. In A. Adamik (Ed.), *Nauka o organizacji. Ujęcie dynamiczne*. Oficyna Wolters Kluwer business.

87 Adamczewski, P. (2013). Funkcjonalne determinanty ICT przedsiębiorstw sieciowych. *Zeszyty Naukowe WSB w Poznaniu*, *49*(4), 121.

88 Zakrzewska-Bielawska, A. (2016). Tworzenie i apropriacja wartości jako cel strategii relacyjnej przedsiębiorstwa. *Prace Naukowe Uniwersytetu Ekonomicznego we Wrocławiu*, *444*, 609–622.

89 Latusek-Jurczak, D. (2014). Sieci międzyorganizacyjne jako struktury współpracy–podstawowe pojęcia analityczne. In A. K. Koźmiński & D. Latusek-Jurczak (Ed.), *Relacje międzyorganizacyjne w naukach o zarządzaniu, wyd. Relacje międzyorganizacyjne w naukach o zarządzaniu* (pp. 23–45), Warszawa: Wolters Kluwer SA.

90 Adamik, A. (2008). Kumulowanie wiedzy organizacyjnej poprzez związki współpracy. In A. Glińska-Neweś (Ed.), *Zarządzanie organizacjami w gospodarce opartej na wiedzy. Zasobowe podstawy rozwoju organizacji* (pp. 17–35), Toruń: TNOIK "Dom Organizatora".

91 Dyduch, W., & Bratnicki, M. (2015). Tworzenie i przechwytywanie wartości w organizacjach współdziałających w sieci. *Prace Naukowe Wałbrzyskiej Wyższej Szkoły Zarządzania i Przedsiębiorczości*, *32*, 77–93.

92 Duysters, G., & Vanhaverbeke, W. (1996). Strategic interactions in DRAM and RISC technology: A network approach. *Scandinavian Journal of Management*, *12*(4), 437–461.

93 Gulati, R. (1999). Network location and learning: The influence of network resources and firm capabilities on alliance formation. *Strategic Management Journal*, *20*(5), 397–420.

94 Poznańska, K. (2014). Sieci współpracy a innowacyjność przedsiębiorstw. In A. Sopińska & S. Gregorczyk (Ed.), *Granice strukturalnej złożoności organizacji* (pp. 151–160). Warszawa: Oficyna Wydawnicza SGH.

95 Lewandowska, M. S. (2018). *Koncepcja otwartych innowacji: perspektywa polskich przedsiębiorstw przemysłowych* (p. 116). Warszawa: Oficyna Wydawnicza SGH.

96 Post, J. E., & Altma, B. W. (1994). Managing the environmental change process: Barriers and opportunities. *Journal of Organizational Change Management*.

97 Ng, S. T., Rose, T. M., Mak, M., & Chen, S. E. (2002). Problematic issues associated with project partnering – The contractor perspective. *International Journal of Project Management*, *20*(6), 437–449.

98 Pachura, A. (2015). Kultura organizacyjna a potencjał kreatywności przedsiębiorstwa. Zeszyty Naukowe Wyższej Szkoły Humanitas. *Zarządzanie*, *3*, 87–97.

99 Nowak, D. (2010). Bariery rozwoju powiązań kooperacyjnych w ocenie polskich przedsiębiorstw. *Zeszyty Naukowe Uniwersytetu Szczecińskiego. Finanse, Rynki Finansowe, Ubezpieczenia*, 34 Uwarunkowania wzrostu wartości przedsiębiorstw w warunkach konkurencji, *34*, 289–302.

100 Gołębiowski, T., & Lewandowska, M. (2010). Kooperacja a sprawność marketingowa przedsiębiorstw na przykładzie polskich przedsiębiorstw przemysłu elektromaszynowego. *Zeszyty Naukowe/Szkoła Główna Handlowa. Kolegium Gospodarki Światowej*, 27, 202–224.
101 Strzyżewska, M. (2011). *Współpraca między przedsiębiorstwami-odniesienie do polskiej praktyki*. Warszawa: Oficyna Wydawnicza SGH.
102 Katz, M. L. (1986). An analysis of cooperative research and development. *The RAND Journal of Economics*, *17*(4), 527–543.
103 Berchicci, L., & Tucci, C. L. (2008). *Entrepreneurship, technology and Schumpeterian innovation: Entrants and incumbents* (pp. 332–351). Oxford: Oxford University Press.
104 Wojcik, P., Obłój, K., Wąsowska, A., & Wierciński, S. (2020). Corporate acceleration process: A systems psychodynamics perspective. *Journal of Organizational Change Management*, *33*(6), 1163–1180.
105 Jackson, P., & Richter, N. (2017). Situational logic: An analysis of open innovation using corporate accelerators. *International Journal of Innovation Management*, *21*(7), 1750062.
106 Kelly, M. J., Schaan, J. L., & Joncas, H. (2002). Managing alliance relationships: Key challenges in the early stages of collaboration. *R&D Management*, *32*(1), 11–22.
107 Weiblen, T., & Chesbrough, H. W. (2015). Engaging with startups to enhance corporate innovation. *California Management Review*, *57*(2), 66–90.
108 Hutter, K., Gfrerer, A., & Lindner, B. (2021). From popular to profitable: Incumbents experiences and challenges with external corporate accelerators. *International Journal of Innovation Management*, *25*(3), 2150035.
109 Blomqvist, K., & Levy, J. (2006). Collaboration capability—A focal concept in knowledge creation and collaborative innovation in networks. *International Journal of Management Concepts and Philosophy*, 2(1), 31–48.
110 Bannerjee S., Bielli S., & Haley C. (2016). *Scaling together: Overcoming barriers in corporate-startup collaboration*. London: Nesta, Startup Europe, The Scale-Up Institute.
111 Hill, C. W., Jones, G. R., & Schilling, M. A. (2014). *Strategic management: Theory & cases: An integrated approach*. Cengage Learning.
112 Blank, S. (2020). *The four steps to the epiphany: Successful strategies for products that win*. New Jersey: John Wiley & Sons.
113 Thiel, P., & Masters, B. (2014). *Zero to one: Notes on startups, or how to build the future*. New York: Crown Currency Publishing Group.
114 Ries, E. (2011). *The lean startup: How today's entrepreneurs use continuous innovation to create radically successful businesses*. New York: Crown Currency Publishing Group.
115 Hirt, M., & Willmott, P. (2014). Strategic principles for competing in the digital age. *McKinsey Quarterly*, *5*(1), 1–13.
116 Zastempowski, M., & Cyfert, S. (2023). A new angle on SMEs' competitiveness. How do agility capabilities affect a firm's competitive position? *Journal of Organizational Change Management*, *36*(4), 635–662.
117 Bańka, M. S., Kukurba, M., Miklaszewicz, S., Trzebiński, A. A., Waszkiewicz, A., & Boulangé, P. (2022). *Crowdfunding: Research & practice*. Warszawa: Difin.
118 Cegielska, E., & Zawadzka, D. (2017). Źródła finansowania startupów w Polsce. *Annales Universitatis Mariae Curie-Skłodowska, sectio H–Oeconomia*, *51*(6), 53–61.
119 Shankar, R. K., & Shepherd, D. A. (2019). Accelerating strategic fit or venture emergence: Different paths adopted by corporate accelerators. *Journal of Business Venturing*, *34*(5), 105886.

120 Fasnacht, D. (2009). *Open innovation: The new business paradigm* (pp. 87–102). Open Innovation in the Financial Services. Berlin, Heidelberg: Springer.
121 Deakins, D., & Freel, M. (1998). Entrepreneurial learning and the growth process in SMEs. *The Learning Organization*, *5*(3), 144–155.
122 Chesbrough, H. W., & Appleyard, M. M. (2007). Open innovation and strategy. California management review, 50(1), 57–76.
123 Euchner, J. (2016). Emerging models for corporate innovation: Insights from the IRI 2015 strategy forum. *Research-Technology Management*, *59*(1), 56–60.
124 Christenson, C. (1997). *The innovator's dilemma*. Cambridge, MA: Harvard Business School Press.
125 Weiblen, T., & Chesbrough, H. W. (2015). Engaging with Startups to Enhance Corporate Innovation.
126 Kanter, R. M. (2006). Innovation: The classic traps. *Harvard Business Review*, *84*(11), 72.
127 Dougherty, D., & Hardy, C. (1996). Sustained product innovation in large, mature organizations: Overcoming innovation-to-organization problems. *Academy of Management Journal*, *39*(5), 1120–1153.
128 Kupp, M., Marval, M., & Borchers, P. (2017). Corporate accelerators: Fostering innovation while bringing together startups and large firms. *Journal of Business Strategy*, *38*(6), 47–53.
129 Richter, N., Jackson, P., & Schildhauer, T. (2018). Outsourcing creativity: An abductive study of open innovation using corporate accelerators. *Creativity and Innovation Management*, 27(1), 69–78.
130 Mocker, V., Bielli, S., & Haley, C. (2015). *Winning Together: A guide to successful corporate-startup collaborations*. London: Nesta.
131 Heinzelmann, N., Selig, C. J., & Baltes, G. H. (2020). Critical actions of and synergies between corporate entrepreneurship programs. In *2020 IEEE International Conference on Engineering, Technology and Innovation (ICE/ITMC)* (pp. 1–9). Cardiff: IEEE.
132 Nandi, A., & Mandernach, M. (2016, February). Hackathons as an informal learning platform. In *Proceedings of the 47th ACM technical symposium on computing science education* (pp. 346–351) Memphis Tennessee.
133 Komssi, M., Pichlis, D., Raatikainen, M., Kindström, K., & Järvinen, J. (2014). What are hackathons for? *IEEE Software*, *32*(5), 60–67.
134 Gawer, A., & Cusumano, M. A. (2014). Industry platforms and ecosystem innovation. *Journal of Product Innovation Management*, *31*(3), 417–433.
135 Zedtwitz, M. V. (2003). Classification and management of incubators: Aligning strategic objectives and competitive scope for new business facilitation. *International Journal of Entrepreneurship and Innovation Management*, 3(1–2), 176–196.
136 Becker, B., & Gassmann, O. (2006). Corporate incubators: Industrial R&D and what universities can learn from them. *The Journal of Technology Transfer*, *31*, 469–483.
137 Becker, B., & Gassmann, O. (2006). Corporate incubators: Industrial R&D and what universities can learn from them. *The Journal of Technology Transfer*, *31*, 469–483.
138 St. Jean, E. (2012). Mentoring as professional development for novice entrepreneurs: Maximizing the learning 1. *International Journal of Training and Development*, *16*(3), 200–216.
139 Clarysse, B., & Yusubova, A. (2014). Success factors of business accelerators. In *Technology business incubation mechanisms and sustainable regional development proceedings*, Toulouse Business School, Toulouse, France.

140 Rigg, C., & O'Dwyer, B. (2012). Becoming an entrepreneur: Researching the role of mentors in identity construction. *Education + Training*, *54*(4), 319–329.
141 Selig, C. J., Gasser, T., & Baltes, G. H. (2018, June). How corporate accelerators foster organizational transformation: An internal perspective. In *2018 IEEE international conference on engineering, technology and innovation (ICE/ITMC)* (pp. 1–9). IEEE, Stuttgart, Germany.
142 Kohler, T. (2016). Corporate accelerators: Building bridges between corporations and startups. *Business Horizons*, *59*(3), 347–357.
143 Clarysse, B., Wright, M., & Van Hove, J. (2015). *A look inside accelerators*. London: Nesta.
144 Reimsbach, D., & Hauschild, B. (2012). Corporate venturing: An extended typology. *Journal of Management Control*, *23*, 71–80.
145 Chesbrough, H. W. (2002). Making sense of corporate venture capital. *Harvard Business Review*, *80*(3), 90–99.
146 Chesbrough, H. W. (2002). Making sense of corporate venture capital. *Harvard Business Review*, *80*(3), 90–99.
147 Drover, W., Busenitz, L., Matusik, S., Townsend, D., Anglin, A., & Dushnitsky, G. (2017). A review and road map of entrepreneurial equity financing research: Venture capital, corporate venture capital, angel investment, crowdfunding, and accelerators. *Journal of Management*, *43*(6), 1820–1853.
148 Harrison, J. S., Hitt, M. A., Hoskisson, R. E., & Ireland, R. D. (2001). Resource complementarity in business combinations: Extending the logic to organizational alliances. *Journal of Management*, *27*(6), 679–690.

2 Startup acceleration programs as a tool for inter-organizational cooperation on open innovations

This part of the book concentrates on the role played by startup acceleration programs as a key tool for inter-organizational cooperation on open innovations. A detailed analysis has been conducted on the various aspects and models of startup accelerators, their structures, activities and methods of functioning as platforms for supporting inter-organizational cooperation. The focal point was the integration of the various approaches and partnership strategies between large organizations and startups. The notion of a startup accelerator has been defined and the frameworks for acceleration programs were discussed in detail while taking into consideration the cooperation models most frequently encountered on the market; from cooperation between corporations and external independent accelerators to establishing corporate accelerators in an organization's structure to the cooperation model between corporate accelerators with external accelerators. Different models for the operating activity of accelerators were presented. This is key to comprehend their capabilities and limitations. Attention was drawn to the funding sources for startup accelerators while emphasizing the various strategies for financing them. Acceleration programs in Central and Eastern Europe (CEE) were compared in terms of their distinct nature in juxtaposition with more developed markets such as the United States and Western European nations. Special attention was directed to the differences stemming from local economic, financial and cultural determinants, including limited access to capital. Further considerations pertain to the presentation of the stages of an acceleration program ranging from planning to recruiting startups to preparatory work to administer tests to the stage of testing a solution in a corporation's environment. At the end of this part, there is a presentation of the possible directions of inter-organizational cooperation during post-acceleration. Attention was paid to how the continuation of cooperation may proceed following the formal completion of an acceleration program in the models: white label, joint offer, reselling, acquisition or some other form of investment in a startup.

DOI: 10.4324/9781003540366-3

2.1 Concept and essence of startup accelerators

The first startup accelerator known as Y Combinator was established in 2005 in the United States. With the elapse of time corporations more and more frequently deemed this type of business activity to be a prospective model for sourcing innovative startups and their solutions into the organization.[1] For that reason they started to create corporate accelerators within their own structures. Startup accelerators became an integral part of the startup ecosystem by offering support to new innovative companies in their development and establishing contacts with corporations and prospective investors. Accelerators were traditionally perceived as programs to support entrepreneurs in developing and marketing products. At present, they are understood in a broader sense as they have developed into a global interdisciplinary phenomenon.[2] Accelerators play a central role in the startup ecosystem as intermediaries by combining many heterogeneous entities.[3] In a broader context accelerators exert an impact on different aspects from shaping entrepreneurial attitudes to influencing economies and societies.[4] Corporations that elect to include startup accelerators in their activities as part of their strategies frequently face the choice of building an acceleration program as part of their own structure (e.g., the Orange corporate accelerator – Orange Fab, or Microsoft – Microsoft Accelerator), entrust this to an external partner/create it in collaboration with other companies (ABN Amro Bank) or join an existing one as a partner (e.g., for AXA Partners – accelerator Accelpoint). It should be noted that there are four major approaches to acceleration taken by corporation that differ from one another in terms of their program. The first one is an accelerator as a *Listening Post*. It focuses on identifying new trends and possibilities. The second accelerator is a *Value Chain Investor* that focuses on supporting startups that may strengthen a corporation's value chain. The third approach involves an accelerator as a *Test Laboratory Accelerator*, which makes it possible to check in practice and develop new technologies and solutions. The final type of accelerator is a *Unicorn Hunter Accelerator* that seeks out investments in the most promising and dynamically developing businesses. It is worth noting that the definition of a startup accelerator is not uniform.[5,6] Corporate accelerators have distinguishing traits that differentiate them from regional accelerators run by companies independent of corporations or universities.[7] Usually, these programs last for a limited time as they selectively enroll a specific number of startups (cohort) in a given period.[8] The scale of operation of accelerators varies; however, an increase in the number of corporate accelerators has been observed on the market.[9] They generally run from one to several programs in an on-site, virtual or hybrid form.[10] Accelerators have their own evaluation criteria for the incoming applications and cooperation framework as part of the acceleration program they run. To select startups corporations customarily rely on the team managing the accelerator backed by employees of the business units of organizations, mentors and trade experts.[11] Program management may take on different forms depending on the adopted framework and the expected final results. It is frequently associated with devising new managerial processes in an organization. These programs are ordinarily set up and run as part of the corporate strategy for cooperating with startups. Moreover, corporate accelerators are frequently global and intersectoral spanning companies from different industries (e.g., Walt Disney, Samsung, Microsoft, Google, Bayer, Orange, Santander Bank, Volvo). In their offer corporate accelerators offer a number of additional services that are useful in the development of new companies. They range from providing office space, mentoring, testing the solutions of startups and establishing business contacts with the partners of large organizations.[12]

Having regard for the variety and fragmented nature of the acceleration program operation models, the following item presents the most frequently encountered framework for inter-organizational cooperation between corporations and startups. This review aims to illustrate the principal schemes and strategies that are utilized for the purpose of supporting mutual interactions and synergies between the parties.

2.2 Frameworks for acceleration programs

Acceleration programs are applicable as part of different operating models. They form the program structure and the *Framework*. The framework established in this manner encompasses goals, tasks, processes and indicators that support an accelerator in program management and the engaged parties such as startups, corporations and possibly investors in effectively running these efforts and achieving the designated goals. That is why devising the framework is a significant step toward understanding and selecting a suitable model for engaging a corporation in an acceleration program. The framework provides a structure and an action plan, which is of great significance from the vantage point of managing an acceleration program and backing inter-organizational cooperation. A properly designed structure helps achieve the intended goals. It supplies the expected values expected to startups, accelerators and corporations that are indispensable when it comes to effectively managing resources and ultimately implementing innovations. Accordingly, the framework should flexible and aligned to specific goals and the context surrounding the acceleration program and the corporation's strategy.

2.2.1 Model of cooperation between a corporation and an independent external accelerator

Under this model a corporation collaborates with an external *Independent Accelerator*. An accelerator becomes the liaison between a corporation and startups. It extends backing on many planes and intermediates between startups and corporations (Figure 2.1).

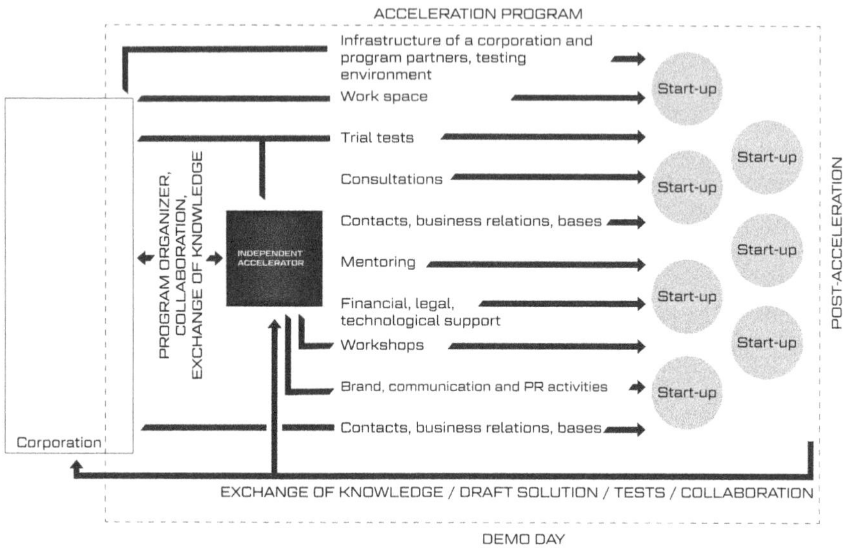

Figure 2.1 Model of cooperation between a corporation and an independent external accelerator.

Source: Proprietary material based on Bańka et al. (2022).

An accelerator's task is to create conditions and cooperation space that curtails and/or eliminates obstacles in the cooperation between startups and corporations. This organization is specialized in acceleration processes and it holds proprietary startup support programs. Such a model is most frequently selected by those corporations which lack experience in acceleration-related activities and knowledge about startups; that is also why they elect to participate in cooperation with an external accelerator.[13] Under a mandate from corporations accelerators recruit startups from the market that are aligned to the challenges and verticals defined by large organizations. The corporation focuses mainly on cooperation with the accelerator and startup team by making its own industry experts, infrastructure and test environment available.

The accelerator has its own management separate from the corporation and a team dedicated to cooperating with startups. The accelerator cooperates with managers experienced in launching, financing and scaling up startups. Table 2.1 depicts a characterization of a model for cooperating with an external accelerator.

2.2.2 *Model for establishing a corporate accelerator in an organization*

The common trait of *in-house accelerators* is their direct access and utilization of a corporation's in-house resources for the purpose of implementing more quickly the innovative solutions of startups.[14] In this case the priority

Table 2.1 Characterization of the model of cooperation between a corporation and an external startup accelerator

Aspects	*Model of cooperation between a corporation and an external start-up accelerator*
Attributes	• Cooperation with an external entity running start-up acceleration; • Independence of an accelerator and its team from a corporation's internal structures; • Accelerator financed using various sources (e.g., funds from investors, corporations, public funds); • Accelerator open to start-ups in different growth phases.
Advantages	• Broader access to the innovations of start-ups than in the case of a corporate accelerator; • Not necessary for a corporation to invest funds in the development of internal structures to pursue start-up acceleration; • Extension of the range of corporations to include start-ups that are customarily off the radar of large organizations; • Enrichment of corporate culture to include an external approach to work with innovations.
Disadvantages/ challenges	• Limited influence on an acceleration program and its participants; • Risk of cultural differences between a corporation's team and an accelerator's team; • Risk of diminished engagement by a corporation's internal teams in the acceleration process; • Dependence on the quality of work of an external accelerator; • Need to develop a path for cooperation between the parties.
Resources	• Access to the external accelerator's technological resources and tools; • Option to take advantage of the contact network of the accelerator and its partners, investors and experts.

Source: Proprietary material.

for the operation of an in-house accelerator is not profit but developing innovation within the structures of a corporation and/or its partners.[15] Corporate accelerators differ from external accelerators set up by private investors, universities and public institutions.[16] Corporate accelerators are programs that are characterized by selective cooperation with startups. Programs are developed and run, in principle, as part of the corporate innovation strategy.

On top of direct support for startups corporate accelerators are the entity responsible for cooperation with innovations within the structures of large organizations. Through their acceleration activities corporations strive to achieve their strategic goals associated with sourcing innovative solutions.[17] In this model corporations offer direct access to an organization's resources,

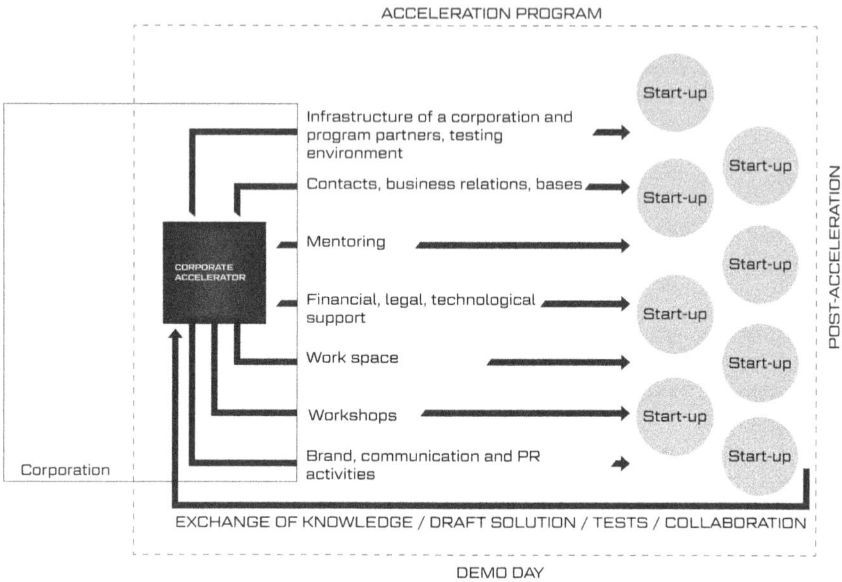

Figure 2.2 Operating model for a corporate accelerator set up in an organization's structure.

Source: Proprietary material based on Bańka et al. (2022).

including its financial resources, strong brand and brand recognition on the market, sales channels, enormous client and supplier database numbering in many instances tens of thousands of clients (Figure 2.2).

A corporate accelerator present in the structure of a large organizations engages an organization's other business units in its activities. A corporation's management (e.g., business unit directors) participates in the process of selecting startups. A corporation's experts offer intense support in product development to startups. In a corporate accelerator one may observe an obstacle in the form of the mentoring offered. This ensues from the fact that experts are usually a corporation's experienced employees who do not necessarily have experience in scaling up a startup's solution. Table 2.2 depicts a characterization of a corporate startup accelerator.

2.2.3 *Model for a corporate accelerator to collaborate with an external accelerator*

The cooperation model (Figure 2.3) characterizes the engagement of a corporate accelerator in cooperation with external independent accelerators. The model aims to source innovations from the market broadly and support development activities to benefit startups by ensuring direct relationships between the startup team and a corporation's business unit. An external accelerator organizes an acceleration program with a defined structure,

Table 2.2 Characterization of an internal corporate startup accelerator

Aspects	*Model of an internal corporate start-up accelerator*
Attributes	• Accelerator's operation within a corporation's structures; • Close integration with a corporation's business and strategy; • Concentration on innovations supporting a corporation's business goals; • Innovations coming from domestic start-ups and the foreign branches of corporations; • Financed from a corporation's own funds; • The accelerator's team consists of the corporation's employees.
Advantages	• Total control over the program and processes; • Option to adopt the program easily to a corporation's distinct needs; • Enhancing the internal culture of innovation; • Start-ups' direct access to a corporation's resources.
Disadvantages/ challenges	• Risk of curtailing the reach of innovations to a corporation's internal structures; • Potential limitation of the activities run by an accelerator in connection with its exposure to only the start-ups that dovetail with the verticals; • Limitation or inability to utilize resources outside the bounds of a corporation;
Resources	• Access limited to a corporation's internal resources such as capital, infrastructure, including its research network and business contact network. • Option to take advantage of the organizational units that are not direct business units, e.g., marketing and the HR department to develop and support start-ups.

Source: Proprietary material.

leaving the freedom to the corporation for the purpose of aligning its own preferences, including the acquisition of a startup at later stages by a corporate accelerator.[18] An external accelerator's tasks include screening and scouting activities, assistance in cooperation with the employees of a corporation to prepare a startup to commence tests.

The cooperation model between a corporate accelerator and an external startup accelerator is treated by large organizations as a way to enhance the chances for gaining access and securing a larger number of valuable projects from the market. Table 2.3 depicts a characterization of this model.

Each one of the described models for the operation of accelerators differs, among other things, by the costs for running an acceleration program, the flow of information between program participants, the impact on the acceleration program and management structures. Corporations may elect to choose any cooperation model with startups, that is, a mandate for running acceleration activities through an external accelerator, organization and conducting acceleration as part of a corporate accelerator or the cooperation of a corporate accelerator with an external startup accelerator. Model selection is dictated

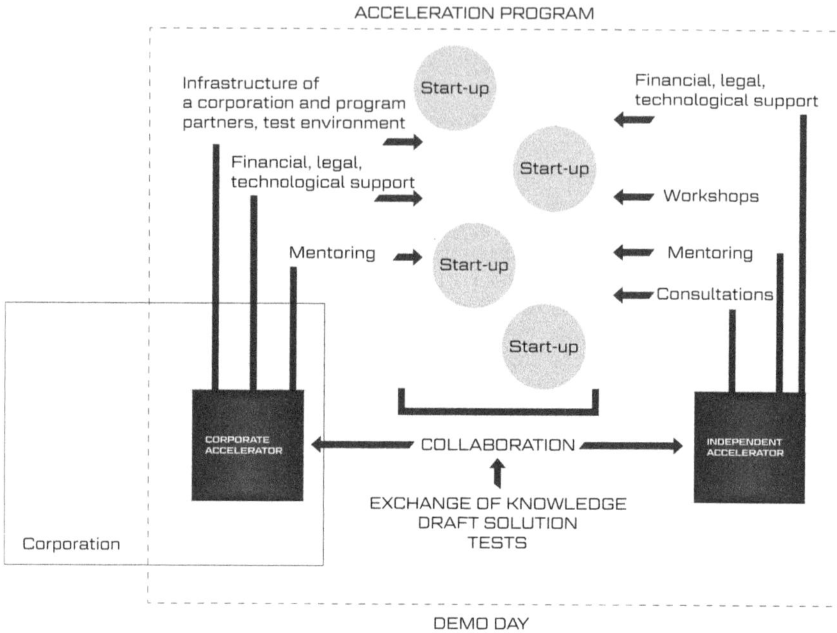

Figure 2.3 Cooperation model between a corporate accelerator and an external accelerator.

Source: Proprietary material based on Bańka et al. (2022).

chiefly by a corporation's abilities to procure organizational, human and financial resources. When making their decisions managers should take into consideration the fact that the required resources will differ significantly depending on the model selected. The model for establishing the internal structure of an accelerator in a corporation will require substantially more resources involving time and finance than operation in the cooperation model with an external independent accelerator. Managers should also be aware that when selecting an accelerator model, startups are guided not only by a firm's brand name but also the scope of support offered by a corporation when they make their decision to submit a project to an acceleration program.

2.2.4 *Operating models for a startup accelerator*

There are many operating models for accelerators where each one of them has its own unique rules for operation, advantages and disadvantages. The most popular operating models are the following:

1 **Equity-based accelerator** – in this model the accelerator makes an equity investment (ranging from several thousand to several tens of thousands of $ or €) in startups in exchange for shares in a company

Table 2.3 Characterization of the cooperation model between a corporate accelerator and an external accelerator

Aspects	*Cooperation model between a corporate accelerator and an external accelerator*
Attributes	• Combining a corporate accelerator through cooperation with independent external accelerators operating outside the environment of a large organization; • Flexibility in selecting the approach to collaborating with start-ups; • Harnessing the advantages of both models to attract start-ups' innovative projects.
Advantages	• Extensive access to innovations and projects; • Greater flexibility and access to various resources, including an external accelerator; • Option to adopt innovations to a corporation's needs while simultaneously reaping benefits from external resources; • Greater recognition in the start-up ecosystem thanks to getting involved in partnerships in other acceleration programs.
Disadvantages	• Potential complications in managing and coordinating both types of accelerators and the programs run; • Risk of divergent goals and organizational culture between the types of accelerators and their programs; • Requirement to provide greater resources and financial expenditures.
Resources	• Combination of corporate resources (infrastructure, capital, expert knowledge) and external resources (networks, mentors, experience in cooperation with various start-ups); • Option to utilize various contact networks, knowledge and technology that up till now has been outside the reach of a corporation.

Source: Proprietary material.

(ordinarily between 3% and 10%). This model leads to a long-term association between the parties, that is, the accelerator and the startup.

2 **Equity-free accelerator** – this model does not require startups to surrender equity in exchange for the received support.
3 **Performance-based model** – this accelerator focuses on measurable goals and results where subsequent decisions depend on them, including potential investments and settlements with startups.
4 **Hybrid accelerator** – this is a combination of various approaches and elements of the operating models of a startup accelerator. This model makes it possible to adopt cooperation to the accelerator's operating strategy in accordance with the accepted conditions prevailing on the market and the startups' expectations.

Table 2.4 characterizes how various operating models affect the activities of an accelerator, startups and how a corporation perceives them. Selecting the

Table 2.4 Characterization of operation models for a startup accelerator

Model	*Key principles of operation*	*Advantages*	*Disadvantages*	*Perception by corporations*
Equity accelerator	• Equity investment in start-ups in exchange for equity • Subscription for shares as prescribed by the acceleration agreement • Long-term engagement in a start-up • Time-limited program	• Greater engagement, strong motivational factor for an accelerator in connection with becoming a shareholder in start-ups • Potential source of income in the event another entity acquires the acquisition	• Start-ups relinquish some control over the firm • Prospective risk of conflict between shareholders stemming from the acceptance of different goals • Greater dilution of shares during subsequent financing rounds	• Corporations perceive this cooperation model as a potential opportunity for a future investment • Investment entails a longer exposure and a corporation's obligations
Equity-free accelerator	• Offering support without having to relinquish shares in a company • Accelerator has no financial obligations to the start-up • Accelerator's short-term exposure to a start-up	• Start-ups retain control over the company • Accelerator available for different types of start-ups	• No motivation for the accelerator to have a long-term involvement in the start-up's project • Spots in the acceleration program are frequently limited and highly desired by start-ups • Start-ups have more difficult access to financing and sometimes it is necessary to secure financial means from outside the program • Accelerator has to secure funds for the program's activity	• Corporations may perceive this model as an opportunity to extend financial support and source innovative solutions • Exposure to the development of the start-up ecosystem, it may produce long-term benefits

Performance-based model	• Performance-based remuneration • Definition and concentration on measurable goals and results • It is possible for an accelerator to subscribe for shares in a start-up in accordance with the clauses of an acceleration agreement	• Focus on results and measurable goals • Effective utilization of resources • Rapid decisions on discontinuing cooperation in a program with a start-up that does not achieve its goals	• It may intentionally sidestep the aspects of long-term development • Difficulty in evaluating all of the aspects of start-ups' success solely on the basis of measurable results • Support may be concentrated on specific areas and not encompass the full spectrum of a start-up's needs • Start-ups without a ready product or clear revenue model may have difficulties with matriculating in an acceleration program	• Corporations may perceive this model as a way of effectively supporting start-ups and monitoring work progress • Model more attractive to corporations that prefer mature solutions of start-ups • A corporation may have better control over the performance of an acceleration program by tying the support provided to the results
Hybrid model	• Combination of various elements of accelerators' other operating models • Cooperation aligned to individual needs	• Aligned to different types of start-ups • Brings together the benefits of various models	• More complicated in management, coordination and monitoring	• Corporations may see this model as a flexible approach that makes it possible to adopt support for various types of projects

Source: Proprietary material.

appropriate model hinges upon an accelerator's individual needs, goals and operational context.

It is worth noting that in terms of how corporations perceive the various operating models of startup accelerators, there are several key factors that affect how they are assessed and its selection preferences. Above all, this is an issue of operating strategy and being aligned to a corporation's goals. For instance, if a corporation has a goal of developing new products or technologies, the equity accelerator model appears to be attractive in this instance as it fosters close cooperation and long-term relationships with innovative startups. If, however, the purpose of a corporation is to gain access to various solutions on the market and experiment quickly, then the equity-free accelerator model is more suitable.

The next thing is the degree of involvement in innovations and the scale of business, including access to financial resources and infrastructure. Organizations that are more technologically advanced and open to innovations frequently elect to choose equity or hybrid models. This approach gives them greater control over the product being developed and the startup's service. In turn, organizations that are less open to innovations may prefer to a greater extent equity-free models so as to mitigate the risk and costs associated with inter-organizational cooperation. In addition, the horizon of the planned cooperation with startups is of importance when it comes to a corporation's perception and choice of the model. If a corporation is striving to attain short-term goals or run specific projects, then the performance-based model may be more suitable.

Having regard for the above, how corporations perceive accelerators' operating models hinges on their needs, goals and operating strategies. When selecting a model corporations must factor in their approach to innovations,[19] the available resources and the actual possibilities of being involved in a program's operating activities and the length of the planned cooperation.

2.2.5 *Startup acceleration programs*

Acceleration programs have become a crucial tool for startups and corporations in terms of combining and developing innovative products and services. In this part the three major types of acceleration programs that are the most frequently encountered on the market have been depicted, that is, a general acceleration program, an industrial acceleration program and a program with topical paths. Each one of these three acceleration programs features a divergent approach to inter-organizational cooperation and focuses on an organization's needs. It is crucial for startups to grasp these differences when deliberating on whether to participate in an acceleration program. Similarly, this is important for corporations that are planning to cooperate with innovative companies and as a consequence to attain the intended goals of cooperation. Table 2.5 depicts a characterization of these programs, their pros and cons and how they are perceived by a corporation have also been detailed.

Table 2.5 Types of startup acceleration programs

Type of an acceleration program	*Description*	*Advantages*	*Disadvantages*	*Perception by a corporation*
General acceleration program	• No split or specialization or limitations related to a specific industry; • Extent of engagement of human and technical resources dependent on the number of participating start-ups and the scope of activity; • Requires extensive knowledge and a sizeable group of mentors and experts.	• Flexibility in enrolling start-ups in the program; • Variety of projects run in the program, also in different areas, industries.	• The dearth of specialization may cause the program to be ineffective;	• Tool and source of diverse innovations; • Opportunity to source an extensive spectrum of solutions from the market; • Requires a flexible approach and procuring diverse resources
Industrial acceleration program	• Focused on a specific industry • Requires specialized staff and experts	• Specialist knowledge and support associated with the industry, sector • Focus support on specific areas customarily agreed with the corporation • Start-ups participating in the program operate in the same industry.	• Limited flexibility in enrolling various types of start-ups; • Changes in the industry may affect the functioning of the program.	• Strategic method of sourcing and developing innovations in an area defined by a corporation; Program perceived as more focused and specialized; • Solving specific problems, expectations of a corporation.
Program with topical paths (hybrid)	• Blends elements of the general and industrial approach; • The engagement of resources hinges on the number and variety of topical paths and their scope.	• Flexibility in enrolling start-ups from different industries • Option to create interdisciplinary solutions dovetailing with the needs of multiple industries	• Necessary to manage different topical paths; • Necessary to procure the simultaneous provision of many types of support.	• Compromise between flexibility and specialization.

Source: Proprietary material

A **general acceleration program** is a solution crafted with sourcing startups from the widest possible circle in mind. In this type of program sector and industrial preferences are not designated, meaning that it is open to innovative companies from different areas. For such a program to enjoy interest it must be recognizable in the startup ecosystem and deliver value to its participants. In the case of a general acceleration program, the accelerator customarily receives many applications from startups at a very early development stage. The large number of submissions also denotes a requirement for the accelerator to secure an extensive group of experts. In a general acceleration program emphasis is placed more on the development of the project's business aspects than on support in the development of technologies. That means that startups in the program receive support in issues such as business strategy, financial model, marketing, management and securing funding. Mentors and experts help entrepreneurs understand the market, identify target customers, devise the marketing strategy, prepare for talks with corporations and build a sustainable business model. It is noteworthy that on account of the variety of areas on which this type of program concentrates, its performance in the long-term perspective may be diminished in comparison to more specialized industrial acceleration programs. An **industrial acceleration program** is characterized by its goal being to stimulate cooperation between startups and corporations by sourcing startups from a specific industry, for example, the space, gaming, fintech, regtech or medtech sector. Such a program concentrates on providing startups with the largest possible degree of support in all the levels of cooperation, including the technological level. Industrial specialization is attractive to startups because support is offered that is directly aligned to the needs of these new companies, their distinct nature and their operating requirements. Startup teams have access to industry experts, they cooperate with them from the stage of preparing to run tests. In that manner a suitable selection of a corporation and its preparation and openness to cooperation are essential for the success of an acceleration program. In the event such a program is launched, it is subordinated to the needs of a large organization. What's important, this model has inherent risk for startups as if it turns out that the solution devised as a result of acceleration is overly niche-driven or, what's worse, a corporation abandons it after completion of the program. An industrial program gives its parties the option of dividing the process into several stages, which allows large organizations to vet work progress sequentially and possible test the solution on a small group of clients, or in a test environment set up for this purpose. These are desirable actions prior to the product, service or technology being implemented by a corporation on a full scale. At the same time, such a program calls for much more extensive informational and promotional efforts than a general acceleration program on account of having to source a suitable number of submissions from startups active in the topical area. **An acceleration program with topical paths**, frequently called a hybrid program is a flexible solution that combines the attributes of general and industrial acceleration programs. It focuses on specific topical areas or issues that may be of significance for corporations operating in various industries or markets. In contrast to industrial acceleration programs that are strictly associated with one specific industry or sector, such a program with topical paths is more flexible. That means that startups from different areas can participate in this acceleration program provided that their projects are associated with the topical areas covered by this support. It is worth noting that the topical paths in a program may overlap and contain shared elements. Thanks to that this type of program is conducive to interdisciplinary innovations. That is also why acceleration programs with topical paths offer the potential of creating innovations with broader application than is the case of programs concentrated on one single industry. The solutions devised by startups in such a program may be applicable in many different areas. What is important in this model is that acceleration programs with topical paths form an intriguing solution for corporations that would like to promote innovations in specific topical areas but that would not like for them to be strictly linked to one single industry. Moreover, such programs afford opportunities for startups to develop their projects in an environment consisting of numerous experts and mentors and partners while retaining flexibility in terms of the area in which they operate. Accordingly, these programs may contribute to developing solutions aligned to the needs of many industries, which will make them an attractive tool to promote innovations on a broad scale.

2.2.6 *Procedures on how to organize the operation of startup acceleration programs*

Selecting a suitable procedure for organizing an acceleration program may entail major consequences for the participating parties. In principle, there are three major procedures for organizing acceleration programs. Each one of them features its own unique advantages, disadvantages and implications. These programs are on-site, virtual and mixed. A characterization of each one of these procedures has been depicted below along with how corporations can look at them in terms of their engagement in cooperation with startups.

On-site program – this is a traditional model in which startups physically participate in an acceleration program in a specific venue. This is a program that frequently consists of workshops, training sessions, physical access to mentors and the ability to cooperate with other startups. The accelerator, possibly joined by other entities must provide the indispensable space to work, infrastructure to conduct acceleration-related activities and meetings with mentors and experts. The following may be treated as the advantages of such a program:

a Close interaction and mentoring. Startups have access to mentors and experts every day and can communicate with them easily.
b Forging relationships. The ability to form relationships with other startups, partners participating in the program including corporations may lead to establishing prospective business partnerships and investments in the future.

c Stronger engagement in the program through physical participation.
d The accelerator and corporation can more easily monitor the progress of the startups' work on account of the cooperation being at close quarters.

However, the following may be treated as the disadvantages of such a program:

a The requirement to relocate. Startups have to move to the venue where the program is run, which may be onerous for the team and generate high costs of participation.
b Limitation of access. Startups that are poised to move to a specific venue elect to participate in an on-site program.
c Organizing and maintaining an on-site program may generate high costs and call for performing logistics efforts.
d On-site programs are limited to the accessibility of local experts and mentors and program partners.

Corporations may perceive on-site programs as an effective method of engaging in direct interaction with promising startups. This gives them an opportunity to cooperate closely and evaluate the potential of these companies directly in a corporation's environment.

A **virtual program** is a remotely run program that allows startups to participate in this initiative without being physically in attendance. Such a program operates online and taps into the tools for remote communication. General classes are customarily run in the form of webinars and individual online sessions. This type of program's advantages are as follows:

a Accessibility for the parties. Startups from any place in the world can take part in the program, which enhances access to innovations and various projects.
b Time and costs savings. Since it is not necessary to travel it is possible to save time and costs related to relocating startups, for example, from one country to another. Additionally, there is no need to finance an office or possibly other infrastructure in connection with this program.
c Scalability. Virtual programs can handle a greater number of startups.
d Greater time flexibility. Corporations, the accelerator's team and mentors have greater flexibility in running acceleration-related activities.

However, the following may be treated as the disadvantages of a virtual program

a No direct interaction. The lack of physical attendance may impede direct interaction between startups, mentors and other program participants, for example, corporations.
b Diminished engagement. Startups may be less engaged in a program, which may affect the efficacy and pace of devising and adapting solutions to market needs.

Corporations may perceive virtual programs as a tool to source startups from different places from around the world and an opportunity to explore diverse innovations. However, on the other hand, they may be concerned by the diminished interaction and engagement on the part of the startups, including possible differences ensuing from cultural differences.

Mixed program – this is a hybrid model for organizing acceleration programs that blends elements of on-site programs and virtual programs. In mixed programs some of the activities take place on-site, which means the physical presence of startups in a specific venue designated by the accelerator or its partners. The accelerator holds regular on-site meetings. This makes it possible to have direct interaction and cooperation. Moreover, under this procedure program, participants ordinarily have the option to choose which elements of the program they would like to complete on-site and which ones they would like to complete virtually, which enables them to adapt the program to their own individual needs and preferences. A portion of the acceleration program is held virtually by using online communication tools. The following may be treated as the advantages of a mixed program:

a Flexibility. This is one of the greatest advantages of mixed programs. Startups and corporations can adapt the program to their needs and conditions regardless of their geographic location.
b Time and costs savings. Since it is not necessary to relocate permanently, it is possible to save time and costs related to travel and lodging.
c Direct access to experts. The on-site portion of the program makes it possible to have direct interaction with mentors, experts and other startups as well as program partners. This type of access is ordinarily more effective than a relationship built on the basis of electronic means of communication.
d Health security. In the event of crisis situations (e.g., pandemics), mixed programs may easily be converted into a virtual procedure. This provides for the smooth continuation of the actions undertaken and mitigates the risk of cancellation of such a program.

In turn, the disadvantages of a mixed program are as follows:

a Complexity of program management: mixed programs can be more complex in terms of their management since they require concurrent coordination of the activities held on-site and virtually.
b It is necessary to organize the physical and virtual aspects of this type of acceleration program.
c The need for ensuring suitable technologies. These programs call for technological tools, platforms for communication and management, which may be costly and require advanced infrastructure.
d Absence of full attendance: the virtual portion of the program may curtail the intensity of interactions and the engagement of the parties.

Corporations may perceive mixed programs as striking a compromise between on-site interaction and virtual accessibility. This gives them the option of benefiting from the best aspects of both models, simultaneously enhancing accessibility and their exposure to the market and innovations. For this reason, mixed programs can be attractive to corporations that want to cooperate with many startups, regardless of their geographic location, while at the same time ensuring a certain level of interaction and integration with program participants. In the case of unexpected circumstances such as a pandemic, mixed programs retain flexibility in continuing efforts and supporting startups.

2.3 Sources of funding for a startup accelerator

Different models for funding startup accelerators are encountered on the market. They differ from one another depending on their operating strategy, the goals imposed on an accelerator, the operating region, the type of startups recruited for the program, etc. The four major models for funding accelerators are presented below:

1 **Partnership and equity-based model** – this is one of the most popular funding models. An accelerator may invest its own equity or secure funds through partnerships from other investors (business angels), venture capital funds or financial institutions, including corporations. In exchange for the funding extended to a startup, the accelerator receives *Equity* in the companies it enrolls in the acceleration program. The terms and conditions for making the investment such as the quantum of capital obtained in exchange for equity and the valuation of the startup are negotiated by the accelerator, the startup and sometimes by investors cooperating with the accelerator in the form of a venture capital fund. As a result of the sale of equity in the startups, the accelerator secures funding for its operating activity. It is noteworthy that in contrast to the public funding model, the model entailing funding solely from private means greatly facilities all of the formalities associated with transferring funds to startups and, additionally, it is not burdened by public aid caps just as that is frequently the case when obtaining public funding as part of funds originating from EU programs.

2 **Corporate-sponsored model** – an accelerator may enter into strategic partnerships with corporations that finance an acceleration program in exchange for access to innovative solutions and technologies. These funds may be earmarked for scouting startups, developing products, expanding a team, marketing, research and development (R&D) as well as for the other developmental needs of startups. The transfer of funds may be accomplished through a cooperation agreement between a corporation and an accelerator. In some instances, the corporation is the sole owner of the accelerator and provides up to 100% of the funding for the operating activity of the startup accelerator.

3. **Fee-based model** – an accelerator may charge fees to startups. The fee may entail remuneration for the startup's participation in an acceleration program and/or future profit-sharing by virtue of the startup establishing cooperation with the corporation.
4. **Government-funded model** – political authorities at the national, regional or local government level and their public programs can co-fund the activity of an accelerator as part of the initiatives supporting the development of the startup ecosystem. The government-funded model is frequently subject to specific limitations and legal regulations. This may encompass the necessity of documenting the results obtained, adhering to regulations concerning the correctness of spending public funds and reporting progress on the intended goals, the product and outcome indicators achieved. This model frequently prohibits the accelerator or other entities with personal or equity ties from subscribing for equity in the startups. A special instance in this model is the funding extended to accelerators by non-profit organizations (foundations, associations), which have goals recorded in their articles of association such as supporting entrepreneurship and innovativeness.

2.4 Model of operation for an acceleration program and the challenges it faces

During the course of creating a startup acceleration program, a corporation's managers frequently face the task of creating a performance-based and sustainable plan to cooperate with startups in a specific time horizon. To attain this goal, the managers must focus on many key aspects and understand that the acceleration program may produce the maximum benefits considering the engagement of the participating parties. Figure 2.4 depicts the general model for inter-organizational cooperation between accelerators, startups and corporations.

When setting up a startup acceleration program a corporation should take into account multiple aspects and questions so that program can be performance-based and contribute to achieving the organization's strategic goals. These aspects may pertain, among others, to the following

1. **Strategy of the acceleration program and the program's goals** – defining strategy and the program's principal goal is indispensable as this forms the basis for the entire undertaking. The team engaged in executing the program should conduct its efforts so that it is aligned to the greatest degree possible to the goals defined by the corporation. The designed acceleration program should also comport with the company's general innovation strategy. Here managers should ponder the following questions

   - Does the corporation have a strategy on how to operate with innovations coming from outside the bounds of the organization?

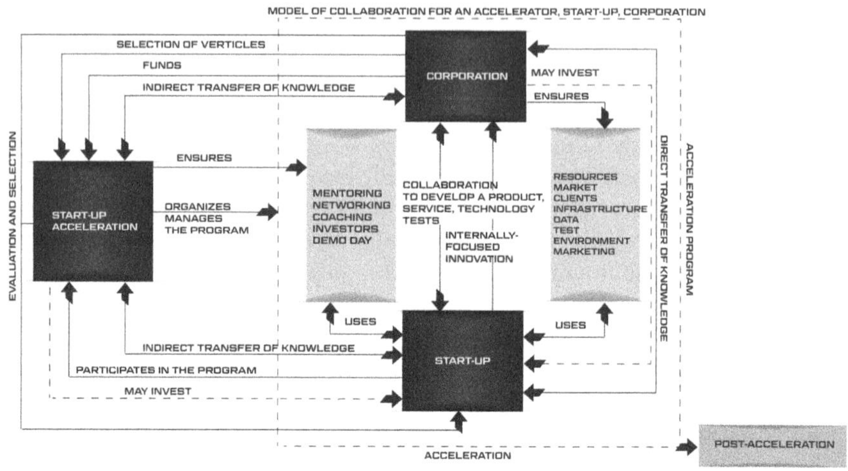

Figure 2.4 Model of cooperation for an accelerator, startup and corporation in an acceleration program.

Source: Proprietary material.

- What is the principal goal of the acceleration program and what are its side goals?
- What specific goals do we want to attain through the program and how will we measure them?
- How does the startup acceleration program fit with the corporation's overall strategy, including its innovation strategy?
- How does the program intend to reach the startups the corporation wants to have?
- Will the program be executed through an in-house accelerator, or will it be run by a cooperating external startup accelerator?

2 **Program structure and organization** – correctly defining the structure and organization of an acceleration program will be of significant importance for its ultimate performance. Defining the organizational structure, the mechanisms for monitoring and managing progress makes it possible to plan how the program will operate on a daily basis. In this context managers should ponder the questions below:

- What will the organizational structure of the acceleration program be?
- Who will manage the program and what will be the roles and tasks of the key persons, other entities from the market engaged in the acceleration-related efforts?
- What will be the mechanisms for monitoring and managing progress in the program?

- What should be done so that the acceleration program is not associated with the daily routine activity of the corporation and makes it possible to develop innovative solutions in the organization's environment?

3 **Planning an acceleration program's resources** – identifying the available human, technical, organizational, including financial and intangible resources (e.g., expert knowledge, access to the client database) helps specify which actions should be safeguarded as part of the acceleration program. Such an activity will make it possible to identify the potential limitations associated with the program and possibly undertake prior remedial steps. In this aspect the management should take into consideration the following questions:

- Where will the startup accelerator be conducted (e.g., acceleration in an on-site or virtual model)?
- What organizational, technical, human and financial resources will be dedicated to the program?
- What other resources (e.g., experts) will be available to the startups taking part in the program?
- Will any sources of program funding, and which ones, be provided in the program and in what amount?
- At what time will the foregoing resources be needed and does the corporation have them at its disposal?

4 **Startup acceleration process** – the process of work and the support extended to startups in the acceleration program should be defined in their entirety. Understanding and planning support in the form, for example, of mentoring and conducting tests on a corporation's infrastructure will be facilitated by the prior planning of activities and safeguarding the required means, tools and resources, respectfully. It is worth taking into consideration the following questions:

- What will be the process for selecting and picking startups to join the program, including the evaluation criteria?
- Is the acceleration process similar to other similar types of instruments launched by the corporation and what conclusions have been drawn from them and can they exert an impact on the acceleration program?
- What specific technical and organizational support and mentoring will be provided to the startups taking part in the program?
- How will cooperation between the corporation's units and the startup and the accelerator take place and is it possible to streamline this cooperation?

5 **Roles, tasks, responsibilities** – precisely defining the roles and responsibilities of program participants and partners, including those from the

corporation, accelerator and startups, is indispensable to ensure the proper coordination of activities. At this time, it is important to consider the following questions:

- What are the specific roles and responsibilities of the program participants?
- Who will be the leader responsible for managing the acceleration program?
- What are the expectations of the participating parties?
- Who will be responsible for communication between the parties to ensure the effective flow of information?
- How will reporting to the corporation's management be done?
- Will the corporation's management be involved in the acceleration program?

6 **Cooperation with the startup ecosystem** – startup acceleration programs are part of the innovation ecosystem. Cooperating with other organizations and ecosystem participants is crucial for the program's ultimate success. Here one should take into consideration the following questions:

- Which partnerships and external relationships will be important in terms of the program?
- Is a corporation open to external partnerships?
- How did a corporation source the innovations and startups thus far, using which models?
- What benefits can cooperation with other organizations, research units and funds produce?

7 **Expected outcomes and the method of calculating them** – specifying the expected outcomes and the method of calculating them is important to evaluate the efficacy of a startup acceleration program involving a corporation. This task enables one to track progress, identify areas for improvement and adapt actions in response to the measurement results obtained. Here managers should take into consideration the following questions:

- What are the expected outcomes of a startup acceleration program?
- Which indicators and measurement methods will be used to evaluate the efficacy of an acceleration program?
- Who will be involved in evaluating the outcomes of the acceleration program and the fulfillment of its objectives?
- Is there a method in the corporation for measuring the impact exerted by innovative solutions of startups on the organization, its clients and its partners?
- What mechanisms will be applied to monitor the program's progress and introduce any possible adjustments?

Considering the foregoing seven aspects and the challenges related to them in terms of the acceleration program involving a corporation supports the organization in terms of a cohesive action plan and reaching the intended targets. This will also make it possible to confirm the justification for taking actions related to launching the program, or decide to cancel it.

2.5 Acceleration programs in Central and Eastern Europe in the background of the global markets

Acceleration programs are gaining more and more significance in CEE. At the same time, this region is grappling with a number of unique challenges and opportunities that distinguish it from other parts of the world such as the United States, Western European countries and Asia. In the CEE region acceleration programs are becoming an inseparable element of the support provided to startups, taking on various operating models ranging from strictly industrial programs to ones that have an extensive scope of application on multiple markets. Most frequently, these programs span key elements such as mentoring, access to technological resources and cooperation with industrial experts for the purpose of accelerating the development of new innovative companies. Nevertheless, one of the aspects distinguishing acceleration programs in the CEE region is the close cooperation with universities and local government agencies. These institutions are playing a crucial role not just by providing new companies with scientific and R&D support but also by giving them access to funds and grants. European Union structural funds play a particular role, especially in terms of acceleration programs. These funds frequently form a key part of funding startups, especially faced with the limited access to private capital in the region.

In terms of the overall structure and goals of the acceleration programs in CEE one may perceive similarities to the models used in more developed economies such as the US or Western European countries. The key assumptions such as support for innovativeness, acceleration, product development and facilitation of new companies' access to resources are universal. The corporations that participate in these programs offer support not just in the form of mentoring or providing technologies, but also by opening doors to their contact networks and international markets that would otherwise be difficult for these new companies to obtain. At the same time, the acceleration programs in CEE differ in many regards from the ones present on more developed markets such as the United States or on Asian markets (e.g., Singapore, South Korea). These differences stem from local economic, cultural and structural determinants. For instance, one of the largest challenges the startup ecosystem in the CEE region is facing is the limited access to capital, especially capital from venture capital funds. Compared to markets such as the United States where private capital and venture capital investors play the prevalent role in financing innovations, in CEE the capital market is much less developed. It is true that countries such as Poland, the Czech Republic, Hungary and Romania have local venture capital investment funds but their scale and resources are incomparably smaller. This means that many startups in the region have limited financing capabilities, which may slow down their development and curtail the scaling up of their business. For that reason, the corporations participating in acceleration programs in the CEE region sometimes fulfill a double role. First, they not only offer mentoring and technological support but also fill the capital gap by financing some stages in startup development. In this manner these corporations become not just partners but also investors in these startups, especially during their early development stages.

Another noticeable difference is the scale and reach of acceleration programs in CEE. In the CEE region these programs are usually smaller and more focused on the local market than their counterparts in the United States and Asia. For instance, acceleration programs in the United States, for example, the ones run by Y Combinator, 500 Startups and Techstars have a global reach and attract startups from around the world. In turn, in CEE most acceleration programs have a regional focus, and their participants are predominantly companies from countries in this region. This local focus stems mostly from the fact that many acceleration programs in the region are financed using public funds, including European Union funds. By definition public funding frequently limits the geographic range of these programs as the funds are allocated with the development of innovations at the local level in mind. Moreover, countries in CEE feature a strong level of engagement on the part of governmental institutions in the development of innovativeness. The governments of these countries actively support acceleration programs through various financial initiatives such as grants and subsidies. The United States is the opposite where public support for acceleration programs is minimal, where most of them are financed by private capital, including venture capital funds and business angels.

Another major difference between the CEE region and more developed ecosystems is manifested by the culture of innovativeness and the approach to risk. In countries in CEE one can observe a more conservative approach to risk in comparison with the startup ecosystems in the United States or Western Europe. This conservative approach may have its roots in the region's historical conditions. It was not until the last several decades that it experienced economic transformation in connection with the collapse of the Soviet Union and its political and economic system.

However, it is noteworthy that despite the regional distinct traits, one of the aspects that binds acceleration programs in the CEE region to those in the United States, Western Europe and Asia is the international nature of the corporations participating in these programs. Major global corporations such as Microsoft, Samsung, Orange, Santander Bank are involved in acceleration programs in different parts of the world, which contributes to similarities in the structure of these programs and the method of cooperation between global entities and new companies. This stems from the fact that corporations are frequently looking for innovative solutions that may be applied regardless of whether the startups are operating on local markets or have international ambitions. Thanks to that the startups hailing from CEE that are taking part in regional acceleration programs may gain access to global markets and developmental opportunities.

2.6 Stages of an acceleration program

An acceleration program forms the key element of supporting the development of business undertakings and merging innovations with corporations. The stages of an acceleration program are diligently planned steps that aim to accelerate the growth and development of a startup that is prepared to cooperate with market participants. In this part of the book the major stages of an acceleration program such as the following are analyzed:

1 **Program planning stage**, which encompasses a discussion among other things on the key aspects of the program's strategy and structure, the desired goals, verticals and resources that are necessary for the effective launch and management of an acceleration program.
2 **Startup recruitment stage**, which is crucial for the success of a program and for the achievement of the intended goals because its outcome is to ensure the high quality of startups in the acceleration program. Here a discussion was held among other things on communication strategies, the criteria used to evaluate the submitted projects and the process of negotiating and entering into cooperation contracts with startups.
3 **Stage of preparatory work for tests** focuses on preparing startups for the practical application and testing of their solutions in a corporation's environment or on its infrastructure. The support offered startups in a program, the activities associated with preparing a development plan, the scope and activities associated with the preparation of the environment or test infrastructure were discussed among others.
4 **Stage of testing startups's solutions** is focused on the practical implementation and evaluation of the innovations delivered by startups in an acceleration program. The rules for testing data, verifying the value of the service, technology and product offered by the startups and the activities associated with a corporation making the decision to continue business cooperation were discussed among others.

Through an analysis of the foregoing four stages it will be possible to become familiar with a comprehensive review of the acceleration process from planning to testing solutions, thereby illustrating how these programs contribute to developing and implementing innovations in large organizations. When analyzing the stages of an acceleration program and their steps one should take into account aspects such as the overlap of decision-making layers, monitoring progress and building relationships and trust between the parties to inter-organizational cooperation. In each one of the four stages of an acceleration program, these three layers are penetrated. They play a material role because they form an integral aspect of an acceleration program as they affect the shape of the cooperation itself in an acceleration program, the evaluation of progress and the quality of the relationships established between the participants.

2.6.1 *Planning stage for a startup acceleration program involving a corporation*

Stage one – planning for a startup acceleration program involving a corporation – forms the basis for the entire undertaking and consists of a series of steps that should be taken to confirm the assumptions and launch the acceleration-related activities. This stage consists of seven steps (Figure 2.5).

2.6.1.1 *Step 1. Securing/confirming the participation of a corporation*

During this step, it is necessary to get a corporation to participate in the acceleration program, while in the case of the operation of a corporate accelerator inside an organization, it is necessary to obtain the required consents

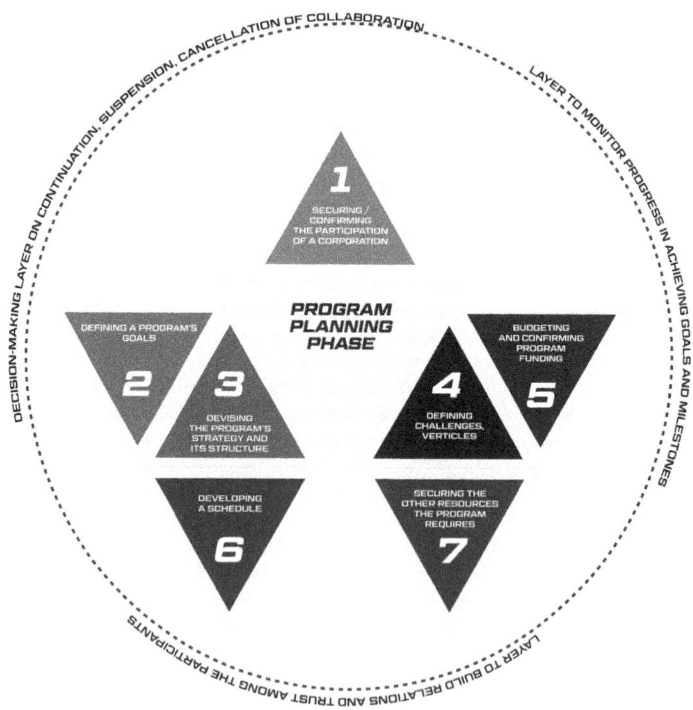

Figure 2.5 Planning stage for an acceleration program.

Source: Proprietary material.

to launch a program or a subsequent edition thereof. If it is necessary to get a large organization to join an acceleration program, it is imperative for an external accelerator to compose an attractive cooperation proposal, conduct negotiations and provide for effective communication. To this end it is necessary to identify the potential corporations that may be interested in cooperation in an acceleration program. This may encompass not just market research but also analysis of industries, confirmation from corporations that actively invest in the development of new innovative products and services. During the next step, contact is established with selected corporations and their interest is piqued in the potential benefits ensuring from participating in an acceleration program. This frequently involves the parties in a negotiation process. During the negotiations, it is important to gain a joint understanding of the expectations for the planned activities. Moreover, it is important to indicate the benefits flowing from the acceleration of the startups' solutions to a corporation along with confirmation which one of the strategic goals may be achieved by a large organization thanks to its engagement in an acceleration program.

2.6.1.2 *Step 2. Defining the program's goals and its desired outcomes*

After confirming the participation of a corporation, the detailed goals which are planned to be achieved along with the intended outcomes in the acceleration program should be defined. The goals being defined should be aligned to the corporation's binding strategy. If possible, the goals should also incorporate the needs by which the startups are guided when joining an acceleration program involving corporations. Some examples of the goals of a corporation may be as follows: sourcing innovative solutions from the market, enhancing the culture of innovativeness in an organization, expanding the product portfolio and acquiring talent. It is worth observing that these goals should be realistic and measurable. The choice of the formula for the operation of the acceleration program and the employed tools and methods of working with startups will also hinge upon the goals a corporation intends to attain.

2.6.1.3 *Step 3. Devising the program's strategy and its structure*

In this step the acceleration program's strategy is articulated to take into account the previously elaborated goals for a corporation and the needs of startups. The directions for further activities in the program are laid down. Moreover, the added values for startups are specified, for example, in the form of the financial support offered, or bringing together a corporation's commercial partners operating on other markets. The rules for recruiting startups to join the program along with the selection criteria are also defined. The program structure and the action program are confirmed, including the duration, number of rounds, planned number of startups to be enrolled in the program, the geographic area of activity, the team engaged in its execution. When approving the assumptions for an acceleration program it is also worthwhile to confirm whether one of the methods will be applied, for instance, customer development, lean startup, design thinking. The communication plan is also approved. It should include not just the planned information and promotional activities but also the rules for communicating with program participants (internal communication) and external partners, for example, prospective investors, entities and the community of the startup ecosystem. The program management model is also confirmed which specifies the organizational structure and key roles of the people involved. In this step the method of monitoring progress and introducing possible adjustments to the acceleration program is also crafted.

2.6.1.4 Step 4. Defining challenges, verticals

Challenges refer to specific topical areas (challenges) in which corporations are seeking innovative solutions. They are defined by corporations based on their strategy goals, current difficulties and market trends. Thereby the acceleration program should have defined areas in which a corporation is looking for startups. A corporation should select those areas which are the most important to it, or whose distinct nature requires the engagement of startups. This may pertain, among others, to potential market opportunities, the application of technologies, problems with which a corporation's employees grapple on an everyday basis. It is important for the solutions sought after by an accelerator to comport with a corporation's challenges and goals and to offer the potential of accruing value to the organization. It is noteworthy that prior to defining the topical areas it is important to conduct a strategic analysis of the corporation for the purpose of appreciating its major goals, priorities, areas of business and also its potential gaps and challenges, which a corporation intends to bolster and address. It is also important to designate those areas and verticals that are consistent with the corporation's activities, and for the sought after startups to have the potential to deliver synergy with a corporation's operations. When defining the verticals and challenges it is worth considering the technologies that will have a chance in the future of affecting a corporation's activities and development. The defined needs form an important part in the process of communicating the program. They serve the purpose not only of advising startups which solutions or innovations are expected of them, but also of interesting them in the scale of the challenges.

2.6.1.5 Step 5. Budgeting and confirming program funding

Under this step the budget of the acceleration program is approved. At the outset, the costs related to the planned program launch should be analyzed. Any possible funding for the startups, the remuneration planned for experts and mentors (if applicable), capital expenditures for promotional and informational activities, technological support and other operating expenditures should be taken into account. It is also worth confirming the split of the budget into the program's various stages related to recruitment, acceleration/preparation for tests, testing of solutions. After estimating the program's costs, it is necessary to secure funding for operations. Funding may be secured, for example, as part of the budgets of the business units of the corporations participating in the program, or from external sources such as EU grant programs obtained for the execution of the program for cooperation between large organizations and startups or from external partners in the form of venture capital funds.

2.6.1.6 *Step 6. Devising the schedule for executing the acceleration program*

Approving the program budget will make it possible to kick off the work related to devising the schedule for the planned activities. The first step to devising the schedule is identifying the key stages and tasks to form the acceleration program. Then, the duration of each one of them should be specified. This schedule may cover among other things the dates of the program's commencement and completion, the dates of recruitment, the dates of workshops, the technical facilities made available, the availability of experts and mentors, the organization of Demo Day, etc. When planning the tasks, it would be worthwhile to set aside a margin of safety so that in the event of delay it is possible to extend or shift a given stage. On account of the fairly short and intensive acceleration program, the devised schedule should be monitored, and the delays or problems encountered in the meantime should be solved on an ongoing basis.

2.6.1.7 *Step 7. Confirming and securing a corporation's other resources*

In this step it is important to provide for the necessary resources on the part of the corporation and accelerator that will be used to support and enrich the acceleration program, and that will also deliver added value to the startups participating in it. For instance, this may refer to seasoned employees of the corporation engaged as experts available to the startups. Experts may also support startups with their experience, familiarity with the corporation and its processes. One should remember that the quantum of resources to be allocated to the acceleration program hinges on the number of startups that are enrolled. Corporations may make their technological/technical resources available in the form of infrastructure, laboratories, test environment, databases, etc. Moreover, as part of the program financial support may be provided in the form of grants, investments, additional benefits, for example, in the form of free software or software made available at a preferential price. Moreover, giving startups access to a corporation's contacts, clients and business partners will enable startups to establish partnership and business relationships. It is worth remembering that the acceleration program symbolizes the corporation and positions it in the startup ecosystem. Working comfort should be provided, and infrastructure should also be secured not just for the accelerator's team and the mentors but above all for the startups to pursue the required tests. The market perception of the program will depend on that, and that may determine whether good projects are attracted for acceleration in the corporation's environment.

2.6.2 *Startup recruitment stage in a program*

Second stage of a startup acceleration program involving a corporation pertains to recruitment activities via the selection of startups and entering into cooperation agreements with them. This stage is important to the extent that the proper selection of entities from the market augments the chances of the parties to achieve success in inter-organizational cooperation. This stage consists of eight steps, where the text under Figure 2.6 depicts its characterization.

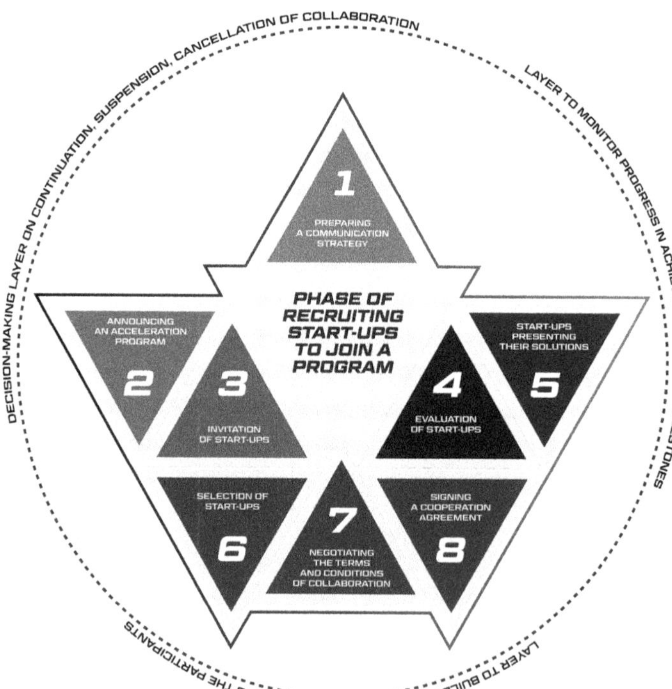

Figure 2.6 Startup recruitment stage in a program.

Source: Proprietary material.

2.6.2.1 *Step 1. Preparing a communication strategy*

The first step is to prepare a communication strategy whose purpose is to reach the appropriate group of interested startups that dovetail to the greatest degree with the corporation's defined topical areas/verticals and as a consequence to attract them to the acceleration program. This activity entails among other things the following:

- identifying the target group of startups. This may be companies for instance from a given industry, geographic region or companies at a defined stage of development;
- selecting the channels of communication. This may for instance mean social media, the program's website (containing at least information regarding the acceleration program, benefits, method of submitting an application, mentors, program partners), industrial events, conferences, trade fairs, newsletters, databases of startups, the corporation's channels of communication, information meetings, web browsers, social media, cooperation with brokers and university technology transfer centers, venture capital funds and business angel networks, organizations with member businesses (chambers of commerce, associations);
- defining the method of distributing communications regarding the program. Drawing up a clear and attractive message to communicate with participants to reflect the value (tangible benefits) and goals of the program. This message should in particular contain information regarding the benefits and possibilities for startups to develop their solution in cooperation with a corporation and an accelerator, the support of mentors and experts and importantly the successes achieved during previous rounds of the program;
- personalization of the communication on the basis of specific benefits. Planning graphic materials containing attractive graphs, video clips and case studies to support communication and persuade startups that program participation offers potential and is attractive;
- preparing a media plan and communication calendar, including the appropriate planning of publications and communication-related activity on the part of the accelerator's team members, the employees of the corporation's business units and the program participants who took part in the program in the past;
- designing tools and indicators to monitor the effectiveness of the adopted communication strategy on an ongoing basis.

Thereby the devised communication strategy should comport with the goals of the acceleration program, including the corporation's expectations and importantly it should also take into account the unique values and benefits offered by the acceleration program.

2.6.2.2 *Step 2. Announcing an acceleration program*

After fixing the communication strategy one should announce the acceleration program. In this step information is provided about the acceleration program involving a corporation, its goals and benefits and the conditions for participation. It is worthwhile to publish the program's rules and regulations containing key information regarding the organization, selection and rules for a startup to participate in the acceleration program. Announcements may be placed on the website, in social media, newsletters and conveyed to partners.

2.6.2.3 *Step 3. Recruiting startups for an acceleration program*

In this step the process of recruiting startups to join the program begins. Interested companies may submit their applications to participate in an acceleration program by a designated deadline. The recruitment process may be open or directed to a closed group of startups depending on the assumptions adopted. This process may encompass filling out application forms or submitting project-related presentations (pitch deck). Suitable tools should be provided to make it possible to submit projects and compile the necessary information from companies interested in participation, for example, on the startup team, the offered solution, and in particular how it fits with the corporation's needs and business model. During recruitment it is important to continue promoting the acceleration program. It is worthwhile to organize webinars and workshops with potential companies interested in participation and run information sessions during which entities can learn more about the program and obtain responses to the questions they have about the recruitment procedure and about cooperation itself. At this time, it is also important to convey information about the challenge put forward by the corporation in a way that is easy for the startups to understand the context.

2.6.2.4 *Step 4. Evaluation of startups*

After completing recruitment one proceeds to evaluate the submissions received. The recruitment committee reviews the projects in accordance with the accepted evaluation criteria aiming to identify the most promising solutions offered by the startups. Generally, the evaluation criteria may be divided into two groups, that is, formal criteria pertaining for instance to a potential conflict linked to personal or equity ties to a corporation or accelerator, the fulfillment of the criterion of the startup being a micro or small business undertaking and qualitative criteria related to the evaluation of the submitted solution. The evaluation criteria may pertain, for instance, to the following:

- compliance with the program's goals and defined topical areas, published challenges;

- stage of development of the solution offered by a startup, including the potential it offers, whether for instance the product, service or technology makes it possible to market a new product which has not been offered by the corporation to its clients to date. What impact the offered solution may exert on the corporation's operating activity and the market;
- the startup team, including the experience and skills of the team members, capabilities to cooperate with a large organization;
- innovativeness of the solution, that is, its feasibility and the ability to implement it in a corporation or with its partners;
- scalability of the solution, that is, whether a given solution can easily be developed and aligned to a bigger scale so as to enlarge its reach and its operating performance;
- the startup's business history on the market to-date, including experience associated with the sale of the submitted solution to other entities on the market.

The sequence of evaluating startups and their solutions according to the criteria is arbitrary. One may take into consideration either issues on the merits or the formal issues first. The decision to be guided by the evaluation on the merits first will require greater involvement on the part of the accelerator and the corporation. In such an approach in the event of a negative formal evaluation the startup team, despite being on the list of projects recommended for support, may ultimately be rejected on account of failing to fulfill the formal evaluation criteria at a later stage. The fourth step ends with the preparation of a list of the startups that will be invited to showcase their solution to the accelerator and/or corporation team.

2.6.2.5 Step 5. Startup presentations during pitching sessions

The startups selected during the fourth step are invited to showcase their solution during a pitching session. This is an important time during the recruitment stage, as during this session the startup team has the opportunity to prove the value and attractiveness of the submitted solution at close quarters with the corporation and clarify why it would be worthwhile to select the submitted project to join the acceleration program. The startups' pitch ordinarily lasts roughly 30 minutes, and the main elements are as follows

- the idea on how to solve the challenge put forward by the corporation, how the startup dovetails with the announced topical area through the product, service or technology it is offering;
- it presents the uniqueness, innovativeness and effectiveness of the offered solution;
- insofar as it is possible it makes a short demonstration of the operating product, service or technology;
- it confirms the market potential of the solution, its scalability.

During this session the recruiting committee has the opportunity to pose questions and clarify all of the doubts related to the project submitted by the startup. This presentation makes it possible to establish initial contact and build a relationship between the startup and representatives of the corporation. This session is also important on account of the possibility of evaluating the communication competences and the presentation skills of the startup team. The communication capabilities of the startup team will be of major significance during subsequent stages of direct cooperation with the employees seconded by the corporation to work on the solution's development. It is worth noting that the pitching session may be preceded by a conversation or meeting focused on verifying the quality, ability to integrate and possibilities for implementing the startup's submission. Sometimes, it is also necessary to confirm the team's motivation when it comes to inter-organizational cooperation.

2.6.2.6 *Step 6. Taking the decision to select startups to participate in an acceleration program*

After analyzing and evaluating the submitted presentation and the pitching session conducted concerning the submitted solutions, the evaluation committee drafts a ranking of the submissions received and selects the startups which will be selected to join the program. This process encompasses an analysis, discussion and selection of the projects that are consistent with the program's assumptions. The recruitment committee's decision is based on qualitative criteria and matches the submitted solutions to the goals of the program and the corporation's challenges. After selecting the startups contact is made with the selected companies to advise them of the decision made. It is noteworthy that it is also important so provide constructive feedback to the startups that are not selected to join the program. This information may entail hints on developing the submitted solution or other suggestions that will assist the startup team in better preparing itself for future rounds of the acceleration program.

2.6.2.7 *Step 7. Negotiating the terms of cooperation*

Under this step the startup teams and representatives of the corporation and possibly the accelerator conduct negotiations for the purpose of agreeing on the detailed terms and conditions of their future cooperation, the scope of the offered support, the parties' obligations and other material issues for participation in the program. This is a key moment for defining the relationships between the parties because the following elements among others are devised in this process:

- the scope of cooperation in the form, for instance, of access to infrastructure and the organizational facilities of the corporation and the accelerator, and access to experts, the contact network and partners;

- any possible financial terms and conditions in the form, for instance, of funding the development stage of the startup's solution during the acceleration program, the quantum and scope of the future investment, the clauses of the future articles of association;
- any possible split of the rights to the product, service, technology and intellectual property;
- duties of the parties, for example, in terms of reporting work progress, matching the solution to the corporation's needs; reporting on the achieved milestones, participation in events organized by the corporation and accelerator;
- potential model for future cooperation after the end of the acceleration program along with affirmation of the possible distribution of future earnings.

It is worth emphasizing that the negotiated terms and conditions, including the rules of participation should be recorded in the form of a framework cooperation agreement along with an action plan and budget for the individual acceleration program. This forms the construct for further inter-organizational cooperation. Insofar as negotiations may pertain to the action plan, budget or goals to be achieved, negotiations on the wording of the template of the general terms and conditions of the agreement should not be permitted. This creates a dangerous precedent, while the very information about amendments to the body of the agreement will very likely reach other participants, who will also be interested in engaging in negotiations on the clauses of the general memorandum of agreement. Such an action may cause delays to triggering program launch. The best practice is to provide the agreement template to the startups at the stage of applying to the acceleration program. At this time, it would also be worthwhile to allow for the appropriate time for the parties to sign the acceleration agreements, especially when it is necessary to collect signatures from the management of the organization and/or collect the signatures and corporate consents of the various business units, respectively.

2.6.2.8 Step 8. Signing an agreement to participate in the acceleration program

On the basis of the arrangements during the negotiations, the final wording of the agreement and the attachments thereto is prepared. Depending on the accepted assumptions, this agreement may be bilateral, that is, between the accelerator and the startup or between the corporation and the startup or trilateral, that is, between the accelerator, the corporation and the startup. The agreement contains the detailed terms and conditions for participation in the acceleration program and lays down the rights and duties of the startup and the corporation/accelerator as part of the inter-organizational cooperation being undertaken. The finalization of the final wording of the agreement and its attachments in the form of the parties signing the same formally ends the negotiation process and opens the path to the next stage of cooperation.

2.6.3 *Preparatory work stage to test solutions*

The third stage of the program pertains to preparing the startups to commence tests of the startups' solutions in the corporation's infrastructure or on a small sample of the corporation's clients/partners. This stage encompasses alignment and technological support, advisory services and planning the scope of tests. This stage consists of eight steps in keeping with Figure 2.7.

2.6.3.1 *Step 1. Onboarding and adapting startups to an acceleration program*

Before the proper acceleration work begins, the team of the accelerator and corporation should familiarize the startups with the rules of cooperation and subsequent activities to gain a better grasp of the goals of the program, communication and the corporation's expectations. During this kick-off meeting the

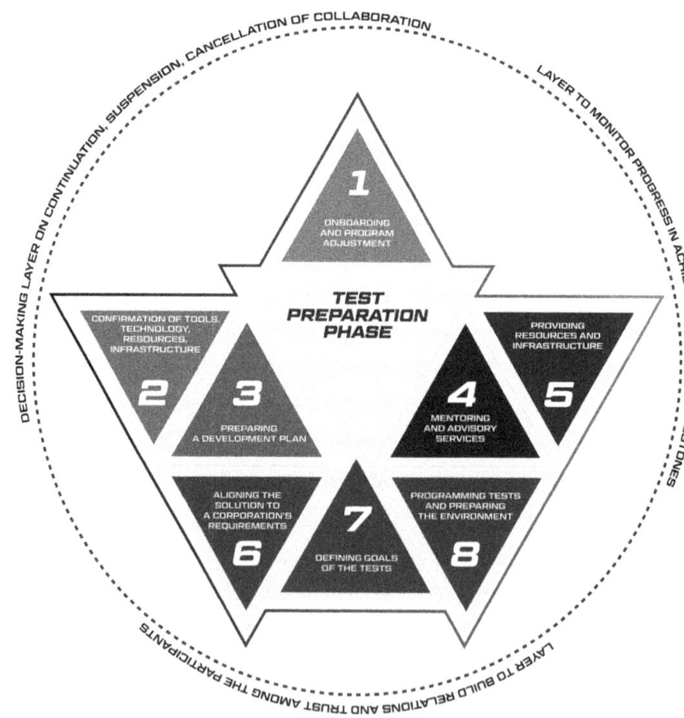

Figure 2.7 Preparation stage for testing a startup's solution in an acceleration program.

Source: Proprietary material.

organizers remind the parties about the overall cooperation framework and help the startup teams align themselves to the program structure and the schedule of the work to be done later. During this meeting the startups become acquainted with the team of the accelerator/corporation, the program's stages and the key events such as workshops, mentoring sessions, meetings with experts and the business owners on the side of the corporation. A program relationship manager is then also assigned to a startup. Mentors and experts are identified giving consideration to the profile, industry, development needs product development stage or also the business model. Cooperation with a corporation in an acceleration program may assume a varying character. The continuous procedure signifies intense work during a designated period which ordinarily means in this case a period of no longer than three to six months for the entire program. The startup team must split its time between operating activity on the market and work on development and adjusting the solution to meet the needs of the corporation. This procedure ordinarily means the startup is cut off from external stimuli and requires it to devote its full attention to cooperation with the accelerator and the corporation. In turn, if we speak about a program characterized by diminished intensity, then we are dealing with regular intervals. This procedure signifies the necessity of having the startup perform the imposed work in accordance with the devised action schedule, the tasks to be performed and the monitoring of work outcomes, including their reporting. Depending on the distinct nature of the projects pending in the organization, an acceleration program may in some startup cases exceed a period of 12 months.

2.6.3.2 *Step 2. Confirming the available tools, technologies and resources in an acceleration program*

The actions in this step concentrate on checking and affirming which tools, technologies and resources of the accelerator/corporation are available and may be used by the startups for the purposes of developing and testing the solutions in a new environment. The option of using physical infrastructure, laboratories, research center or other facilities, specialized infrastructure that may be made available to the startups is subject to analysis. The parties precisely analyze and identify the available tools and technologies and the analytical data, for example, regarding the corporation's clients that may be used as part of the acceleration program. They subsequently confirm that they are compliant with the requirements and fit to the future planned activities in accordance with the startup's acceleration plan that has been sketched out. The available tools and technologies are estimated with an eye to their potential in terms of enhancing performance and innovativeness and improving the quality and competitiveness of the solution, including the possibility of application by the startup. A plan for using the available tools, technologies and resources of the corporation and accelerator is also written for the purpose of maximizing the usage of the potential offered by these resources and accelerating the development of the solution offered by a startup. The startup team also has the option of running consultations with the experts, mentors and persons responsible for supplying the foregoing resources.

2.6.3.3 Step 3. Preparing the development plan

During this step the startups confirm the work plan for the upcoming period with the business units of the corporation and the accelerator, the team's engagement and they specify in detail the tasks and the milestones that are to be achieved. To this end the team prepares a detailed analysis of the offered solution identifying its strengths and weaknesses, the possibilities of development and the areas in need of streamlining or change, which are indispensable with an eye to performing future tests in the corporation's environment. Potential streamlining may encompass, for example, functional modifications, aligning the interface or also take into account integration of the solution offered by a startup with the existing corporate infrastructure or with one of its partners. It is worth noting that at this stage the business model is also subject to verification. Adaption and flexibility in reacting to the changing market conditions are vital to the success of the overall undertaking. In the event of a requirement to change the business model the startup conducts an analysis thereof and introduces the pertinent adjustments so that the business model is better matched to market needs and the corporation's strategy. The very procedure of the cooperation undertaken in the acceleration program depends on the accepted work model. Several types of situations may transpire along with the program's advancement, that is:

- **Changing the concept for the operation of a solution, business model forming the subject matter of inter-organizational cooperation** (*Pivot*). This may stem from undertaking cooperation with a corporation's business unit and the results obtained, talks with mentors and is frequently the result of the experience gained, feedback from users, the corporation's business partners, market analysis and observation of the competition. A pivot occurs when the startup team becomes aware that the embraced path will not produce the expected outcomes for the corporation or that it does not correspond to market needs. For the startup this denotes a change of direction in development in the form of even just a change to functionality, technology, the embraced business strategy, for example, focusing on a different group of clients, changing the business model in terms of the scope of generating revenue, or some other key elements of the offered solution, for example, changing the distribution channel. The acceleration program itself encourages startups to test their assumptions and hypotheses pertaining to the market and the product quickly. The results of these tests may indicate the need to pivot. It is worth noting that during the cooperation one can also observe the drive to achieve the maximum level of performance and the attempt to curtail risk. This may incline the startup team to alter the accepted path of cooperation if it turns out that there are more promising paths for the development and implementation of the solution in the future. In this manner the purpose of pivoting is to enhance the opportunities for achieving market success, including success in the cooperation with a corporation.

- **Withdrawal of a startup team from participating in a program.** A startup may withdraw from participation in the program on account of the following reasons

  - failing to achieve the intended milestones or goals in the acceleration program;
  - dynamic changes on the market, including evolving trends in the industry in which the corporation operates;
  - a misfit in the startup's operational approach to differences stemming from having a different culture or operational philosophy from the corporation;
  - financial problems associated with the excessive costs of participation in the program;
  - a change in the startup's goals that do not comport with the intended benefits at the outset of participation in the acceleration program;
  - the emergence of other business opportunities that are more attractive to the startup.

- **Cancelling a startup's participation in a program.** Participation is cancelled in the event the accelerator or business unit of the corporation issues a notification on ceasing and desisting from further cooperation with a startup. The reasons for making this decision are as follows:

  - the analyses performed on the potential of the startup's solution in terms of the corporation's needs, including the expected product, service and applied technology;
  - the overly slow pace in achieving the goals set forth at the outset of the acceleration program or in the meantime by the corporation and/or accelerator;
  - a difference of opinion on the vision, goals or business strategy of the corporation with the startup;
  - discovering problems related to ethics, the law or compliance with the regulations applicable to the solution offered by a startup;
  - violation of the terms and conditions of the cooperation agreement as part of the acceleration program; lack of engagement on the part of the startup in the acceleration-related activities and cooperation with a corporation or accelerator;
  - wish to optimize the portfolio of startup projects. The corporation focuses on those projects which in its opinion offer the greatest growth potential and have a better match with its business strategy. This action allows for directing greater attention and resources to those startups that may contribute to the maximum degree to improving the corporation's activities.

Regardless of the reason for cancelling participation in the program, it is important for the startup to receive a clear message on the reasons underlying this decision since the team may escalate the problem to the media or the partners of the corporation or its clients.

2.6.3.4 *Step 4. Mentoring and advisory services*

As part of the acceleration program a startup receives advisory support from experts from the corporation, accelerator and other mentors invited to join the program. This support may encompass, for example, technological expert (pertaining, e.g., to system architecture, the choice of technology, licenses), market, business or legal and financial opinions in terms of optimizing the solution being worked on and its integration in the corporation's environment. The startup team jointly with the mentors and experts identifies the major challenges associated with project development and works on effective strategies for overcoming them. It adapts its efforts to the evolving market conditions and the needs of the corporation and its clients and partners. Mentors and experts also help startups forge business relationships not only with the corporation's units but also other market participants. It is noteworthy that regular sessions with mentors and experts also constitute part of monitoring progress and evaluating a startup's accomplishments as part of the program.

2.6.3.5 *Step 5. Making infrastructure and resources available*

In accordance with the second step a corporation and/or accelerator give startups access to infrastructure, resources and tools that may include office space, laboratories, space to conduct tests, servers, analytical tools and databases. In some cases, training sessions and workshops are also held in which startups are instructed on how they should take advantage of the available tools, technologies and infrastructure furnished by corporations. Moreover, startups may gain access to the knowledge base of a corporation or accelerator, which may contain documentation, case studies, best practices and the experiences of other startups coming from the historically performed tests.

2.6.3.6 *Step 6. Adapting solutions to the requirements of corporations*

In this place startups modify their solutions under the watchful eyes of experts so that they correspond better to the needs and requirements of a corporation or its clients/partners. Adaptation may entail, among other things:

- analysis of requirements for a solution forming the subject matter of acceleration in terms of technical, organizational, legal and business aspects.

The analysis may encompass issues pertaining to the business model of a corporation, its market strategy, target group, preferred technology, infrastructural capabilities;

- consultations, sessions with experts, relationship managers and mentors appointed by the accelerator/corporation for the purpose of preparing the solution for the slated tests. Confirmation of the proposed modifications in terms of their suitability to the requirements in play, including evaluations of adherence to the rules, regulations and policies of a corporation;
- technical and functional reviews that concentrate on improving and optimizing the solution offered by a startup, for example, for the purpose of integration with other information systems, improving the interface of the solution being designed or integrating the solution with existing corporate infrastructure so as to facilitate smooth cooperation and data exchange;
- implementation of the changes that have been affirmed by the corporation for the purpose of preparing the solution for future tests of the startup's product, service and technology.

2.6.3.7 Step 7. Defining the goals of the tests of the solution undergoing acceleration

The corporation and the startup jointly confirm the intended goals of the tests, that is, what specifically is to be verified and what the expected desirable outcomes are. Therefore, the goals of the tests should be measurable and realistic and they should comport with the documents forming attachments to the acceleration agreement. The activities in this place concentrate on the following:

- understanding the goal of the tests, for example, verifying functionality, evaluating performance, checking the utility of the solution offered by the startup, or adapting the product or service to a corporation's specific requirements;
- identifying the key criteria on whose basis the efficacy and utility of the solution subject to acceleration will be assessed. Confirming the key metrics and indicators in connection with the necessity of measuring the performance of the solution subject to acceleration, for example, the number of transactions handled, client conversion, performance improvement, revenue increase, bug rectification, shortening the time to handle complaints, waste reduction, augmentation of customer satisfaction, speed of action;
- confirming the success factors for the planned tests which must be fulfilled to deem the results to be significant and determining the ability to begin talks on implementation in the corporation at the post-acceleration stage.

2.6.3.8 *Step 8. Devising the test program and preparing the test environment*

This step contains the requirement of taking the following actions in connection with the planned tests on the corporation's infrastructure or on a small sample of the corporation's clients/partners:

- precisely stating the test scenarios that will include descriptions of the instances of using the solution subject to acceleration. These scenarios describe which steps should be taken during testing to test various functions and aspects of the solution so as to obtain the most representative results. It is worth identifying the most important areas that will require special oversight and attention during testing from the vantage point of their materiality in the success of the tests.
- selecting testing methods and techniques. Here the startup team and the corporation specify the testing methods and techniques to be applied during the tests. This may include functional and performance tests, or loading, utility or compliance tests.
- selecting the group of persons or entities participating in the tests. In other words, the persons or entities to participate in the solution tests are specified. They may be employees of the corporation or accelerator, selected clients or business partners of large organizations. It is worth noting that in the event of testing a startup's solution on the basis of actual data, it will be necessary to secure and anonymize the data in accordance with GDPR regulations and information security rules[20];
- confirming and configuring the test environment in the form of corporate infrastructure, test platforms, test tools and test data, or the specially prepared simulation environment that will help run the tests and analyze the results obtained. Based on the analysis performed possible shortcomings related to the requirements pertaining to the test environment are identified. Corporations undertake here an attempt at running the tests based on a virtual environment. This makes it possible to isolate the tested solution from actual production, meaning the services that are supplied to the market. Thanks to that a safe and controlled test environment is assured. The access rights to the test environment are also defined in accordance with the roles of the members of the startup team and the corporation/accelerator. The purpose of this activity is to maintain control over access and introduce any possible unauthorized changes. It is also important to roll out along with the tests a change management procedure in the test environment. The purpose of this procedure is to control any and all modifications and updates that may be introduced and that could affect the nature of the tests. One should tend to oversight over the performance and accessibility of the test environment to ensure that the tests can be performed efficiently and seamlessly from the vantage point of the corporation's business;
- putting together the schedule and test plan. Here the test schedule (dates and stages of the tests), the roles and responsibilities of the participants,

the procedures for evaluating and reporting the results and the conduct of the organization in the event of encountering problems are defined;

- mapping prospective risks associated with running the tests. The potential factors that may affect the flow of the tests and the results ultimately obtained, including their credibility should be identified.

2.6.4 *Solution-testing stage*

The fourth stage concentrates on practically testing the startup's solution in the corporation's environment (infrastructure, test environment, clients and partners). This is a critical point in the acceleration program as a startup has the ability to verify and improve its solution in a corporation's genuine operating conditions. In turn, thanks to the results of the tests obtained and the analysis performed, a large organization holds data in its possession that will help the corporation's business unit to evaluate the value and effectiveness of the product, service or technology offered by the startup and make the decision on further cooperation. This stage consists of four steps in keeping with Figure 2.8.

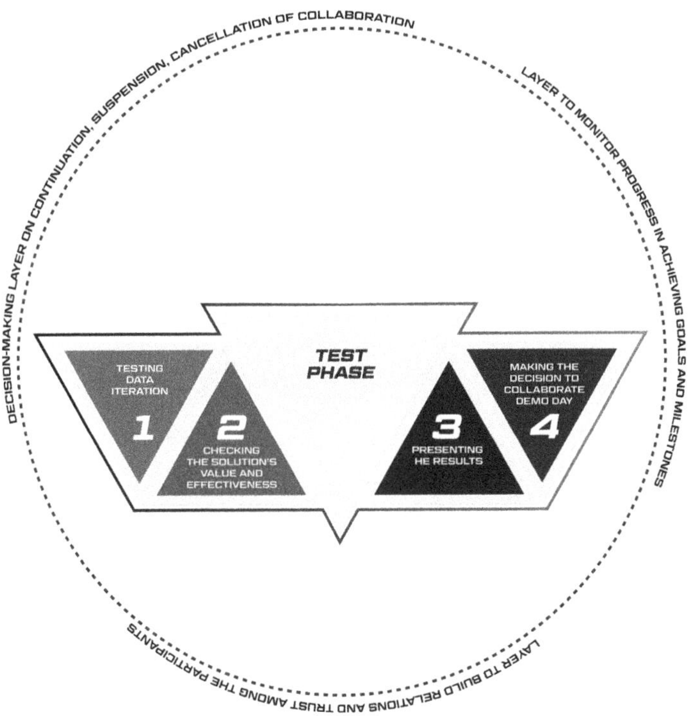

Figure 2.8 Stage to conduct tests on a startup's accelerated solution in a corporate environment.

Source: Proprietary material.

2.6.4.1 *Step 1. Testing, data compilation and iteration*

Here the process of tests on the solution in a controlled corporate environment begins. This process aims to achieve the highest possible quality and utility of the startup's solution prior to making the decision on possible full-scale implementation in the corporation. Testing should take place in an environment that approximates to the greatest possible extent genuine usage conditions. This means that startups attempt with the support of a corporation to replicate the situations in which users will encounter on an everyday basis. This process encompasses, among other things, the usage of the corporation's infrastructure to test functions, performance, security and other technical and business aspects. During the testing startups may consult with a corporation's or accelerator's experts who may furnish valuable hints and suggestions on the solution being tested and track how users take advantage of the solution. The utility of the solution, the user's interface, ease of use, method of receipt and communication with users are among the aspects subject to testing. Different versions, modules and functionalities of the solution subject to acceleration may be tested. Special emphasis is placed here on monitoring the solution's performance and stability when under a load to ensure that the solution behaves in a stable fashion and does not crash in different conditions, for example, in cases when end users or the corporation's partners are more active. During this work tests of security should also be taken into account as they identify possible gaps, for example, in personal data protection and in avoiding any possible breaches of privacy. In the meantime, the startup team has the possibility of rolling out iterative corrections and modifying the solution being tested on the basis of the findings of the tests and the feedback from users. These modifications aim to enhance its efficacy, utility, performance and adaptation to the corporation's expectations to the greatest possible degree. After making corrections the tests are continued. At the same time, it is verified whether the new corrections have made an adverse impact on other parts of the solution and whether the solution is still aligned to the intended goals of the tests.

2.6.4.2 *Step 2. Checking the solution's value and effectiveness*

The testing process should be documented, as should the result obtained. This is vital from the vantage point of preserving the transparency of the process. After the conducted rounds of testing, the startup prepares documentation based on the compiled data in the form of a report on the tests for the corporation, for instance. At this stage it is verified whether the startup's solution fulfills the pre-defined requirements that were fixed not only at the stage of negotiating the participation agreement in the acceleration program but also during the preparations for testing in accordance with the test scenarios. This is checked on the basis of data on whether the solution generates value for the organization and fulfills the intended goals. Accordingly, the solution's value and effectiveness should be duly checked in several dimensions according to Table 2.6.

The performed analysis of the dimensions involving the value and effectiveness of the startup's solution forms the basis for presenting the results and ultimately for making the decision on future cooperation by the corporation's management.

Table 2.6 Dimensions for verifying the value and effectiveness of a startup's accelerated solution

Dimension	*Actions*
Impact on the organization and its environment, including a forecast of its long-term impact	• The organization's ability and willingness to implement the solution should be evaluated. • The impact of the solution on a corporation's clients and partners should be evaluated and whether the start-up's product or service will generate added value for the organization. • Whether the results of the solution subject to acceleration effectively address the specific needs of end users should be verified. • Whether the solution can be scaled up, e.g., in terms of growing the number of users should be evaluated. • Other areas in the organization where one could possibly introduce additional changes to be able to leverage the implementation of the solution subject to acceleration in full in the future should be identified.
Fulfillment of expectations	• An analysis of the compliance with expectations should be conducted, that is, whether the solution fulfills the expectations associated with its functionality, quality and other parameters established at the outset of cooperation and at the stage of preparing for the tests.
Utility and effectiveness	• An analysis of the indicators matched to the solution subject to acceleration in the following areas should be performed: • performance indicators such as for instance reaction time, speed, number of transactions handled by a product in a unit of time; • utility indicators such as ease of use, interface coherence, user reaction speed; • user satisfaction indicators.
Viability of the solution	• The business goals should be verified, that is, evaluate whether the solution subject to acceleration achieves the intended business goals. The goals may pertain e.g. to revenue growth, enhancing client engagement, enhancing the effectiveness of processes, generating savings of time and resources. • An analysis of the solution's viability should be performed in terms of the costs of product implementation and maintenance, including accessibility to resources compared to the derived benefits.

Source: Proprietary material.

2.6.4.3 Step 3. Presentation of the results obtained from the conducted tests

This step focuses on presenting the startup's solution and the obtained results of the tests. The presentation of the results enables the corporation to understand and confirm the achievements, possible challenges and the potential for future cooperation regarding product development and implementation or the startup's service. A sample test report should contain, among others: a description of the conducted tests, the scope thereof and the goal as well as the results of the conducted tests. Moreover, a startup should insert an assessment of the compliance with the requirements imposed by the corporation. It should also conduct a risk analysis including an identification of the potential threats. The presentation of the results takes place in the headquarters of the corporation or the accelerator. This meeting may assume the form of a video conference. During the presentation a question and answer session will be held during which representatives of the corporation and invited experts may pose questions and request additional explanations. It is important for the presentation of the results to contain accurate data and conclusions because the report itself, in the event a corporation makes the decision to roll out the solution, will be the subject of further analyses, also by external entities such as law firms and patent agents, etc.

2.6.4.4 Step 4. Making the decision on further cooperation and organizing Demo Day

In the fourth step, on the basis of the results of the conducted tests, the analysis of the potential offered by the solution and the startup team, the risk benefit analysis and the experiences compiled during the program, the corporation makes the decision on continuing or discontinuing cooperation with a given startup. The decision made affects the subsequent fate of inter-organizational cooperation, the investment in a startup, the possible further development of the product or service, the implementation of the solution on a grander scale and the achievement of the parties' business goals. It should be noted that if a decision is made to discontinue cooperation, startups and corporations may consider other alternative scenarios, even if it entails submitting an offer of employment in the corporate to the entire startup team. If a decision to continue is made, then the startup and the corporation kick off business negotiations and proceed to a new chapter in inter-organizational cooperation meaning post-acceleration. Frequently, an accelerator and a corporation hold a Demo Day at the end of a given round of an acceleration program. A Demo Day is an event during which startup teams have the opportunity of showcasing their solutions to a broad auditorium for a few minutes. The organization of a Demo Day for startups may assume various forms depending on the goals, resources and preferences of its organizer and encompasses forms such as the following ones:

1 Physical large-scale event in a major conference center or some other space.
2 Conducting a virtual event utilizing a platform for a video conference, which makes it possible to have a broader reach and to have people from different parts of the world participate.
3 Narrow industry event concentrated on a specific industry or technology.
4 Network events constituting a combination of a presentation of startups with networking sessions, which will make it possible to facilitate contact between the founders of startups and investors, mentors and employees of corporations.
5 Combination with some other industry event such as part of a conference, for instance.
6 Event for selected representatives of an organization's business units.

The foregoing forms may be utilized in a hybrid form, that is, on-site and virtually. The auditorium ordinarily consists of investors, mentors, representatives of corporations, the media, government administration and other potential stakeholders. This event is an opportunity for startups to showcase their achievements and the potential offered by their products and services. It is possible that during a presentation representatives of a corporation will join the startups to emphasize their joint work and achievements. During an event the startup teams receive valuable hints from more seasoned entrepreneurs, industry experts and investors. Participating in a Demo Day helps augment the visibility of startups on the market and allows new companies to continue building their relationships with a corporation and other ecosystem participants while networking with other entrepreneurs, mentors and industry experts. The participation of corporations in Demo Day helps build their image as businesses open to innovations and supportive of new technological firms, which is attractive to their clients and prospective employees. Demo Day may also inspire the employees of a corporation to think in a more entrepreneurial and innovative fashion, which translates into the organization's internal development. By supporting startups corporations contribute to the development of the startup ecosystem from which they may in the future reap benefit.

2.7 Inter-organizational cooperation during post-acceleration

Post-acceleration is a period that usually lasts up to 12 months counting from the end of the acceleration program (e.g., the Demo Day event). During the acceleration program the startup receives expert support, access to resources, infrastructure and the corporation's contact network in connection with the defined development program (test preparation stage) or solution testing stage. The post-acceleration stage is vital to the extent that it creates an opportunity to continue the established cooperation between a startup and a corporation, while at the same time it allows the startup team to continue conducting business and operational activity on the market, solicit new clients and position its solution. In contrast to the acceleration program, during the post-acceleration period the startup does not have constant and intense support from the corporation; however, it does have the possibility of using the network of partners involved in the acceleration program, depending on the decisions made by the corporation and the accelerator, and in some cases it also has access to the corporation's resources. It should be observed that startups that complete the acceleration program may also support and share knowledge with subsequent startups that commence the acceleration program. It is worthwhile to engage program graduates in the program as they share knowledge not only on how to cooperate with a corporation's business units but also on how to utilize the resources made available by a corporation in the program as best as possible. The negotiation process during post-acceleration may pertain to various aspects of prospective inter-organizational cooperation. Several key issues forming the axis for negotiation are portrayed below:

1 **Form of further business cooperation.** Further cooperation between a startup and a corporation may assume the form of a capital investment, a service provision agreement, the provision of the startup's product to the corporation or its partners, or a cooperation agreement with the corporation on product or service development.
  Business cooperation may also span issues relating to integrating the startup's technologies with the corporation's products, placing the startup's product and service in the distribution channels of a large organization or its partners and marketing activities.
2 **Intellectual property rights.** The negotiations conducted by the parties frequently concern intellectual property rights in the form of patents and copyrights to the final solution.
3 **Financial conditions.** During the post-acceleration period the financial conditions for future cooperation are also subject to agreement. Negotiations may pertain to the conditions for the investment, including: quantum and timing of the investment, number of rounds, share of potential earnings, capital structure and possibly the formation of a joint venture.
4 **Access to a corporation's resources, including experts.** A startup may also negotiate the terms and conditions for access to a corporation's infrastructure and resources to enable it to continue any possible further work.

Depending on the type of cooperation, various parties can be involved in the negotiation process. Representatives of the startup (e.g., management board and representative of the shareholders), representatives of the corporation/members of the accelerator's team, and possibly other entities invited to participate, for example, law firms, financial advisors, transaction advisors customarily participate. The parties endeavor to find the shared points and strike an agreement regarding the future clauses of the agreement. There are many different approaches to the potential models of cooperation between a startup and a corporation depending on both parties' goals and the nature

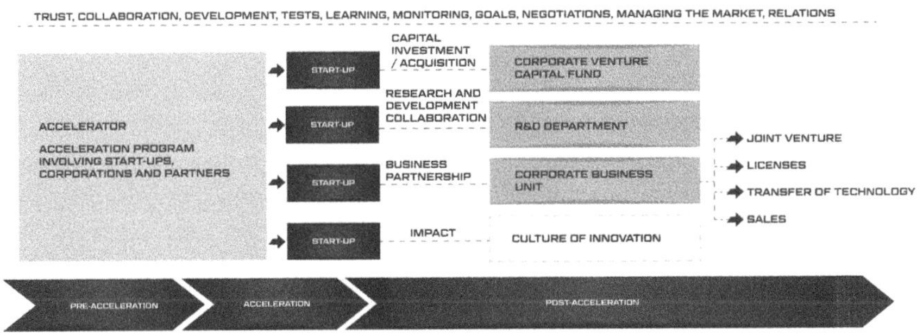

Figure 2.9 Cooperation model in the post-acceleration period.

Source: Proprietary material.

of the business conducted. Figure 2.9 depicts the cooperation model during the post-acceleration period.

The approaches to cooperation during the post-acceleration period that are popular on the market may pertain to the following:

1 **A corporation's capital investment in a startup.** A capital investment made by a corporation in a startup is a desirable outcome of inter-organizational cooperation. Corporations may elect to purchase equity in the startup. This enables them to gain a certain degree of control over the activities of the startup and a share in the startup's potential earnings. This type of investment may have a varying scale – from a minority stake to the full acquisition of all of the equity in a startup. An investment may be part of the corporation's long-term strategy aiming to expand its footprint on the market and penetrate new markets or secure the option of buying a startup if its technology or product is successfully rolled out in the corporation.
2 **R&D cooperation.** The startup and the corporation may further combine their strengths and cooperate on R&D projects that may accrue benefits to both parties. Such partnerships make it possible to combine unique resources and competences for the purpose of continuing cooperation and jointly developing innovative products, services or technologies, and also conducting R&D work.
3 **Business partnership, licensing technologies, etc.** A startup and a corporation may establish cooperation to supply raw materials, products and services and to offer the startup's solutions in the corporation's sales channels, which may accrue benefit to both parties. As they have greater resources and a distribution network, corporations may provide startups with greater reach and scale of operation. These types of business partnerships allow startups to scale up their innovations and technological solutions while they allow corporations to enrich their offering, gain access to new and frequently more technologically advanced products and services

that may then be resold to end users. This form of cooperation is a win-win for both parties.

4 **Activity contributing to enhancing the culture of innovativeness in an organization.** In this aspect of cooperation corporate culture may be transformed by incorporating the approach to entrepreneurship and openness to innovations characteristic of the startup community. As a consequence, corporations gain new possibilities of constantly developing their employees and maintaining their competitiveness in a rapidly evolving environment thanks to continuing their cooperation with new innovative companies. In this sense corporations may for instance adapt new methods of work, approaches to solving problems and strategies for implementing innovations. They draw inspiration from creativity, flexibility and the agile approach that is typical of startups. Such cooperation may manifest itself in different forms, for example, in the form of organizing workshops for the employees of corporations on designing and implementing innovations, programs for exchanging knowledge and experience, approaching the risk of cooperation with external entities. It is noteworthy that insofar as the acceleration program refers to a pre-defined time period, the evaluation of a program's effectiveness should take into account the results of such cooperation after the completion of a program round. The goals of an acceleration program that do not translate into improvement in the activity of a corporation evidence the erroneously articulated assumptions of a program. From the perspective of parties taking part in an acceleration program, it is necessary to analyze the final profits and losses resulting from the established inter-organizational cooperation.

On the basis of the conducted analysis of the literature and proprietary experience, Table 2.7 depicts the four main cooperation models that are associated with the flow of financial resources between parties.

Negotiations and the selection of the cooperation model should take into account the needs and strategies not just of the corporation but also of the startup. The cooperation models described aim to foster a win–win situation in which both parties derive benefits from their cooperation after the completed acceleration program. The key element is to weigh their interests and understand their mutual expectations. To recap, the white label model is attractive to startups that obtain access to a corporation's clients and resources and to a corporation that may enlarge its offering to include innovative solutions. However, the effectiveness of this model depends on properly managing the relationships between the organizations and the conducted communication.

In the event of a joint offering this cooperation may be beneficial because it makes it possible to utilize the strengths of the startup and the corporation in the process of developing and promoting the product or service and during its distribution. However, just as in the white label model, the success of this model depends on effective communication, cooperation and skills of

Table 2.7 Cooperation models between corporations and startups following the termination of the acceleration program

Model of cooperation	*Type of partnership*	*Assumptions*	*Responsibility and profit sharing*
White label	Intermediary	• A corporation distributes through its own channels the solutions created by start-ups under its own brand name. This is supposed to contribute to better reception on the market of the product or service and higher sales than if the start-up were to do this in a traditional manner (greater trust and interest from the side of clients). • On the basis of cooperation with a start-up a corporation enlarges its offering, which may contribute to enhancing its competitiveness and the attractiveness of its offering. • A corporation is an intermediary in transferring the start-up's product or service to the final client. • The risk associated with customer dissatisfaction and the related image losses rest on the corporation. • The start-up's task is to deliver the product in accordance with the requirements prescribed by the corporation (compliance with the guidelines and standards defined by a large organization for the products and services rendered in its distribution channels).	• The corporation has greater responsibility on account of selling the start-up's solution under its own brand name. • In the event of problems or failures the image-related losses are borne by the corporation. • The responsibility for supplying the product belongs to the start-up. • The parties share the sales revenue and square accounts in accordance with the concluded business agreement. The financial conditions and the percentage share of profits due to the start-up and the corporation are confirmed through negotiation.

(*Continued*)

Table 2.7 (Continued)

Model of cooperation	*Type of partnership*	*Assumptions*	*Responsibility and profit sharing*
Joint offering	Business partner	• This model is based on preparing a joint product and service offering. As part of this model both parties combine their resources, knowledge and skills to create a joint product or service offering that is the outcome of synergy between a corporation and a start-up. • The object forming the joint offering may be the outcome of intense actions instigated at the acceleration stage. • The mutual understanding of the needs and goals of each one of the parties and proper communication between a corporation and a start-up is vital.	• The corporation and the start-up alike share responsibility at all stages of the sales process, including production, marketing, distribution and customer service. • Each party contributes its own unique competences and resources. • Parties share the profits on sales and square accounts on the effects of their cooperation in accordance with the executed business agreement.
Reselling	Intermediary	• The idea behind reselling is that a corporation purchases products from a start-up, and then resells them through its channels to its partners, the final clients at a price higher than the purchase price. Corporate business experience, familiarity with the target market and the extensive distribution network and the customer database should assist in this activity. • A start-up is solely the supplier of the solution to the corporation. The corporation undertakes further decisions on what to do with the purchased product. In this manner a start-up does not have much influence over what happens with its products after a corporation purchases it.	• Responsibility for the success of reselling the products or services belongs to the corporation. • The risk associated with failure in sales, customer dissatisfaction or problems related to the product or service is transferred to the corporation. • When it makes delivery of the solution the start-up receives payment for it. • The corporation earns a sales margin. The final price at which the products are sold to partners or clients is higher than the price of purchase from the start-up, which allows the corporation to turn a profit.

Acquisition or some other form of investment in a start-up	Equity partner	• A corporation acquires a portion/all of the equity in a start-up. It acquires a partial or total right to the start-up's product, service or technology. • In the event of a total acquisition the corporation may fully integrate the start-up with its own activity, while tapping into innovations for strengthening its own market position. • This approach may also contribute to accelerating innovation processes inside a corporation through direct access to the technologies and talents originating from a start-up. • Cooperation between a corporation and a start-up may accrue synergy effects. For a corporation this is a method of diversifying its portfolio and investing in new promising market areas. In turn, a start-up has access to the corporation's resources, market and knowledge, ability to obtain the required financial means for further development and expansion. • Capital investments are helpful in forging long-term and strategic relationships between corporations and start-ups, thereby producing financial, developmental and image-related benefits to the parties. • Risk of protracted negotiations concerning a transaction's business conditions	• Responsibility for the success of the start-up's operating business is transferred to a large extent to the corporation. • Profits in accordance with the dividend policy.

Source: Proprietary material.

solving any possible conflicts. The properly construed partnership agreement is critical to specify clearly roles, duties and profit sharing.

In turn, the reselling model is attractive to startups that may find a large client and receive stable revenue for the delivery of their solutions. This model is also attractive to corporations that may expand their offering to include new products or services. Undoubtedly, the success of this model depends on a corporation's ability to distribute effectively and promote the solutions purchased from startups.

The model in which a corporation becomes an equity partner of a startup is the least frequently encountered model on the market. A corporation gains access to innovative solutions and technologies, and it secures its position on the market. In turn, a startup obtains stable financing and access to the corporation's environment, including its infrastructure, clients and partners. However, it should be remembered that a corporation's greater control over a startup may introduce certain challenges related to the loss of independence experienced by the startup and engender potential conflicts against this backdrop, also including the team's diminished engagement in the startup's further development.

This part of the book illustrates the role played by startup acceleration programs with the involvement of large organizations as a key tool supporting inter-organizational cooperation on open innovations. Diverse aspects and operating models of startup accelerators have been analyzed while giving consideration to their structure, functioning and funding methods. The frameworks for acceleration programs have been depicted in detail. The stages of an acceleration program have been submitted to a meticulous analysis, starting from planning to testing solutions in a corporate environment. The differences in the functioning of acceleration programs in the CEE region have also been discussed in comparison with their counterparts in more developed economies. The acceleration programs in CEE differ in terms of scale and structure alike. They frequently rely on local funding models such as public funds, including EU grants. Despite these differences, the common element of acceleration programs across the world is the international nature of the corporations participating in them, which facilitates startups' access to global markets and broader development opportunities. The end of this part of the book presents the possible directions of cooperation following the completion of an acceleration program, including the most frequently encountered cooperation models at the post-acceleration stage.

The foregoing issues form a robust basis for further research for the purpose of gaining a more profound appreciation for the cooperation between startups and corporations as part of acceleration programs with special emphasis on the cognitive aspect of this process. In the subsequent chapters of this book this will be reflected through analysis of how inter-organizational cooperation is perceived as part of acceleration programs from the vantage point of corporations and startups alike. This constitutes a natural development of the issues discussed in this part of the book. It will be possible to investigate to what extent the assumed goals are achieved by the parties and what obstacles impede effective cooperation in acceleration programs. Additionally, this research will make it possible to identify the attributes that have a potential impact on cooperation between startups and corporations. This will be a development of prior analyses making it possible to indicate which specific predictors may potentially be of importance for the success of cooperation with corporations.

Notes

1 Mahmoud-Jouini, S. B., Duvert, C., & Esquirol, M. (2018). Key factors in building a corporate accelerator capability: Developing an effective corporate accelerator requires close attention to the relationships between startups and the sponsoring company. *Research-Technology Management*, *61*(4), 26–34.
2 Veit, P., Kramer, A., Kanbach, D., & Stubner, S. (2021). Revising the taxonomy of corporate accelerators: Moving towards an evolutionary perspective. *International Journal of Entrepreneurial Venturing*, *13*(6), 568–599.
3 Clayton, P., Feldman, M., & Lowe, N. (2018). Behind the scenes: Intermediary organizations that facilitate science commercialization through entrepreneurship. *Academy of Management Perspectives*, *32*(1), 104–124.
4 Autio, E., Kenney, M., Mustar, P., Siegel, D., & Wright, M. (2014). Entrepreneurial innovation: The importance of context. *Research Policy*, *43*(7), 1097–1108.
5 Crişan, E. L., Salanţă, I. I., Beleiu, I. N., Bordean, O. N., & Bunduchi, R. (2021). A systematic literature review on accelerators. *The Journal of Technology Transfer*, *46*, 62–89.
6 Prexl, K. M., Hubert, M., Beck, S., Heiden, C., & Prügl, R. (2019). Identifying and analysing the drivers of heterogeneity among ecosystem builder accelerators. *R&D Management*, *49*(4), 624–638.
7 Cohen, S. (2013). What do accelerators do? Insights from incubators and angels. *Innovations: Technology, Governance, Globalization*, *8*(3), 19–25.
8 Shankar, R. K., & Shepherd, D. A. (2019). Accelerating strategic fit or venture emergence: Different paths adopted by corporate accelerators. *Journal of Business Venturing*, *34*(5), 105886.
9 Hochberg, Y. V., & Fehder, D. C. (2015). Accelerators and ecosystems. *Science*, *348*(6240), 1202–1203.
10 Mahmoud-Jouini, S. B., Duvert, C., & Esquirol, M. (2018). Key Factors in Building a Corporate Accelerator Capability: Developing an effective corporate accelerator requires close attention to the relationships between startups and the sponsoring company. *Research-Technology Management*, *61*(4), 26–34.
11 Kohler, T. (2016). Corporate accelerators: Building bridges between corporations and startups. *Business Horizons*, *59*(3), 347–357.
12 Hochberg, Y. V. (2016). Accelerating entrepreneurs and ecosystems: The seed accelerator model. *Innovation Policy and the Economy*, *16*(1), 25–51.
13 Moschner, S. L., Fink, A. A., Kurpjuweit, S., Wagner, S. M., & Herstatt, C. (2019). Toward a better understanding of corporate accelerator models. *Business Horizons*, *62*(5), 637–647.
14 Trotter, A. (2013). Six Lessons for Corporations Building Innovation Accelerators. *Strategy & Innovation*, *11*. https://www.innosight.com/insight/six-lessons-for-corporations-building-innovation-accelerators/
15 Pauwels, C., Clarysse, B., Wright, M., & Van Hove, J. (2016). Understanding a new generation incubation model: The accelerator. *Technovation*, *50*, 13–24.

16 Cohen, S. (2013). What do accelerators do? Insights from incubators and angels. *Innovations: Technology, Governance, Globalization*, *8*(3), 19–25.
17 Urbaniec, M., & Żur, A. (2021). Business model innovation in corporate entrepreneurship: Exploratory insights from corporate accelerators. *International Entrepreneurship and Management Journal*, *17*(2), 865–888.
18 Bańka, M., Salwin, M., Kukurba, M., Rychlik, S., Kłos, J., & Sychowicz, M. (2022). Start-up accelerators and their impact on sustainability: Literature analysis and case studies from the energy sector. *Sustainability*, *14*(20), 13397.
19 Hallen, B. L., Bingham, C. B., & Cohen, S. (2014). Do accelerators accelerate? A study of venture accelerators as a path to success? In *Academy of management proceedings* (Vol. 2014, No. 1. 12955). Briarcliff Manor, NY: Academy of Management.
20 Bańka, M., Soczyński, T., & Wasiak, D. (2021). Practical methods of implementation for the indispensable mechanism of GDPR compliance. *Wroclaw Review of Law, Administration & Economics*, *11*(2), 31–47.

3 Research methodology

This part of the book pertains to defining the research gap on inter-organizational cooperation between corporations and startups in terms of acceleration programs. This chapter begins with a systematic literature review conducted in accordance with the PRISMA methodology (*Preferred Reporting Items for Systematic Reviews and Meta-Analyses*). This review encompasses an analysis of the publications available in the scientific databases called Web of Science (WoS) and Scopus. Additionally, an analysis of the database BazEkon[1] and of the database of projects financed by the National Science Center in Cracow was conducted. The results of the ninth edition of the report investigating Polish startups in terms of the available research on cooperation between companies in acceleration programs were also incorporated. Later in the book the research process was depicted in detail, including a description of the research tool, the data collection procedure and the methods applied to analyze the data. The last part of the chapter concentrates on a characterization of the researched groups, that is, startups and large organizations that took part in the acceleration programs.

3.1 Systematic literature review

In this part of the book a systematic review of scientific literature was conducted, which is crucial to gain an appreciation for the inter-organizational cooperation between corporations and startups in terms of acceleration programs. The research conducted not only enriches the current state of knowledge but also forms the foundation for defining the research gap. The exploratory research stage was done as desk research. It served the purpose of recognizing the state of knowledge pertaining to current information and the justification for examining the inter-organizational cooperation between corporations and startups in terms of acceleration programs. A systematic review of literature was used to attain this goal.[2] The review made it possible to prepare a critical and objective review of the body of scientific knowledge in the selected research area.[3] Verifying the literature made it possible to identify and evaluate the theoretical approaches used to date, and as a consequence it contributed at a later stage to extract the knowledge gap and

DOI: 10.4324/9781003540366-4

limitations in the previously conducted research. To do the review of scientific literature a search was applied whose structure was inspired using the PRISMA methodology.[4] PRISMA is a widely recognized method recommended in scientific research.[5] It structures the reporting of results for systematic reviews of literature and it provides for substantial transparency in the process of selecting results in the conducted review of scientific publications. Transparency and clarity of the research methodology, including the search strategy, inclusion/exclusion criteria and a flowchart illustrating the number of publications identified and evaluated with an eye to qualifications, as well as those included in the review and the reasons for exclusion at various stages, are key aspects of the PRISMA methodology.[6] Table 3.1 depicts the logic underlying the search query. The columns show the operator OR, which means that at least one of the words in the column should appear as a part of the title, keywords or abstract. The rows also show the operator AND, which means that each one of the words in these rows should appear as a part of the title, keywords or abstract. The first area of focus for the search was accelerators and the synonyms related to them, which are used to describe these types of undertakings. This group contains the English counterparts of words such as business accelerator, venture accelerator, start-up accelerator, entrepreneurship accelerator, seed accelerator and corporate accelerator. Additionally, using the character "*", the search was extended to include difference endings for the designated keywords. The second area of focus for the search was startups (startup* and start-up). The two foregoing areas should eliminate records not associated at all with startup accelerators such as entries related to physics or mechanics, for example, particle accelerator. Additionally, entries related to corporations ("corporate") and accelerators ("accelerator*") were required in the search.

A search in the titles, abstracts and key works was conducted in the Scopus knowledge base using the query:

TITLE-ABS-KEY ("business accelerator*" OR "venture* accelerator*" OR "start-up* accelerator*" OR "entrepreneurial accelerator*" OR "seed accelerator*" OR "corporate accelerator*" OR "startup* accelerator*") AND ("startup*" OR "start-up*") AND (corpor*) AND "accelerator*") AND PUBYEAR > 2003 AND PUBYEAR < 2023 AND (LIMIT-TO (LANGUAGE, "English").

In turn, the query in the WoS knowledge base was similar. The search was conducted in the parameter "Topic", which contains the title, abstract and keywords. The query in WoS covered the following:

TS = ("business accelerator*" OR "venture* accelerator*" OR "start-up* accelerator*" OR "entrepreneurial accelerator*" OR "seed accelerator*" OR "corporate accelerator*" OR "startup* accelerator*") AND ("startup*" OR "start-up*") AND (corpor*) AND "accelerator*").

After doing a search using this query, the period of publications was set in the filters in the two databases to cover the scope from 1 January 2003 to

Table 3.1 Logic for searching for articles pertaining to inter-organizational cooperation in acceleration programs

	OR						
A N D	Business accelerator	Venture accelerator	Start-up accelerator	Entrepreneurial accelerator	Seed accelerator	Corporate accelerator	Startup* accelerator
	Startup* Corpor* Accelerator*	Start-up*					

Source: Proprietary material.

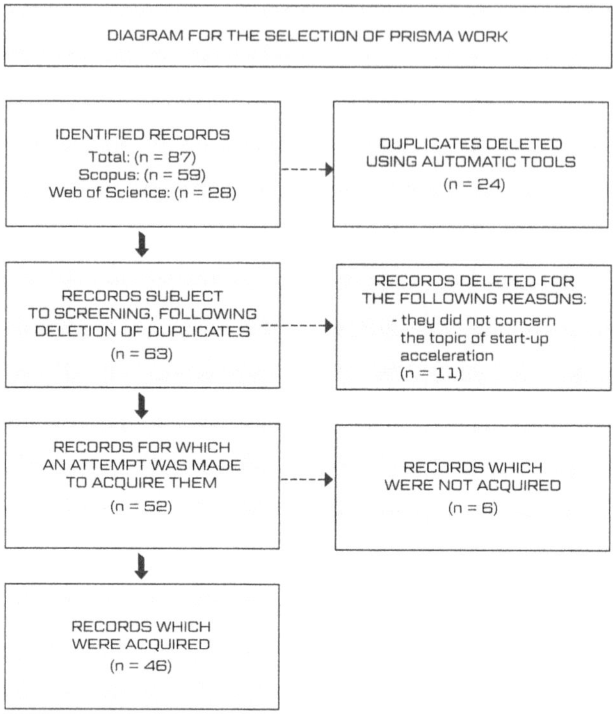

Figure 3.1 Schematic for the adopted work selection according to the PRISMA methodology.

Source: Proprietary material.

31 December 2022, and the results were limited to the English language. The outcome of this search led to the receipt of a total of 87 works with 59 of them in the Scopus database and 28 in the WoS database. Figure 3.1 depicts the scheme for selection. The records were exported to a csv and Excel file, and then 24 redundant items were removed using automatic functions. Sixty-three records went through the screening of abstracts and summaries. Eleven papers were rejected as they did not concern the topic of startup acceleration involving the participation of corporations. Then, an attempt was made to search for 52 publications in generally accessible libraries or directly from the co-authors. Ultimately, 46 papers were sourced as they were available in libraries or offered open access in the internet or were made available thanks to the kindness of their authors.

All 46 scientific papers pertained to accelerators and their programs. They include topics such as definitions and a characterization of accelerators, the benefits stemming from their operation from the perspective of corporations and startups as well as the risks associated with running an acceleration program. The conclusions in these papers were based on survey research, in-depth interviews and sporadically on case studies.

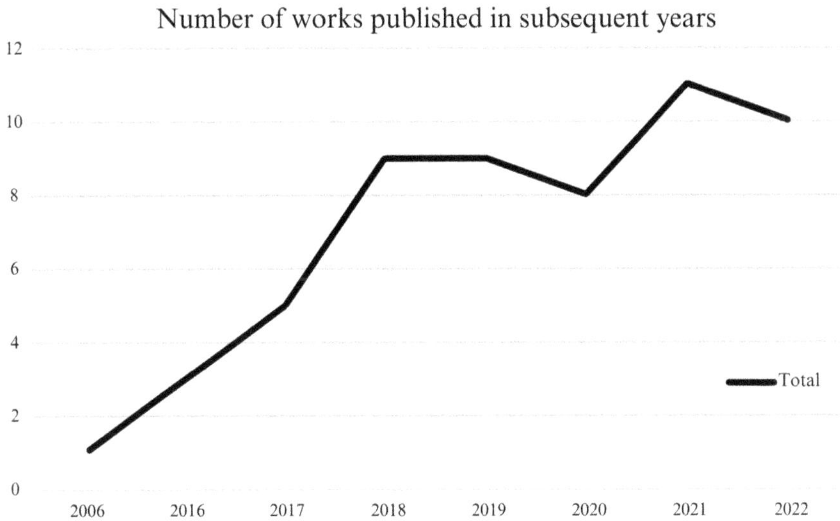

Figure 3.2 Number of publications in subsequent years in the Scopus and Web of Science databases according to data as at the end of 2022.

Source: Proprietary material.

Interest in the topic of accelerators and their programs climbed gradually from 2006 with a slight decline in 2020 and 2022. In total, however, over the years 56 scientific papers were published on this subject matter, and since 2018 an average of 9 articles have been published annually and which are indexed in the Scopus and/or WoS databases. These numbers, and the growth since 2018, illustrate that the literature is characterized by being recent, and the topic still constitutes a research area that has been explored to a limited extent (Figure 3.2).

Even though the applied method for identifying the key literature satisfied the criteria for a systematic review, the Author deemed it to be limited. Since inter-organizational cooperation in terms of acceleration programs in explanatory research will pertain to acceleration programs involving the participation of corporations operating in Poland, it was also vital to review the state of knowledge in research projects financed by the National Science Center in Cracow and local scientific literature, which is not always indexed in the foregoing international scientific databases. According to the following:

1 NCN database[7] as at the end of December 2023 only three scientific research projects related to startups received financing in Poland, including two in the HS4 panel (economics, finance, management, demography, socio-economic geography, urbanistics) and one in HS6 (psychology, pedagogics, sociology). The scientific centers in which the research was done were the Jagiellonian University, the Warsaw School of Economics and the

Kraków University of Economics. None of the foregoing projects pertains to inter-organizational cooperation between corporations and startups.

2 BazEkon database[8] as at December 2023 indexing magazines and publication series in the economic sciences in 1982–2023. As part of the query to search using keywords: accelerator or akcelerator or words in the title: accelerators or akcelerator, 28 scientific publications appeared. After reviewing the full titles, keywords and abstracts for these 28 publications, only 5 of them pertained to acceleration programs, of which none of them pertained to the issues that are the subject matter of this monograph. The first one of the articles pertained to the evaluation and comparison of factors affecting the results of startups as part of the leading business accelerators in three countries: Brazil, India and the United States by employing the Resource-Based View concept. It was observed that the financial contribution of accelerators in the form of seed capital played a significant role and increased the chance of survival, growth and the financial results of startups.[9] The second article whose co-author is the author of this publication pertains to a systematic literature review with a bibliometric analysis in terms of the general reconnaissance of the operation of startup accelerators and support extended to new companies.[10] The third article concentrates on comparing Poland' startup environment with that of other European Union countries in the context of the functioning of startup accelerators and incubators.[11] The next article pertains to a scientific literature review on startup accelerators. The discussion concerned the definition of accelerators, their functions, the offered value proposition and the functioning of the accepted business model of an organization in comparison with other models for supporting startups such as incubators. Later in the article the author concentrated on research pertaining to the effectiveness of accelerators. Attention was drawn to the measurement of the performance of startup accelerators should take into account the goals and assumptions underlying their operation.[12] The fifth article pertained to the issue of financial institutions such as banks launching corporate accelerators (Wells Fargo Startup Accelerator, Barclays Accelerator, Nordea Startup Accelerator, Catalyst belonging to Société Générale), dealing with the search for and the support of startups active in the fintech sector. The term fintech refers to companies supplying innovative technologies to the financial industry encompassing financial tools and related services, customarily through internet platforms. It was observed that on account of their unique nature, startup accelerators may offer solutions with a better fit than other instruments available on the market.[13]

An analysis of the data in the NCN and BazEkon databases unambiguously indicates a noticeable shortfall of domestic scientific research devoted to the cooperation between corporations and startups in terms of acceleration programs. Accordingly, publications from international databases such as WoS and Scopus were selected for further literature analysis. For the broader context of the impact exerted by acceleration programs on inter-organizational cooperation in Poland, the results of the ninth annual report entitled Polish Startups 2023 released by the Startup Poland Foundation were also presented.

3.1.1 Results of the literature review conducted

The verification of the literature conducted in response to the defined criteria for the inquiry revealed the presence of publications that are not directly associated with the specific research areas discussed in this monograph. Therefore, in the latter portion of this review, articles were selected that, in the author's opinion, dovetail with the conducted research. The literature selection was based on criteria such as the topical consistence with the area under research and the potential impact on subsequent research within the scope of the research described in this monograph. Based on the research conducted to-date the assertion was made that the considerations of the authors pertained to three areas:

1 goals, advantages and benefits ensuing from the execution of acceleration programs involving corporations;
2 challenges with which corporate acceleration programs are grappling;
3 factors that are significant from the point of view of strategy, management and the structure of operation of the startup acceleration programs.

In reference to the first point, the research focused on the following:

1 Goals and competitive advantages of corporations associated with sourcing and implementing external innovations.[14] The authors drew attention to the fact that corporations endeavor to cooperate with startups above all to obtain access to innovations, track the innovations appearing on the market, monitor technological trends, absorb the culture of innovativeness characteristic of startups in the organization, create potential investment opportunities, source talents and reorganize internal organizational processes. It was emphasized that these are only parts of a broader spectrum of motivation. It was pointed out that there are probably many reasons why large organizations get involved in such partnerships, which evidences the complexity and diversity of corporations' approaches to innovativeness and cooperation with the startup community. Improving financial results in the long-run, a learning organization and having a corporation's staff gain unique competences were also identified as some of the benefits on top of the ones listed above when thinking about the achievement of the intended goals of cooperation.
2 Company's reputation and image, reconnaissance in the startup ecosystem.[15] Corporations by getting involved in projects with startups were

perceived as modern companies that are inclined to innovate, and that are also meeting trends and the expectations of consumers head on. This attracts the attention of new and innovative companies. Corporations by getting involved in cooperation with startups may also be perceived as leaders in their industry and as partners for the innovative solutions of startups. Additionally, their recognition in the startup ecosystem is bolstered. Thanks to this recognition the corporation's established cooperation with startups leads to long-term business relationships, creates an opportunity for corporations to be the first to gain access to innovations emerging outside the bounds of large organizations.

In respect of the second point, the research concentrated on the following:

1 Human capital, including the requirement to provide for the engagement of the corporation's employees in corporate acceleration programs.[16] It was observed that on top of the challenges relating to the engagement of the senior management ensuing from the rooted methods of thinking and managerial habits, the shortage of competence and experience may also be a challenge. These shortfalls frequently result from limited knowledge concerning the functioning of acceleration programs, which additionally hinders their effective implementation and execution in corporate structures. It is a challenge to find employees in a corporation who are capable of effective cooperation with startups and who hold skills in terms of navigating the corporate structures. Capable of supporting startup teams when they come upon deadlocks in relationships with a corporation's business units, also in the process of identifying the key decision makers.
2 Providing partnerships, a varied and attractive value proposition and a suitable and flexible organizational structure for the acceleration program. Preparing the organization to evaluate startups and carry out acceleration programs, also ensure the appropriate approach to cooperation with startups.[17] The significance of providing for easy access to a corporation's resources, its partners and experts and mentors was emphasized, which constitutes a key distinguishing factor and the added value of acceleration programs for new companies. Corporations should, to the extent possible, rely not only on local resources but also benefit from the knowledge and international partner networks with which they cooperate. It was also observed that large corporations have a tendency to avoid risk and are characterized by limited flexibility and freedom of operation, which forms a significant challenge in the context of inter-organizational cooperation. These traits contrast with the dynamic and flexible nature of startups, which may additionally complicate cooperation. Moreover, attention was drawn to the significance of the process of evaluating and selecting startups' applications as a key stage that has a direct impact on the success of the overall cooperation. Tapping into an extensive partner network when seeking startups enhances the chances of a corporation sourcing

a higher number of submissions, which on one hand may translate into cooperation with more valuable startups, while on the other hand partners may offer support in executing the program at later stages. Attention was drawn to startup projects being diverse, even if they fall within the area of business prescribed by a corporation, which means that the evaluation of an application calls for the corporation to have interdisciplinary knowledge and cooperate with diverse experts. Moreover, corporations should tend to the startup selection process being competitive and recurring. It was pointed out that corporations and startups differ from one another in terms of their decision-making pace. Corporations are characterized by a multi-level decision-making process that frequently requires the engagement of different organizational units, which protracts the decision-making period. In turn, startups prefer rapid decision-making, which results from their more flexible and dynamic structure. The research also encompassed analysis of corporations' willingness to cooperate with innovative companies, their ability to work with innovative solutions and the degree of adaptation of innovations in their organizational structures.

In reference to the third point, on account of the variegation of the topics undertaken by researchers it turned out to be necessary to divide the factors into two parts that exert an impact on strategy, the structure of an acceleration program and its management. The first part pertains to those factors that are associated with the strategic goals of the corporation's business. These aspects refer to assigning a direction to the acceleration program from the perspective of the organizational strategy and the organization's achievement of its intended goals.[18] Research was conducted in this context in the following scope:

- business model analysis covered aspects such as concentration on selected areas and important problems for corporations. It was noted that in some instances the researched corporations did not have clearly defined challenges or needs, which a startup was supposed to solve with its product, service or technology. Instead of that large organizations expected that the corporate accelerator would find a *perfect match*. Accelerators should engage representatives of the organization's business units and procure their full involvement in a program from the very outset, that is, from defining the need, priority areas and verticals. In a short-term perspective corporate accelerators and their programs generate new market knowledge pertaining to clients' expectations, industrial trends and new technologies;
- orientation on the market needs of an organization and its clients, building scalable solutions, creating new markets for products, services and technologies created as a result of inter-organizational cooperation;
- impact exerted by a corporation's reputation and credibility on the capacity to attract the most innovative solutions offered by startups from the market. The research analyzed how a corporation's reputation and

credibility influence the efficacy of sourcing high quality startups and their innovative solutions.

The latter part concentrates on the key factors for the approach to managing an acceleration program.[19] When it comes to management special attention should be paid to the process of selecting startups to an acceleration program which is perceived as a key factor determining the success of the overall undertaking. A prerequisite for the effectiveness of a corporate accelerator and its program is the effective identification and recruitment of suitable startup teams. Moreover, the area of acceleration program management was investigated by scientists with reference to the following:

a defining the goals of cooperation and the expectations of the parties, starting from the program's concept and ending with the perception of success, performance criteria and the expected outcomes for an acceleration program. Cooperation at the various stages should combine the interests of corporations and startups for the purpose of engendering mutual benefits. According to researchers precisely setting the goals for the term of startup acceleration in a corporation's environment helps define and structure the relationship, and duly align the startup's solution to the needs of the corporation's business unit. Clear communication in respect of the success factors during an acceleration program is equally important. It allows not just a corporation's managers but also its teams to monitor progress;

b operational management of an acceleration program starting from recruitment until Demo Day and any additional activities after completing the acceleration program. Corporations should strive to foster a specific value which takes into consideration specific resources and assets such as access to markets, stakeholders, resources and program partners. The observation was made that the performance of accelerators and their acceleration programs hinges not just on the suitable physical infrastructure but above all on the procurement of support required for the development of startups and the testing of their products, services and technologies in a corporate environment. Startups should have access to corporate experts, mentors, contact networks, corporate infrastructure and other facilities, which as a consequence contributes to accelerating the development of innovations and sets up suitable conditions for implementing the solutions of startups. The assertion was made that the management's engagement is crucial for a corporation to get involved in a program and provide for the availability of the indispensable resources for the purposes of cooperating with startups. Engaging the management to play the role of mentors or relationship managers for startup teams is an action aiming at transforming corporate culture in the direction of a more open environment that is conducive to the integration of internal and external innovations. Engaging the management in this way curtails the risk of opportunistic behavior on the part of a corporation's employees toward the startup teams and their solutions.

c procuring the effective flow of information and communication, as well as shaping mutual trust between the participants of an acceleration program. Decisions should be made in a decentralized manner, which enables the team of an accelerator to preserve its autonomy in cooperation with startups.

3.1.2 *Report entitled Polish startups 2023*

The ninth edition of the report entitled *Polish Startups 2023* was drafted using the SurveyLab tool. This survey research was conducted in the period from July to September 2023. 44% of the respondents emphasized the need for increasing the number of specialized acceleration programs in Poland in the part of the report devoted to the indispensable changes for the purpose of accelerating startup development. Nearly an equal percentage of subjects (45%) flagged the necessity of creating a more stable legal system. 76% of the surveyed startups invested their own funds in the company's development in terms of funding. Higher risk Venture Capital funds enjoyed the greatest popularity among the forms of external financing, with 25% of the firms in the research having utilized that form. The more pronounced role of acceleration programs was observed. Since 2016 they have been developed to an ever greater magnitude in Poland. In 2016 the Polish Agency for Enterprise Development launched a pilot instrument supporting startup accelerators. According to the report entitled *Polish Startups 2023*, 21% of Polish startups took advantage of the support offered by domestic accelerators, while 9% took advantage of foreign programs.[20] These results emphasize the key role played by acceleration programs in the startup ecosystem and the climbing demand for this type of support in Poland. As the report observed, acceleration programs not only play a significant role in supporting developing startups but also form a fundamental element in building a strong and sustainable innovation ecosystem in Poland.

3.2 Defining the research gap and research goals

The analyses conducted by the author of domestic scientific literature and research projects funded by the National Science Center in Cracow revealed a significant gap not just in Polish research but also in international research. This gap is particularly interesting in terms of the fact that international literature, in accordance with the systematic review conducted in the databases WoS and Scopus, is limited, fragmented and is just beginning to develop.[21], [22] For this reason it is an area that calls for meticulous analysis and in-depth research that could substantially contribute to developing knowledge in this field (scientific problem area).[23],[24] Researching this gap constitutes a significant novelty that may exert an impact on the development of science, especially in terms of the open innovation theory.[25] The author's taking up of this subject will make it possible to gain a better appreciation for how corporations and startups may collaborate effectively. Moreover, the findings of these analyses may reveal new templates in the dynamics of this cooperation, which is extraordinarily important for the researchers dealing with innovations, their transfer and corporate entrepreneurship. Appreciating the cooperation model between corporations and startups may also lead to devising better management practices. It may also support the shaping of state policy and economic development strategy. Cooperation between large and well-established companies with innovative startups that are frequently the source of landmark solutions and technologies may be critical in understanding how to support inter-organizational cooperation effectively and reap benefits from it. It is noteworthy that the author's taking up of the topic of inter-organizational cooperation may lead to an interdisciplinary approach bringing together various fields of knowledge such as management, economics and sociology. This may blaze the path to refining new methodological approaches and theoretical frameworks to be applied in varying contexts. Cooperation between corporations and startups in acceleration programs may be crucial when it comes to generating innovations, accelerating technological development and advancing business growth. Understanding these processes may supply valuable information regarding the efficacy of acceleration programs and the identification of best practices. In this manner the research findings proffer the potential not just to enrich scientific literature but also to translate into widespread application in economic practice. This may precipitate better design and implementation of acceleration programs involving corporations. Accordingly, the author's ongoing research on this topic will exert a significant impact on the development of the open innovation theory and on practice, opening up new horizons for the management of corporations, accelerators and startups. Having the above in mind further work will concentrate on filling the identified research gap, which will be critical to the development of scientific knowledge in three important areas[26] (**research problem**):

First area: perception of inter-organizational cooperation between startups and corporations as part of acceleration programs and its importance.

The research in the first area will focus on the following:

a how respondents perceive the research on the significance of corporations and startups establishing inter-organizational cooperation as part of acceleration programs along with a specification of the importance of the difficulties that may potentially appear;
b specifying the opinion of the research respondents regarding the topic of the meaning of acceleration programs for assistance in establishing cooperation between startups and corporations and supporting the implementation of startups' solutions in corporations;
c verifying whether the participation of startups and large organizations in acceleration programs engenders greater benefit than the expenditures incurred to establish and maintain their cooperation.

Second area: goals of cooperation between startups and corporations, the difficulties and the challenges encountered along with an analysis of the goals of cooperation achieved by the parties.

The research in the second area will pertain to fixing the opinions of the representatives of the startups and corporations in respect of the following:

a importance of the goals guiding startups and corporations in establishing cooperation as part of acceleration programs;
b importance of the difficulties encountered by corporations and startups during their cooperation in acceleration programs;
c importance of the challenges encountered by corporations and startups when they participate in acceleration programs;
d verifying whether the assumed goals of inter-organizational cooperation are achieved by the parties as a result of participating in acceleration programs.

Third area: identifying the attributes characterizing startups that potentially may be predictors of enhancing their chances for successful inter-organizational cooperation in acceleration programs.

The scientific literature review performed in the WoS and Scopus databases demonstrated that researchers have not defined in detail the traits of startups that could potentially contribute to enhancing the effectiveness of inter-organizational cooperation in acceleration programs. Accordingly, research in the third area will encompass a verification of the six main blocks of variables and attributes that may potentially influence the effectiveness of cooperation. The following blocks of variables were analyzed:

1 Predictive block – demographic variables of founding members;
2 Predictive block – demographic variables of a startup;
3 Predictive block – measures taken and established cooperation;
4 Predictive block – cooperation with a corporation;
5 Predictive block – evaluation of readiness to cooperate with a corporation;
6 Predictive block – evaluation of the goals of cooperation with a corporation.

3.3 Organization and conduct of research

The innovative nature of the discussed problem area of inter-organizational cooperation, inability to apply the fragmented research findings to-date and the high currency of the research problem triggered the necessity of concentrating on the appropriate designing of the research process. In accordance with the literature, decisions made at the stage of designing research exert an impact not only on the quality of the research project,[27] but above all on the credibility of the conclusions drawn on their basis.[28] The topics of cooperation between corporations and startups in acceleration programs discussed in previous chapters have been submitted to empirical verification. This research is a natural continuation of the author's prior interests pertaining to the cooperation between large organizations and startups in light of the open innovation theory. This chapter relies chiefly on the findings of the quantitative research performed among representatives of startups and corporations. To provide for a high quality research tool, a number of steps preceding the research itself were taken

1 A systematic scientific literature review covering 2003–2022 (until the end of December) was completed. Its results are presented in this chapter.
2 On the basis of the subject literature and several years of the author's experience gleaned from his work with startups, accelerators and corporations, and also from participation in Demo Day wrapping up acceleration programs, a proprietary survey questionnaire was devised.
3 The purpose was to gain a deeper understanding of the research topic and capture the most important issues from the perspective of the acceleration program participants. The author conducted individual interviews with representatives of the startups, accelerators and corporations regarding inter-organizational cooperation. These interviews constituted a supplement to the survey research, where their purpose was to refine and expand the research questionnaire.
4 Field observations of the startup acceleration programs conducted with the participation of corporations were conducted, and an analysis of the outcomes of inter-organizational cooperation was conducted on the basis of the findings presented during Demo Day. The purpose of the field observations and of the participation in Demo Day was to refine further and supplement the research questionnaire.
5 Pilot research was administered among representatives of the startups and corporations. The task of the administered pilot research was to gain final confirmation of the utility of the research tool, and also to remove any and all possible imperfections and errors from the structure of the questionnaire.

The first version of the questionnaire was the subject matter of an interview with seven representatives of startups, four representatives of startup accelerators and three representatives of corporations. The purpose of these interviews was, on one hand, to gain a more profound understanding of the phenomenon under examination based on varying cognitive perspectives and, on the other hand, to ensure the full understanding of the survey questionnaire in terms of the findings of the analysis. The decision to invite a given entity to participate in the research followed from the recognition which an entity enjoys in the startup ecosystem. Additionally, an entity had to take part in one of the acceleration programs involving corporations. The deliberate selection of the researched entities was justified by the need for obtaining a broader perspective of the parties participating in acceleration programs (Table 3.2).

Table 3.2 Entities involved in the process of verifying the correctness of the contents of the research questionnaire

No	*Company*	*Activity*	*Selected corporations in the acceleration program or area of activity*	*Position*
Representatives the accelerators				
1	Fundacja Przedsiębiorczości Technologicznej – Akcelerator MIT Enterprise Forum Poland	Start-up accelerator	Coca-Cola, Adamed, PKO BP, MCX	Manager of the acceleration program
2	Fundacja Polska Przedsiębiorcza	Start-up accelerator	Maspex, Olewnik, Wierzejki, Putka, Laude	Managing Director; manager of the acceleration program
3	Accelpoint Sp. z o.o.	Start-up accelerator	Orange Polska, Santander Bank, Santander Consumer Bank, AXA Partners	Management Board member of the Accelerator; manager of the acceleration program
4	Krakowski Park Technologiczny Sp. z o.o.	Start-up accelerator	PGNiG, Tauron, Warbud, Solaris, Grupa Azoty, VOX	Deputy Director of the Industry 4.0 Department; manager of the acceleration program
Representatives of the corporations				
1	Santander Polska	Corporation	Bank	Innovation Department Manager
2	AXA Partners	Corporation	Insurance and reinsurance broker	Management Board member
3	Orange Polska	Corporation	Telecommunications	Innovation Department Manager
Representatives of the start-ups				
1	Alphamoon	Start-up	Document processing automation	President of the Management Board
2	AI Busters	Start-up	Automation and enhancement of customer service processes	Management Board Member
3	PBG Management	Start-up	Insurance	Management Board Member

(*Continued*)

Table 3.2 (Continued)

No	*Company*	*Activity*	*Selected corporations in the acceleration program or area of activity*	*Position*
4	Symmetrical	Start-up	Supplier of headless payroll technologies to facilitate automation of payroll processes	Management Board Member
5	Cashy	Start-up	Supplier of B2B solution streamlining the management of financial relations with vendors	President of the Management Board
6	Plenti	Start-up	Access to electronics in a subscription model	President of the Management Board
7	Revdebug	Start-up	Detection and correction of software bugs	Management Board Member

Source: Proprietary material.

In this portion of the research a total of 14 interviews lasting from 31 to 72 minutes were conducted. The outcome of the conducted interviews was as follows:

1 New research questions were added to the questionnaire, for example, in respect of the evaluation of startup representatives on whether participation in an acceleration program substantially increases the chances of implementing innovation and entering into commercial agreements to sell products and services. Another survey question added to the survey pertained to the evaluation of the costs and benefits of the cooperation between corporations and startups in acceleration programs.
2 Modifying the research questions to add new items to the content thereof, for example, in terms of the importance of the goals of establishing cooperation with a startup to the representatives of a corporation – the topic of developing the company that will potentially be acquired by a corporation was appended. In the second instance, regarding the importance of the specified goals for establishing cooperation with a corporation from the viewpoint of the representatives of startups – the topic of the startup's product penetrating foreign markets was appended. In terms of the part pertaining to the research on the predictive block: a startup's demographic variables – the topic referring to the presence of foreigners among the founders/persons holding key positions in a startup was introduced. In turn, the block pertaining to the following: undertaken actions and established cooperation – prior cooperation with mid-sized businesses on the part of a startup was taken into consideration.
3 Grouping some research questions in the questionnaire pertaining to questions for corporations in terms of their strategy, procedures for cooperating with startups and the adjustment to the wording of the research questions pertaining to the startups' measurement indicators.
4 Introducing a more comprehensible vocabulary for research participants to reflect more precisely the sense underlying the aspects of inter-organizational cooperation being analyzed, that is, the term – road map has been replaced with the term devise an implementation plan.

According to the established procedure for administering survey research the process was begun with conducting pilot research. The researchers' questionnaire was tested on a small sample during this early phase. The sample consisted of three startups and three corporations. The purpose of the pilot research was not just to verify the utility of the research tool with finality but also to eliminate any and all potential unclearness and errors in how the survey was construed. Moreover, the research made it possible to evaluate the actual time respondents need to fill out the survey, which was critical for planning the effective data compilation process during the main research stage. It should be emphasized that considering the limitations to-date in research on the cooperation between startups and corporations as part of acceleration programs, the research questionnaire was intentionally designed so as to investigate inter-organizational cooperation broadly. Nevertheless, the subsequent part of the monograph focuses on aspects of cooperation between corporations and startups (micro and small businesses) that are significant in the research undertaken in this book. The findings of the analyses not used in this monograph will serve the author for the purpose of doing further research work. The survey questionnaire for corporations numbers 53 questions and is divided into three parts. The first part concentrates on the research topics related to corporations cooperating with startups. The questions in this section pertain among other things to the significance of cooperation with startups, the methods for establishing it and the goals and achieved results of cooperation. Additionally, the issues of corporations holding a strategy for their cooperation with startups, the procedures devised in this respect, the challenges and obstacles to cooperation, the pursuit of pilot implementations of startups' solutions and the stage of a startup's development were touched upon as they are important to a corporation in terms of establishing cooperation. The purpose of the first part was to examine and understand the aspects of cooperation between corporations and startups, including the reasons for establishing this cooperation, its goals and the results achieved. The second part of the survey concentrates on a corporation's cooperation with startup accelerators and the preferred cooperation model with startups. It contains questions regarding the evaluation of a corporation's participation in acceleration programs and the preferred model of business cooperation with startups. The purpose of this part was to appreciate how corporations evaluate their participation in acceleration programs for startups and determine which business cooperation model with startups they prefer. The final part of the questionnaire concentrated on the characterization of corporations. It contains questions pertaining among other things to the industry in which an organization operates, the length of cooperation with startups, having a corporate venture capital fund, the number of employed persons, the units involved in cooperation with startups and the quantum of financial means allocated for such cooperation per annum. The purpose of this part was to compile detailed information regarding the profile and resources made available by corporations for the purposes of cooperation in acceleration programs. This made it possible to gain a better appreciation for the potential of large organizations and their engagement in inter-organizational relationships with startups.

In turn, the research survey designated for startups consisted of 61 questions and it was also divided into three parts. The first part concentrates on issues and experiences of startups in terms of their participation in acceleration programs involving corporations. The questions pertain to aspects of cooperation, including the reasons for establishing it, the goals for joint actions with corporations, the readiness of startups to engage in such cooperation and the stage of a startup's development at the time of launching the cooperation. Moreover, topics associated with the obstacles in the process of establishing cooperation, the difficulties encountered during this period, the experience gleaned during cooperation and the benefits ensuing from the established relationship. The purpose of this part of the survey was to examine and appreciate the various aspects of inter-organizational cooperation and gain a comprehensive picture of cooperation between startups and corporations. The second part of the survey concentrates on evaluating cooperation between startups and accelerators and on the preferred cooperation model with corporations. It includes questions referring to the evaluation of the support offered by acceleration programs as well as the possibilities of recommending participation in such programs to other companies in the future. This part aims to appreciate how startups perceive value and the efficacy of acceleration programs and what are their preferences and expectations in terms of their cooperation with larger corporations. The final part of the survey concentrates on the compilation of information characterizing startups and their founders. The questions covered various operating aspects of these companies such as the industry in which they operate, the time of functioning on the market, the revenue generated, the number of employed persons, funding sources when participating in an acceleration program, cooperation with other market entities, holding patents, business cooperation with foreign clients, etc. Moreover, this research also encompassed a profile of the startup founders. Questions were posed regarding their age, gender, presence of foreigners in the group of co-founders, education and professional experience. The purpose of this part was to obtain in-depth insight into the profile and characterization of the startups participating in the acceleration programs involving corporations. The correct definition of the research population and the selection of an appropriate sample were an important aspect of the conducted quantitative research. The target research population, that is, startups participating in acceleration programs involving corporations in Poland had not been identified to-date; it was not subject to indexation separated in the Polish Business Classification System (PKD), nor was it subject to other criteria applied by the Central Statistical Office in Poland. An attempt was made to source information about the number of startups taking part in acceleration programs involving corporations from the Polish Agency for Enterprise Development (PARP) as the entity overseeing the implementation of acceleration programs involving corporations in Poland. PARP entered into contracts with ten startup accelerators for a total amount of projects worth EUR 35 million. Sourcing this data from PARP was important to define the research population precisely. The separation and the analysis of the group subject to research made it possible to obtain representative results that may be useful in a scientific and economic context. The data obtained from PARP indicate that 356 startups were included in acceleration-related activities involving large corporations during the research. Ultimately 101 startups filled out the questionnaire. In turn, the number of corporations involved in acceleration programs as the clients of the products, services and technologies offered by the startups was 137. Results were collected from 25 corporations. A request to obtain access to data was addressed to the management of each one of the ten startup accelerators that were engaged in pursuing acceleration programs with corporations at that time (Table 3.3).

Table 3.3 Startup accelerators pursuing acceleration programs involving corporations

No	*Name of the accelerator managing the acceleration program involving corporations*	*Title of the project*	*Total cost of the start-up acceleration project (EUR)*
1	Fundacja Przedsiębiorczości Technologicznej	MIT Enterprise Forum Poland Acceleration Program	3.98 million
2	FundingBox Accelerator Sp. z o.o.	IMPACT_Poland (2.0)	3.66 million
3	Blue Dot Solutions Sp. z o.o.	Space3ac Scale Up II	3.77 million
4	DGA S.A.	INDUSTRYLAB II Industrial Innovation Accelerator	3.78 million
5	Accelpoint Sp. z o.o.	Accelpoint ScaleUp – technological accelerator combining innovative solutions with technology clients	3.48 million
6	Fundacja Polska Przedsiębiorcza	Program to accelerate and commercialize start-ups' solutions with the participation of technology clients	3.26 million
7	HugeTECH Sp. z o.o	IDEA Global Accelerator	3.12 million
8	Krakowski Park Technologiczny Sp. z o.o.	KPT ScaleUp	2.75 million
9	Łódzka Specjalna Strefa Ekonomiczna S.A.	Startup Spark 2.0	3.48 million
10	Brinc Limited Sp. z o.o. Branch in Poland	Brinc's individual acceleration program dedicated to startups in the hardware, IIoT, AI, AR sector	4.06 million

Source: Material based on the following: https://www.parp.gov.pl/storage/grants/documents/21/Lista_projektow_wybranych_do_dofinansowania.pdf (retrieved: 30.10.2023).

The very process of sourcing quantitative data was based on the following steps:

1 Identifying and confirming the target research population with the Polish Agency for Enterprise Development and ten accelerators – the startups and corporations that took part in acceleration programs. This stage ended with building a database of startups and corporations participating in acceleration programs.
2 Confirmation with accelerators, corporations and startups – CAWI research technique – as the most suitable technique to run the research

process. These entities flagged the computer assisted web-based online interview as the preferred research technique on account of the innovative nature of these companies, their method of operating on the market and the universal usage of information and communication technologies by these entities. The survey questionnaire itself is a universally applicable tool to collect data in the social sciences,[29] also in the management sciences.[30] The usage of CAWI in the research made it possible to obtain accurate and representative data that are indispensable to conduct a precise analysis and draw credible conclusions. In the context of research on inter-organizational cooperation CAWI afforded the ability to reach respondents quickly and effectively, which is critical in the dynamically evolving startup ecosystem.

3 Generating individual links for startups and corporations and forwarding them by electronic mail to accelerators for the purpose of further distribution. Corporations and startups were invited by the accelerators to fill out the survey by forwarding an invitation to them with individual links. On account of the limitations stemming from GDPR regulations, the author did not have access to the sensitive personal data of the entities under examination such as first and last names and e-mail addresses. Thanks to the generated individual links to the surveys, it was possible to monitor the number of filled out questionnaires. If no response was given, the management of the accelerators was asked to re-send this request to the startups and large organizations that had not yet filled out the surveys for them to do so. It should be indicated that the data were collected from one representative of each one of the entities under examination, by applying a single informant approach.[31]

The startups and corporations that participated in the individual acceleration program in the model: startup – accelerator – corporation were included in this research. In accordance with the literature, 100 observations are accepted as the critical minimum sample size[32]; therefore, all of the requirements for this analytical approach were fulfilled.[33] In respect of the corporations it was not possible to examine 100 entities because the entire population numbered 137 large organizations engaged in the startup acceleration programs. Despite the limitations ensuing from the size of the corporation population, the sample was selected in such a way so that the results obtained would be as representative as possible and valuable for analysis. The limited number of available entities did not affect the accuracy of the research as the compiled data reflects the distinct nature and differentiation of industries for the population of corporations participating in the startup acceleration programs. The vast majority of the empirical material itself was obtained from startup owners/managers and employees in corporations' management level. It was accepted that they constitute the best source of information regarding cooperation with large organizations as part of the individual acceleration program (*key informants*).[34] An acceleration program dedicated to a specific startup lasting three to six months based on intense cooperation between a new company, an accelerator and a corporation (technology clients) is assumed to be an individual acceleration program spanning in particular advisory and mentor support and support in a financial form aiming to accelerate the product development process (service, too) or technology, and in particular their validation in conditions similar to actual conditions (using the infrastructure of a large organization and its test environment). A startup should satisfy the criteria designated in art. 22 sec. 2 of the EU Commission's regulation no. 651/2014 of 17 June 2014, which defines the notion of a startup up to a micro or small businessman not listed on the stock exchange, beginning business activity or conducting the same for no longer than five years (counting from the date of registration in the pertinent register), which has not distributed profits and has not been established as a result of a merger.

The analyses of the findings were conducted using the IBM SPSS Statistics 25 analytical software.[35] A number of statistical analyses were conducted using this tool that made it possible to prepare an in-depth and accurate interpretation of the compiled data. The descriptive statistics and the Kolmogorov–Smirnov tests, which check the normality of the distributions of the quantitative variables being analyzed, as well as the dependent samples t-test, single factor analyses of variance in an intergroup scheme, analyses of the Spearman Rank Correlation Coefficient ρ, the Mann–Whitney U tests and the Kruskal–Wallis tests, were performed with its usage. The ρ Spearman rank correlation coefficient was used. The classical threshold of $\alpha = 0.05$ was taken as the significance level in the research; however, test statistics probability results at the level of $0.05 < p < 0.1$ were interpreted as significant at the statistical trend level. The results presented for the frequency analyzes were rounded off to one place after the decimal point.

3.4 Characterization of the research groups

This point was devoted to a special description of the two main research groups: startups and corporations participating in the startup acceleration programs. The goal is to present a profile of each one of these groups, which will make it possible for the reader to gain a better appreciation of their distinct nature, as well as the needs and challenges they are grappling. A precise characterization of these groups is indispensable to understand the dynamics in the cooperation between them and the impact the exert on one another within the context of inter-organizational cooperation.

3.4.1 Characterization of the startups

One hundred and one representatives of startups took part in the research. On account of the fact that the respondents could simultaneously discharge

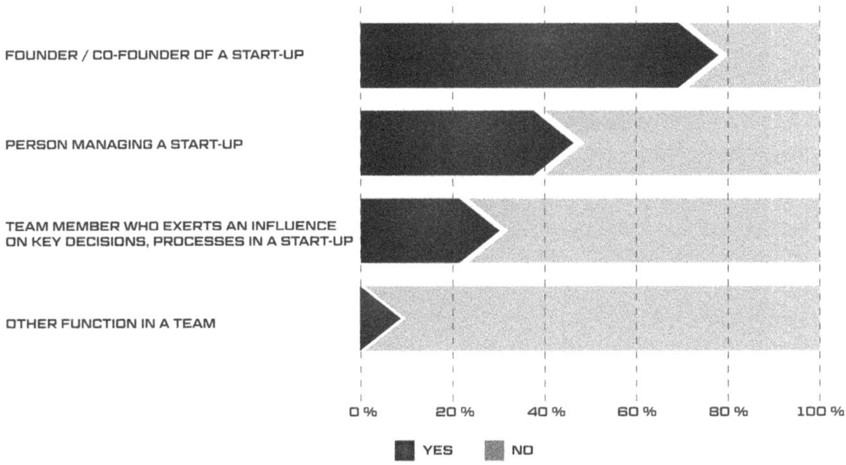

Figure 3.3 Functions discharged by the researched persons in startups.

Source: Proprietary material.

more than one function in a company under examination, the data were presented as a percentage of the persons who indicated or did not indicate that they play a given role. As one may observe in Figure 3.3 the percentage of persons who are founders/co-founders of a startup (81 persons, 80.2%) was the largest. Thirty-three subjects (32.7%) declared that they have a decisive influence on the decisions and processes in the startup.

The vast majority of the startups in the research, that is, 96 companies (95%) declared that they are cooperating with a corporation at the time of the research. In turn, 60 startups (59.4%) had already previously cooperated with a corporation. At what development stage a startup is was also checked. As can be seen in Figure 3.4, the largest percentage of startups in the research were at the development stage (49 instances, 48.5%), 32 startups were at the idea/minimum viable product (MVP) stage (31.7%) and 20 were at the scale up stage (19.8%).

Idea/MVP stage is the first stage of a startup's development. The MVP is the first basic version of a product or service, which contains the most important functionalities and allows an entrepreneur to test the produced solution among clients and obtain the feedback needed for further development. At this stage an entrepreneur refines the idea for a new product or service that may accrue unique value to future clients. The startup team concentrates its efforts on market research and understanding clients' needs to design an idea that will respond to their needs to the greatest possible extent. In turn, the **growth stage** is characterized by the startup already having a designed product or service whose value has been affirmed by the clients, and the business model has been tested and verified in business practice. The growth stage is a period of intense development and marks the startup's attempt

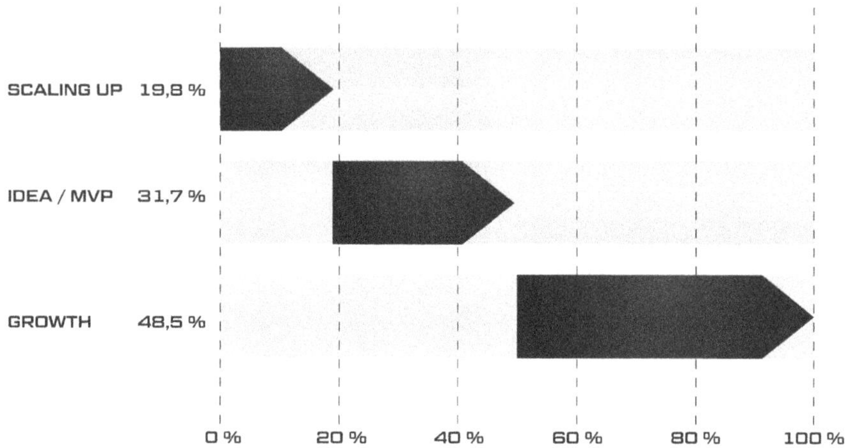

Figure 3.4 Phase of startup development.

Source: Proprietary material.

at commencing the scaling up of the business it is running. At this stage the entrepreneur concentrates on gaining the largest possible number of clients/users and expanding the market on which it operates. Sometimes this also marks the time of developing proprietary infrastructure. The purpose of this stage is to achieve profitability in the business being run and maintaining market competitiveness. **Scaling up** is the last and third stage of a startup's development. At this stage the company has a tried and tested business model, it has confirmed the value of the solution it offers on the market and it has procured funding, including a client database. The purpose of this stage is to extend the product or service offering and pursue market expansion or penetrate new markets by ramping up the magnitude of operation based on a higher number of clients. To this end scalable processes are rolled out that allow the management of a startup to manage a substantially larger number of contracts and purchase orders.

The decision was also made to present at which stage of the acceleration program the startup of the subjects is to be found. In 55 instances the subjects evaluated that their startup completed the acceleration program and executed their POC but did not sign an agreement with a corporation (54.4%). In 24 instances the startup signed a contract with a technology client for commercial implementation of a product/technology (23.8%). In 22 instances the startup participated in an acceleration program but it did not execute its POC (21.8%). Figure 3.5 compiles the results.

Detailed data pertaining to the founders of startups were depicted in the next step. The entities in the research clearly differed from one another in terms of the number of founders. There was one person in 21 cases (20.8%), while in 48 cases (47.5%) there were two co-founders, in 24 cases

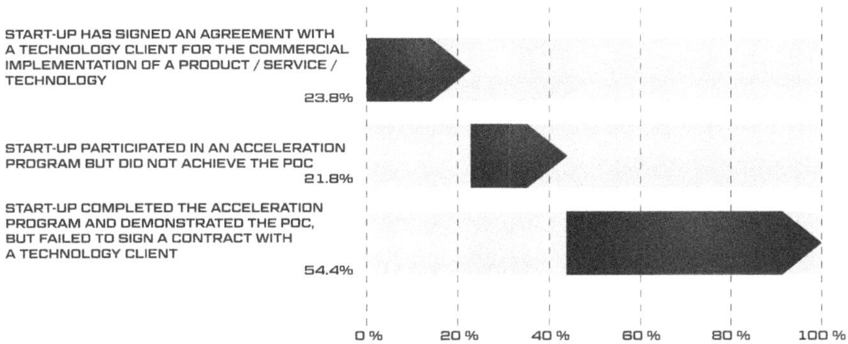

Figure 3.5 Categories specifying the type of cooperation between a startup and a corporation in an acceleration program.

Source: Proprietary material.

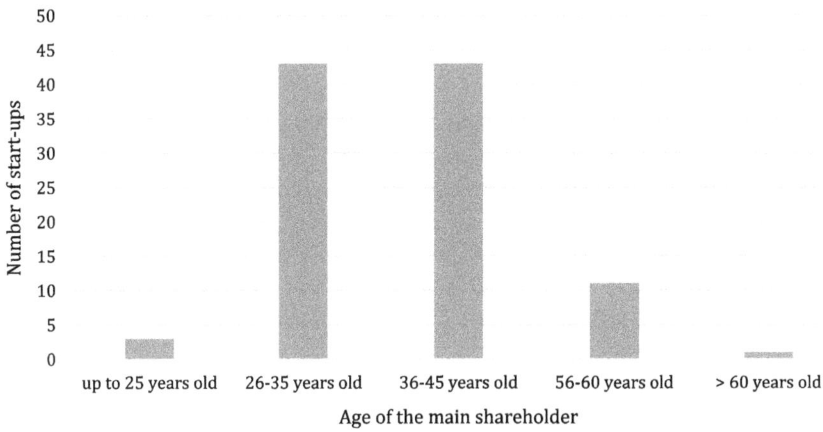

Figure 3.6 Age of a startup's principal shareholders.

Source: Proprietary material.

(23.8%) there were three and in eight cases (7.9%) there were more than three co-founders. After that, data concerning the largest shareholder in the startup was compiled. In 90 instances they were men (89.1%). In merely 11 instances they were women (10.9%). As can be seen in Figure 3.6 two dominants were recorded in terms of the age of the main startup shareholders – there were 43 persons (42.6%) aged 26–35 and 36–45. There were only three main shareholders up to 25 years of age.

It is worth observing that the clearly dominant level of education among the main startup shareholders was a master's degree (79 persons, 78.2%). The percentage of persons with a scientific title (doctor, habilitated doctor,

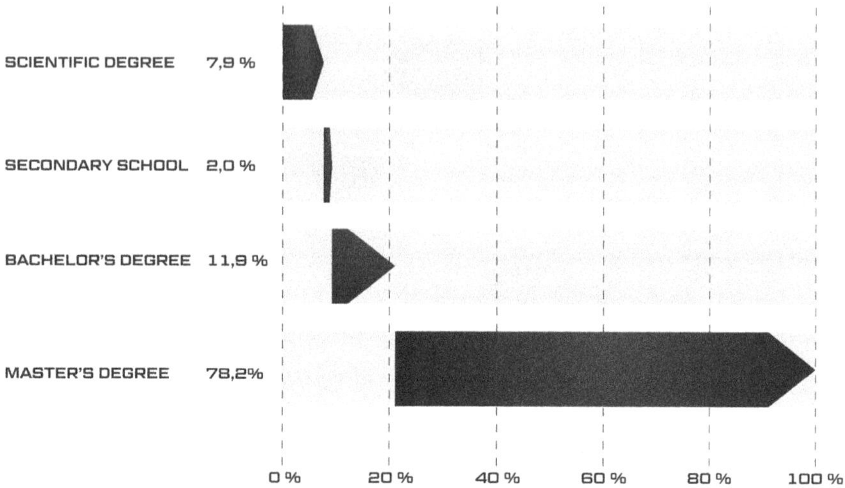

Figure 3.7 Level of education of a startup's principal shareholders.
Source: Proprietary material.

professor) was minimal with eight cases (7.9%). Figure 3.7 depicts the detailed distribution of data.

The area in which the main founder of the startup was educated in three areas of science: technical and engineering sciences (47 persons, 46.5%); social and economic sciences (28 persons, 27.7%) and exact and natural sciences (13 persons, 12.9%). Other areas were represented much more seldomly. In the vast majority of cases the main founders were persons who had professional experience. Only five persons indicated that their professional experience was shorter than three years. Figure 3.8 depicts the detailed data.

During the next step what the main founder of the startup did prior to its formation was checked (Figure 3.9). Since this question was a multiple choice question, the percentages of persons indicating and not indicating specific types of activity were compiled. The fraction of main shareholders who prior to establishing a company taught in school/university (five persons) or were engaged in scientific or teaching work (nine persons) was very small. The vast majority of the main founders were recruited from corporations (52 persons, 51.5%), or from companies: private companies (48 persons, 47.5%) and their own/family companies (32 persons, 31.7%) alike. Thirty people declared having worked historically in a different startup (29.7%).

What portion of their professional activity the main founders devote to development of the startup was also checked. As can be seen in Figure 3.10 nearly one-half of the responses indicated that they almost entirely subordinated their professional activity to the startup under examination (47.5%).

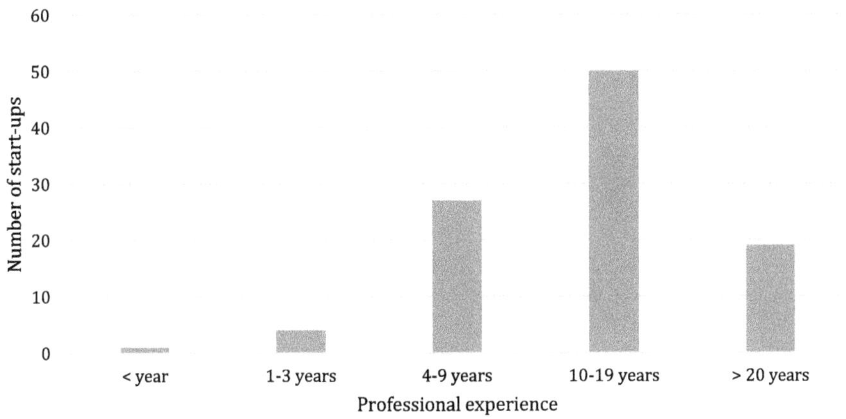

Figure 3.8 Professional experience of a startup's principal shareholders.
Source: Proprietary material.

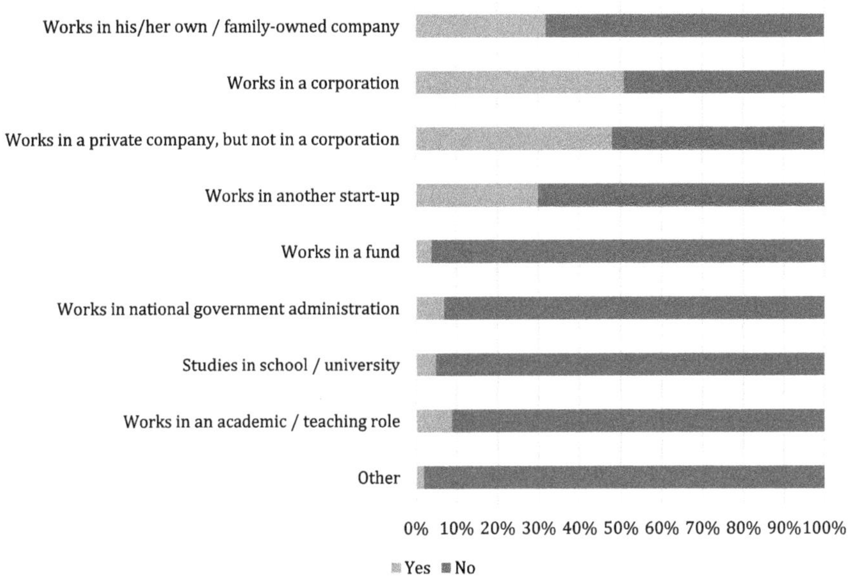

Figure 3.9 Activities of the principal shareholders prior to setting up a startup.
Source: Proprietary material.

3.4.2 *Characterization of the activities of the startups*

Then, the detailed data concerning the characterization of the startups under examination were analyzed. Startups that had been functioning on the market from two to three years (30 instances, 29.7%) were prevalent in

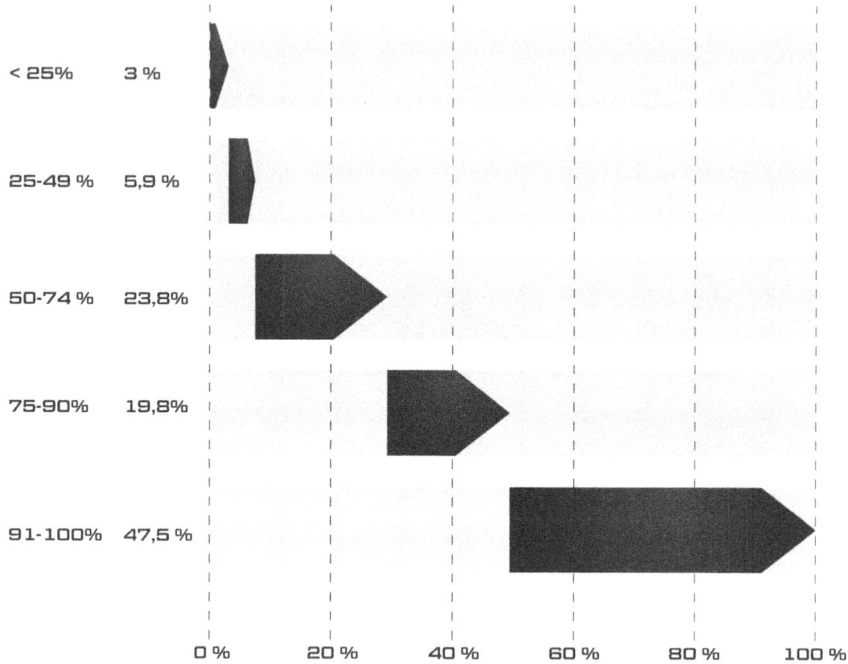

Figure 3.10 Time of professional activity devoted by a principal founder to a startup.
Source: Proprietary material.

the research. Twenty-six startups had been in operation on the market from three to five years (25.7%) while 22 had been in operation from one to two years (21.8%). Startups with a shorter or longer period of activity were also represented in the research, but they were clearly less numerous. Figure 3.11 depicts the distribution of the results.

The examined startups were highly varied in terms of the number of employed persons. As can be seen in Figure 3.12 the most frequently recorded startups employed two to five persons (38 instances, 37.6%) and six to ten persons (33 instances, 32.7%). Single-person companies (11 cases, 10.9%) and companies with 11–20 employees (16 cases, 15.8%) were represented in relatively strong numbers. There were only three cases in which headcount exceeded 20 persons. In 12 startups (11.9%) there were foreigners among the founders or persons holding key positions.

It is worth pointing out that more than one-half of the startups had been financed up to this point solely using their own funds (51 cases, 50.5%). There were only seven instances (6.9%) in which the founders had not spent their own money on financing the startup at the stage of its formation. Support coming from European Union programs (35 cases, 34.7%), venture capital funds and funds from business angels (18 cases a piece, 17.8%) should be mentioned among the relatively frequently indicated sources of

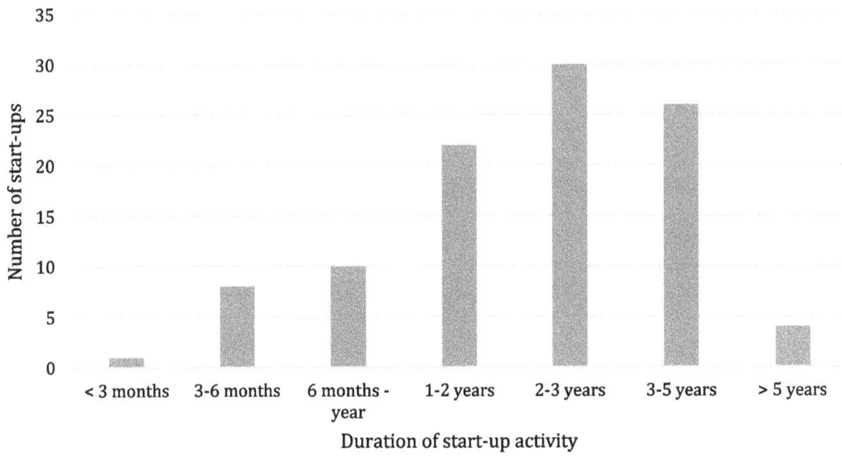

Figure 3.11 Length of operations of the startups covered by this research.

Source: Proprietary material.

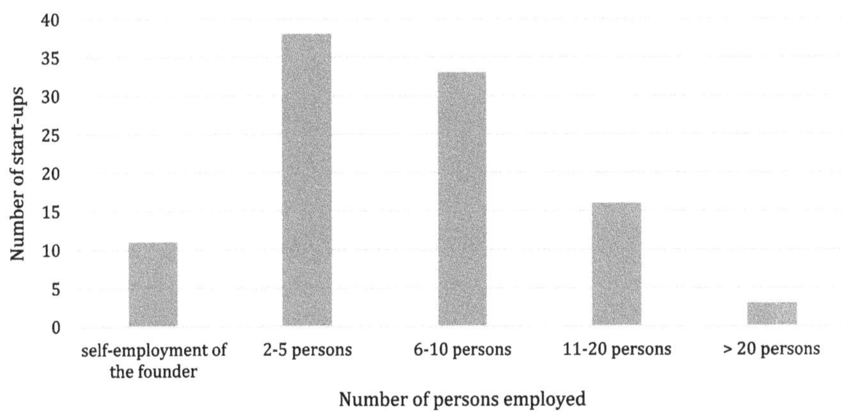

Figure 3.12 Employment of persons in the startups covered by the research.

Source: Proprietary material.

co-funding. What is interesting is that the research sample did not include a single startup that used crowdfunding or loan funds at the formation stage. Figure 3.13 depicts the foregoing data.

It is worth comparing these data with the current sources of funding startups, which are depicted in Figure 3.14. Even though the founders' own funds were the main source of funding a startup (68 cases, 67.3%), the second most frequently source of funding indicated by the representatives of the startups was revenue generated in its own business (34 cases, 33.7%). Support originating from European Union funds was designated in third

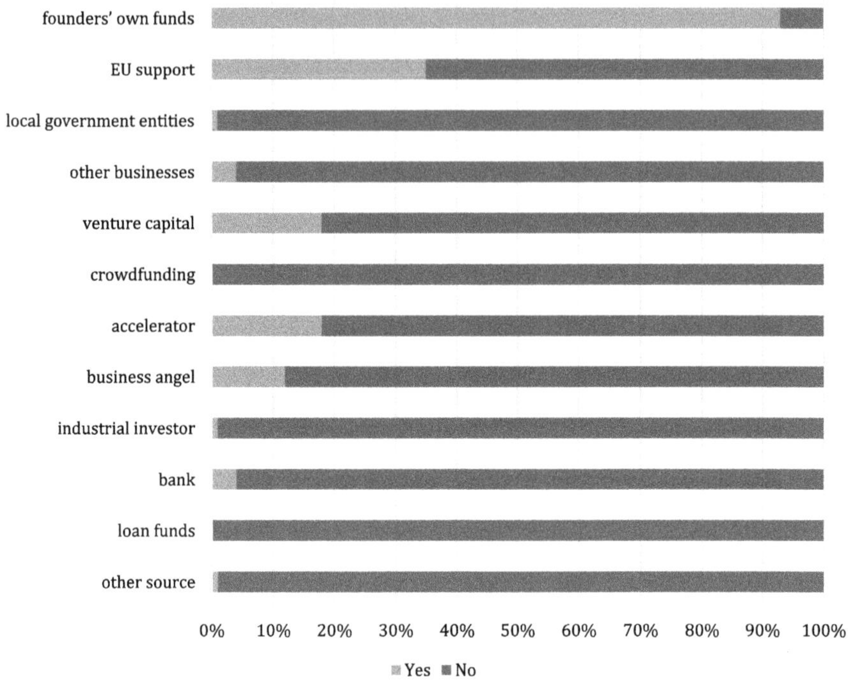

Figure 3.13 Startup's funding sources at the stage of its formation.

Source: Proprietary material.

place (30 cases, 29.7%). Responses indicating cases in which accelerators financed startups (19 cases, 18.8%) and venture capital funds financed them (12 cases, 11.9%) were also numerous.

In the next step a check was made on with which entities/institutions the startups under examination had cooperated. As can be seen in Figure 3.15 responses indicating cooperation with corporations were prevalent. Some 87 startups under examination (86.1%) indicated this type of cooperation. Seventy-two companies participating in an acceleration program undertook cooperation with mid-sized businesses (71.3%), while only 31 did so with micro/small businesses (30.7%). Sixty startups cooperated with an accelerator (59.4%). Others responses were clearly more seldomly indicated by the representatives of the startups. It is noteworthy that some 44 (43.6%) of the 101 startups under examination had cooperated with foreign entities.

Whether startups have foreign clients was checked during the last step. As can be seen in Figure 3.16 the responses given here varied strongly. Only nine companies (8.9%) had foreign clients constituting more than one-half of their portfolio. In 44 cases (43.6%) startups did not have any foreign clients, while in 31 cases (30.7%) the percentage of foreign clients was below 10% of the total number of clients.

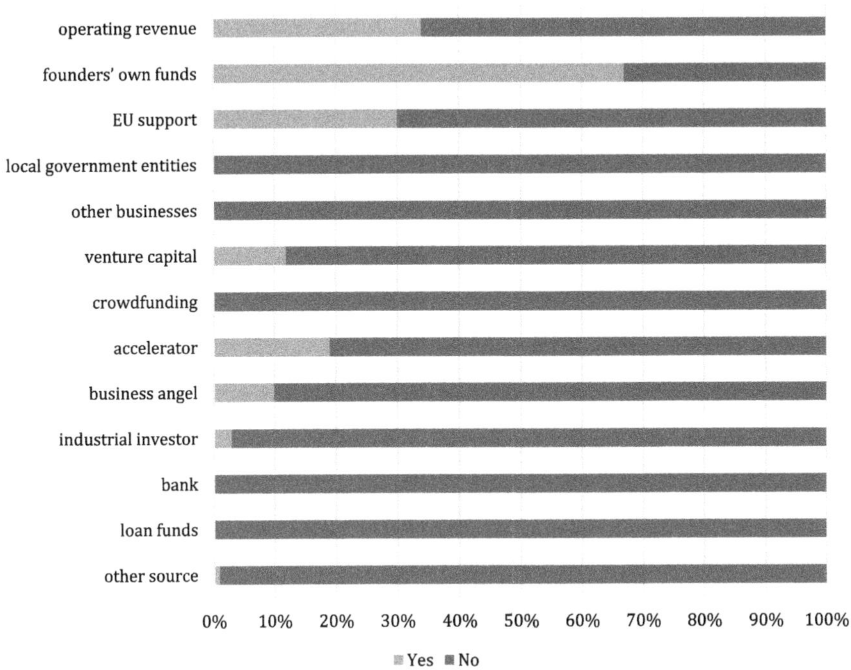

Figure 3.14 Startup's current funding sources.

Source: Proprietary material.

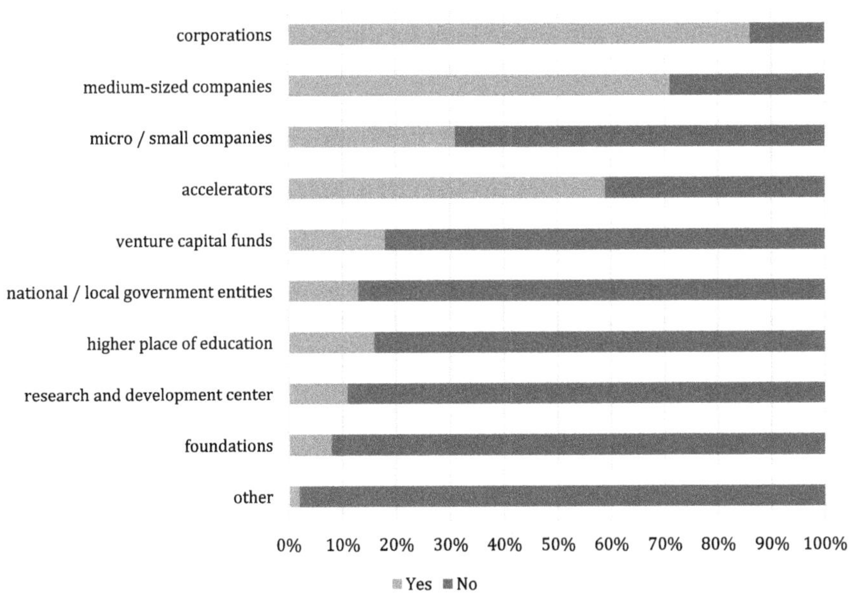

Figure 3.15 Entities with which startups established cooperation.

Source: Proprietary material.

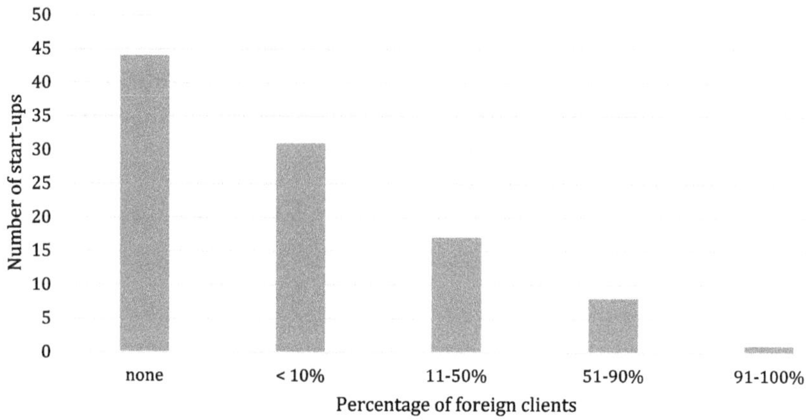

Figure 3.16 Percentage of foreign clients in startups.
Source: Proprietary material.

3.4.3 *Characterization of the corporations*

Twenty-five representatives of corporations participated in the research – six directors (24%), seven team managers (28%), four experts/specialists (16%) and eight people discharging other functions (32%). The business under examination was characterized by a high level of differentiation in terms of the number of employees (Figure 3.17).

All of the organizations in the research declared their historical cooperation with startups as part of the acceleration programs. Six representatives of the companies constituting 24% of the subject sample declared that their period of cooperation has lasted from six months to one year. In five cases (20%) their period of cooperation was from one to two years. In eight cases (32%) the length of cooperation fell within the range of two to three years, while in six businesses it exceeded three years (24%).

In 40% of the cases (ten businesses) from among the large organizations in the research they had a strategy or procedures pertaining to cooperation with startups, while in 64% (16 companies) of the cases they confirmed that they had defined a method for sourcing startups for cooperation. The share of businesses, however, was clearly lower when there was a rapid path for the solutions offered by startups whose budget does not exceed a predefined value set by the company and ones where a company had an internal acceleration program other than the program administered in cooperation with accelerators independent of that company. The percentage of these businesses was 16% (four businesses) and 12% (three businesses), respectively. One in five of the corporations in the research had their own fund or some other internal unit that makes investments in startups. What percentage of companies have implementations of solutions conducted by startups was also checked. Twenty-one representatives provided a response in the affirmative. Figure 3.18 depicts the number of such implementations in large

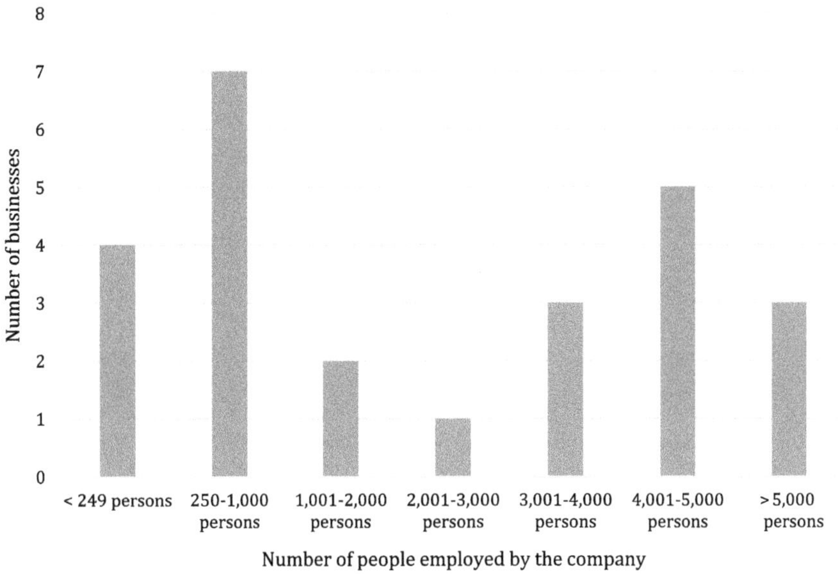

Figure 3.17 Headcount in the researched organizations that are clients of startups' solution.

Source: Proprietary material.

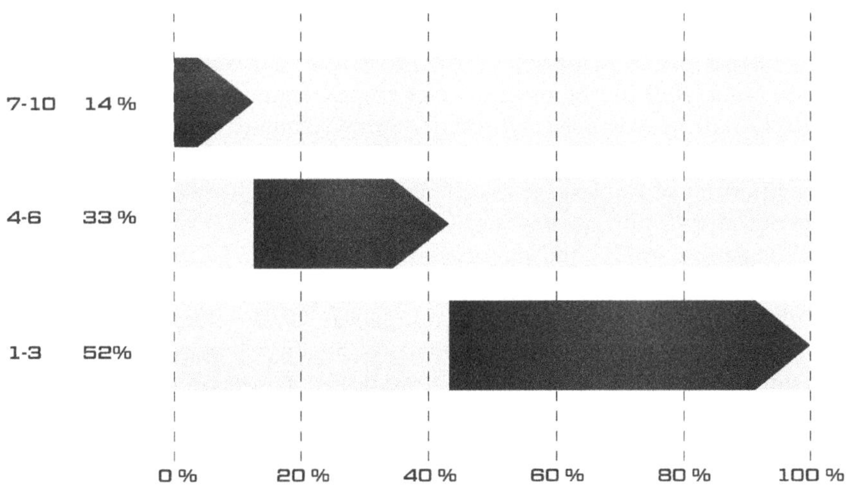

Figure 3.18 Percentage of organizations with a specified number of implementations of startups' solutions.

Source: Proprietary material.

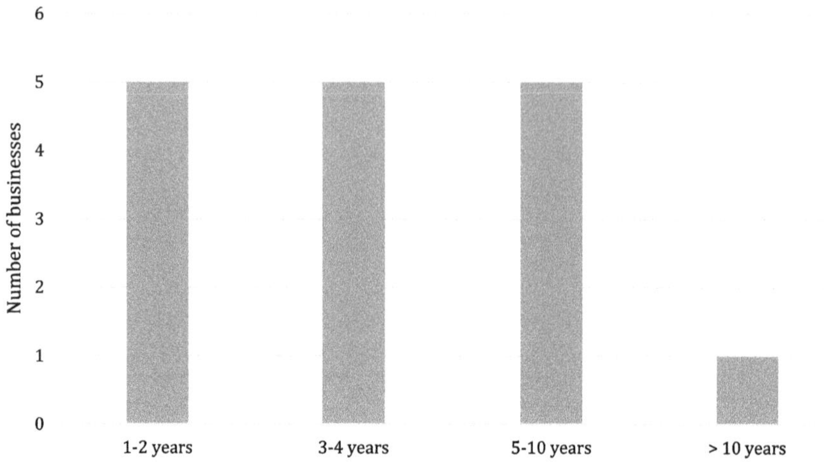

Figure 3.19 Length of operation of an innovation department in an organization.
Source: Proprietary material.

organizations, where companies that had at least one implementation were taken into consideration.

In 16 instances (64%) the researched businesses have their own innovation/research and development (R&D) department, or the organization seconds people to cooperate with startups. Figure 3.19 depicts the length of operation of such a department.

Six of the researched companies representing 24% had a management board that was directly and regularly involved in cooperation with startups. In 14 instances, the management board's occasional contact with startups was declared while in five instances such engagement did not transpire at all. Figure 3.20 depicts detailed information on which units were responsible for managing cooperation with startups.

The portion of the budget allocated by the researched organizations for cooperation with startups was also examined. As can be seen in Figure 3.21, in 15 instances (60%) the quantum was under 1% of the corporation's budget.

This part of the book conducts an analysis for the purpose of defining the research gap in inter-organizational cooperation between corporations and startups in terms of acceleration programs. This process began with a systematic literature review in accordance with the PRISMA requirements. It entailed an analysis of the publications available in the leading scientific databases such as WoS and Scopus. This review facilitated the identification of existing research and the identification of areas which require further exploration. Additionally, an analysis of the domestic sources of data was conducted. This made it possible to capture the overall state of the research pertaining to cooperation between companies in acceleration programs.

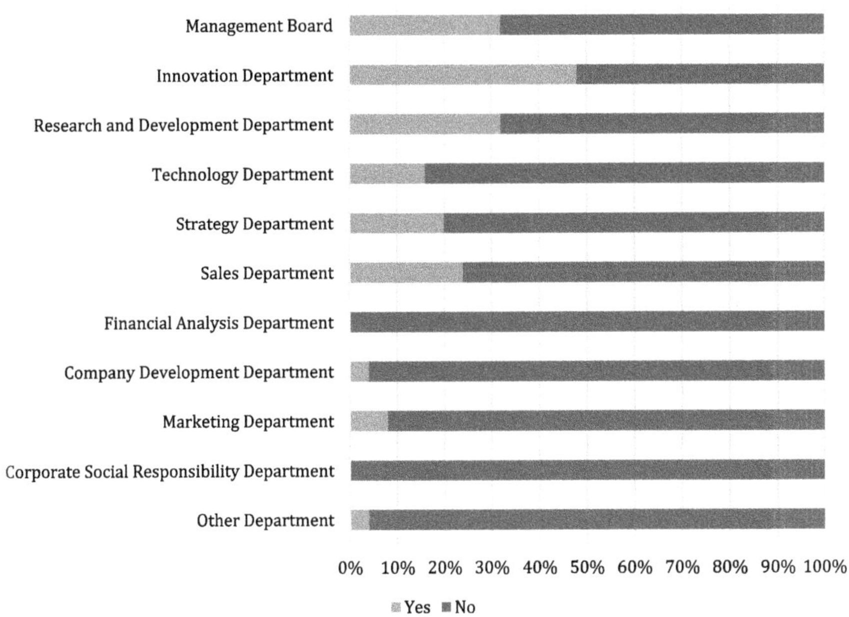

Figure 3.20 Percentage of firms pointing to specific intraorganizational entities responsible for managing cooperation with startups.

Source: Proprietary material.

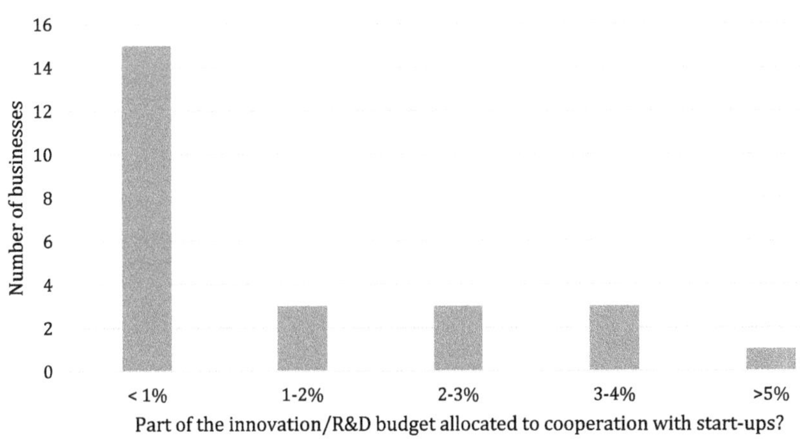

Figure 3.21 Portion of the budget allocated for innovation/R&D in the organizations under research.

Source: Proprietary material.

Then, the research process was described in detail, covering the selection and adaptation of the research tool, the data compilation procedure and the statistical analysis methods used. The depiction of these elements aimed to provide for the accuracy and credibility of the results obtained. The last part of the chapter is dedicated to a detailed characterization of the groups under examination, that is, startups and large organizations participating in acceleration programs. This analysis made it possible to gain an appreciation for the distinct nature of these entities in connection with investigating the interactions taking place between these groups in terms of the open innovation theory.

Notes

1 Database: Bazekon is co-created as part of a consortium of university library centers, inter alia: Main Library of the Economic University in Wrocław, Main Library of the Economic University in Cracow, Library of the Warsaw School of Economics, Main Library of the Economic University in Poznań, Main Library of the Economic University in Katowice and the Faculty Libraries of the University of Szczecin.
2 Czakon, W. (2011). Metodyka systematycznego przeglądu literatury. *Przegląd organizacji*, *3*, 57–61.
3 Levy, Y., & Ellis, T. J. (2006). A systems approach to conduct an effective literature review in support of information systems research. *Informing Science*, *9*, 181–212.
4 https://www.prisma-statement.org/.
5 Liberati, A., Altman, D. G., Tetzlaff, J., Mulrow, C., Gøtzsche, P. C., Ioannidis, J. P., & Moher, D. (2009). The PRISMA statement for reporting systematic reviews and meta-analyses of studies that evaluate health care interventions: Explanation and elaboration. *Annals of Internal Medicine*, *151*(4), W-65.
6 Rethlefsen, M. L., Kirtley, S., Waffenschmidt, S., Ayala, A. P., Moher, D., Page, M. J., & Koffel, J. B. (2021). PRISMA-S: An extension to the PRISMA statement for reporting literature searches in systematic reviews. *Systematic Reviews*, *10*, 1–19.
7 https://projekty.ncn.gov.pl/ (retrieved: 16.12.2023).
8 https://bazekon.uek.krakow.pl/wyniki (retrieved: 16.12.2023).
9 Shetty, S., Sundaram, R., & Achuthan, K. (2020). Assessing and comparing top accelerators in Brazil, India, and the USA: Through the lens of new ventures' performance. *Entrepreneurial Business and Economics Review*, *8*(2), 153–177.
10 Bańka, M., Salwin, M., Waszkiewicz, A. E., Rychlik, S., & Kukurba, M. (2022). Startup accelerators. *International Journal of Management and Economics*, *58*(1), 80–118.
11 Serwatka, A. (2018). Accelerators for startups in Europe. *Copernican Journal of Finance & Accounting*, 7(1), 67–81.
12 Mishigragchaa, B. (2017). Accelerators as a tool to support startup ventures: Assessing their performance and success factors. Literature Review. *Studia i Prace WNEiZ US*, *48*(1), 9–19.
13 Świeszczak, K. (2017). Akceleratory przedsiębiorczości tworzone przez banki jako instytucjonalna forma wsparcia sektora FinTech. *Finanse*, *1*, 239–250.
14 Jung, S. (2018). Cooperating with start-ups as a strategy: Towards corporate entrepreneurship and innovation. *Technology entrepreneurship: Insights in new technology-based firms, research spin-offs and corporate environments* (pp. 283–298).Jung, S. (2018). Cooperating with start-ups as a strategy: Towards corporate

entrepreneurship and innovation. In: Presse, A., & Terzidis, O. (eds) *Technology entrepreneurship. FGF studies in small business and entrepreneurship*. Springer, Cham. https://doi.org/10.1007/978-3-319-73509-2_15

15 Jung, S. (2018). Cooperating with start-ups as a strategy: Towards corporate entrepreneurship and innovation. *Technology entrepreneurship: Insights in new technology-based firms, research spin-offs and corporate environments* (pp. 283–298) London; Kohler, T. (2016). Corporate accelerators: Building bridges between corporations and startups. *Business Horizons*, *59*(3), 347–357; Euchner, J. (2016). Emerging models for corporate innovation: Insights from the IRI 2015 strategy forum. *Research-Technology Management*, *59*(1), 56–60; Mocker, V., Bielli, S., & Haley, C. (2015). *Winning Together: A guide to successful corporate-startup collaborations*. Nesta; Urbaniec, M., & Żur, A. (2021). Business model innovation in corporate entrepreneurship: Exploratory insights from corporate accelerators. *International Entrepreneurship and Management Journal*, *17*(2), 865–888; Shankar, R. K., & Shepherd, D. A. (2019). Accelerating strategic fit or venture emergence: Different paths adopted by corporate accelerators. *Journal of Business Venturing*, *34*(5), 105886; Arreola, F., Favre-Bonte, V., & Tran, S. (2022). The Corporate accelerator: A new kind of strategic factor market to access strategic resources. *Management*, *24*(1), 56–71.

16 Kupp, M., Marval, M., & Borchers, P. (2017). Corporate accelerators: Fostering innovation while bringing together startups and large firms. *Journal of Business Strategy*, *38*(6), 47–53.

17 Kohler, T. (2016). Corporate accelerators: Building bridges between corporations and startups. *Business Horizons*, *59*(3), 347–357.

18 Shankar, R. K., & Shepherd, D. A. (2019). Accelerating strategic fit or venture emergence: Different paths adopted by corporate accelerators. *Journal of Business Venturing*, *34*(5), 105886.

19 Hutter, K., Gfrerer, A., & Lindner, B. (2021). From popular to profitable: Incumbents experiences and challenges with external corporate accelerators. *International Journal of Innovation Management*, *25*(3), 2150035.

20 Dziewit, W. (2023). *Polskie start-upy 2023*. Warszawa: Fundacja Startup Poland. https://startuppoland.org/report/luki-w-ekosystemie-startupowym/.

21 Heinzelmann, N., Selig, C. J., & Baltes, G. H. (2020, June). Critical actions of and synergies between corporate entrepreneurship programs. In *2020 IEEE International Conference on Engineering, Technology and Innovation (ICE/ITMC)* (pp. 1–9). Cardiff: IEEE.

22 Veit, P., Kramer, A., Kanbach, D., & Stubner, S. (2021). Revising the taxonomy of corporate accelerators: Moving towards an evolutionary perspective. *International Journal of Entrepreneurial Venturing*, *13*(6), 568–599.

23 Hausberg, J. P., & Korreck, S. (2020). Business incubators and accelerators: A co-citation analysis-based, systematic literature review. *The Journal of Technology Transfer*, *45*, 151–176.

24 Kupp, M., Marval, M., & Borchers, P. (2017). Corporate accelerators: Fostering innovation while bringing together startups and large firms. *Journal of Business Strategy*, *38*(6), 47–53.

25 Richter, N., Jackson, P., & Schildhauer, T. (2018). Outsourcing creativity: An abductive study of open innovation using corporate accelerators. *Creativity and Innovation Management*, *27*(1), 69–78.

26 Niemczyk, J. (2009). Chciałbyś coś odkryć? *Przegląd Organizacji*, *10*, 3–5.

27 Czakon, W. (2016). W kierunku rozwoju badań ilościowych w naukach o zarządzaniu. *Organizacja i Kierowanie*, *173*(3), 41–52.

28 Niemczyk, J. (2016). Formułowanie i wartościowanie problemów naukowych. In W. Czakon (Ed.). *Podstawy metodologii badań w naukach o zarządzaniu* (pp. 103–118), Warszawa: Wydawnictwo Nieoczywiste.

29 Ekiz, E. H., & Bavik, A. (2008). Scale development process: Service quality in car rental services. *Electronic Journal of Business Research Methods*, 6(2), 161–174.
30 Venkatraman, N., & Grant, J. H. (1986). Construct measurement in organizational strategy research: A critique and proposal. *Academy of Management Review*, *11*(1), 71–87.
31 Kaufmann, L., & Astou Saw, A. (2014). Using a multiple-informant approach in SCM research. *International Journal of Physical Distribution & Logistics Management*, *44*(6), 511–527.
32 Hair, J. F., Black, W. C., Babin, B. J., & Anderson, R. E. (2014). *Multivariate data analysis: Pearson new international edition* (Vol. 1(2)). Essex: Pearson Education Limited.
33 Hinkin, T. R., Tracey, J. B., & Enz, C. A. (1997). Scale construction: Developing reliable and valid measurement instruments. *Journal of Hospitality & Tourism Research*, *21*(1), 100–120.
34 Yuan, F., & Woodman, R. W. (2010). Innovative behavior in the workplace: The role of performance and image outcome expectations. *Academy of Management Journal*, *53*(2), 323–342.
35 George, D., & Mallery, P. (2019). *IBM SPSS statistics 26 step by step: A simple guide and reference*. New York: Routledge.

4 Diagnosis regarding the perception of inter-organizational cooperation between startups and corporations in acceleration programs

Cooperation between startups and corporations is more and more visible in the current day of an economy based on innovation and digital technologies. The phenomenon of corporations launching various models for attracting new innovative companies and their innovations has been observed in recent years. One instrument that has gained particular popularity on the market involves acceleration programs which, as discussed in the second chapter, form the structural framework for cooperation between startups and corporations.

Accordingly, the purpose of this chapter (first area of the research gap) is to introduce the diagnosis on how these programs are perceived by both parties, that is, startups and corporations. In total, it consisted of five research goals. The purpose of the research was to demonstrate the significance and importance of establishing cooperation between startups and corporations in terms of implementing the solutions offered by startups in large organizations. This consists of the following:

1 Specifying the essence of startups establishing cooperation with corporations while confirming the existence of impediments to achieving that.
2 Specifying the importance of corporations establishing cooperation with startups.
3 Specifying the importance of acceleration programs to assist in establishing cooperation between startups and corporations.
4 Specifying the importance of acceleration programs to support the implementation of startups' solutions in corporations.
5 Verifying whether the participation of startups and large organizations in the acceleration programs organized by accelerators engenders greater benefit for the parties than the expenditures incurred to establish and maintain their cooperation.

The following assumptions were accepted at the time of proceeding to realize the foregoing research goals:

Assumption 1: Establishing cooperation with corporations is important to startups and this constitutes a challenge for the firms participating in the

DOI: 10.4324/9781003540366-5

acceleration program. The verification of the foregoing assumption involved answering the following three questions:

- How important is it to establish cooperation with corporations according to the representatives of the startups?
- Is the establishment of cooperation between startups and corporations rated as being difficult?
- Would it be plausible to develop a solution offered by a startup without cooperating with a corporation?

Assumption 2: Establishing cooperation with startups is important to corporations and this is an arduous undertaking. The verification of the foregoing assumption involved answering the following three questions:

- How important is it to establish cooperation with startups according to the representatives of corporations?
- Is the establishment of cooperation with startups by corporations difficult for corporations?
- Would it be possible to implement innovations in a corporation without cooperation with a startup?

Assumption 3: Acceleration programs play a crucial role in bringing startups together with large organizations. The verification of the foregoing assumption involved answering the following two questions:

- How is cooperation established with corporations most frequently and do acceleration programs play a crucial role and do they serve as a mechanism in bringing together startups and corporations?
- Is it worthwhile to recommend to other startups that they participate in an acceleration program involving technology clients for the purpose of establishing cooperation with them?

Assumption 4: Accelerators and their acceleration programs significantly contribute to establishing cooperation between startups and corporations in connection with the need for startups to test their solutions on the market and as a result they greatly enhance the opportunities for startups to enter into commercial arrangements to implement innovations and sell their products and services to corporations. The verification of the foregoing assumption involved answering the following four questions:

- Is faster project commercialization plausible through cooperation with accelerators as part of acceleration programs?
- Is an accelerator the sole opportunity for startups to launch cooperation with corporations?

- Does participation in an acceleration program make it substantially easier for a startup to establish cooperation with a corporation and test its product, service and technology?
- Does participation in an acceleration program substantially increase the chances of startups entering into commercial agreements to implement innovations and sell products and services to corporations?

Assumption 5: The participation of startups and large organizations in the acceleration programs organized by startup accelerators engenders greater benefit than the expenditures incurred to establish and maintain their cooperation. The verification of the foregoing assumption involved answering the following four questions:

- How beneficial has your startup's collaboration with corporations been so far?
- Have the benefits from your startup's collaboration with a corporation outweighed the expenditures incurred?
- How beneficial has your company's collaboration with startups been so far?
- Have the benefits from your company's collaboration with a startup outweighed the expenditures incurred to establish and sustain this collaboration?

The subsequent sub-sections in this part of the book constitute an attempt at answering the foregoing research questions and verifying the assumptions made.

4.1 Essence of startups establishing cooperation with corporations

In the first step the decision was made to investigate how important it was according to the representatives of the startups to establish cooperation with a corporation. As can be seen in Figure 4.1 responses indicating the high importance of such cooperation were prevalent – 49 respondents (48.5%) indicated that such action was very important, 34 persons (33.7%) evaluated this as being important, but not required, 13 persons (12.9%) checked the response "to a certain degree" and 3 persons (3%) found it to be hard to say while single representatives of the startups checked the response "rather unimportant" and "unimportant".

Such high results evidence the perception of cooperation with corporations as a significant factor driving product development, the implementation of innovation and reaping benefits that are not only financial in nature but also in other areas – for instance in the form of lending credibility to the business being conducted, building trust in the solution being offered among prospective clients and extending the business contact network. Access to the corporate partner's infrastructure and technical and technological center

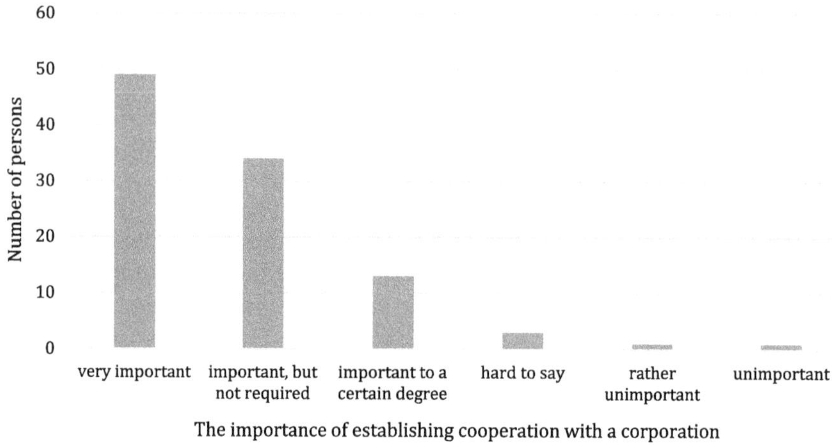

Figure 4.1 Evaluation of how important it was for a startup to establish cooperation with a corporation.

Source: Proprietary material.

is particularly important for those startups that operate in an industry other than IT, for example, in the chemical, food, automobile and furniture industries.

The next question concerned the difficulties involved with establishing cooperation with a corporation (Figure 4.2). Responses were given using the classic Likert scale. A response was obtained to this question from 95 representatives of the startups. The other six persons were not capable of evaluating the level of difficulty and they were not incorporated in the table below. Once again, responses in the affirmative were prevalent in the test sample. Thirty-five respondents selected the response "rather difficult" while another 26 persons selected the response "decidedly difficult". However, it is worthwhile to observe that slightly more than ¼ of the responses obtained to this question were ambiguous (27 cases). Responses in the negative appeared much more rarely – six persons flagged the response "rather easy", while one person flagged the response "definitely easy". The average result obtained for this question was 3.83 points (SD = 0.94).

The research indicated that it was difficult to establish cooperation between the parties. The divergent organizational culture of startups and corporations is most assuredly not conducive to this, nor is the difference between the teams working on both sides. The organizational culture in the two groups of entities under examination is characterized by different processes, experience in mindset toward goals. Moreover, the mere fact that acceleration programs and the cooperation between startups and larger businesses are also a new experience for the parties does not at all facilitate this cooperation. The market still has very few disseminated prime examples illustrating the advantages of such cooperation and the benefits it accrues. Examples of such solutions

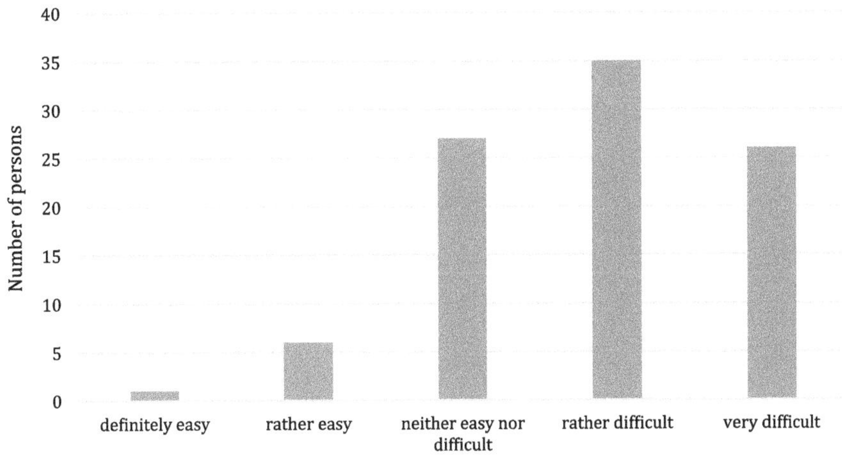

Figure 4.2 Evaluation of whether establishing cooperation between startups and corporations is difficult.

Source: Proprietary material.

may be the cooperation between the startup Dropbox and Hewlett-Packard (HP) in 2011. Dropbox offered access to space in the cloud to the users of HP laptops. Thanks to that Dropbox obtained access to millions of HP clients at the drop of a hat. The example of the acquisition of the startup Instagram by Facebook in 2012, or the solutions known from the Polish market entailing the e-signature offered by the Autenti platform, which is being successfully used by banks, such as PKO BP, BNP Paribas and Alior Bank or the combination of InPost's courier services with procurement platforms. Despite the positive examples of executing joint projects and the implementation of startups' services by corporations, the market still lacks the critical mass required to change this picture. Respondents also rated whether it would be possible to develop their startup or product without cooperating with a corporation. The responses given to this question using the classic Likert scale were clearly more varied (Figure 4.3). The most frequent response was "neither no nor yes", which was posted in 41 cases (40.6%). The responses "rather not" were slightly more prevalent than the responses "rather yes" (26 cases vs 20 cases, respectively). In turn, extreme responses appeared with the same frequency – in seven cases (6.9%). The average result obtained for this question was 2.94 points (SD = 1.01).

The differences in responses may follow from the development stages of the startups that are participating in the acceleration programs. Some of the startups are in the phase of having the first version of their product and for them further business development is significant. In turn, startups in the scaling up phase, having a product aligned with market needs and pursuing market expansion, are not interested in its further development. Instead, their primary interest lies in establishing business contacts with a corporation

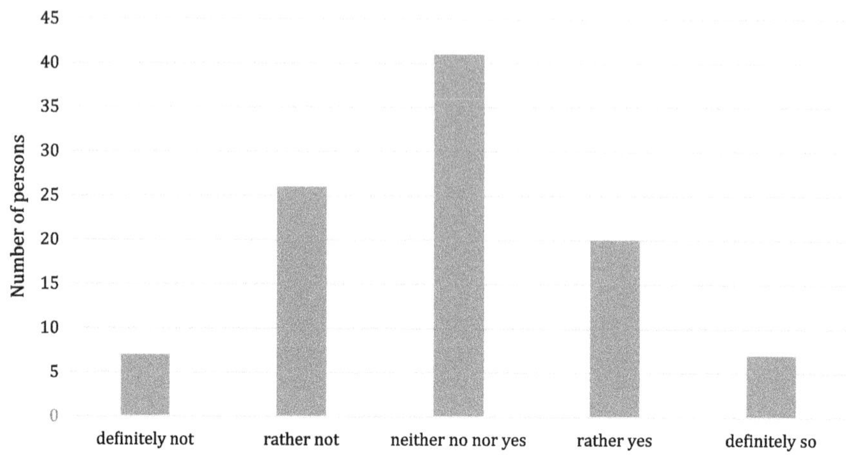

Figure 4.3 Evaluation of whether it would be plausible to develop a startup/product of the researched persons without cooperating with a corporation.

Source: Proprietary material.

and commencing sales in the distribution channels of a large organization as soon as possible (under the *Plug and Play* model).

4.2 Essence of corporations establishing cooperation with startups

The responses provided by startups regarding the essence of cooperation have been compiled with the results obtained from corporations. Figure 4.4 depicts the distribution of responses to questions concerning the importance of establishing cooperation with a startup. The response "Important to a certain degree" was the most frequent response – 14 instances (56%). Eight respondents (32%) indicated that such cooperation is important but not required, while in three instances (12%), it was evaluated as being very important.

The scores received differ from the ones obtained from the representatives of the startups. For corporations establishing cooperation with startups is not fundamentally perceived as a key element of innovation processes. The challenge appears to be implementing the products offered by startups. This may stem from internal relationships and complicated structures that frequently appear in large organizations. Proprietary observations of the startup acceleration programs under execution in a corporation's environment indicate that the process of working out innovations is not always formally structured. The assignment of suitable resources is lacking, and the employees engaged in this process perceive cooperation with a new organization not so seldomly more as an "adventure" or experiment than as a strategic partnership. Employees in multiple instances become discouraged

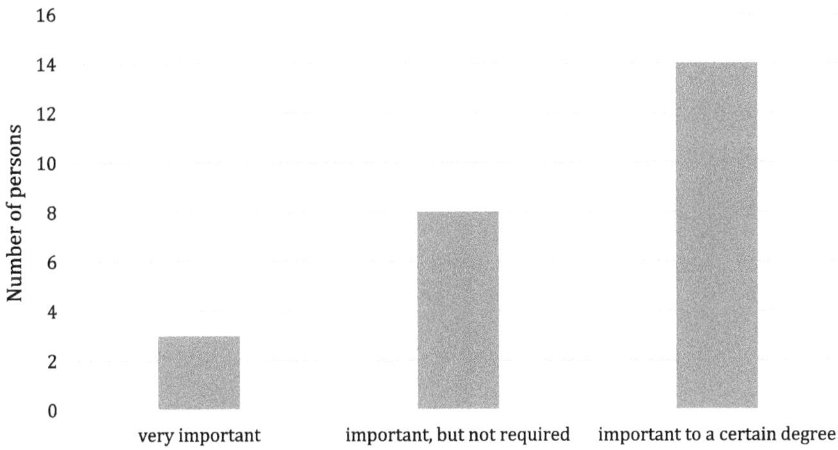

Figure 4.4 Evaluation of how important it was for a corporation to establish cooperation with a startup.

Source: Proprietary material.

in terms of cooperation with startups, especially when an organization concentrates on core business, while the management's expectations are related to quickly achieving measurable successes. Even though one may observe a positive approach to cooperation in corporations, a properly structured process for implementing innovations is frequently lacking, even when the results of tests suggest that the startup's solution is promising. This lack of structure and formalization of the innovative process may lead to failing to tap into the potential offered by cooperation with new innovative companies, which in turn may curtail the possibilities of achieving long-term benefits for both parties. It is also worth observing that a relatively large number of responses pointing to the lack of a priority-guided approach to cooperation with startups may stem from the fact that large corporations frequently have their own research and development (R&D) departments that are dedicated to creating innovations. Accordingly, large organizations have greater comfort in operating and they do not have to concentrate their resources to a substantial degree on supporting external innovative projects.

The next question concerned the difficulties involved with establishing cooperation with a corporation. Responses were given using the classic Likert scale. As can be seen in Figure 4.5 the responses indicating substantial difficulty in that cooperation were prevalent. Eleven respondents (44%) flagged the response "rather difficult", while another two people (8%) rated it as very difficult. Six people (24%) each flagged the response "rather easy", along with an intermediate response. The average result obtained for this question was 3.36 points (*SD* = 0.95).

Similar to the responses given by startups, representatives of corporations also evaluated that establishing cooperation is generally not straightforward.

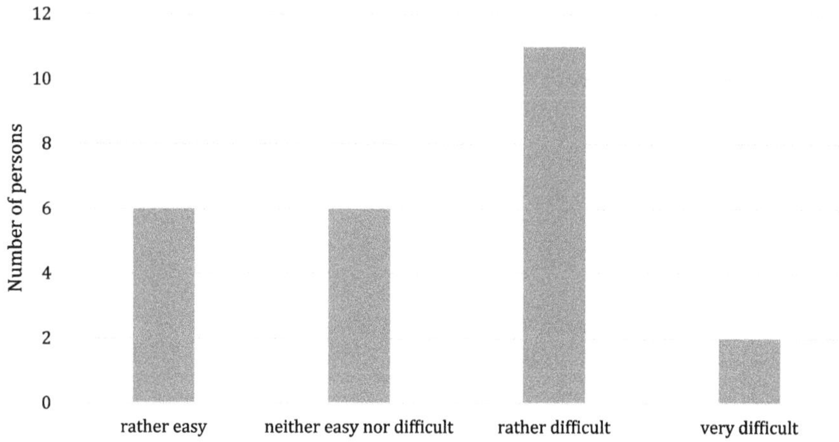

Figure 4.5 Evaluation of whether establishing cooperation between startups and corporations is difficult.

Source: Proprietary material.

Here we may speak of different possible obstacles, for example, procedural (e.g., decision-making process lasting many months, rigidity of processes), cultural (striving to curtailing risk to the greatest possible degree, noticeable absence of a culture of entrepreneurship), structural (e.g., many decision-making centers and their lack of transparency), strategic (e.g., mismatch with goals) and frequently cross-sectional obstacles (combining the obstacles enumerated above). In the next step, respondents evaluated in turn whether it would be possible to implement innovation in a corporation without cooperation with a startup. As can be seen in Figure 4.6 nearly one-half of the sample under examination (12 persons, 48%) flagged an intermediate response. Eight respondents flagged the response "rather yes" (32%), three representatives flagged the response "definitely not" (12%), while two persons (8%) rated this possibility as rather negative. The average result obtained for this question was 3 points (SD = 0.96).

The results obtained may be explained by citing the experience of large organizations in creating innovations and implementing them on the market. Before startup accelerators and acceleration programs appeared in the innovation ecosystem corporations were capable of responding to the needs of clients stemming from the market. The R&D departments functioning in these organizations fill the role of suppliers of innovations, forming an alternative to the solutions offered by startups. This probably explains the prevailing opinions among respondents that the innovation process may be pursued while overlooking startups. Additionally, one should take into account that large organizations may also benefit from the solutions offered by other vendors who frequently hold a well-established position on the market and supply tried and tested solutions. Companies specializing in the digitization of documents

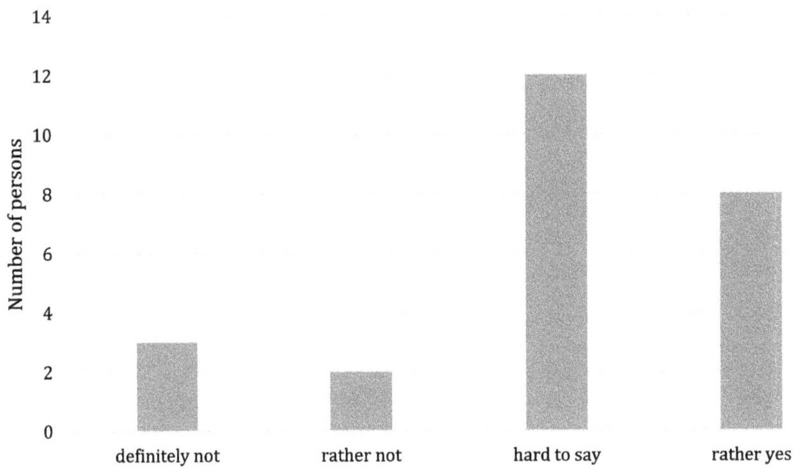

Figure 4.6 Evaluation of whether it would be possible to implement innovation in a corporation without cooperation with a startup.

Source: Proprietary material.

in workflow may serve as an example. They offer finished and tested tools forming an alternative to the innovations being developed by startups.

4.3 Acceleration programs and their role in bringing startups and corporations together

Then, the decision was made to check in the research how cooperation is most frequently established with corporations. Whether, in fact acceleration programs are ones that play a crucial role and serve as a mechanism in bringing together startups and corporations. A similar question was posed to startups (Figure 4.7) and corporations (Figure 4.8) alike. In both cases the response indicating that the acceleration program under execution led to the commencement of cooperation between the parties clearly prevailed (100% of the responses for the startups and 96% of the responses for the corporations). Such a high percentage of responses in the affirmative for both parties comports with market observations. It is precisely the participation of corporations and startups in acceleration programs that substantially opened up the two parties to engage in cooperation. This will allow the parties to get to know one another and devise a framework for future cooperation. This is also visible in the official communications concerning the sources of obtaining innovations used by large organizations that do not only more and more willingly participate in external acceleration programs but recently some of them have elected to launch activities associated with setting up their own corporate accelerators whose task it will be to attract startups and work with them and coordinate cooperation between the organization's business units and the startups.

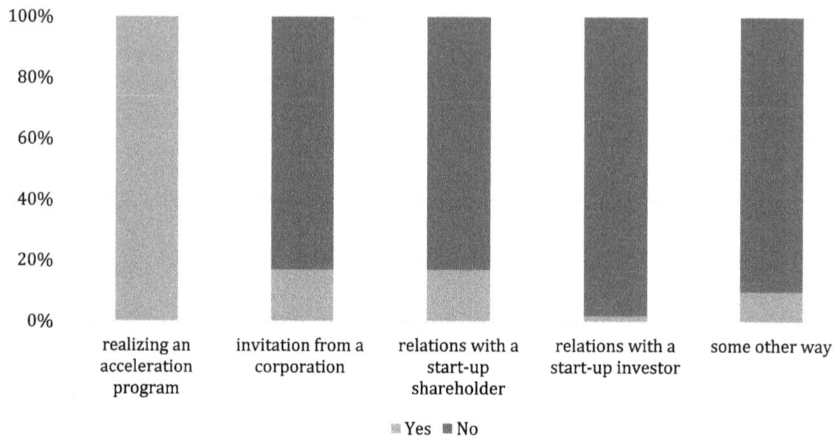

Figure 4.7 Method of establishing cooperation between a startup and a corporation.
Source: Proprietary material.

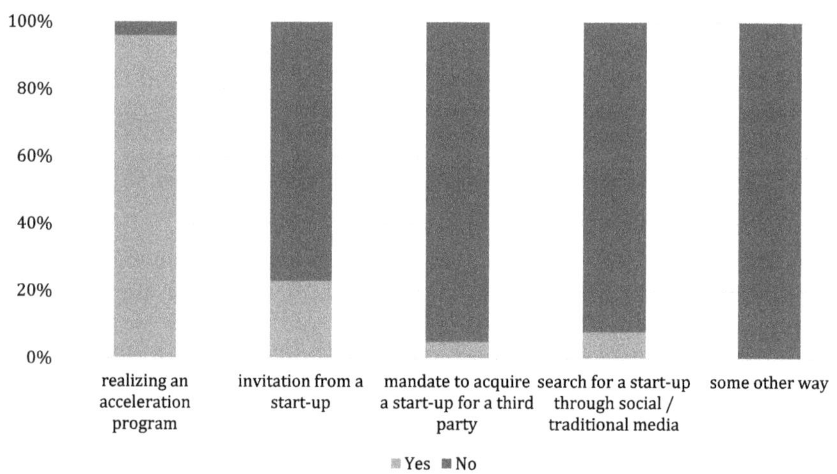

Figure 4.8 Method of establishing cooperation between a corporation and a startup.
Source: Proprietary material.

It is noteworthy that both sides also undertook attempts at making contact in a different way. In 15 cases (14.9%) startups were invited to cooperate by corporations that with the awareness that they are participating in an acceleration program elected to steer the applying entities directly to such programs. It is worth pointing out that startups also actively put forward a proposal of direct cooperation. 24% of the large organizations under examination indicated that startups were the ones to instigate the establishment of cooperation and they were the first ones to submit an offer to a corporation.

During the next step how startups generally perceive their participation in acceleration programs was checked. As can be seen in Figure 4.9 the responses given by the representatives of the startups were resoundingly positive. Seventy-one respondents (70.3%) responded "decidedly yes". Furthermore, no response in the negative was recorded.

The positive reception of participating in an acceleration program involving corporations stems from the following:

1 Structuring the program that offers a well-organized process giving the possibility of cooperation with prospective clients of the solutions offered by startups. Clearly defined program stages and goals enhance the chance of the parties entering into a business contract, affording the possibility of rapidly marketing an innovation based on a corporation's resources and sales channels.
2 Effective management of an acceleration program in which the startup accelerator is directly responsible for organizing and managing the acceleration process. It endeavors to maximize the efficacy of the overall process. Procures that the communication between startups and the representatives of corporations will proceed seamlessly. In the event of encountering difficulties, an accelerator is capable of actively getting involved in the negotiation process, helping solve a possible deadlock in talks.
3 Possibility of testing solutions in real market conditions. Participation in an acceleration program frequently creates a non-recurring chance for startups to test their products or services in an actual corporate environment. This possibility allows for rapid iterations and refining the solution on the basis of actual data and feedback from the corporation's management and end users.

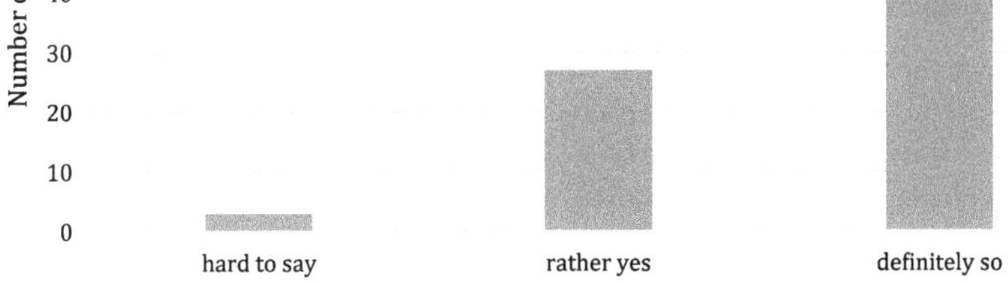

Figure 4.9 Evaluation of whether it is worthwhile to recommend to other startups that they participate in an acceleration program involving large organizations.

Source: Proprietary material.

4 Access to a corporation's technological and infrastructural resources: corporations may give startups access to their sophisticated technological resources, laboratories, equipment and IT infrastructure, which greatly enhances the possibilities of developing and testing the products, services and technologies offered by startups.
5 Provides financial funds for startups depending on the formula adopted by the program. Access to financial means allows them to focus on developing innovations and aligning the products to market needs.
6 Engagement of mentors and experts to support startups at every one of the stages of an acceleration program.
7 Support provided by former program participants. Startups that previously participated in an acceleration program frequently share their experiences with new participants during networking sessions. These seasoned entrepreneurs may offer valuable hints on how to prepare for talks with a corporation's business units and what to watch out for in communication.
8 Building long-term business relationships. Acceleration programs may serve as a platform to establish sustainable business relationships not only with corporations but also with other partners taking part in the program. These relationships may survive beyond the formal acceleration period and lead to further cooperation and investments.

A decision was also made to check whether, in the opinion of the representatives of corporations, the business would have run the project with startups had it not participated in an acceleration program. The results of the research in which 36% of the representatives of the corporations responded in the affirmative and 64% in the negative suggest that acceleration programs discharge a crucial function in instigating cooperation between large organizations and new innovative companies. Acceleration programs serve as catalysts that not only facilitate the establishment of contacts between startups and corporations but also create structures and processes that may not exist outside of these programs.

4.4 Acceleration programs managed by accelerators and their importance in supporting startups' solutions in corporations

In this part the decision was made to analyze the aspect of the functions of accelerators in the eyes of the representatives of the startups slightly more precisely. Therefore, the responses examining the significance of participating in acceleration programs entailed were investigated. Each sub-point was evaluated on a scale of 1–10. First, the responses supporting the assertion that "thanks to cooperation with accelerators one can commercialize a project more quickly" were analyzed. As can be seen in Figure 4.10 the responses in the affirmative clearly prevailed, even though some individual representatives of the startups also expressed disparaging opinions. The average result for this question was 8.02 points (SD = 2.08).

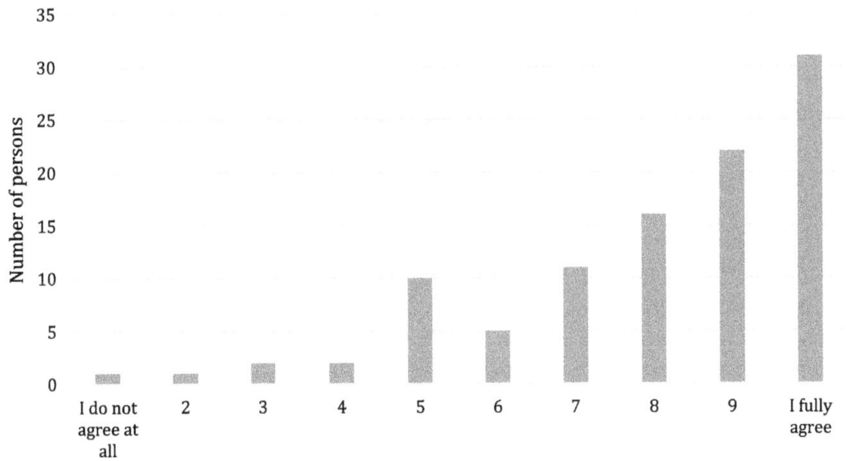

Figure 4.10 Evaluation of startup representatives contending that thanks to cooperation with accelerators one can commercialize a project more quickly.

Source: Proprietary material.

It seems that such a high level of perception of the significance of acceleration programs for the purposes of implementing startups' solutions is linked, among other things, to the following:

1 Professional approach on the part of the parties to the acceleration program. The acceleration program is defined in advance and aims to bring together startups and corporations. In principle, the framework and conditions of cooperation are known. The accelerator team, as part of the workshops held with corporations, collaborates to define the program, identify and confirm the needs and challenges faced by large businesses, understand their expectations of startups and establish the desired outcomes of the acceleration program.
2 Establishing relations and having accelerators enter into contracts with large organizations. Accelerators are responsible for bringing corporations and startups together.
3 Defining the goals of an acceleration program. The parties participating in the program were poised to carry out at least trial implementations. Once they have elected to choose startups along with an accelerator, corporations strive to test the maximum quantum of solutions offered by new companies that are aligned to the needs of large companies from the outset.
4 Accelerator's support in a negotiation deadlock. The accelerator team may play the role of mediator between the parties. The accelerator may clear a path through obstacles in cooperation between the parties at the stage of the acceleration program and the pending innovation process.
5 Exchange of experience and networking that would not have occurred without participation in an acceleration program.

Moreover, without the corporation's engagement in acceleration programs, there probably would not have been teams defined in large organizations with a designated responsibility for cooperation with startups and making it easier for them to reach the right managers of the business units who could also be interested in the solutions offered by startups. If a corporation takes part in an acceleration program, then corporations most frequently designate a team or organizational unit within its structure that would be responsible for cooperation with startups and thereby they become the organizational guides for those companies. The responses to the assertion that an accelerator is the sole option for startups to commence cooperation with corporations were then analyzed. As can be seen in Figure 4.11, there was a very high differentiation among the results obtained in the case of this question. Scores indicating greater or lesser agreement with the stated assertion (responses giving 7–10 points) accounted for 45.5% of the research sample. However, in parallel, responses disagreeing with this content (responses giving 1–4 points) accounted for 31.7% of the responses. Thus a portion of the representatives of the startups actually deemed accelerators to be the sole possibility for startups but a sample that was not much smaller did not agree with this way of framing the matter. The average result for this question was 5.84 points (*SD* = 2.88). This result may be interpreted in the context of the diversity of business models and operating strategies of startups. Startups operating in different industries can have different needs and possibilities, which affects how they perceive the value of accelerators and organized programs involving corporations. For some, especially those in more niche-like or technologically advanced industries, accelerators may not be the only or the best path to cooperation with corporations. Others, especially new startups

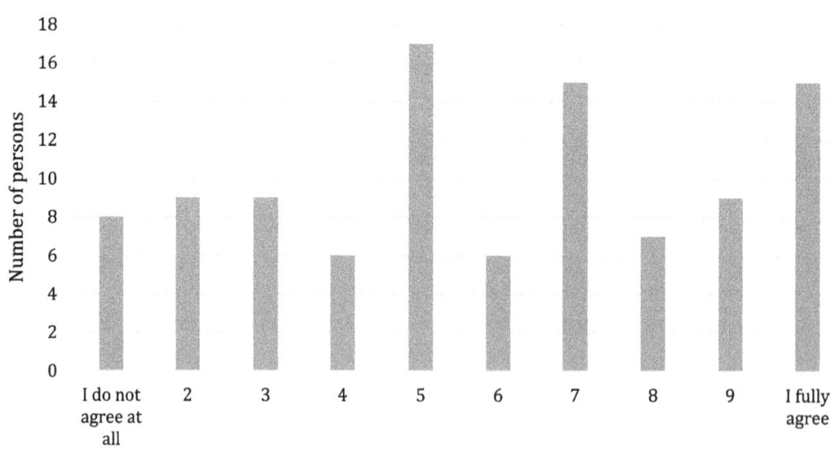

Figure 4.11 Evaluation of startup representatives contending that an accelerator is the sole opportunity for startups to launch cooperation with corporations.

Source: Proprietary material.

without an extensive contact network may perceive an acceleration program as a key stage on the path to establishing strategic partnerships with large organizations. Accordingly, even though accelerators play an important role in the startup ecosystem and in implementing innovations in corporations, they are not always seen as a one-size-fits-all solution for all new innovative companies. For some startups they may be indispensable while others may find alternative paths of reaching and establishing inter-organizational cooperation.

The next question pertained to the evaluation of whether participation in an acceleration program makes it substantially easier for a startup to establish cooperation with a corporation and test its products, services and technologies. As can be seen in Figure 4.12 the responses in the affirmative clearly prevailed. The dominant for this distribution, that is, the most frequent response had the value of 10, or the maximum value, indicating that it fully comported with the wording of the assertion under discussion. Thirty-five persons (34.7%) responded in this manner. The average result for this question was 8.01 points (SD = 2.07).

That startups have such a good perception of participating in acceleration programs most assuredly ensues from the engagement of dedicated resources and units on the part of the corporation and accelerator in the cooperation. The program provides experts, people with market experience working in corporations, who are dedicated to cooperation with startups. In this

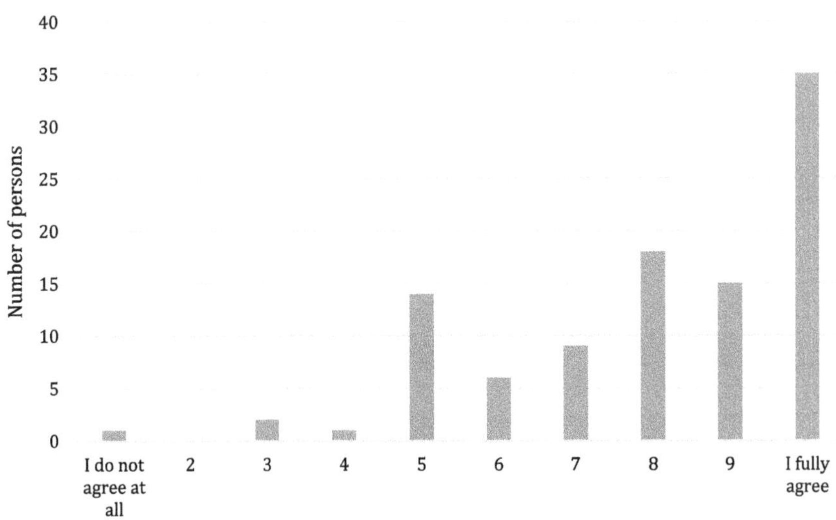

Figure 4.12 Evaluation of startup representatives contending that participation in an acceleration program makes it substantially easier for startups to establish cooperation with corporations and test their products, services and technologies.

Source: Proprietary material.

manner the adverse phenomena associated with the secondment of people who do not fully appreciate the process and their role in such a program is averted. By engaging the right human resources, meetings with experts are organized, covering various areas such as technical, technological and pricing, for instance. Moreover, startups frequently have procured access to a test environment, laboratories to work with the corporation's clients (e.g., a laboratory belonging to the telecommunications company T-Mobile – Edge Computing Lab). The mere participation in an acceleration program may also augment the credibility of a startup in the eyes of a corporation, which will facilitate the future establishment of sustainable business cooperation.

The last topic analyzed pertained to increasing the chances for implementing innovation and entering into commercial agreements to sell products and services by participating in an acceleration program. As can be seen in Figure 4.13 the responses in the affirmative once again prevailed. The dominant for this distribution once again had a value indicating that it fully comported with the wording of the assertion under discussion and was tagged by 32 people (31.7%). The average result for this question was 7.71 points (*SD* = 2.29).

A characteristic feature of acceleration programs involving corporations is that the corporation's needs and the solutions it seeks are known and communicated from the outset. The projects submitted correspond to the needs of the corporations. Startups participating in such a program know from the beginning what the need is and whether the product, service or technology they offer falls within the corporation's area of interest. Moreover, during the program,

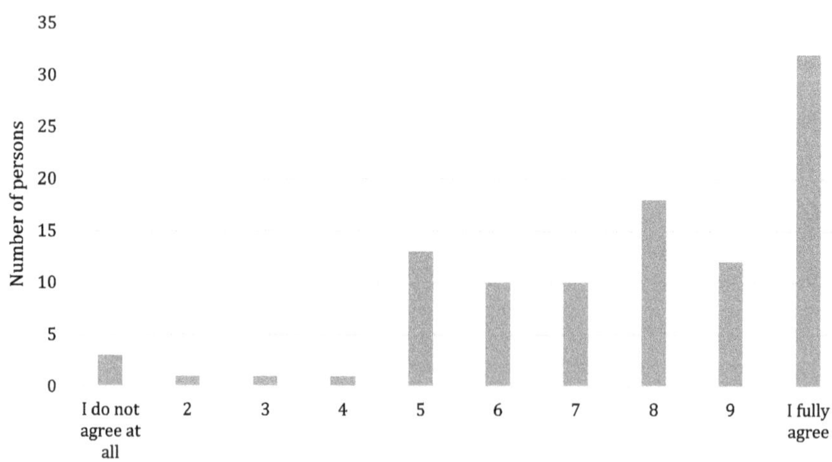

Figure 4.13 Evaluation of startup representatives contending that participation in an acceleration program substantially increases the chances of implementing innovation and entering into commercial agreements to sell products and services.

Source: Proprietary material.

tests are held and their outcome is known. If the tests are positive, it is easier for the parties to strike an agreement, and accordingly, the startup has good chances of entering into a commercial contract. Moreover, participation in a program allows the parties to get to know one another, plan their cooperation and put together a schedule for implementing the innovation, including preparations for satisfying the criteria and procurement procedures in force in a corporation, which is also important. The obstacles encountered during cooperation are subject to limitation, while the potential risks are duly addressed during the acceleration program that lasts for several months. The acceleration program itself is frequently treated by the parties as a joint effort, whereby the parties involved subconsciously endeavor to strike an agreement at its termination.

4.5 Acceleration programs versus the costs and benefits of cooperation

To recap the foregoing considerations, it is necessary to verify in this chapter whether participation in an acceleration program produced benefits surpassing the expenditures incurred and how this cooperation was generally evaluated by startups and corporations. These questions were first posed to representatives of the startups. Their responses were evaluated on a scale from 1 (the worst possible score) to 10 points (the best possible score). The results indicate a generally positive score – the average score on the beneficial nature of cooperation to-date was 7.25 points (SD = 2.11), while the average score of the excess benefit over costs was 6.68 points (SD = 2.66). As Figure 4.14 shows, positive responses were prevalent, though it is worth

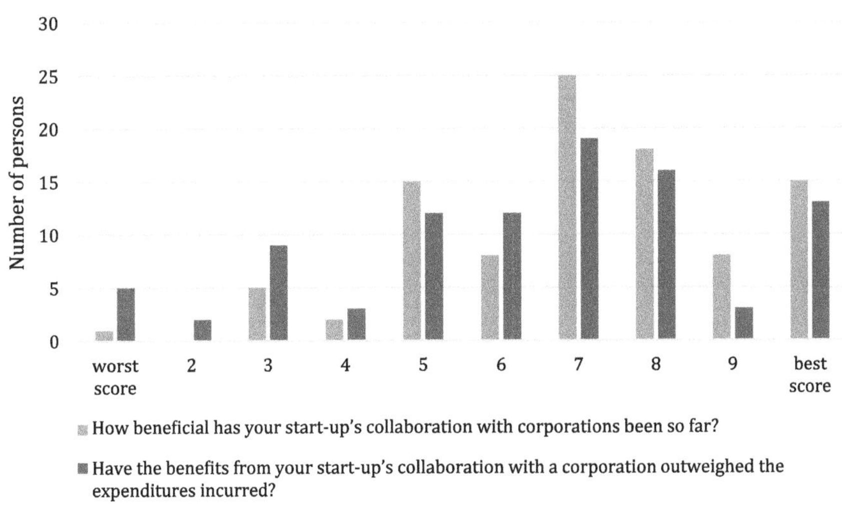

Figure 4.14 Evaluation of the costs and benefits of the cooperation between startups and corporations.

Source: Proprietary material.

noting that five startups gave an extremely negative evaluation of the ratio of benefits to the expenditures incurred.

The high positive responses given by startups may be associated with the benefits these small companies have achieved thanks to establishing cooperation as a result of participation in an acceleration program involving corporations. Participation in a program gives them the possibility of matching the offered product or service to the genuine needs of large organizations. Thanks to that startups can vet their product and its fit. Even though the result itself of this verification may be positive or negative, it nevertheless gives startups a chance to save time and financial means in connection with vetting the offered solution against market demand and specifics. Startups have the option of implementing and frequently sourcing their first reference client for their solutions. Testing the solution, gaining references and know-how during cooperation gives them the opportunity to win this organization as a client which can provide the means for further development or sell the solution offered by a startup. Similar questions posed to representatives of the corporations revealed similar findings. The responses were generally positive for both questions – in the case of the evaluation of the beneficial nature of cooperation to-date the average score in the research sample was 6.54 points ($SD = 1.29$), while the evaluation stating that the benefits outweigh the costs was rated on average as 6.05 points ($SD = 2.01$). As can be seen in Figure 4.15, the scores were focused in the region of moderate to positive values, while extreme opinions showed up much more seldomly. A single

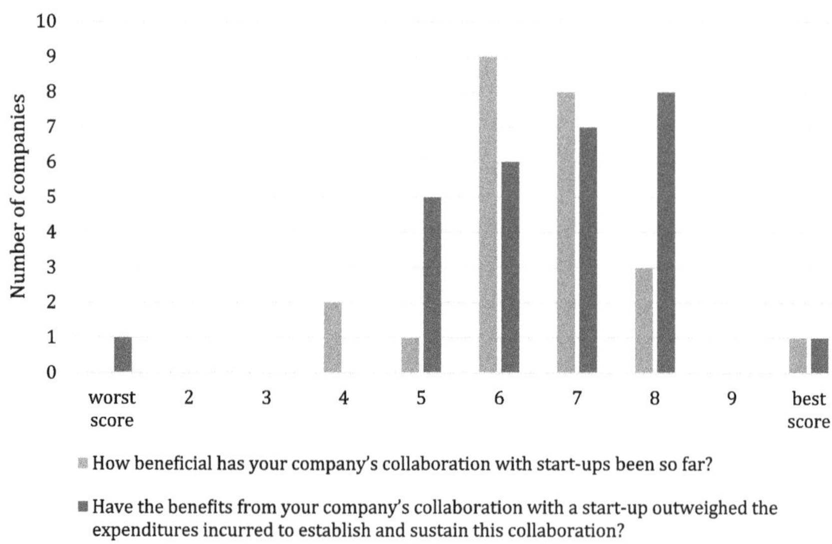

Figure 4.15 Evaluation of the costs and benefits of the cooperation between corporations and startups.

Source: Proprietary material.

technology client evaluated the cooperation and the benefits as extremely good and extremely negative.

Based on the analysis of the results obtained one can assert that despite large organizations incurring costs (e.g., engaging persons for cooperation with startups), the benefits from the cooperation with startups as part of the acceleration programs nevertheless outweighed the incurred expenditures. Examples of the benefits achieved by an organization may pertain to the following:

1 Reducing risk in terms of sourcing and testing the innovative solutions offered by startups.
2 Improving processes and enhancing the culture of innovativeness, for example, by performing tasks in the corporation in accordance with the *Agile* methodology approach to work.
3 Exploring the solutions and technologies offered by startups coupled with the minimum engagement of one's own resources.
4 Acquiring the ability to work with small companies and suppliers, which usually leads to a more effective utilization of new technologies in terms of costs and timing, and thereby to building sustainable market advantages.
5 Possibility of vetting the internal procedures for choosing suppliers and entering into business contracts.
6 Image-related aspects related to the perception of corporations as entities open to innovations originating from outside the bounds of an organization.

As part of the first research task a diagnosis was performed on how startups and corporations perceive the acceleration programs managed by startup accelerators. The analysis of the results obtained formed the basis for responses to the following five questions.

1 Is establishing cooperation between startups and corporations important to new companies and does it constitute a challenge for them?
2 Is the corporations' establishment of cooperation with startups important to large organizations and is this an arduous undertaking?
3 Do acceleration programs play a crucial role in bringing new firms together with large organizations and are they recommended by startups?
4 Do accelerators and their acceleration programs significantly contribute to establishing cooperation between startups and corporations, particularly in relation to the need for startups to test the solutions they offer on the market? As a result, do they greatly enhance the opportunities for startups to commercialize their project and enter into commercial arrangements to sell their products and services to corporations?
5 Does the participation of startups and large organizations in acceleration programs engender greater benefit than the expenditures incurred to establish and maintain this cooperation?

Responding to the first research question, one may assert that establishing cooperation with corporations is important to startups. Roughly 82% of the businesses in the research selected this response. Equally, establishing cooperation between business partners is difficult in principle. Roughly 64% of the businesses in the research selected this response.

The second question concerned the importance of corporations establishing cooperation with startups and how the process itself is perceived (how difficult it is). The research demonstrated that 56% of the respondents flagged the response that cooperation is important to a certain degree, 32% indicated that such cooperation is important but not required, while 12% evaluated it as being very important. Therefore, one may deem that corporations affirm their interest in cooperation with startups and work on their solutions; however, this process is not a top priority for them, just as in the case of startups. Representatives of corporations rated the process of establishing cooperation as less than easy.

The scores for the responses given to the third question confirmed that acceleration programs play a crucial role and serve as a mechanism in bringing together startups and corporations and contribute to the commencement of cooperation between them. More than 95% of the research respondents on the part of the startups and the vast majority of the corporations confirmed the efficacy of the acceleration programs in bringing the parties together. Moreover, the startups positively welcome participation in such programs involving corporations. More than 70% of the startups in the research would recommend participation in the program to other new companies. However, participation in an acceleration program is less important for corporations than for startups.

The response to the fourth question is as follows: the initiatives undertaken by accelerators in connection with launching and running acceleration programs substantially contribute to establishing cooperation between startups and corporations. Startups confirmed that thanks to participation in acceleration programs involving corporations they can more quickly commercialize their product or service (84% of the entities in the research). Moreover, the respondents confirmed that participation in an acceleration program increases the chances of implementing innovation and entering into commercial agreements to sell products and services to corporations in the future. The average result for this question was 7.71 points ($SD = 2.29$). The final and fifth question referred to the benefits and the expenditures incurred by startups and large organizations in connection with establishing and maintaining cooperation. In both instances the respondents in the research conducted confirmed that cooperation was beneficial to both parties, and that the benefits outweigh the expenditures incurred.

The responses given to the various questions formed the basis for vetting the research assumptions that were embraced in reference to the diagnosis on how startups and corporations perceive acceleration programs. Table 4.1 depicts the list of assumptions and their verification

Table 4.1 Verification of the adopted research assumptions

No	*Research assumption*	*Result of verifying the research assumption*
1	Establishing cooperation with corporations is important to start-ups and this constitutes a challenge for the firms participating in the acceleration program.	Assumption confirmed
2	Establishing cooperation with start-ups is important to corporations and this is an arduous undertaking.	Assumption confirmed
3	Acceleration programs play a crucial role in bringing new firms together with large organizations.	Assumption confirmed
4	Accelerators and their acceleration programs significantly contribute to establishing cooperation between start-ups and corporations in connection with the need for start-ups to test their solutions on the market and as a result they greatly enhance the opportunities for start-ups to implement innovations and enter into commercial arrangements to sell their products and services to corporations.	Assumption confirmed
5	The participation of start-ups and large organizations in the acceleration programs organized by start-up accelerators engenders greater benefit than the expenditures incurred to establish and maintain their cooperation.	Assumption confirmed

Source: Proprietary material.

5 Cooperation between corporations and startups in acceleration programs – cognitive basis

The aspect indicated in the previous sub-chapter concerning the significance of acceleration programs for startups and corporations in terms of rolling out innovation and also confirming that the benefits ensuing from the established cooperation surpass the expenditures incurred to establish and sustain it triggered the in-depth analysis of inter-organizational cooperation between startups and corporations. This analysis was conducted with respect to key dimensions such as the goals, difficulties and challenges that the parties encounter during cooperation in acceleration programs. Accordingly, in this part of the book, the following research goals were formulated (second area of the research gap):

Goal 1 – Specifying the importance of the goals for establishing cooperation guiding startups and corporations as part of acceleration programs.
Goal 2 – Specifying the importance of the difficulties encountered by corporations and startups during their acceleration programs.
Goal 3 – Specifying the importance of the challenges encountered by corporations and startups when they participate in acceleration programs.
Goal 4 – Researching whether the intended goals of cooperation are achieved by the parties.

Having in mind the goals defined above, eight research questions were formulated, with two for each goal

1 What are the most important goals of corporations establishing cooperation with startups (**goal 1**)?
2 What are the most important goals of startups establishing cooperation with corporations (**goal 1**)?
3 What are the most important difficulties in corporations establishing cooperation with startups (**goal 2**)?
4 What are the most important difficulties in startups establishing cooperation with corporations (**goal 2**)?
5 What are the greatest challenges encountered by corporations during an acceleration program with the participation of startups (**goal 3**)?

DOI: 10.4324/9781003540366-6

6 What are the greatest challenges encountered by startups during an acceleration program with involving corporations (**goal 3**)?
7 Do corporations achieve the intended goals of cooperation with startups (**goal 4**)?
8 Do startups achieve the intended goals of cooperation with corporations (**goal 4**)?

Later in this book an attempt was made at responding to the various research questions.

5.1 Strategic goals for corporations to establish cooperation with startups

In the first step the importance of the goals of establishing cooperation by both parties was investigated. The goals were evaluated on a scale. Since these goals may diverge in the two groups of entities under research, the questions posed to the representatives of the startups and of the corporations were not identical. The responses were therefore analyzed separately in the two groups. First, the importance of the goals specified by corporations was scrutinized in the context of establishing cooperation with startups. As can be seen in Figure 5.1, 17 potential goals were sorted from the most important to the least important. What is noteworthy is that among the 25 corporations, there was no goal that could be deemed critical. The average result in the event of the most important goal – creating or developing an innovative technology/product/service/process/sales channel – was 7.6 points of 10 possible points. Only two other goals – minimizing a company's operating expenses and optimizing internal processes – had an average importance above 7 points (7.44 and 7.28 points, respectively). These three goals may be deemed to be important in terms of cooperation with startups. Additionally, another goal – maintaining or enhancing customer satisfaction – scored an average of 6.96 points, and thus very close to the value assumed to be the borderline for high scores. In the case of the next three goals, the value obtained was in the range of 6–7 points. Therefore, they may be deemed to be elevated. The goals of growing revenue on the activity conducted (6.64 points), creating the image of a modern company (6.24 points) and gaining access to innovative business models and trends (6.08 points) were rated within this range. The other goals were rated within a range of 4–6 points, meaning they were moderately important. No goal was scored below 4 points meaning that the representatives of the corporations taking part in the acceleration programs did not deem any aspect of the cooperation to be totally insignificant. Analyzing the average values assigned to the various goals one may observe that the goals of a clearly business-related nature were rated the highest as they have the potential to defend themselves, for instance, against project committees by demonstrating their potential economic benefits to the organization on the execution of selected projects.

Nice-to-have goals are lower in the hierarchy as they are perceived as less important to large organizations. Managers of corporations therefore place emphasis on identifying startups and their products that have a specific business case for their organizations. They believe that cooperation based on these projects has greater chances of achieving positive outcomes, which in turn translates into allocating to these undertakings the appropriate priority and assigning them the requisite resources – tangible and intangible alike.

Generating a financial return on the capital expenditures incurred for venture capital (4.04 points) and learning the approach from a startup for implementing innovations (4.20 points) were rated as being the least important goals. This may stem from several factors. First, corporations frequently have brittle structures that impede the implementation of agile operating models. Second, large organizations may not be fully poised to extract all of the benefits from these projects, especially when it comes to what are referred to as the "on-top business case". This means that even though corporations may see the prospective benefits inherent in the science of the agile methodologies for implementing the innovations adopted from startups, they encounter difficulties in finding the space and resources to implement them. In addition, one can frequently run into the conviction in corporations that certain activities are difficult or simply impossible to implement on account of the existing limitations stemming from procedures or the business model in-force. Consents must be obtained at different levels of the organization, which slows down the pace of decision-making and contributes to the impossibility phenomenon, that is, the conviction that the organization is incapable of phasing in innovative change. This feeling of impossibility is rooted in organizational structures and the culture of corporate work alike. When it comes to the return on capital expenditures, venture capital corporations are more frequently inclined to invest larger amounts in one tried-and-true business, such as USD 1 billion, rather than carrying out a number of smaller investments, such as 100 projects with a budget of USD 10 million each. This type of approach stems from the fact that a larger investment in a tried-and-true business is customarily less risky than the dissemination of capital to many smaller startup projects that may have less chance of survival and effective scaling up their business. Investing in smaller startups also entails the necessity of making many more investment decisions, which in turn increases the complexity of managing an investment portfolio. From the vantage point of large corporations, one larger investment in a tried-and-true business may better correspond to their strategic objectives in contrast to many smaller capital injections that require greater capital expenditures to monitor and support the various startups. It is also worthy of emphasis that corporations ordinarily have greater financial resources at their disposal than traditional venture capital funds and they can allow themselves to allocate greater means to an individual undertaking that portends well. In turn, venture capital funds, having regard for their distinct nature, must frequently diversify their investment portfolios to mitigate risk and enhance the chances of a return on their investment. For this reason widespread investing in startups and acquiring them from the market is not the principal goal of corporations. Additionally, one should observe that it is still the case that few corporations have their own in-house venture capital funds dedicated to making investments in new companies, which means that these investments are frequently outside the area of their core competences and strategic interests. It is also worth keeping in mind that a return on a capital investment of under 20 million dollars is relatively small given the scale of a large corporation, which means that these types of investments are less attractive to them. From the perspective of large organizations, equity exposure to startups may not accrue sufficiently substantial benefits so as to justify the efforts associated with monitoring and managing such investments. Additionally, it is worth drawing attention to one research finding depicted in Figure 5.1, namely the extensive variation in the scores given by the individual representatives of the companies participating in the acceleration programs. This is manifested by a large standard error. This means that there is no one general model for the goals of establishing cooperation with startups among the representatives of large organizations. Analysis of the minimum and maximum scores for each one of the subordinated goals demonstrated that only for three goals – creating or developing an innovative and specialized technology/product/service/process/sales channel, creating the image of a modern company and maintaining or enhancing customer satisfaction, the minimum score was more than one point. In the case of the first of these goals the minimum score was 5 points. Therefore, no representative of a corporation deemed this goal to be insignificant, but in the other two instances the lowest assigned score was 2 points. In the case of the other 14 goals, at least one company representative assigned the value of 1, in other words, that person indicated that a given goal was not at all valuable to that person. On the other hand, there was only one goal (generating a financial return on the capital expenditures incurred for venture capital) where the assigned maximum score was 8 points. In all of the other goals at least one representative of a corporation indicated that it was very important or outright crucial for that person. The maximum score was 10 points in the case of nine goals.

Considering the foregoing, one should note that on the market there is diversity in the approaches of corporations to the goals of establishing cooperation with startups. This diversity stems from a host of factors that shape the strategies and priorities of these organizations. Above all, these goals may differ depending on the operating strategy embraced by a corporation. Organizations placing emphasis on innovations may perceive cooperation with startups as crucial for their own ability to market new products. In turn, corporations with a more conservative approach may treat these partnerships as incremental but not as indispensable support in executing their main business goals. The history of collaboration as part of acceleration programs may also affect how corporations define their goals for cooperation. Organizations that already have experience in successful cooperation with

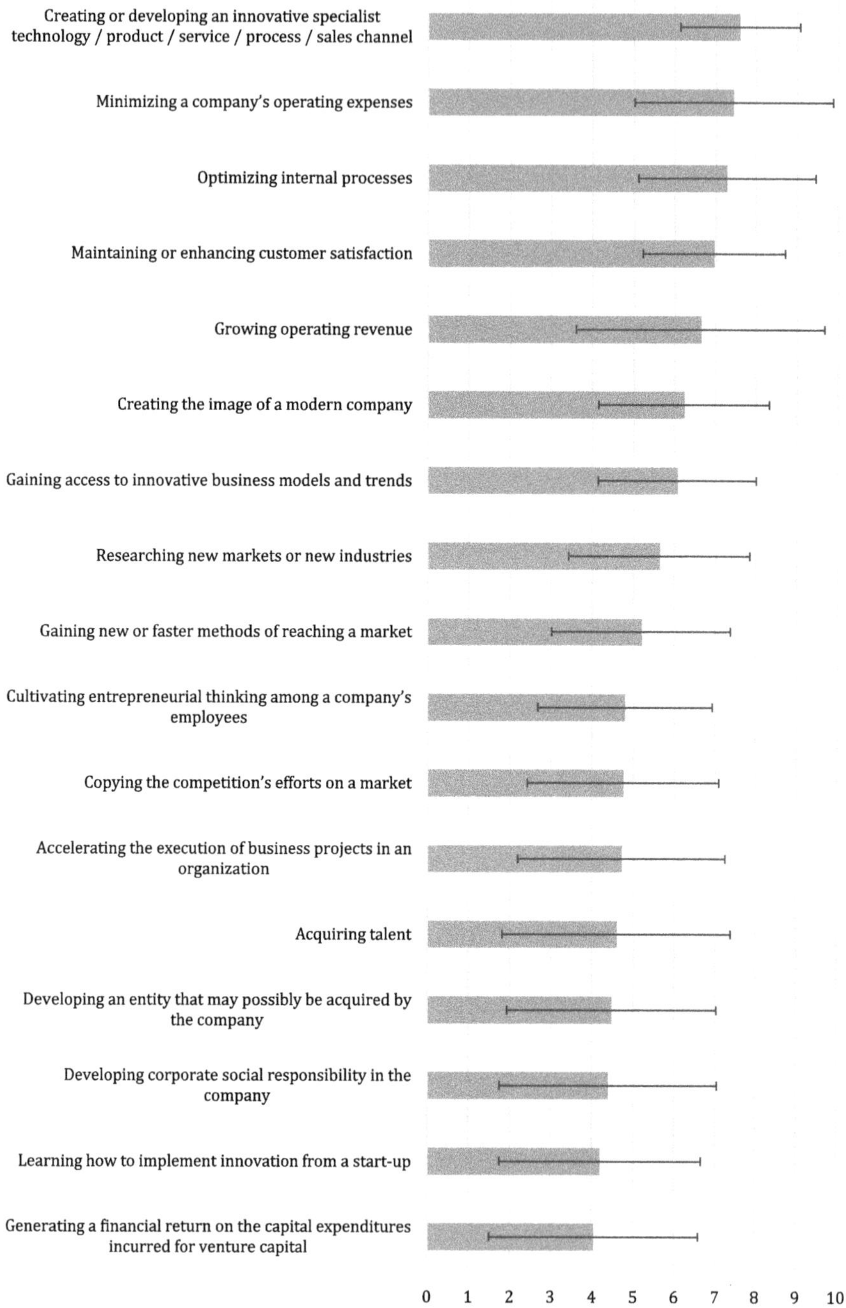

Figure 5.1 Importance of the specific goals for establishing cooperation with a startup from the viewpoint of the representatives of corporations. The average value (bar) and the standard deviation (hooks) are depicted.

Source: Proprietary material.

startups may have more precisely defined goals and greater expectations of these programs. In turn, corporations that are just starting their adventure with accelerators may be more cautious and have more varied expectations. For that reason, the experience gleaned during previous rounds of cooperation with startups also plays a major role in shaping goals. Corporations that have encountered difficulties or limitations in prior projects may draw conclusions from them and more precisely define their goals in future acceleration programs thereby endeavoring to avoid previous mistakes. Moreover, observation indicates that the organizational culture of a corporation also affects how the goals of cooperation are articulated. Corporations with an innovative culture that are open to change will be more inclined to establish flexible partnerships with startups. In turn, organizations with a more hierarchical and conservative culture may have a more formalized and restrictive approach to such cooperation. In the end the industry in which the corporation operates also determines the goals for cooperation. Cooperation with startups may be perceived as indispensable to maintain competitiveness in industries with a high technological dynamic such as IT. In other industries, such as heavy industry, the goals for cooperation may be more oriented on optimizing processes and reducing costs, and not necessarily at product-related innovations.

5.2 The goals of startups in cooperation with corporations

A similar question posed to the representatives of the startups revealed the existence of three goals which may be deemed to be critical for these types of businesses because their mean was above 8 points. The most important goal unambiguously identified by respondents was product or service development with the highest mean of 8.42 points. Goals related to verifying a product's market match (8.29 points) and obtaining a reference for later sales (8.28 points) were in the next positions. Another goal, though rated slightly lower, was product testing or Minimum Viable Product (MVP) with a score of 7.99 points, which also points to it being of crucial importance to representatives of the startups in terms of cooperation with a corporation.

The managers of startups when they elect to participate in an acceleration programs involving corporations embrace a pragmatic business approach. They treat large organizations not only as experts in a given market area but also as prospective future business partners. Participation in such programs is perceived as a strategic opportunity for the development, vetting and sales of their product, which is critical to the long-term success of the startup. In their activities the managers of startups think in a dual-track mode in terms of carrying out their pilots. First, they focus on cooperation directly with a given corporation, counting on subsequent implementation and commercialization of their solution as part of a large organization. Second, they perceive a corporation as a partner in reaching a broader market.

This approach enables startups to augment the scale of their activity and also to gain valuable references, which may open the doors to new markets and more contracts.

In the case of the next three goals, the mean values recorded were in the range of 7–8 points. Therefore, one may also deem them to be high. These goals are in order as follows: image-related benefits, marketing and PR (7.81 points), gaining access to markets or extending pre-existing sales channels (7.57 points) and sourcing funding, or not having to search for external grants and investors (7.22 points).

The next four goals were rated on average at 6–7 points, therefore one may consider this value to be elevated, though in three cases these results are closer to the lower value in this range. These goals are as follows: acquiring clients/access to a client database (6.85 points), refining a product or MVP (6.13 points), getting to know the market and mentoring (6.08 points) and launching the product on foreign markets (6.02 points). The other goals were rate on average at 4–6 points, thus the value for startups was moderate. Just as in the case of the results obtained from research on corporations in respect of the goals of cooperation one may assert that none of the goals under examination can be deemed to be totally unimportant. The minimum values were 1 point and the maximum values were 10 points for each one of the 16 goals rated by the startups. This means that within the group of 101 startups, some rated the most important goal as totally insignificant, while others deemed the least valuable goal to be crucial. Even though the template for critical goals appears to be more uniform among startups, one should remain cautious when defining general templates for the goals of cooperation since they may vary depending on the internal factors that are characteristic of the various startups.

The difference in the goals of startups with respect to cooperation with corporations may ensue from several factors. Above all, startups participating in acceleration programs ordinarily are at different growth stages and therefore they have varying priorities. For instance, new startups in the MVP phase may concentrate principally on the desire to test their products and secure their first references. This will enable them to secure further funding for business development. In the case of more mature startups that already have certain market accomplishments on their account, their goals may be more complicated and encompass scaling up business and winning new markets. Similarly, the distinct nature of a product, service or market on which a given startup operates also has in principle a major impact on the setting of goals as part of acceleration programs. Startups developing advanced technologies such as artificial intelligence or biotechnology may have different needs from ones offering consumer products. In the former instance the crucial goal may be validation of technology and adapting it to the distinct requirements while in the latter instance the goal may be to win new sales markets. Figure 5.2 depicts the results of the importance of the specified goals of cooperation for startups.

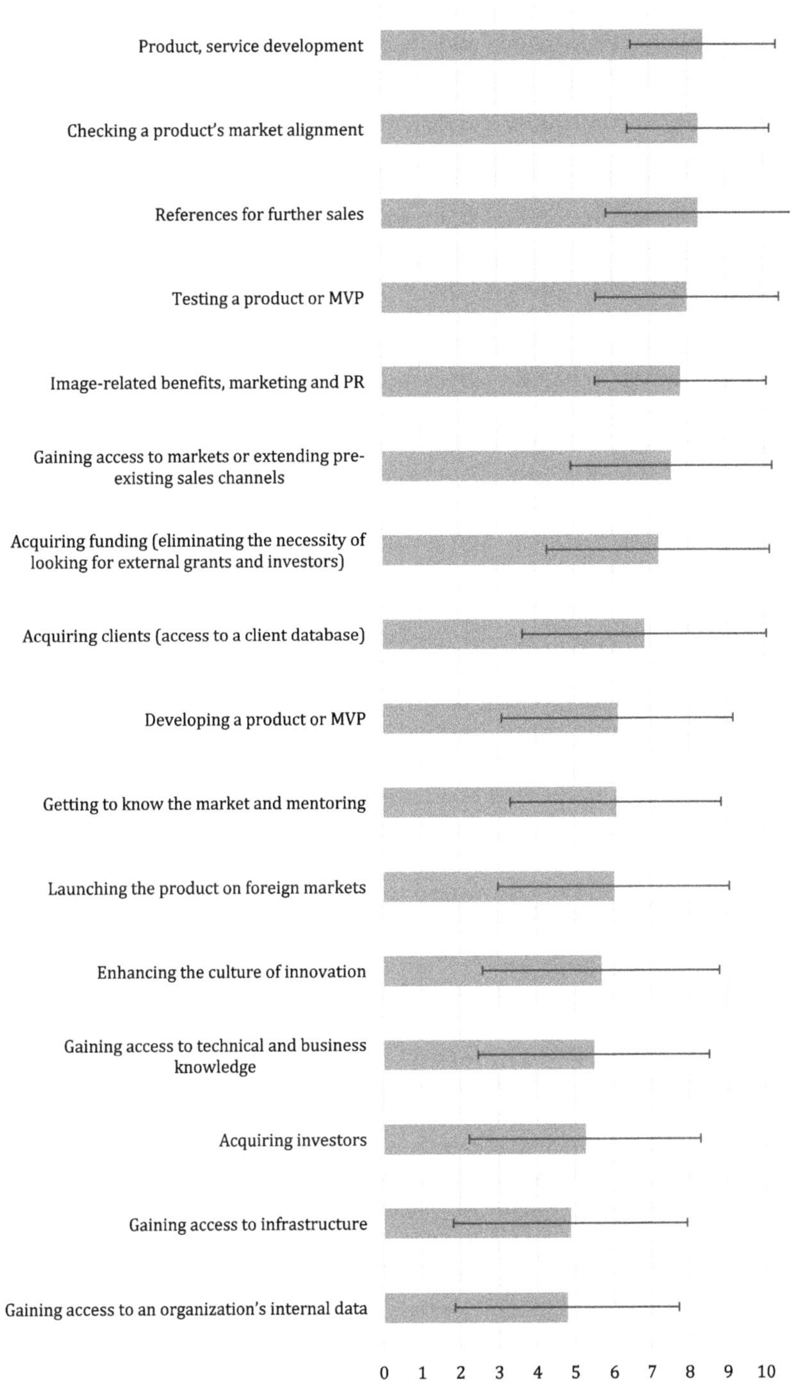

Figure 5.2 Importance of the specific goals for establishing cooperation with a corporation from the viewpoint of the representatives of startups. The average value (bar) and the standard deviation (hooks) are depicted.

Source: Proprietary material.

5.3 Difficulties involved with shaping partnerships between corporations and startups

Next, we checked what difficulties are encountered in establishing cooperation according to corporations and startups. These difficulties were rated on a scale. These difficulties were articulated differently in the two groups (though some of them could overlap). That is why the responses given by the two parties were discussed first. It was not until the next step that they were directly juxtaposed with one another. Figure 5.3 depicts the importance of a difficulty for corporations when establishing cooperation with startups. The responses provided by the representatives of corporations were balanced – in no event did we find any dimension that would be extremely difficult or very easy for the representatives to handle. One aspect was rated above 7 points – namely the difference in the pace of decision-making between the company and startups. This may be deemed to be a relatively high level depicting the importance of this difficulty (7.24 points). What's more, this difficulty was not rated by any respondent as not being very problematic – the minimum ascribed rank was 5 points. Representatives of the corporations are aware that their organizations operate slowly but they deem this attitude to be an equitable approach to startups. It should be noted that certain exceptions from this rule can appear on the market – persons managing the innovation area are capable of building what are referred to as "rapid action paths" to implement innovations coming to corporations from the outside world. The next two dimensions – the aspect of bureaucracy and the overly excessive expectations of startups pertaining to the forms of support provided by a technology client – were rated at a level from 6 to 7 points (specifically 6.68 and 6.04 points). One may therefore deem that the evaluation of the importance of these difficulties was elevated. Corporations are characterized by the fact that they are bureaucratized, while their approach to startups must proceed in a fixed similar fashion as in respect to other business partners (the audit path is preserved). Large organizations ordinarily apply procedures that are identical and are in force with respect to projects for EUR 3 million and for ones with budgets of roughly EUR 100,000.

In turn, only one aspect was deemed to be not very significant – the absence of a geographical match was identified by representatives of corporations at the level of 3.96 points on average. The pandemic altered the approach, and the corporation's management is placing ever greater emphasis on solutions that can have a supraregional nature. Frequently, the employees of the research and development (R&D) and innovation departments and the units cooperating with startups exhibit greater openness to change than is encountered in other business units (e.g., production or sales). Employees employed in R&D departments are usually responsible for the development of new products or services and the R&D activities related to that. This work requires them to demonstrate creativity, innovativeness and openness to change. Moreover, the process of creating new solutions frequently calls for experimenting, testing and introducing changes. Similarly, employees of

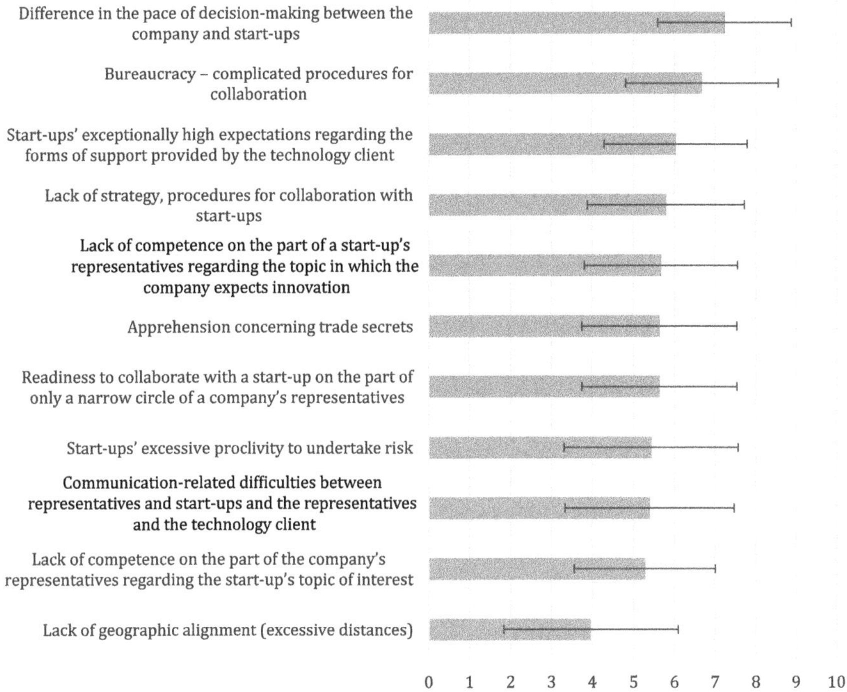

Figure 5.3 Importance of the specific difficulties in establishing cooperation with a startup from the viewpoint of the representatives of corporations. The average value (bar) and the standard deviation (hooks) are depicted.

Source: Proprietary material.

units cooperating with startups deal with new companies that are frequently more innovative and flexible in their decision-making than large organizations. Cooperation with these companies demands openness to new ideas and approach to work and cultivating relationships with the environment. That is why these persons are not necessarily focused on solutions originating from the given country in which their organization functions.

It is worth noting that the pressure of competition on corporations is more and more frequently originating not from similar companies operating in the same sector but from their broader surroundings. The openness of corporations and of acceleration programs to solutions transcending the boundaries of a country may accrue better outcomes and the achievement of the intended goals of cooperation between corporations, accelerators and startups. The domestic market (e.g., the Polish market) is smaller than the German market, for instance. If the scouting of startups is under way in a given region, then over time it turns out that a given market has been exploited in full and does not generate new valuable projects for large organizations. That is why corporations and accelerators should more broadly open themselves up to cooperation than just focus on the local market. Furthermore, the progressing digitization of businesses and globalization have substantially contributed to attenuating the significance of geographic match in terms of establishing cooperation.

The other dimensions were rated as being less problematic, with a mean result of 5–6 points. Once again, in 3 of the 11 difficulties under examination, the full spread of responses given by the representatives of corporations was recorded – the minimum was 1 and the maximum was 10 points. Thus these difficulties, such as communication problems between representatives of the startups and representatives of the technology client, startups' overly excessive proclivity to undertake risk and the lack of competences on the part of the representatives of the startups in a subject area in which the company expects innovation were rated as being insignificant, while others deemed this to be crucial.

The spread in the responses given by representatives of the corporations may stem from the varying approach, experience and values or its absence in respect to specific difficulties in establishing cooperation. An organization operating on many markets may have a totally different approach to perceiving startups in terms of the possibilities of cooperation and the identified difficulties than a corporation operating solely on one market. As may be observed, representatives of the corporations demonstrated an even-keeled approach without identifying any aspect of cooperation as extremely difficult or easy. In particular, the difference in the decision-making pace between corporations and startups has been rated as the most problematic, which reflects the complexity of decision-making processes in large organizations. The additional difficulties ascertained in the conducted research such as bureaucracy and the overly excessive expectations of startups in terms of support from corporations also received elevated scores. This highlights that cooperation with startups requires of corporations not just flexibility but also the skill of managing the expectations of new companies that may frequently overvalue their needs and the possibilities of support on the part of large organizations.

5.4 The key difficulties involved with startups building cooperation with corporations

The responses given by the representatives of the startups displayed in Figure 5.4 demonstrate the existence of two very important dimensions defining the key difficulties in establishing cooperation with a corporation. The time-consuming decision-making process applied by corporations has received a mean rating of 8.56 points of the maximum ten possible. It is worth observing that even though both parties, that is, startups and corporations have defined the possible difficulties in a heterogeneous manner, the key problem of cooperation has proven to be time and the disconnect relating to the pace of operation. This aspect was flagged by the representatives of the

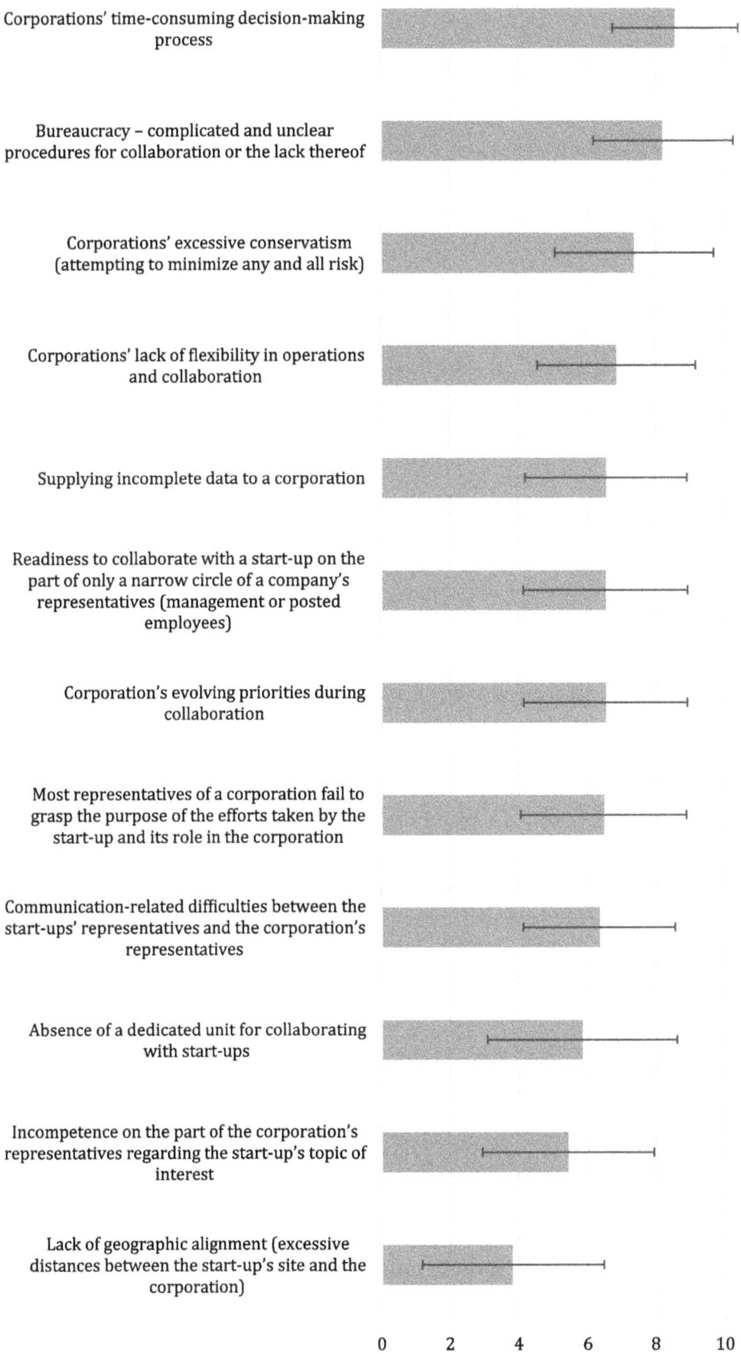

Figure 5.4 Importance of specific difficulties experienced by the representatives of startups involved with establishing cooperation with a corporation. The average value (bar) and the standard deviation (hooks) are depicted.

Source: Proprietary material.

startups as being more problematic, as the foregoing mean assigned to this group of respondents indicates. The perception of time substantially differentiates the two parties to cooperation. For a startup the main unit of time is frequently "15 minutes", while for corporations that same 15-minute period may signify "1 week". The managers of startups, to be able to stay afloat on the market, frequently must make decisions to suspend negotiations with corporations to focus on the execution of current projects, especially when they have other clients or they perceive prospective clients on the horizon with whom they can achieve business success more quickly. Nevertheless, it is worth remembering that for the management of startups the time dedicated to talks with corporations implies not just a potential risk associated with doing business but also an opportunity of dynamic growth and the possibility of greatly scaling up the business.

In turn, for corporations, the slower pace is part of the embraced operating strategy and above all it constitutes a form of securing its position. Corporations must operate in accordance with established procedures, which frequently entails longer decision-making processes for the purpose of mitigating risk and procuring compliance with internal standards. This collision of differences in terms of the perception of time may constitute a major challenge in the cooperation between startups and large organizations. Another very important dimension of the indicated difficulties is the aspect of bureaucracy (8.21 points). This dimension once again overlaps with the second largest difficulty also shown by corporations. This result is also very interesting and shows that problems with formalities impede the lives of both parties in this process and these parties are aware of their existence. The awareness of this problem and its importance for both parties appears to be crucial when it comes to drafting simpler procedures for the purposes of cooperation in acceleration programs. Another important dimension of difficulty identified by representatives of the startups is the excessive conservatism of corporations rated on average at 7.37 points. This conservatism is predicated on striving to mitigate any and all risk and may ensue from the absence of a developed culture of innovation and limited openness to new ideas in corporations, including the absence of what is referred to as "consent to failure". In terms of innovation this process frequently spans trying multiple solutions where not all of them prove to be effective at the end of the day. Introducing an approach based on a "consent to failure" could substantially improve the climate of cooperation between corporations and startups. Such a culture promulgates openness to experimentation and learning by mistake, which is crucial for the development of innovations. Corporations that are capable of understanding and adapting to this approach may not just cooperate better with startups but they may also gain a competitive edge on the market. Moreover, striving to mitigate any and all risk may be associated with the fact that the managers in corporations frequently lack a mandate to make decisions encumbered with greater risk. They must submit the project to different types of committees multiple times so as, on one hand, to secure the engagement of the corporation's proper organizational units and their resources and, on the other hand, obtain all of the corporate consents.

Difficulty in almost all of the other dimensions was rated as being moderate or slightly elevated (results in the range of 5–7 points). Only one dimension – lack of geographic match – was flagged as being insignificant (mean of 3.82 points). What is interesting, a similar score given by representatives of the startups and of the corporations is visible in this scope, too – this aspect was rated similarly as being not very problematic in both groups.

The results obtained indicate that representatives of the corporations and of the startups alike similarly rate the difficulties associated with cooperation. The depiction of these results and their discussion with both parties participating in acceleration programs may contribute to overcoming existing obstacles, which as a consequence may elevate the effectiveness of the cooperation being established.

The table with the overall evaluation of the level of difficulty of cooperation between startups and large organizations proved to be interesting. The Student's *t*-test for independent samples demonstrated a statistically significant difference in evaluating difficulty – representatives of the startups rated it as more demanding (mean of 3.96 on a 5-point scale of difficulty) compared to the representatives of corporations (mean of 3.36), $p = 0.010$. This outcome comports with the evaluation of the individual difficulties presented above – representatives of the startups generally assigned greater importance to specified difficulties of cooperation than the representatives of the corporations. Figure 5.5 depicts the result.

To gain a better grasp on the evaluation of the aspects of cooperation and the related difficulties, it is worth noting that startups must customarily adapt to corporations' operating models, schemes of conduct, prevailing

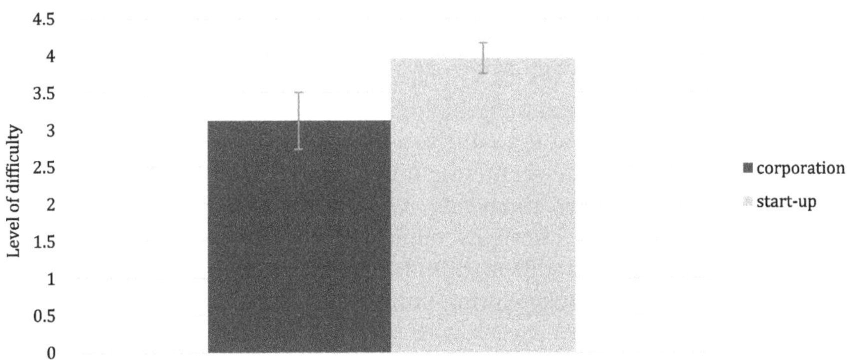

Figure 5.5 Comparison of the general difficulty encountered in cooperation between a startup and a corporation on the part of the two partners in acceleration programs. The average value (bar) and the standard error (hooks) are depicted.

Source: Proprietary material.

procedures and processes, not vice versa. For corporations cooperation with startups frequently does not constitute the main components of their strategy but is rather treated as an auxiliary activity. In turn, for startups cooperation with a corporation and the pursuit of shared projects are frequently a priority that may determine the new company's "to be or not to be". As a result, startups feel greater pressure to attain rapid results and ordinarily they are the party with a poorer position in their relationships. Besides that, a smaller startup team also forms a certain type of limitation to achieving cooperation. In many instances startups have merely a few key persons at their disposal – one person responsible for technology, one for sales and one for operating activity. In the meantime, in corporations, teams are much more sizable, which translates into greater resources and specialization. For instance, the legal department in a corporation frequently hires more people than the entire startup team. In many cases, the startup faces experts, corporate departments, etc. in the cooperation process. Therefore, it appears that this may be the source of the evaluation stated above of the level of difficulty related to cooperation between startups and large organizations.

5.5 Challenges faced by corporations and startups during an acceleration program

In the next step the decision was made to take a look at the dimensions of the challenges in cooperation between a corporation and a startup during the established inter-organizational cooperation. The challenges have been evaluated on a scale; Figure 5.6 depicts the evaluations rendered by representatives of corporations. The first thing that draws attention is the fact that no challenge has been rated very high. The highest average score was recorded for the challenge related to agreeing on the appropriate sales cycle for a commercial agreement after completing the Proof of Concept (POC) phase, whose average score is 6.52 points. This may ensue from the fact that the switchover from the POC phase to the commercial phase requires the engagement of a substantially higher number of organizational units on the part of the corporation than at the previous stage meaning the acceleration program. The process of entering into a contract following POC during the post-acceleration stage frequently involves the engagement of a totally new team, including new business units, the security department and the legal department, which are brought in for negotiations and form an integral part of the process of implementing innovations. This stage is highly time-consuming since it calls for stating with precision the details of future efforts so that the startup's product is complete and above all becomes an effectively functioning part of a corporation.

In turn, the challenge presented by the rivalry between the startup and the development department of a large organization has been unambiguously rated as not being very important (average score of 3.36). The other challenges should be deemed to be of average importance.

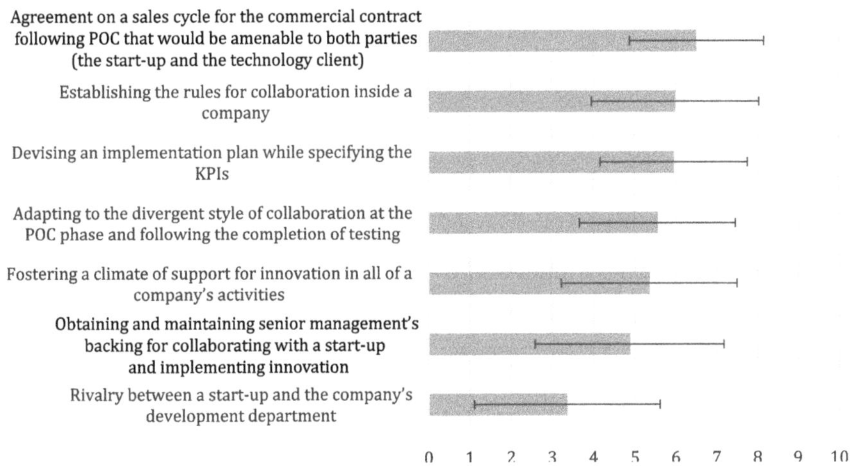

Figure 5.6 Importance of specific challenges experienced by representatives of a corporation in the cooperation between a corporation and a startup. The average value (bar) and the standard deviation (hooks) are depicted.

Source: Proprietary material.

The solutions devised by startups are in principle complementary with the operations of corporations. The innovation and R&D departments in corporations do not directly compete with startups and their products as part of acceleration programs as there is a clearly defined line of demarcation pertaining to cooperation with startups in the open innovation model. Strategic projects of crucial importance continue to be executed in-house by the R&D Department and the Innovation Department of large organizations, which makes it possible to retain control over the most important initiatives. In turn, solutions of lesser importance, lower budgets and priorities are carried out in cooperation with external partners such as startups. This approach based on a clear split between strategic projects and the ones of lesser importance is beneficial to corporations and startups. It is important for corporations to be flexible when defining this demarcation line. The innovation market is dynamic and some projects initially deemed to be less significant may over time take on strategic meaning.

A similar analysis in the group of representatives of the startups demonstrated an even greater flattening of the evaluation concerning the challenges posed by cooperation with corporations (Figure 5.7). All of the dimensions were rated as being important on average. What is crucial is that each of the nine dimensions received at least 1 point, while the maximum score was 10 points. This means that all of the challenges could simultaneously be treated as insignificant and critical for the various representatives of the startups. It, therefore, seems that in contrast to the analysis of difficulties the ability to draw conclusions and assumptions for the future based on the answers given by the respondents is greatly restricted when dealing with challenges.

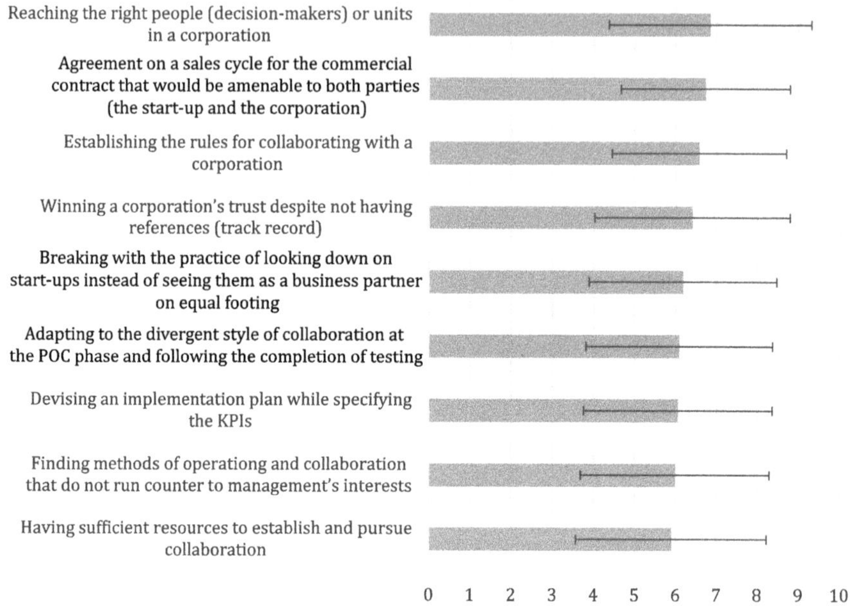

Figure 5.7 Importance of specific challenges experienced by representatives of startups in the cooperation between a corporation and a startup. The average value (bar) and the standard deviation (hooks) are depicted.

Source: Proprietary material.

It is worth noting the three challenges rated the highest by representatives of the startups in terms of inter-organizational cooperation. In this research the following were named as the largest challenges: reaching the right people or units in a corporation, agreement on a sales cycle for the commercial contract that would be amenable to both parties and establishing the rules for collaborating with a corporation. These challenges reflect the key difficulties that startups face in establishing and maintaining relationships with large organizations. First, reaching the appropriate decision makers in a corporation is frequently time consuming and complicated, which forms a significant obstacle for startups that operate under the pressure of time and limited resources. Shortening the decision-making process may be critical for saving time and resources, which in turn influences the effectiveness of cooperation. In the case of large organizations that have expansive structures and hierarchies, identifying the right units and persons responsible for business decisions is a challenge that may postpone negotiation and implementation processes.

Second, agreeing on a sales cycle and cooperation rules is a key challenge as marketing a startup's product through a corporation calls for precisely defining the terms and conditions of cooperation, including the budget, resources and key performance indicators (KPIs). The business units in corporations that are responsible for these negotiations may have other priorities and expectations than the startups, which may engender difficulty in striking an agreement. In these instances, the lack of understanding for the distinct nature of the operation of startups may lead to putting forward conditions that would be difficult to fulfill, which may threaten the further functioning of the startup and lead to it being excessively dependent on a single corporation. Attention should also be paid to market practices that may additionally complicate cooperation. Frequently corporations insert clauses in contracts that ban competition or place a requirement of having exclusivity. This may curtail the possibilities of development and scaling up the startup's business on the market. These clauses may constitute a grave risk for new companies that are endeavoring to diversify their client database and become independent of single business partners.

5.6 Evaluation of the level to which corporations and startups achieve their goals for cooperation under acceleration programs

In the final step the level of achieving the intended goals of establishing cooperation by both parties in acceleration programs was investigated. Since these goals may diverge in the two groups of entities under research, the questions posed to the representatives of the startups and of the corporations were not identical. The responses were therefore analyzed separately in the two groups.

First, the level of achieving a corporation's specific goals was scrutinized in the context of establishing cooperation with a startup. As can be seen in Figure 5.8 the representatives of corporations evaluate the level of achieving their goals as relatively average. The average scores for these 17 potential goals fall within a range of 4.35–6.64 points. Substantial variation of the scores has been recorded for each goal as illustrated by the value of standard deviation. Therefore, among the corporations in the research that participated in startup acceleration programs, there was more than one case in which the very same goals were not achieved at all by one of the large organizations or were achieved in full by another corporation. The differences in the evaluation probably stem from the corporations' approach to acceleration programs. Different units and lines of business are in play in the organizations in the research, while decision makers can set different goals for them to achieve. The open innovation formula makes it possible to pursue a broad spectrum of goals. There are organizations that may have nearly 20 goals and there are businesses that may have a mere 3 goals for instance. However, endeavoring to draw general conclusions, the average values presented below have been analyzed.

Two goals were rated much worse than the other goals: sourcing talent and generating a financial return on the expenditures incurred for venture capital. The representatives of corporations gave these goals low scores of 4.35 and 4.48 points, respectively, out of a possible 10 points. It appears

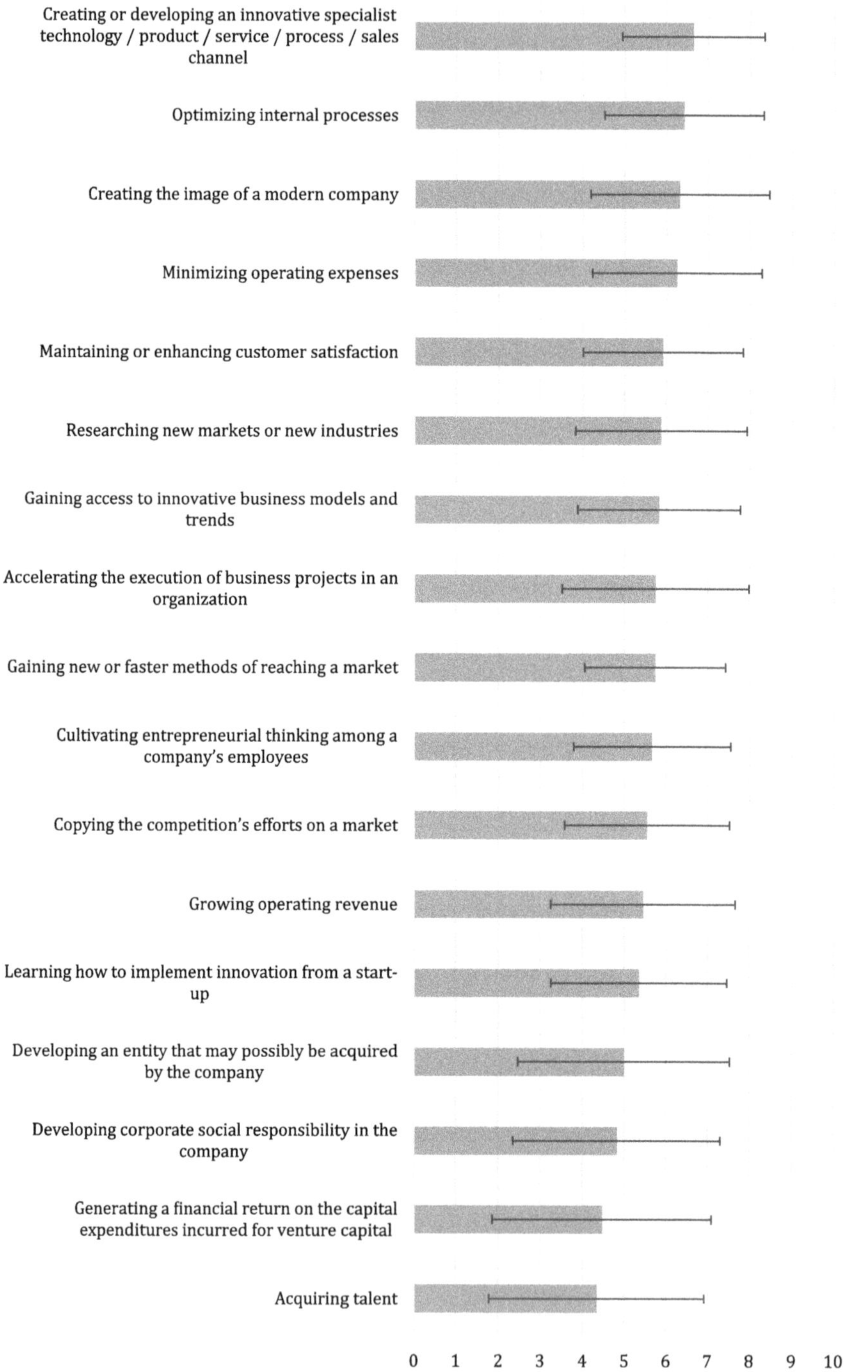

Figure 5.8 Level of corporations achieving their goals for inter-organizational cooperation in acceleration programs.

Source: Proprietary material.

that corporations are not capable of sourcing talents from startup teams for several reasons. The first one is the fact that startup teams join acceleration programs with the intention among other things of developing and testing their own product in a corporate environment, sourcing resources and funding and finding a client. The goal of the startup team is therefore not to move to the corporation. Additionally, the goal of sourcing talents is usually within the mandate of the departments responsible for employee recruitment and development and they do not generally take part directly in acceleration programs. The author's experience indicates that sourcing talent is frequently treated as an "incremental" goal for a corporation to participate in an acceleration program, but not as a priority. That means that corporations may not attach sufficient importance to this aspect, which consequently engenders the low scores given to this goal. Moreover, startups can have several options to choose from when talking about business partners and investors, and therefore their teams do not have to be interested in switching jobs to move to a corporation. Startups that are capable of sourcing resources and financing on their own have greater freedom in maintaining their independence, which additionally diminishes the probability of their members being interested in job offers in a corporation. That is also why corporations that want to benefit effectively from acceleration programs as a tool to source talent may find it necessary to employ a more integrated approach in which recruitment departments will work more closely with the teams responsible for innovations. In this manner they could better identify and attract valuable talents from the startup ecosystem.

Referring to the goal of generating a financial return on the expenditures incurred for venture capital, just as was mentioned before, one should record the fact that there continue to be few corporations on the market that have such an investment vehicle. Besides that, the goal of generating a return on investment may be achieved in a longer period (e.g., ten years), where that is a distant perspective, which transcends the scope of the acceleration program. For that reason, even if a corporation covered by the research has an investment fund that invests in startups, it may not yet perceive the benefits flowing from its engagement in the startup acceleration program at the time of evaluating the fulfillment of this goal.

The goals of developing corporate social responsibility in the company (4.83 points), developing the entity that may potentially be acquired by the company (5 points), learning the approach taken to implement innovations from a startup (5.36 points) and enhancing revenue on the business activity conducted (5.46 points) were also evaluated as being below the average value of 5.5 points (the potential scale fell within the range of 1–10 points). It is noteworthy that the revenue stemming from cooperation between a corporation and startups may not emerge immediately, but rather at a later stage during post-acceleration where negotiations and product commercialization are of critical significance. During the initial phase of cooperation, the corporate teams dealing with external innovations may not perceive the generation of revenue as a top priority goal. Rather, they concentrate on testing and implementing innovative solutions that may produce financial benefits in the long-term perspective, most frequently over a two or three years horizon. This strategy enables corporations to build a robust technological and market base before it begins to expect measurable financial gains on cooperation with startups.

Representatives of the corporations deemed creating or developing an innovative specialist technology/product/service/process/sales channel (6.64 points) to be the goal achieved to the greatest extent. This result confirms the most frequent goal for a corporation to join acceleration programs. The goals of optimizing internal processes (6.42 points), creating the image of a modern company (6.32 points) and minimizing a company's operating expenses (6.26 points) were also rated relatively well. The above goals (optimizing processes, company image, minimizing costs) should be juxtaposed with the goal of enhancing revenue by establishing cooperation. It appears that it would be easier to demonstrate that a solution developed by a startup contributes to reducing expenses or optimizing processes than to prove that a product, service or technology developed by a startup contributes to growing the topline of a corporation. This is related to the innovations arising from running acceleration programs pertaining more to tasks involving optimization and cutting the operating expenses of corporations. It is assumed that it is easier to engage in these types of implementations and thereby for the management of large organizations to demonstrate success. The other goals were rated as slightly positive. The scores ranged from 5.5 to 6 points.

A similar analysis conducted on a sample of representatives of the startups demonstrated higher fulfillment in terms of the achievement of self-set intended goals. Only 3 of the 16 proposals considered received a negative rating. The fulfillment of the goal of sourcing investors (4.49 points) and launching the product on foreign markets (4.62 points) was rated the worst. The unsatisfactory results in these two areas clearly stood out against the backdrop of the other responses. As was observed when discussing the results on the goals achieved by corporations, acceleration programs involving corporations are clearly more poised to developing a startup business than to sourcing investors. Similarly, the internationalization of a startup is not the principal goal of these programs. The internationalization process calls for an in-depth analysis of the future market, and it frequently also calls for aligning the current solution to the preferences of new buyers and establishing business relationships with local partners. This may generate a need for incurring substantial financial expenditures and requires a lot of time and knowledge, which startups, especially ones at their initial stage of operation or in the growth phase most frequently do not ordinarily have. The internationalization process also unseldomly transcends the framework and resources of standard acceleration programs.

The third goal for which the level of achievement was recorded below the theoretical average value was gaining clients (access to a database of clients). The average score for this goal was 5.48 points. This may stem from the fact that startups frequently base their products on technologies that have not yet been widely marketed, meaning that these solutions are not generally known to prospective customers (no recognition). Additionally, startups frequently consist of technological teams with a preponderance of scientists, meaning that they may have limited experience in the sale of products and services, which in turn impedes the process of establishing relationships with prospective partners and clients. Additionally, startups ordinarily have limited resources at their disposal (e.g., poorly developed sales channels or low expenditures for marketing activity) whereby they may encounter difficulties in reaching prospective clients. It is also worth drawing attention to the possibility of employing an incorrect sales strategy and business model embraced for the startup's operation. This may entail concentrating sales efforts on the wrong clients, operating on the wrong markets and as a consequence on failing to win clients. One interesting aspect may also be the situation in which startups did not have the goal of winning clients when they joined an acceleration program. Their main goal could be product or service development, as well as testing a solution in a large organization. In such an instance the "client" in the traditional meaning of this word may not be present on the other side since the startup's priority was not sales, but rather developing and vetting a product, service or technology.

It is noteworthy that the representatives of the startups were capable of clearly identifying the goals which they managed to achieve in the vast majority of cases in comparison to the corporations. Three goals stood out in terms of the level of their fulfillment versus the other goals, that is, testing a product or MVP (8.03 points), followed by product/service development (7.80 points) and product or MVP design (7.76 points). The foregoing results confirm the idea that stands behind acceleration programs involving corporations. Most frequently, the goal of these programs is the possibility of conducting a pilot on the basis of an existing solution in a test environment, on a selected sample of a large organization's clients and utilizing the knowledge of the industrial experts working for large entities who may help in product development (e.g., proposing changes to the startup's technology or business strategy and its effective implementation). The next three goals were rated above 7 points – checking a product's market alignment (7.42 points), image-related benefits, marketing and PR (7.31 points) and references for further sales (7.28 points). The other goals were rated as slightly positive. The average scores were in the range from 5.5 to 6.7 points. Figure 5.9 depicts all of the results.

As part of the second research task an analysis was conducted of startups' cooperation with corporations in acceleration programs. The importance was stated for the goals, difficulties and challenges in inter-organizational cooperation, and an evaluation was conducted on whether the parties achieve

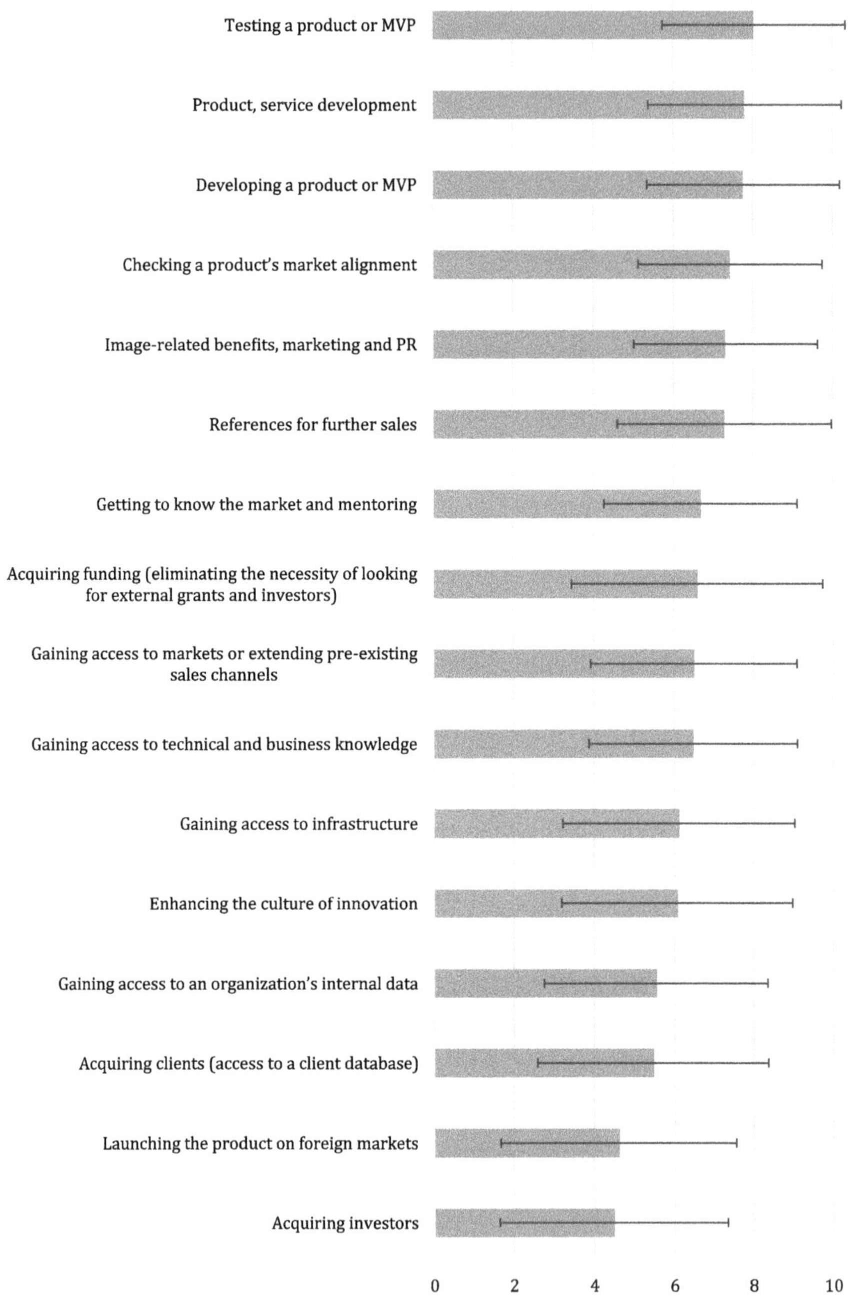

Figure 5.9 Level of startups achieving their goals for inter-organizational cooperation in acceleration programs.

Source: Proprietary material.

their intended goals by participating in acceleration programs. The analysis of the results obtained formed the basis for responses to the following eight research questions as part of the four research goals.

Responding to the first question: What are the most important goals of corporations establishing cooperation with startups? – large organizations rated the following goals the highest:

1 creating or developing an innovative specialist technology/product/service/process/sales channel;
2 minimizing a company's operating expenses;
3 optimizing internal processes;
4 maintaining or enhancing customer satisfaction.

In response to the second question: What are the most important goals of startups establishing cooperation with corporations? – the representatives of the startups flagged:

1 product or service development;
2 ability to check a product's market alignment;
3 obtaining references for further sales;
4 ability to test a product or MVP.

The third research question pertained to indicating the greatest difficulties in corporations establishing cooperation with startups. Representatives of large organizations specified the following as their greatest difficulties:

1 difference in the pace of decision-making between the company and startups;
2 aspect of bureaucracy – complicated procedures for collaboration;
3 startups' exceptionally high expectations regarding the forms of support provided by the technology client.

In respect of the fourth question, the following should be deemed to be the greatest difficulties in startups establishing cooperation with corporations:

1 corporations' time-consuming decision-making process;
2 aspect of bureaucracy – complicated and unclear procedures for collaboration or the lack thereof;
3 corporations' excessive conservatism (large organizations attempting to minimize any and all risk).

The responses provided to the fifth question indicate that corporations report the largest challenges in cooperating with startups in the following aspects:

1 agreement on a sales cycle for the commercial contract following POC that would be amenable to both parties (the startup and the technology client);

2 establishing the rules for collaboration inside a company;
3 devising an implementation plan while specifying the KPIs.

The largest challenges for the representatives of the startups according to the sixth question are as follows:

1 reaching the right people or units in a corporation;
2 agreement on a sales cycle for the commercial contract that would be amenable to both parties;
3 establishing the rules for collaborating with a corporation.

However, it is worth having in mind that on account of the extremely divergent evaluations of the nine dimensions ranging from totally immaterial to crucial, the conclusions regarding challenges are difficult to generalize, which limits the ability to formulate unambiguous assumptions.

Regarding the seventh question, giving consideration to the values received on corporations achieving the goals of the established inter-organizational cooperation as part of the acceleration programs, one should observe that the fulfillment of goals was evaluated as being the highest for the following:

1 creating or developing an innovative specialist technology/product/service/process/sales channel;
2 optimizing internal processes;
3 creating the image of a modern company;
4 minimizing a company's operating expenses.

It is noteworthy that the representatives of corporations evaluated the level of achieving the intended goals of cooperation on a relatively average level.

The last research question pertained to checking whether startups achieve the intended goals of cooperation with corporations. The degree of achieving the goals intended by startups proved to be higher than for corporations. The fulfillment of the goals intended by startups was rated the highest in the following areas:

1 ability to test a product or MVP;
2 ability to develop a product/service;
3 development of a product or MVP;
4 ability to check a product's market alignment.

On the basis of the results obtained in this part, which covered the achievement of the goals intended by corporations and startups alike, one may formulate the following conclusion: the average results achieved by corporations as part of acceleration programs may adversely affect the quality of cooperation and lead to program participants wasting tangible and intangible resources. Even though corporations reap some benefits from participating in these programs, startups, however, are the ones that usually derive greater benefits and achieve their goals to a greater degree. This circumstance may stem from the extensive support and various benefits offered to startups by accelerators and the corporations cooperating with them. Startups are by nature more inclined to undertake risk and experiment. They are capable of marketing new and innovative products and services even if corporations do not demonstrate greater interest in these solutions following the conclusions of an acceleration program. This flexibility and willingness to adapt quickly to evolving market conditions forms a major strength of startups. It may explain their higher level of achieving their goals in comparison with corporations.

Nevertheless, there is a need to revise the current formula used in acceleration programs so as to align them better to the needs of all of their participants and mitigate the risk of squandering resources. The average results achieved by corporations may suggest the necessity of altering the approach to the selection of startups as one of the major factors contributing to the failure of achieving the expected results is enrolling startups in the program that are not suitably picked in terms of their potential business cooperation, that is, they do not have the attributes that are conducive to effective cooperation with large organizations.

Accordingly, startup accelerators and corporations should place greater emphasis on the process of selecting startups to enroll in the program. Suitably selected startups may enhance the opportunities for achieving the program's key goals such as entering into a business agreement concerning the commercial implementation of a product, service or technology, or the sale of equity in the startup to a corporation after completion of the acceleration. In light of the foregoing findings, the purpose of the subsequent part of this monograph will be to recognize and analyze in detail the attributes of startups that may exert a potential impact on the success of inter-organizational cooperation in acceleration programs.

6 Attributes of startups that may affect the effectiveness of inter-organizational cooperation

Research findings demonstrated that the goals of corporations in cooperation with startups in acceleration programs are achieved at a medium level. Accordingly, identifying the attributes of startups that may potentially contribute to enhancing the effectiveness of this cooperation is vital. Identifying the attributes (predictors) of startups that potentially enhance their chances for successful cooperation may accrue the following benefits. First, the risk of the failure of inter-organizational cooperation is diminished through better selection of program participants. Second, optimization of the resources made available by the accelerator and the corporation for the program's needs is better, which translates into more effective management of the overall acceleration process. Choosing the right startups will also contribute to growing the value of the program itself. It will build its reputation and position it as an attractive platform for innovative companies and their solutions on the domestic market and the international market.

Accordingly, the principal purpose of this chapter (third area of the research gap) is to identify the key attributes (predictors) characterizing startups that may potentially enhance their chances of effective inter-organizational cooperation in acceleration programs. Execution of Proof of Concept (POC) and signing a business agreement by a startup for commercial implementation of a product, service or technology are above all treated as an indicator of the effectiveness of cooperation. This indicator may be treated as an ordinal variable divided into three classes defining the intensity of its level. The scale spans: (1) total lack of effectiveness – failure to execute POC, (2) partial effectiveness of cooperation (partial success) in the form of executing the POC with a corporation, although ultimately no agreement signed with a technology client and (3) complete effectiveness defined as execution of POC with a corporation and signing an agreement for commercial implementation of a product, service or technology. Alternatively, this indicator may be examined as a dichotomous variable pointing to the absence of cooperation or the achievement of full cooperation (in other words, the failure or the execution of commercial implementation

DOI: 10.4324/9781003540366-7

of a product, service or sale of the company's equity to a corporation). For the purposes of this research the scenario with three classes was accepted as the one best corresponding to the characterization of acceleration programs involving corporations.

To identify the attributes of startups that may foster effective cooperation, an analysis of the literature available in the databases Web of Science and Scopus was conducted at first. In-depth literature research showed that to-date this topic has not been fully explored by researchers. Additionally, the author took advantage of his own experience gleaned during his observation of the acceleration programs carried out for various international corporations such as the Santander Group (Santander Bank Polska, Santander Consumer Bank, Santander Leasing), Insurer AXA, Telecom Orange and Bank PKO BP. Moreover, a number of talks were held with the representatives of the corporations responsible for cooperation in acceleration programs and with the representatives of the startup accelerators and the startups themselves. The information obtained in this manner made it possible to create a database of possible attributes that may influence inter-organizational cooperation. This database consisted of six major blocks of variables containing a total of 66 possible attributes. Each block groups attributes whose actual link to the examined dependent variable was subject to further verification. Figure 6.1 depicts the schematic presentation of the blocks grouping potential predictors.

Later in this chapter the findings of the research for the various blocks of variables were discussed. In every sub-section the prospective attributes

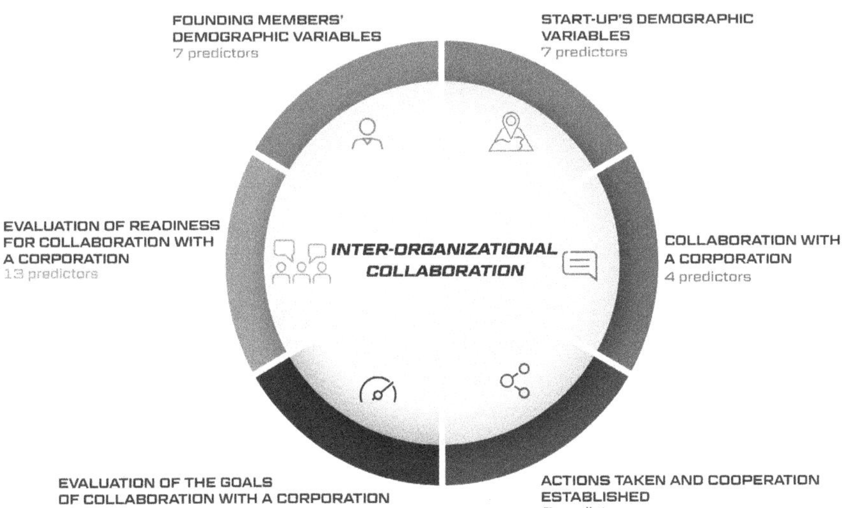

Figure 6.1 Schematic presentation of the blocks grouping potential predictors.

Source: Proprietary material.

under analysis were portrayed, which were duly marked in the following manner on the summary figure:

- statistically significant predictors remained unchanged;
- statistically insignificant predictors were deleted;
- predictors at the level of a statistical trend were marked with a star.

6.1 Predictive block – demographic variables of founding members

The specific goal was to identify those demographic variables of a startup that may potentially constitute valuable predictors of establishing effective cooperation with corporations. In the block verifying the linkage of the demographic variables, the following were taken into account (Figure 6.2):

1 number of a startup's founding members;
2 age of a startup's founding members;
3 gender of a startup's founding members;

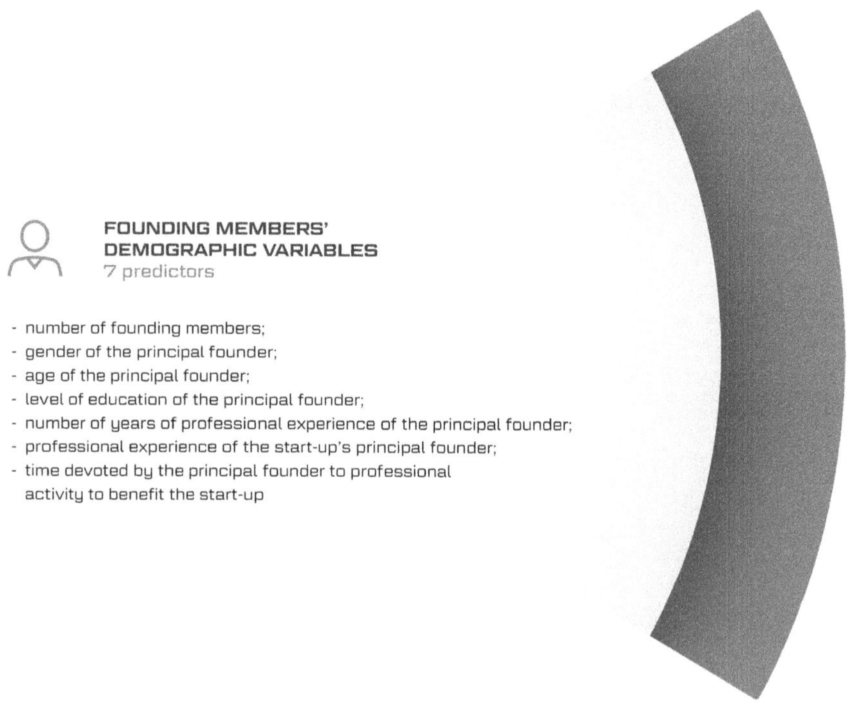

Figure 6.2 Verified variables as part of a predictive block of demographic variables pertaining to the founding members of a startup.

Source: Proprietary material.

4 level of education of the principal founder;
5 professional experience;
6 time devoted to actions related to professional activity for the startup.

The number of a startup's founding members was taken into consideration as the first variable. The Kruskal–Wallis test was performed, which turned out to be statistically significant, $H(2) = 6.19$; $p = 0.045$. Consequently, a post hoc analysis using the Dunn–Sidak tests was performed. One statistically significant difference was noted. Startups that did not execute their POC featured a smaller number of founding members than startups that executed their POC but did not sign an agreement with a technology client ($p = 0.021$).

Startups that signed an agreement with a technology client for commercial implementation did not differ substantially from the two other groups. Table 6.1 displays the detailed distribution of the obtained data. Therefore, even though the number of founding members was in a certain way associated with the level of effectiveness of cooperation (testing the solution offered by a startup with a corporation), there are no unambiguous indications that a greater number of founding members in a startup may lead to the execution of POC with a corporation and the signing of an agreement for commercial implementation of a product, service or technology, or the sale of the company's equity to a corporation.

Then the gender of the principal founder was taken into consideration. This time the performed Fisher's exact test proved not to be statistically significant, $p = 0.578$. Gender of the principal founder was not related to the level of inter-organizational cooperation achieved (Table 6.2).

Then the age of the principal founding member was taken into consideration. The performed Kruskal–Wallis test proved not to be statistically

Table 6.1 Number of founding members and the achieved level of a startup's cooperation

Number of founding members		*Start-up participated in an acceleration program but did not achieve the POC*	*Start-up completed an acceleration program and delivered the POC, but failed to sign a contract with a technology client*	*Start-up has signed an agreement with a technology client for commercial implementation*
One	N	7	7	7
	%	31.80%	12.70%	29.20%
Two	N	11	26	11
	%	50.00%	47.30%	45.80%
Three	N	4	17	3
	%	18.20%	30.90%	12.50%
More than three	N	0	5	3
	%	0.00%	9.10%	12.50%

Source: Proprietary material.

Table 6.2 Gender of the principal founding member and the achieved level of a startup's cooperation.

Gender		*Start-up participated in an acceleration program but did not achieve the POC*	*Start-up completed an acceleration program and delivered the POC, but failed to sign a contract with a technology client*	*Start-up has signed an agreement with a technology client for commercial implementation*
Female	N	3	7	1
	%	13.60%	12.70%	4.20%
Male	N	19	48	23
	%	86.40%	87.30%	95.80%

Source: Proprietary material.

Table 6.3 Age and education of the principal founding member and the level of a startup's achieved cooperation

Age of a start-up's principal founding member		*Start-up participated in an acceleration program but did not achieve the POC*	*Start-up completed an acceleration program and delivered the POC, but failed to sign a contract with a technology client*	*Start-up has signed an agreement with a technology client for commercial implementation*
<25 years old	N	1	1	1
	%	4.50%	1.80%	4.20%
26–35 years old	N	8	28	7
	%	36.40%	50.90%	29.20%
36–45 years old	N	10	19	14
	%	45.50%	34.50%	58.30%
46–60 years old	N	3	7	1
	%	13.60%	12.70%	4.20%
>60 years old	N	0	0	1
	%	0.00%	0.00%	4.20%
Level of education of a start-up's principal founding member		Start-up participated in an acceleration program but did not achieve the POC	Start-up completed an acceleration program and delivered the POC, but failed to sign a contract with a technology client	Start-up has signed an agreement with a technology client for commercial implementation
Secondary school	N	0	2	0
	%	0.00%	3.60%	0.00%
Bachelor's degree	N	4	4	4
	%	18.20%	7.30%	16.70%
Master's degree	N	16	47	16
	%	72.70%	85.50%	66.70%
Doctorate/status of professor	N	2	2	4
	%	9.10%	3.60%	16.70%

Source: Proprietary material.

significant, $H(2) = 1.25$; $p = 0.536$. There was no clear relationship between the age of the main shareholder and the level of achieved cooperation. A similar analysis was conducted on the level of that person's education (Table 6.3); once again, however, no statistically significant relationship was identified, $H(2) = 0.52$; $p = 0.772$.

The number of years of professional experience of the principal founder was also not linked to a substantial degree to the level of achieved cooperation, $H(2) = 2.74$; $p = 0.254$. Table 6.4 displays the distribution of the obtained data.

Whether the type of activity of the startup's principal founding member prior to its formation is linked to the level of achieved cooperation was also checked. A series of χ^2 tests were performed and – if the assumptions of this test were not satisfied – Fisher's exact tests were performed. As can be seen in Table 6.5, one statistically significant relationship was found. As the level of achieved cooperation rose, persons with a history of working in government administration were recorded more seldomly. In the case of the other types of previous places of work of the startup's main founder, statistically significant ties were not found, although it is worth indicating two more results at the level of a statistical trend – in respect of studying in school/at university and scientific and teaching work. In the first instance a decline in the percentage of persons with such a past was once again recorded as the level of achieved cooperation grew. In turn, in the second case, the percentage of such persons was the lowest for a partial level of achieved cooperation.

In the last step the percentage of time designated for professional activity, which was devoted by the main founding member to the startup's activity was taken into consideration. The performed Kruskal–Wallis test proved not

Table 6.4 Number of years of professional experience of the principal founder and the level of achieved cooperation

Number of years of professional experience of the principal founding member		*The start-up participated in an acceleration program but it did not execute its POC*	*Start-up completed an acceleration program and delivered the POC, but failed to sign a contract with a technology client*	*Start-up signed a contract with a technology client for commercial implementation*
<1 year	N	0	1	0
	%	0.00%	1.80%	0.00%
1–3 years	N	1	2	1
	%	4.50%	3.60%	4.20%
4–9 years	N	5	18	4
	%	22.70%	32.70%	16.70%
10–19 years	N	10	26	14
	%	45.50%	47.30%	58.30%
>20 years	N	6	8	5
	%	27.30%	14.50%	20.80%

Source: Proprietary material.

Table 6.5 Activity of the principal founding member prior to establishing a startup and the level of achieved cooperation

		Start-up participated in an acceleration program but did not achieve the POC	*Start-up completed an acceleration program and delivered the POC, but failed to sign a contract with a technology client*	*Start-up has signed an agreement with a technology client for commercial implementation*	
Work in one's own or family company	*N* %	5 22.70%	18 32.70%	9 37.50%	$\chi^2(2) = 1.22$ $p = 0.544$
Works in a corporation	*N* %	12 54.50%	27 49.10%	13 54.20%	$\chi^2(2) = 0.28$ $p = 0.870$
Works in a private company, but not in a corporation	*N* %	11 50.00%	25 45.50%	12 50.00%	$\chi^2(2) = 0.21$ $p = 0.901$
Works in another start-up	*N* %	6 27.30%	16 29.10%	8 33.30%	$\chi^2(2) = 0.22$ $p = 0.894$
Works in a fund (e.g., venture capital)	*N* %	1 4.50%	3 5.50%	0 0.00%	Exact Fisher Test $p = 0.651$
Works in national government administration	*N* %	4 18.20%	3 5.50%	0 0.00%	**Exact Fisher Test** $\boldsymbol{p = 0.049}$
Studies in school/university	*N* %	3 13.60%	2 3.60%	0 0.00%	Exact Fisher Test $p = 0.083$
Works in an academic/teaching role	*N* %	4 18.20%	2 3.60%	3 12.50%	Exact Fisher Test $p = 0.056$

Source: Proprietary material.

to be statistically significant, $H(2) = 3.53$; $p = 0.172$. Table 6.6 displays the distribution of the obtained results.

To recap, it should be observed that only two statistically significant relationships were identified from among the analyzed demographic variables pertaining to founding members with special emphasis on the main shareholder – between the achieved level of cooperation and the number of founding members and the work of the main founding member in government administration prior to its establishment. Figure 6.3 depicts a graphic summary of the results obtained.

Table 6.6 Percentage of time set aside for the professional activity of the principal founding member devoted to the startup and the achieved level of cooperation

Percentage of time		*Start-up participated in an acceleration program but did not achieve the POC*	*Start-up completed an acceleration program and delivered the POC, but failed to sign a contract with a technology client*	*Start-up has signed an agreement with a technology client for commercial implementation*
<25%	N	0	1	2
	%	0.00%	1.80%	8.30%
25–49%	N	2	2	2
	%	9.10%	3.60%	8.30%
50–74%	N	4	13	7
	%	18.20%	23.60%	29.20%
75–90%	N	5	10	5
	%	22.70%	18.20%	20.80%
>90%	N	11	29	8
	%	50.00%	52.70%	33.30%

Source: Proprietary material.

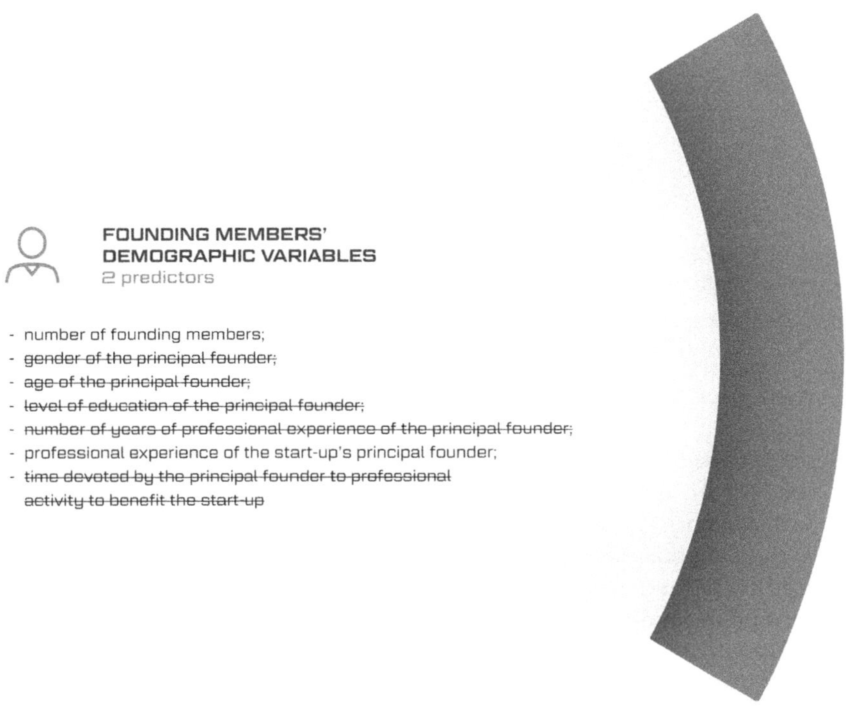

Figure 6.3 Summary of a startup's material predictors as part of the block of demographic variables of founding members.

Source: Proprietary material.

6.2 Predictive block – demographic variables of a startup

In the block verifying the linkage of a startup's demographic variables, the following were taken into account (Figure 6.4):

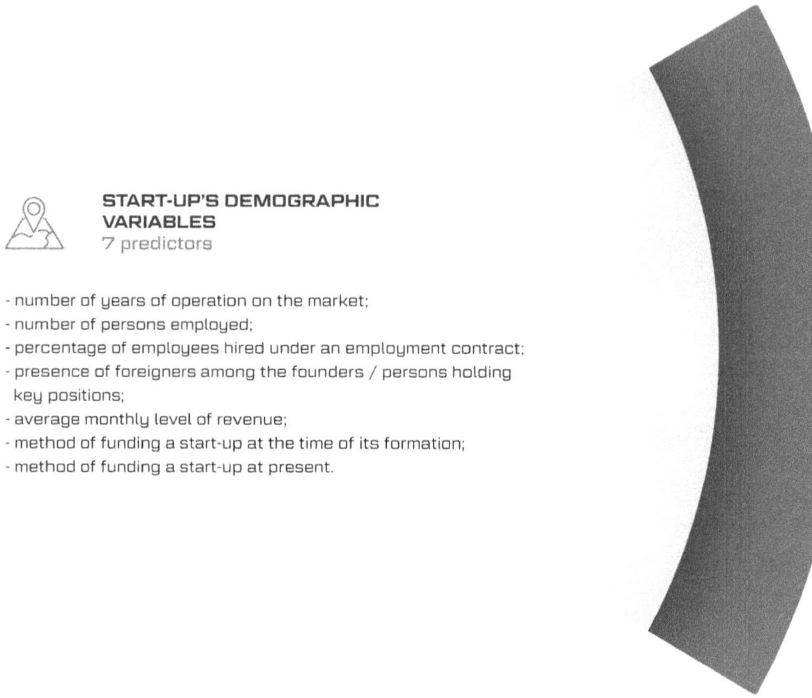

Figure 6.4 Verified variables as part of a predictive block of demographic variables pertaining to a startup.

Source: Proprietary material.

1 number of years of a startup's operation on the market;
2 number of persons employed;
3 percentage of employees hired under an employment contract;
4 presence of foreigners among the founders/persons holding key positions in a startup;
5 average monthly level of revenue during the most recent year;
6 method of funding a startup at the time of its formation;
7 method of funding a startup at present.

Whether there is a tie between the length of a startup functioning on the market and the level of achieved cooperation by a startup was checked first. The Kruskal–Wallis test was performed. A statistically significant result was recorded, $H(2) = 6.84$; $p = 0.033$. Consequently, a post hoc analysis using the Dunn–Sidak test was performed. Two statistically significant differences were

Table 6.7 Duration of a startup's activity and the level of achieved cooperation

Duration of start-up activity		*Start-up participated in an acceleration program but did not achieve the POC*	*Start-up completed an acceleration program and delivered the POC, but failed to sign a contract with a technology client*	*Start-up has signed an agreement with a technology client for commercial implementation*
<3 months	N	1	0	0
	%	4.50%	0.00%	0.00%
3–6 months	N	4	3	1
	%	18.20%	5.50%	4.20%
6 months to year	N	3	3	4
	%	13.60%	5.50%	16.70%
1–2 years	N	6	12	4
	%	27.30%	21.80%	16.70%
2–3 years	N	4	20	6
	%	18.20%	36.40%	25.00%
3–5 years	N	4	14	8
	%	18.20%	25.50%	33.30%
>5 years	N	0	3	1
	%	0.00%	5.50%	4.20%

Source: Proprietary material.

noted. The startups that did not execute their POC were characterized by a shorter period of functioning on the market in comparison with the startups that executed their POC, but did not sign an agreement with a technology client (p = 0.011) and those that signed an agreement with a technology client for commercial implementation of products/services/technologies (p = 0.041). The difference between these two groups was not even close to being statistically significant. Table 6.7 depicts the results.

Whether there is a tie between the number of persons employed by a startup and the level of achieved cooperation in a program by a startup was checked first. The Kruskal–Wallis test was performed. A result that was only close to being statistically significant was recorded, $H(2) = 5.47$; $p = 0.065$. Therefore, one cannot conduct a post hoc analysis. As one may observe, the startups that did not execute a POC were characterized by having the smallest number of employed persons (Table 6.8). These startups were also characterized by having clearly the largest percentage of the founder's self-employment.

In the next step the percentage of employees hired in the startup under an employment contract was taken into consideration. This time the Kruskal–Wallis test proved not to be statistically significant, $H(2) = 0.31$; $p = 0.855$. Table 6.9 displays the distribution of the obtained results.

Nor did Fisher's exact test demonstrate that the level of cooperation hinged to a substantial degree on the presence of foreigners among the founders or among the persons holding key positions, $p = 0.456$ (Table 6.10).

Table 6.8 Number of persons employed and the level of achieved cooperation

Number of persons employed		*Start-up participated in an acceleration program but did not achieve the POC*	*Start-up completed an acceleration program and delivered the POC, but failed to sign a contract with a technology client*	*Start-up has signed an agreement with a technology client for commercial implementation*
Self-employment of the founder	N	6	2	3
	%	27.30%	3.60%	12.50%
2–5 persons	N	8	25	5
	%	36.40%	45.50%	20.80%
6–10 persons	N	6	16	11
	%	27.30%	29.10%	45.80%
11–20 persons	N	2	10	4
	%	9.10%	18.20%	16.70%
>20 persons	N	0	2	1
	%	0.00%	3.60%	4.20%

Source: Proprietary material.

Table 6.9 Percentage of persons employed under an employment contract and the level of achieved cooperation

Percentage of persons employed under an employment contract		*Start-up participated in an acceleration program but did not achieve the POC*	*Start-up completed an acceleration program and delivered the POC, but failed to sign a contract with a technology client*	*Start-up has signed an agreement with a technology client for commercial implementation*
Nobody	N	11	24	12
	%	50.00%	43.60%	50.00%
<50%	N	4	20	8
	%	18.20%	36.40%	33.30%
50%–99%	N	6	8	3
	%	27.30%	14.50%	12.50%
100%	N	1	3	1
	%	4.50%	5.50%	4.20%

Source: Proprietary material.

What is surprising is also the average monthly revenue in the last half year was not substantially linked to the level of achieving cooperation, $H(2) = 3.10$; $p = 0.212$. Table 6.11 displays the distribution of the obtained results.

Whether the fact that a startup had been financed to this point solely using the own funds of founders was associated with the level of achieving cooperation was then investigated. The performed test χ^2 proved not to be statistically significant, $\chi^2(2) = 3.77$; $p = 0.152$. Table 6.12 displays the results.

Table 6.10 Presence of foreigners on key positions and the level of achieved cooperation

Presence of foreigners		*Start-up participated in an acceleration program but did not achieve the POC*	*Start-up completed an acceleration program and delivered the POC, but failed to sign a contract with a technology client*	*Start-up has signed an agreement with a technology client for commercial implementation*
Yes	N	1	7	4
	%	4.50%	12.70%	16.70%
No	N	21	48	20
	%	95.50%	87.30%	83.30%

What is surprising is also the average monthly revenue in the last half year was not substantially linked to the level of achieving cooperation, $H(2) = 3.10$; $p = 0.212$. Table 6.11 displays the distribution of the obtained results.

Table 6.11 Revenue during the last half year and the achieved level of cooperation

Revenue during the last half year		*Start-up participated in an acceleration program but did not achieve the POC*	*Start-up completed an acceleration program and delivered the POC, but failed to sign a contract with a technology client*	*Start-up has signed an agreement with a technology client for commercial implementation*
None	N	9	5	4
	%	40.90%	9.10%	16.70%
<10,000	N	2	8	6
	%	9.10%	14.50%	25.00%
10,000–20,000	N	2	9	3
	%	9.10%	16.40%	12.50%
20,000–50,000	N	3	19	4
	%	13.60%	34.50%	16.70%
50,000–100,000	N	4	9	2
	%	18.20%	16.40%	8.30%
100,000–500,000	N	1	3	5
	%	4.50%	5.50%	20.80%
500,000 to 1 million	N	0	1	0
	%	0.00%	1.80%	0.00%
>1 million	N	1	1	0
	%	4.50%	1.80%	0.00%

Source: Proprietary material.

In the next step it was checked whether startups at a varying level of achieved cooperation differ from one another in terms of the frequency of being funded from specific sources at the time of commencing their activity. The test χ^2 was performed and – if the assumptions of this test were not satisfied – Fisher's exact tests were performed. As can be seen in Table 6.13, one statistically significant result was posted – in respect of the number of startups benefiting

Table 6.12 Funding a startup solely from the founders' own funds and the achieved level of cooperation

Funding a start-up solely from the founders' own funds		*Start-up participated in an acceleration program but did not achieve the POC*	*Start-up completed an acceleration program and delivered the POC, but failed to sign a contract with a technology client*	*Start-up has signed an agreement with a technology client for commercial implementation*
Yes	N	14	23	14
	%	63.60%	41.80%	58.30%
No	N	8	32	10
	%	36.40%	58.20%	41.70%

Source: Proprietary material.

Table 6.13 Funding a startup at the phase of its formation and the level of achieved cooperation

Source of funding		*Start-up participated in an acceleration program but did not achieve the POC*	*Start-up completed an acceleration program and delivered the POC, but failed to sign a contract with a technology client*	*Start-up has signed an agreement with a technology client for commercial implementation*	
Founders' own funds	N	20	52	22	$p = 0.647$
	%	90.90%	94.50%	91.70%	
EU support	N	3	24	8	$\chi^2(2) = 6.27$
	%	13.60%	43.60%	33.30%	$\mathbf{p = 0.044}$
Local government entities	N	1	0	0	$p = 0.226$
	%	4.50%	0.00%	0.00%	
Other businesses	N	0	2	2	$p = 0.517$
	%	0.00%	3.60%	8.30%	
Venture capital	N	3	10	5	$p = 0.832$
	%	13.60%	18.20%	20.80%	
Crowdfunding	N	0	0	0	–
	%	0.00%	0.00%	0.00%	
Accelerator	N	4	12	2	$p = 0.368$
	%	18.20%	21.80%	8.30%	
Business angel	N	2	6	4	$p = 0.706$
	%	9.10%	10.90%	16.70%	
Industrial investor	N	0	0	1	$p = 0.455$
	%	0.00%	0.00%	4.20%	
Bank	N	0	4	0	$p = 0.328$
	%	0.00%	7.30%	0.00%	
Loan funds	N	0	0	0	–
	%	0.00%	0.00%	0.00%	

Source: Proprietary material.

from EU support. The percentage of startups benefiting from EU support was clearly lower among units that did not execute their POC. In the case of other funding sources, no statistically significant results were posted.

Similar analyses were performed for the current funding source. As can be seen in Table 6.14, one statistically significant result was posted once again – in respect of the number of startups benefiting from EU support. This time, once again, the percentage of startups currently benefiting from EU support was clearly lower among units that did not execute their POC.

A relationship was also found at the level of a statistical trend on staying afloat using revenue from its own activity. The largest percentage of these units was posted among startups that achieved partial cooperation. In the case of other funding sources, no statistically significant results were posted.

Table 6.14 Funding a startup at the current phase and the level of achieved cooperation

Source of funding		*Start-up participated in an acceleration program but did not achieve the POC*	*Start-up completed an acceleration program and delivered the POC, but failed to sign a contract with a technology client*	*Start-up has signed an agreement with a technology client for commercial implementation*	
Revenue from their own activity	N	4	24	6	$\chi^2(2) = 5.62$
	%	18.20%	43.60%	25.00%	$p = 0.060$
Founders' own funds	N	16	34	18	$\chi^2(2) = 1.69$
	%	72.70%	61.80%	75.00%	$p = 0.429$
EU support	N	2	20	8	$\chi^2(2) = 5.80$
	%	9.10%	36.40%	33.30%	$\mathbf{p = 0.040}$
Local government entities	N	0	0	0	–
	%	0.00%	0.00%	0.00%	
Other businesses	N	0	0	0	–
	%	0.00%	0.00%	0.00%	
Venture capital	N	2	7	3	$p = 1$
	%	9.10%	12.70%	12.50%	
Crowdfunding	N	0	0	0	–
	%	0.00%	0.00%	0.00%	
Accelerator	N	4	11	4	$p = 1$
	%	18.20%	20.00%	16.70%	
Business angel	N	0	9	1	$p = 0.066$
	%	0.00%	16.40%	4.20%	
Industrial investor	N	1	1	1	$p = 0.595$
	%	4.50%	1.80%	4.20%	
Bank	N	0	0	0	–
	%	0.00%	0.00%	0.00%	
Loan funds	N	0	0	0	–
	%	0.00%	0.00%	0.00%	

Source: Proprietary material.

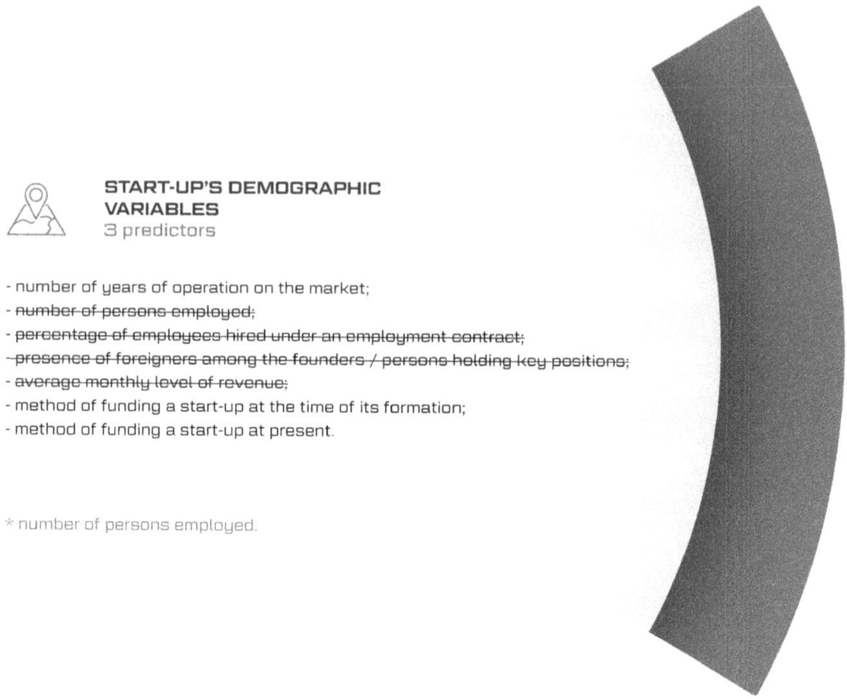

Figure 6.5 Summary of a startup's material predictors as part of the predictive block of demographic variables pertaining to a startup.

Source: Proprietary material.

Summarizing the analyses performed for the demographic variables pertaining to a startup, it should be observed that statistically significant relationships were found – between the level of achieved cooperation and the length of operation and the usage of EU support at the stage of formation and also at present. One predictor at the level of a statistical trend was also recorded. Figure 6.5 depicts a graphic summary of the results obtained.

6.3 Predictive block – measures taken and established cooperation

In the block verifying the linkage of variables concerning a startup's activities as part of undertaking cooperation, the following were taken into account (Figure 6.6):

1 institutions with which a startup cooperates;
2 holding patents/trademarks/utility designs or the startup had launched the process to secure them;

Figure 6.6 Verified variables as part of a predictive block of demographic variables pertaining to the undertaken actions and the established cooperation.

Source: Proprietary material.

3 collaboration with foreign entities;
4 startup having foreign clients;
5 history of collaboration with accelerators.

Institutions (Table 6.15) cooperating with a startup were considered first. The test χ^2 was performed or – if the assumptions of this test were not satisfied – Fisher's exact tests were performed. One statistically significant result was posted – in respect of the number of startups establishing cooperation with mid-sized businesses. The percentage of startups having that type of established cooperation was clearly lower among units that did not execute their POC. In the case of other types of established cooperation, no statistically significant results were posted.

In the next step having patents/trademarks/utility designs or being in the process of running the procedure to obtain them was taken into account. The Fisher test performed did not, however, demonstrate a statistically significant

Table 6.15 Established cooperation with market entities and the level of achieved cooperation

cooperating institutions		*Start-up participated in an acceleration program but did not achieve the POC*	*Start-up completed an acceleration program and delivered the POC, but failed to sign a contract with a technology client*	*Start-up has signed an agreement with a technology client for commercial implementation*	
Corporations	N	18	48	21	$p = 0.863$
	%	81.80%	87.30%	87.50%	
Medium-sized companies	N	11	42	19	$\chi^2(2) = 6.29$
	%	50.00%	76.40%	79.20%	$\mathbf{p = 0.043}$
Micro/small companies	N	9	16	6	$\chi^2(2) = 1.51$
	%	40.90%	29.10%	25.00%	$p = 0.470$
Accelerators	N	12	34	14	$\chi^2(2) = 0.36$
	%	54.50%	61.80%	58.30%	$p = 0.835$
Venture capital funds	N	3	10	5	$p = 0.833$
	%	13.60%	18.20%	20.80%	
National/local government administration	N	4	6	3	$p = 0.671$
	%	18.20%	10.90%	12.50%	
Higher place of education	N	2	7	7	$p = 0.134$
	%	9.10%	12.70%	29.20%	
Research and development center	N	2	6	3	$p = 1$
	%	9.10%	10.90%	12.50%	
Foundations and other non-profit organizations	N	1	4	3	$p = 0.618$
	%	4.50%	7.30%	12.50%	

Source: Proprietary material.

relationship with the level of achieved cooperation by a startup, $p = 0.800$. Table 6.16 displays the distribution of the obtained results.

The level of achieved cooperation was displayed along with the history to-date of activities with foreign entities. Once again, however, no statistically significant relationship was identified, $\chi^2(2) = 1.95$; $p = 0.377$, Table 6.17.

Then, the percentage of foreign clients was displayed with the achieved level of cooperation. The Kruskal–Wallis test was performed, it turned out that it was close to being statistically significant, $H(2) = 4.60$; $p = 0.100$. This result did not facilitate the performance of a post hoc analysis. However, analysis of Table 6.18 demonstrated that the percentage of these types of

Table 6.16 Holding patents/trademarks/utility designs and the level of achieved cooperation

Holding patents/ trademarks/ utility designs		*Start-up participated in an acceleration program but did not achieve the POC*	*Start-up completed an acceleration program and delivered the POC, but failed to sign a contract with a technology client*	*Start-up has signed an agreement with a technology client for commercial implementation*
Yes	N	4	6	4
	%	18.20%	10.90%	16.70%
In the process of registration	N	2	7	5
	%	9.10%	12.70%	20.80%
No, but we are planning that	N	10	29	9
	%	45.50%	52.70%	37.50%
No	N	6	13	6
	%	27.30%	23.60%	25.00%

Source: Proprietary material.

Table 6.17 Collaboration with foreign entities and the level of achieved cooperation

History of collaboration with foreign entities		*Start-up participated in an acceleration program but did not achieve the POC*	*Start-up completed an acceleration program and delivered the POC, but failed to sign a contract with a technology client*	*Start-up has signed an agreement with a technology client for commercial implementation*
Yes	N	7	27	10
	%	31.80%	49.10%	41.70%
No	N	15	28	14
	%	68.20%	50.90%	58.30%

Source: Proprietary material.

clients was lower among those startups that did not execute their POC in comparison with the other two groups of startups.

In the final step of this series of analyses, the history of a startup's cooperation with accelerators was taken into consideration. The test χ^2 was performed and it proved not to be statistically significant, $\chi^2(4) = 0.99; p = 0.912$. Table 6.19 depicts the distribution of the obtained data.

Summing up the research performed in this part one should observe that only one statistically significant relationship was found among the analyzed variables pertaining to the block of undertaken actions and the established cooperation – it was between the level of achieved cooperation and undertaking cooperation with mid-sized businesses. In this case establishing cooperation with a mid-sized business enhanced a startup's chances of achieving final cooperation. Figure 6.7 depicts a graphic summary of the results obtained.

Table 6.18 Percentage of foreign clients and the level of achieved cooperation

Percentage of foreign clients		*Start-up participated in an acceleration program but did not achieve the POC*	*Start-up completed an acceleration program and delivered the POC, but failed to sign a contract with a technology client*	*Start-up has signed an agreement with a technology client for commercial implementation*
None	N	13	20	11
	%	59.10%	36.40%	45.80%
<10%	N	7	19	5
	%	31.80%	34.50%	20.80%
11%–50%	N	2	10	5
	%	9.10%	18.20%	20.80%
51%–90%	N	0	5	3
	%	0.00%	9.10%	12.50%
91%–100%	N	0	1	0
	%	0.00%	1.80%	0.00%

Source: Proprietary material.

Table 6.19 History of collaboration with an accelerator and the level of achieved cooperation

		Start-up participated in an acceleration program but did not achieve the POC	*Start-up completed an acceleration program and delivered the POC, but failed to sign a contract with a technology client*	*Start-up has signed an agreement with a technology client for commercial implementation*
Yes, we made contact and held talks	N	7	23	8
	%	31.80%	41.80%	33.30%
Yes, we were covered by an acceleration program in a different accelerator	N	5	11	6
	%	22.70%	20.00%	25.00%
No	N	10	21	10
	%	45.50%	38.20%	41.70%

Source: Proprietary material.

Figure 6.7 Summary of a startup's material predictors as part of the predictive block of variables pertaining to the undertaken actions and the established cooperation.

Source: Proprietary material.

6.4 Predictive block – cooperation with a corporation

In the block verifying the linkage of variables concerning cooperation with a corporation with the level of inter-organizational cooperation it achieved, the following were taken into account (Figure 6.8).

1 history of prior cooperation between a startup and a corporation;
2 stage of a startup's development in which the search for a partner in the form of a client for the solutions offered by a startup was begun;
3 phase of a startup's development and the time of establishing cooperation;
4 method of establishing it.

At the beginning, a startup's previous partnership with a corporation (Table 6.20) was taken into consideration. The performed test χ^2 proved to be close to being statistically significant, $\chi^2(2) = 5.53$; $p = 0.063$. The largest percentage of startups with a history of cooperation with corporations was recorded among units with partially achieved cooperation, while the lowest was recorded among startups that did not at all execute their POC.

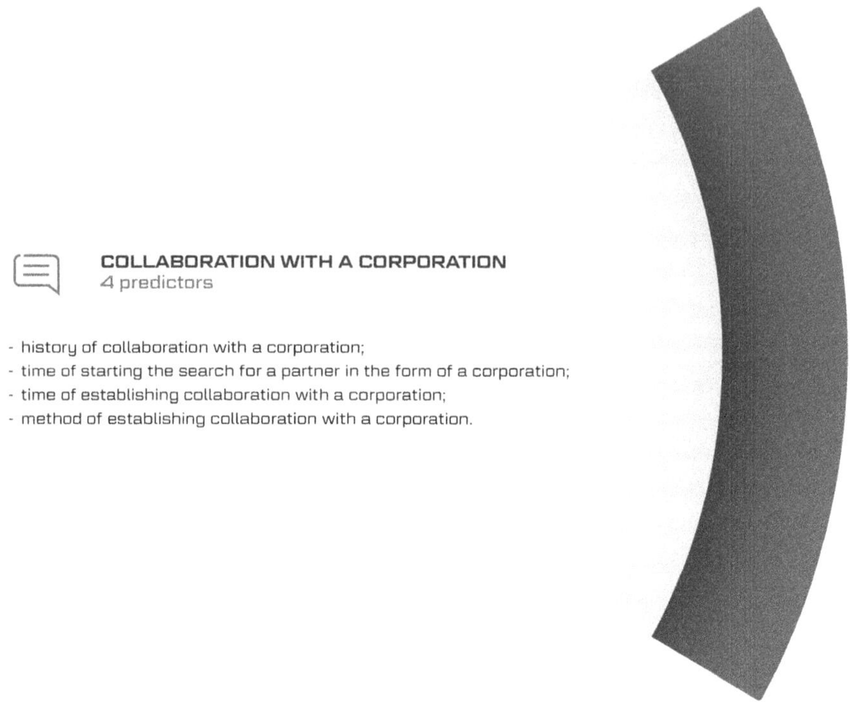

Figure 6.8 Verified variables as part of a predictive block of variables pertaining to cooperation with a corporation.

Source: Proprietary material.

In the next step the time when the startup started the search for a partner in the form of a corporation was taken into consideration. However, no statistically significant relationship with the level of achieved cooperation was recorded, which is indicated by the result of Fisher's exact test, $p = 0.679$. Table 6.21 displays the distribution of the results.

Similar research was performed for the time of commencing such cooperation. This time Fisher's exact test proved to be statistically significant, $p = 0.045$. As can be seen in Table 6.22, in the event of units that did not execute their POC, this activity was clearly taken the most frequently during the idea/Minimum Viable Product (MVP) phase. Thereby those startups that went through the idea/MVP phase and have completed a finished solution for implementation or are engaged in its sale on the market have the greatest chances for achieving cooperation with corporations. In turn, the difference between startups that achieved partial cooperation and those that achieved full cooperation was observed predominantly in the percentage of units that established cooperation during the scale up stage. There were more of these

Table 6.20 History of prior partnership with a corporation and the level of achieved cooperation

History of prior cooperation between a start-up and a corporation		*Start-up participated in an acceleration program but did not achieve the POC*	*Start-up completed an acceleration program and delivered the POC, but failed to sign a contract with a technology client*	*Start-up has signed an agreement with a technology client for commercial implementation*
Yes	N	9	38	13
	%	40.90%	69.10%	54.20%
No	N	13	17	11
	%	59.10%	30.90%	45.80%

Source: Proprietary material.

Table 6.21 Time of starting the search for a partner in the form of a corporation and the level of achieved cooperation

Time of starting the search for a partner in the form of a corporation		*Start-up participated in an acceleration program but did not achieve the POC*	*Start-up completed an acceleration program and delivered the POC, but failed to sign a contract with a technology client*	*Start-up has signed an agreement with a technology client for commercial implementation*
Idea/MVP	N	18	38	15
	%	81.80%	69.10%	62.50%
Growth	N	3	13	6
	%	13.60%	23.60%	25.00%
Scaling up	N	1	4	3
	%	4.50%	7.30%	12.50%

Source: Proprietary material.

in the group of startups that had signed an agreement with a technology client for commercial implementation.

In the last step the method of establishing cooperation was taken into account. A series of Fisher's exact tests were performed. However, as can be seen in Table 6.23, no statistically significant relationships were found.

Summing up the research performed for the block of cooperation with a corporation one should observe that only one statistically significant relationship was found among the analyzed variables pertaining to undertaken actions and cooperation – it was between the level of achieved cooperation and the time of establishing cooperation with a corporation. Figure 6.9 depicts a summary of the results obtained.

Table 6.22 Time of establishing collaboration with a corporation and the level of achieved cooperation

Time of establishing collaboration with a corporation		*Start-up participated in an acceleration program but did not achieve the POC*	*Start-up completed an acceleration program and delivered the POC, but failed to sign a contract with a technology client*	*Start-up has signed an agreement with a technology client for commercial implementation*
Idea/MVP	N	17	26	12
	%	77.30%	47.30%	50.00%
Growth	N	4	25	7
	%	18.20%	45.50%	29.20%
Scaling up	N	1	4	5
	%	4.50%	7.30%	20.80%

Source: Proprietary material.

Table 6.23 Method of establishing collaboration and the level of achieved cooperation

Method of establishing cooperation		*Start-up participated in an acceleration program but did not achieve the POC*	*Start-up completed the acceleration program and demonstrated the POC, but failed to sign a contract with a technology client*	*Start-up has signed an agreement with a technology client for commercial implementation*	
Thanks to the acceleration program under execution	N	22	55	24	–
	%	100.00%	100.00%	100.00%	
The corporation invited us to cooperate	N	3	10	2	$p = 0.566$
	%	13.60%	18.20%	8.30%	
Thanks to the relationships of our shareholder	N	5	6	3	$p = 0.431$
	%	22.70%	10.90%	12.50%	
Thanks to the relationships of our investor	N	2	1	0	$p = 0.171$
	%	9.10%	1.80%	0.00%	

Source: Proprietary material.

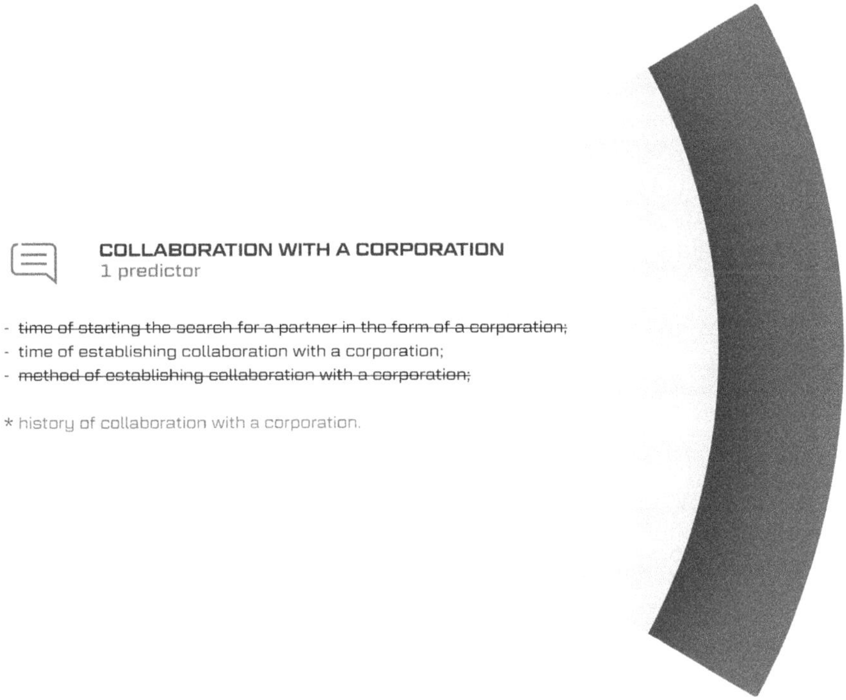

Figure 6.9 Summary of a startup's material predictors as part of the predictive block of variables pertaining to cooperation with a corporation.

Source: Proprietary material.

6.5 Predictive block – evaluation of readiness to cooperate with a corporation

In the block verifying the linkage of variables concerning a startup's readiness to participate in cooperation with a corporation with the level of achieved cooperation, 13 dimensions were taken into account (Figure 6.10):

1 Has a defined goal for collaboration;
2 Has a complete team;
3 Ensures that team members have available time;
4 Has a finished product or MVP;
5 Openness to collaboration, including readiness to make a PIVOT;
6 Startup has a technology base for collaborating with a corporation;
7 Startup has infrastructure for collaborating with a corporation;
8 Having in its offering a product/service/technology with a high level of utility;
9 Has a tried and tested business model (recurring, scalable);

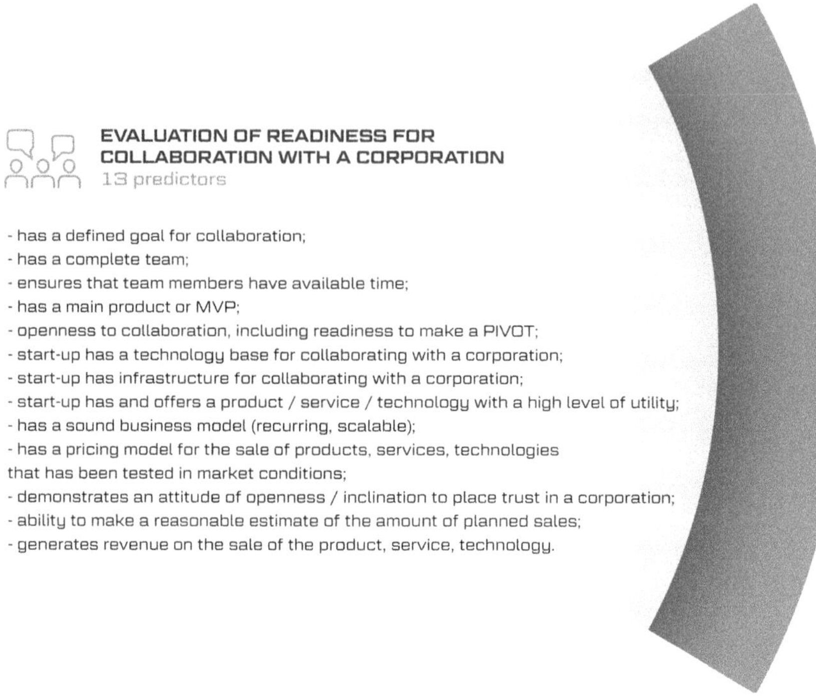

Figure 6.10 Verified variables as part of a predictive block of variables pertaining to the evaluation of the readiness to engage in cooperation with a corporation.

Source: Proprietary material.

10 Has a pricing model for the sale of products, services and technologies that has been tested in market conditions;
11 Demonstrates an attitude of openness/inclination to place trust in a corporation;
12 Ability to make a reasonable estimate of the amount of planned sales;
13 Generates revenue on the sale of the product, service and technology.

The various dimensions of readiness were taken first. The Kruskal–Wallis tests performed demonstrated only one result at the level of a statistical trend among the 13 that were analyzed, that is, in respect of having a finished product or MVP. The evaluation of readiness in this respect climbed along with the level of achieved cooperation. In respect of other dimensions, results were not recorded even at the level of a statistical trend (Table 6.24).

Figure 6.11 compiles the foregoing results. This figure depicts the dimensions of a startup's readiness to cooperate with corporations having in mind the final result of participating in an acceleration program.

Table 6.24 Level of readiness to establish cooperation with a corporation and the level of achieved cooperation

Dimensions of readiness	*Start-up participated in an acceleration program but did not achieve the POC*		*Start-up completed an acceleration program and delivered the POC, but failed to sign a contract with a technology client*		*Start-up has signed an agreement with a technology client for commercial implementation*			
	M	SD	M	SD	M	SD	H	p
Had a specific goal for cooperation	8.14	2.17	8.15	2.00	8.92	1.35	2.56	0.278
Has a complete team	7.50	2.18	8.04	1.75	8.38	1.38	1.84	0.399
Ensures that team members have available time	7.00	2.31	7.78	2.13	8.17	1.66	3.17	0.205
Has a finished product/MVP	6.73	2.83	7.71	2.27	8.29	2.01	5.00	0.082
Openness to cooperation, including PIVOT	7.86	1.58	7.75	2.15	8.00	2.02	0.31	0.859
Has a technological base for cooperation with a corporation	7.64	1.99	7.49	2.08	7.33	2.20	0.17	0.918
Having the infrastructure for cooperation with a corporation	7.55	2.15	7.16	2.26	6.88	2.25	1.53	0.466
Having in its offering a product/service/technology with a high level of utility	7.77	2.00	8.00	1.71	7.96	1.83	0.11	0.945
Has a tried and tested business model (recurring, scalable)	7.09	1.66	6.76	2.46	6.79	2.15	0.11	0.947
Has a pricing model for the sale of products, services and technologies that has been tested in market conditions	5.86	2.17	6.38	2.45	6.46	2.17	1.03	0.599
Has an attitude of openness/inclination to place trust in a corporation	7.68	1.59	7.40	2.15	7.25	2.07	0.37	0.833
Ability to make a reasonable estimate of the amount of planned sales	6.95	1.53	6.89	2.04	7.00	1.79	0.05	0.973
Generates revenue on the sale of the product, service, technology	4.95	3.30	6.55	2.71	6.00	3.12	3.74	0.154

Source: Proprietary material.

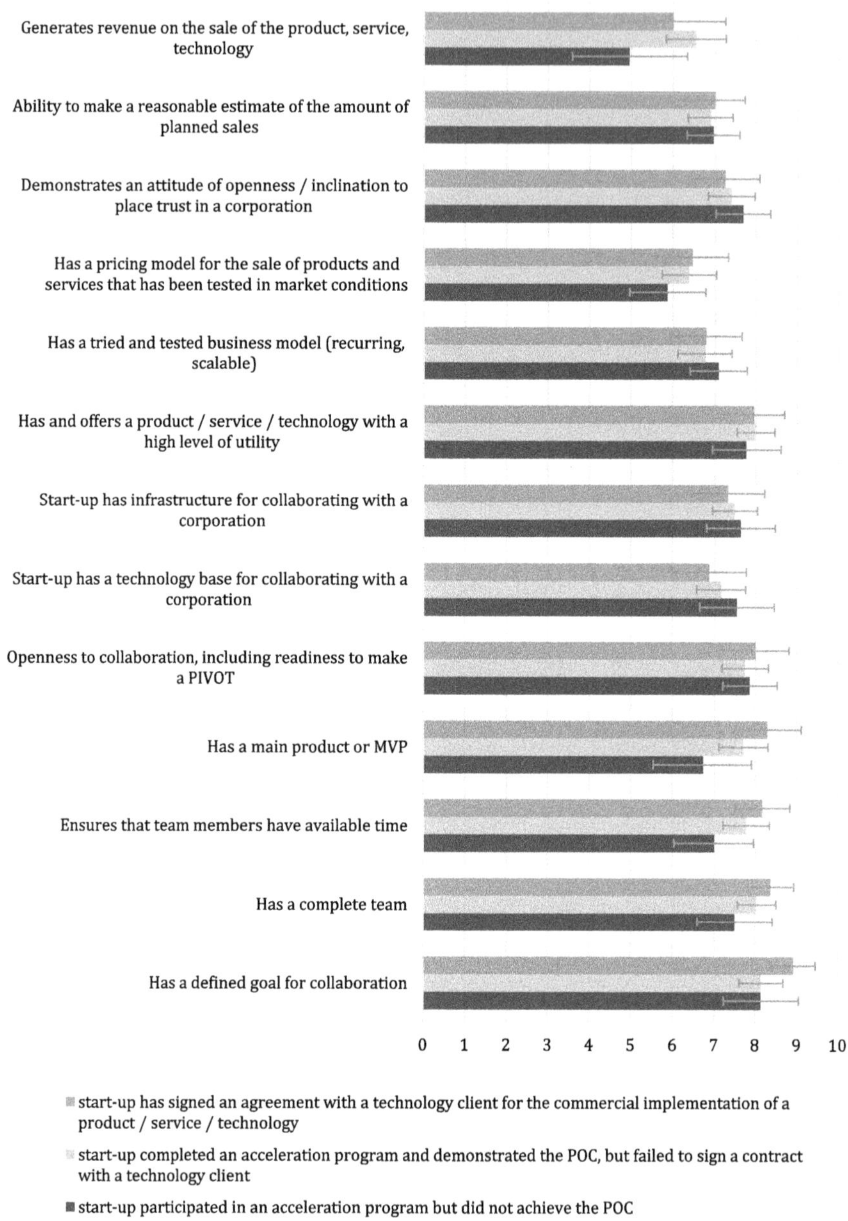

Figure 6.11 Level of readiness to establish cooperation with a corporation and the level of achieved cooperation

Source: Proprietary material.

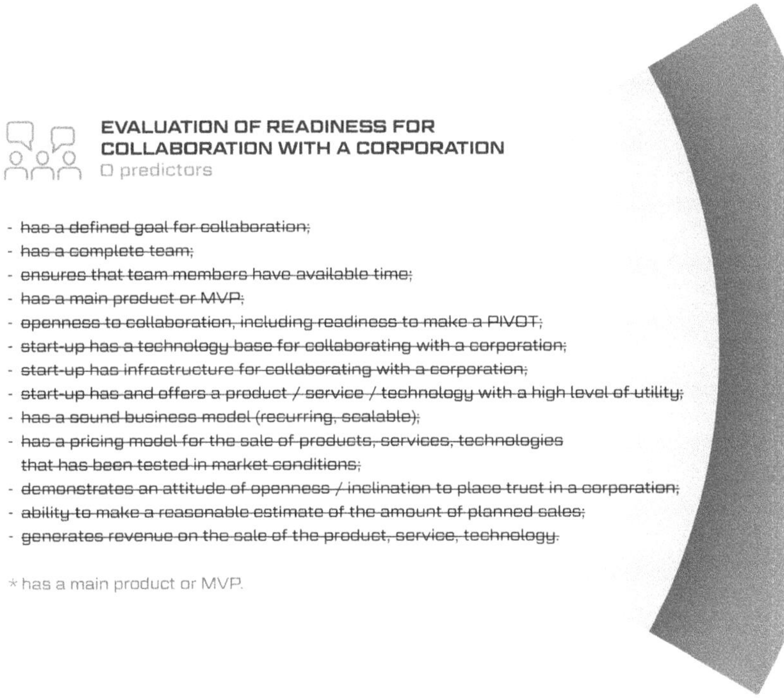

Figure 6.12 Summary of a startup's material predictors as part of the predictive block of variables pertaining to the evaluation of the readiness to engage in cooperation with a corporation.

Source: Proprietary material.

To recap the analyses performed, it should be noted that none of the variables investigated in this block were statistically significant predictor for referencing in future cooperation with a corporation in an acceleration program. Merely one result was posted at the level of a statistical trend and it pertained to the dimension of having a finished product or MVP (Figure 6.12).

6.6 Predictive block – evaluation of the goals of cooperation with a corporation

As part of the block investigating the linkage of variables pertaining to the goals of a startup's cooperation with a corporation with the level of achieved cooperation, the general evaluation of having defined goals prior to engaging in cooperation and the importance of the various goals was incorporated (Figure 6.13).

First, the general level of a startup defining a goal for the cooperation was taken into consideration. The Kruskal–Wallis test was performed, it turned out that it was not statistically significant, $H(2) = 1.38$; $p = 0.502$. As can

Figure 6.13 Verified variables as part of a predictive block pertaining to the evaluation of the goals of cooperation with a corporation

Source: Proprietary material.

be seen in Figure 6.14 the differences between the three groups under comparison were very small – the vast majority of units declared a high level of declaring goals for cooperation.

In the next step the importance of the 15 various goals startups for establishing cooperation with corporations was taken into consideration:

1 product, service development;
2 checking a product's market alignment;
3 testing a product or MVP;
4 acquiring funding (eliminating the necessity of looking for external grants and investors);
5 acquiring investors;
6 getting to know the market and mentoring;
7 gaining access to markets or extending pre-existing sales channels;
8 references for further sales;
9 launching the product on foreign markets;
10 acquiring clients (access to a client database);
11 gaining access to an organization's internal data;
12 gaining access to infrastructure;

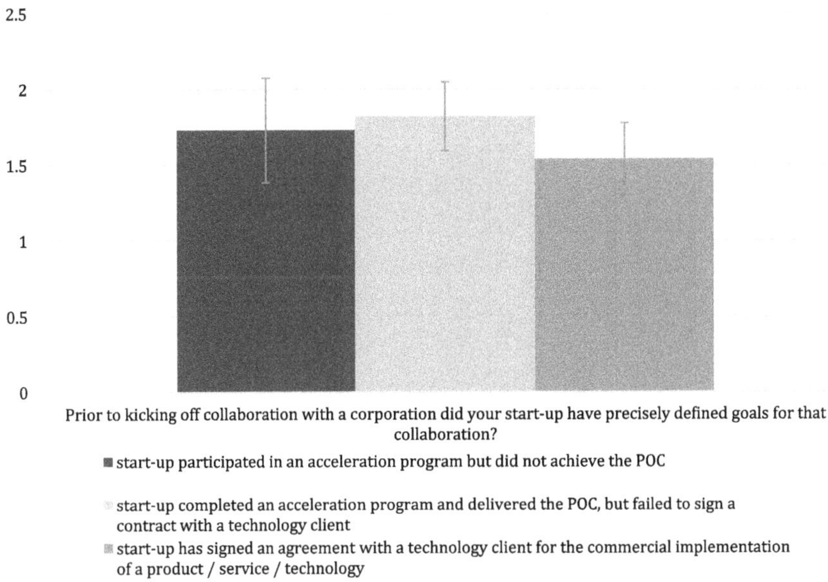

Figure 6.14 Overall level of defining the goals of cooperation with a corporation and the achieved level of cooperation.

Source: Proprietary material.

13 gaining access to technical and business knowledge;
14 image-related benefits, marketing and PR;
15 enhancing the culture of innovation.

The Kruskal–Wallis tests performed (Table 6.25) did not demonstrate any material findings, even at the level of a statistical trend.

Therefore, the level of importance of none of the investigated goals for cooperation significantly influenced the level of achieved cooperation at the end of the acceleration program. Figure 6.15 provides a detailed portrayal of this analysis with a graphic depiction of the results.

Next, the importance of the 13 various goals for cooperating with a corporation with which a startup established an agreement, as seen through the eyes of startups, was taken into consideration. Two statistically significant findings were identified (Table 6.26) – with respect to the factor growing revenue and sustaining or enhancing customer satisfaction. Consequently, a post hoc analysis using the Dunn–Sidak test was performed.

Two statistically significant differences were noted in respect of the importance of the goal of growing revenue. The units that did not execute their POC ascribed to this goal a lower importance than the startups that signed an agreement for commercial implementation ($p = 0.020$) and those that executed their POC but did not sign an agreement with a technology client ($p = 0.010$). These two groups did not, however, differ from one another in a statistically significant manner.

Table 6.25 Level of importance of the goals defined for the cooperation with a corporation and the achieved level of cooperation

Goals for cooperation	*Start-up participated in an acceleration program but did not achieve the POC*		*Start-up completed an acceleration program and delivered the POC, but failed to sign a contract with a technology client*		*Start-up has signed an agreement with a technology client for commercial implementation*			
	M	SD	M	SD	M	SD	H	p
Product, service development	8.18	1.74	8.65	1.81	8.08	2.24	2.50	0.286
Checking a product's market alignment	8.45	1.63	8.15	2.13	8.46	1.41	0.08	0.959
Testing a product or MVP	8.09	2.43	7.98	2.41	7.92	2.50	0.06	0.971
Acquiring funding (eliminating the necessity of looking for external grants and investors)	7.27	2.98	7.22	2.86	7.17	3.13	0.02	0.991
Acquiring investors	5.86	3.01	4.85	3.05	5.67	2.97	2.57	0.277
Getting to know the market and mentoring	6.86	2.68	5.95	2.87	5.67	2.53	2.67	0.263
Gaining access to markets or extending pre-existing sales channels	7.73	2.49	7.40	2.79	7.83	2.50	0.45	0.801
References for further sales	8.45	2.18	8.45	2.15	7.71	3.17	0.35	0.838
Launching the product on foreign markets	5.95	2.95	5.98	3.09	6.17	3.09	0.13	0.939
Acquiring clients (access to a client database)	7.32	3.00	6.84	3.29	6.46	3.24	0.78	0.678
Gaining access to an organization's internal data	4.91	3.25	4.96	2.97	4.29	2.54	0.90	0.638
Gaining access to infrastructure	4.82	3.19	4.98	3.12	4.71	2.91	0.23	0.891
Gaining access to technical and business knowledge	5.59	3.07	5.49	3.11	5.42	2.90	0.07	0.966
Image-related benefits, marketing and PR	8.14	2.17	7.56	2.28	8.08	2.30	2.09	0.352
Enhancing the culture of innovation	5.86	3.03	5.78	3.21	5.33	3.02	0.56	0.756

Source: Proprietary material.

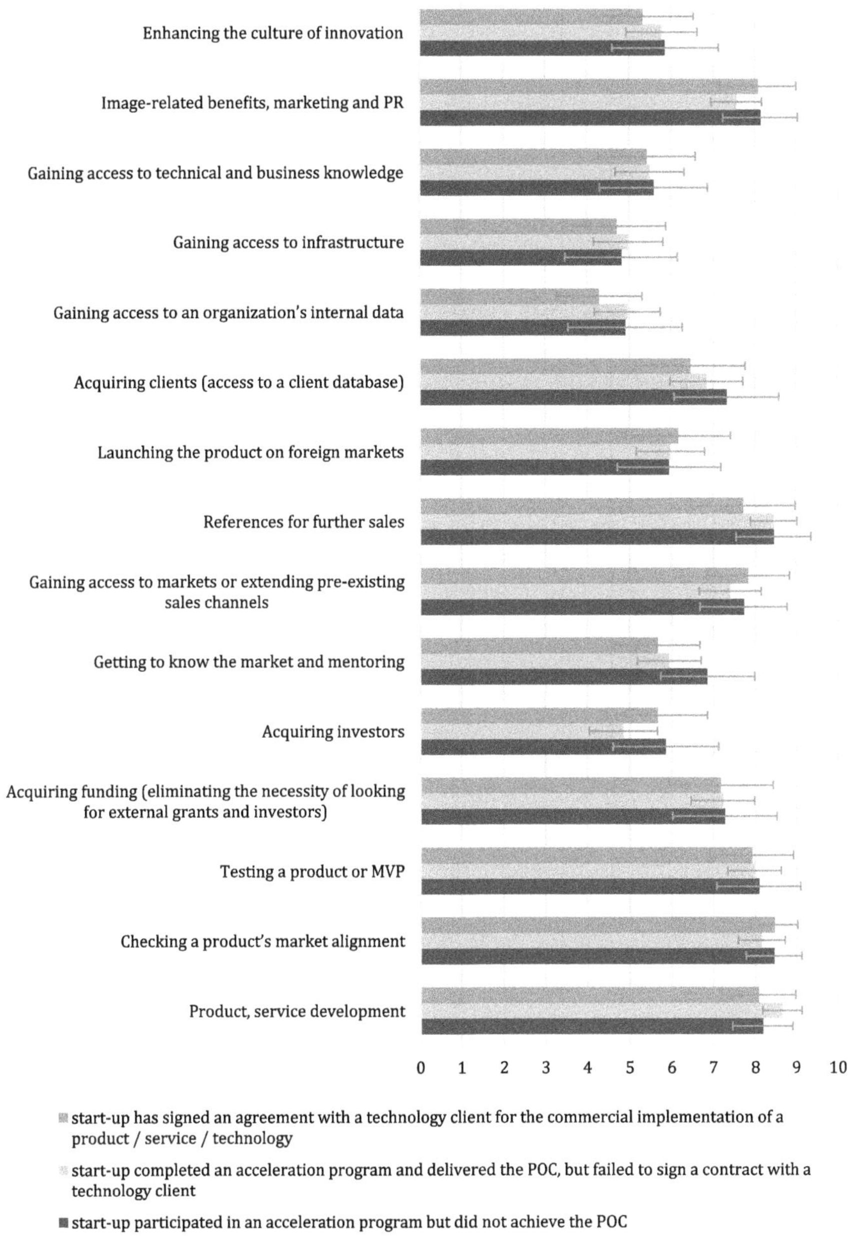

Figure 6.15 Level of importance of the goals defined for the cooperation with a corporation and the level of achieved cooperation.

Source: Proprietary material.

Table 6.26 Importance of the goals for a corporation with which a startup has established collaboration and the level of achieved cooperation

Cooperation factors	*Start-up participated in an acceleration program but did not achieve the POC*		*Start-up completed an acceleration program and delivered the POC, but failed to sign a contract with a technology client*		*Start-up has signed an agreement with a technology client for commercial implementation*			
	M	SD	M	SD	M	SD	H	p
Readiness of a product/service for implementation (extending the proprietary offering)	7.41	2.79	7.64	2.53	7.71	2.14	0.09	0.956
Existence of a need for a startup's product or service	8.23	2.27	8.18	2.09	8.46	1.69	0.21	0.899
Applied technology, innovation (access to technology, innovation)	7.27	2.55	7.51	2.18	7.29	2.24	0.24	0.889
Team competences	7.05	2.48	7.60	2.29	7.54	1.84	1.02	0.600
Growing revenue	5.36	3.11	7.24	2.83	7.42	2.50	7.60	**0.022**
Growing profitability and cost effectiveness	6.09	3.08	7.51	2.85	7.38	2.55	4.78	0.092
Possibility to test a product/service/technology inexpensively	6.64	2.77	7.62	2.35	7.58	2.06	2.47	0.291
Streamlining the operation of a corporation's organizational units	5.36	2.92	5.85	3.22	5.79	2.86	0.47	0.789
Developing a corporation's staff	4.23	3.02	4.65	2.95	5.25	2.82	1.82	0.402
Cultivating the image of a corporation open to innovation	5.95	3.03	7.40	2.44	7.21	2.06	3.87	0.144
New business/clients	5.14	3.38	6.71	2.86	6.54	2.45	3.71	0.156
Maintaining or enhancing customer satisfaction	5.32	3.03	7.29	2.92	6.75	2.40	8.09	**0.018**
Securing a technology, product from the competition	4.18	3.03	6.00	3.12	5.58	2.45	5.93	0.051

Source: Proprietary material.

In respect of the importance of the goal of maintaining or enhancing customer satisfaction, one statistically significant difference was posted. The units that did not execute their POC ascribed to this goal a lower importance than the startups that executed their POC but did not sign an agreement with a technology client ($p = 0.005$). In turn, the startups that signed an agreement for commercial implementation did not differ substantially from the two groups under comparison.

Additionally, the Kruskal–Wallis test proved to be close to statistical significance with respect to the evaluation of two goals on the part of the corporation – grow profitability and cost effectiveness and secure technology and a product from the competition. These results (Figure 6.16) made it impossible

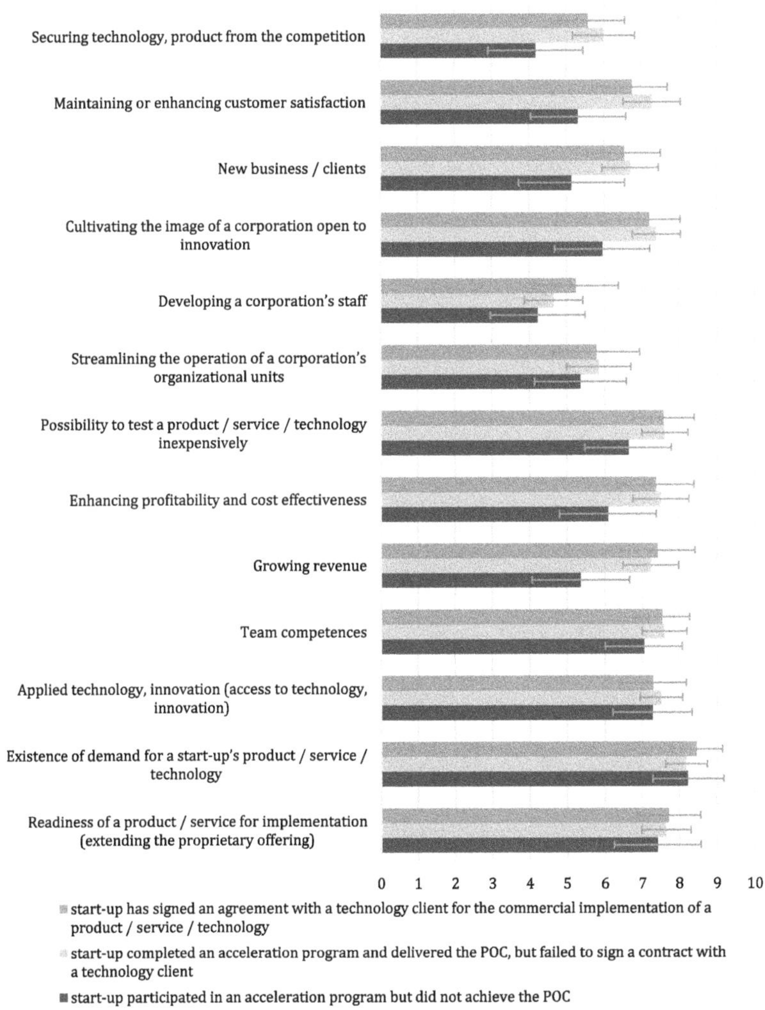

Figure 6.16 Importance of the defined goals for a corporation with which startups have established collaboration and the level of achieved cooperation.

Source: Proprietary material.

to conduct post hoc analyses. Nevertheless, the data obtained indicate that the startups that did not execute their POC ascribed a lesser importance to these goals in comparison to the other two groups. In reference to the other variables no statistically significant differences were posted.

When recapping the analyses performed one should note that two statistically significant dependencies were found among the investigated variables pertaining to the goals of cooperation with a corporation. Figure 6.17 depicts a graphic table of the results obtained.

In this part of the book, the predictors of startups were identified (Figure 6.18) that potentially enhance the chances of elevating the effectiveness of cooperation in acceleration programs with the involvement of corporations. Identifying predictors is crucial because it makes facilitates a better match of startups to cooperation with large organizations.

Figure 6.17 Summary of a startup's material predictors as part of the analyzed block of variables pertaining to the evaluation of the goals for cooperation with a corporation.

Source: Proprietary material.

Figure 6.18 Schematic presentation of the results of the analyses for blocks grouping the predictors of startups achieving cooperation.

Source: Proprietary material.

The following predictors may be counted among the possible determinants of startups achieving success in cooperation in acceleration programs with the involvement of corporations:

1 **Time of commencing cooperation with a corporation** – undertaking inter-organizational cooperation in an acceleration program at a premature stage in the development of a startup may serve as a predictor of this cooperation not achieving effectiveness.

At an early stage of development, a startup may not have a fully tested business model, and the offered product or service may not be in the development phase yet. The key functions, attributes or elements of the solution may be lacking or simply unavailable. Moreover, the lack of full functionality, insufficient quality or untested technologies may lead to the failure of the tests administered by a corporation as part of an acceleration program. In such a circumstance a corporation may observe material imperfections in the solution offered by a startup, which may result in the termination of inter-organizational cooperation.

Moreover, the early phase of startup development frequently entails limitations regarding production capabilities and supplies of products, services and technologies. If a startup is not able to deliver products or services at the required scale and quality, the results of tests may prove to be unsatisfactory. This may incline a corporation to abandon further cooperation with a startup.

It is also noteworthy that at an early stage of a startup's development, there are frequently resource-related limitations such as a dearth of sufficient financial, technical and staff-related means. If a team has been operating on the market for a short period, there may be internal strife among the members and deconcentration during testing. On top of that, a startup first strives to procure funding, which may lead to a shortage of resources for properly securing cooperation with a corporation. As a result, the lack of suitable resources may potentially adversely affect a startup's ability to fulfill the requirements of a corporation and deliver the expected results during the testing of a solution.

2 **Undertaking cooperation with mid-sized businesses** may potentially serve as a predictor of achieving success in inter-organizational cooperation in an acceleration program.

First, this is linked to mid-sized businesses sometimes having a scale of activity similar to a corporation in some areas. Cooperation with such firms allows startups the opportunity to gain valuable experience. It is also helpful in better understanding the operation of large organizations and makes it possible to adapt and align to the requirements and processes that are characteristic of much larger economic entities.

Second, cooperation with mid-sized businesses gives startups the opportunity to test a solution more quickly. This allows for a more efficient process of checking hypotheses and assumptions regarding a startup's business cooperation. As a result, startups obtain faster access to key data that are indispensable for the optimal matching of the model for future cooperation with large organizations.

Additionally, cooperation with such businesses enables startups to gain valuable experience pertaining to negotiations, running projects and forging lasting relationships, which are crucial in cooperation with corporations. Cooperation with mid-sized firms, in principle, affords the possibility of holding more frequent meetings with the key people in an organization (at the level of the management board or directors). This makes it possible to devise a vision and shape the approach to cooperation with corporations where access to decision makers is more difficult.

Medium-sized companies frequently maintain business relationships with corporations as they act as their suppliers or render services to them. Thanks to that startups can benefit from their knowledge and experience, which further strengthens their position. Moreover, through cooperation with mid-sized businesses startups gain valuable experience in adapting to a corporation's evolving needs and requirements.

3 **Meaning of the factor of growing revenue** – a startup's failure to appreciate this aspect may potentially serve as a predictor of not achieving success in inter-organizational cooperation in an acceleration program.

To achieve success in cooperation with corporations, startups should be aware from the very outset that growing revenue is crucial for large organizations. A corporation's internal processes are frequently concentrated on this goal in terms of the cooperation being undertaken. Large organizations naturally prefer those solutions of startups that contribute to achieving the goal of growing business revenue. If a startup is not capable of delivering value to a corporation that translates into revenue growth, that corporation may not be interested in continuing cooperation. The solutions of startups whose outcome is revenue growth are ordinarily easy to justify within a corporation, especially in talks with the financial director. In principle, all other avenues of cooperation (except for cost optimization) may be perceived as less important for a corporation's main business, which may lead to a shortage of appropriate attention on the part of the key decision makers.

It is worth highlighting that a startup's solution focused on revenue growth can easily be integrated with the adopted operating strategy of large organizations. This approach may attract the appropriate attention from the management, which in turn leads to the engagement of the right business units, which have clearly defined revenue targets linked to a system of indicators and bonuses in a corporation. Enhancing revenue is also associated with delivering value to a corporation's clients. If a startup does not offer products or services that are attractive to a corporation's clients, this may lead to low sales and the absence of revenue growth. Therefore, the failure to appreciate this factor may indicate a lack of understanding for the needs and preferences of a corporation's clients and an inability to deliver valuable solutions.

It is also worth noting that cooperation with a corporation may also signify a rivalry between a startup and the other partners of large organizations. If a startup is not capable of effectively competing in terms of revenue growth, then it may be squeezed out into marginal cooperation by more competitive companies that also operate in partnership with a large organization. The failure to appreciate this factor may point to the absence of an effective marketing strategy, an inability to source clients or a lack of competitive prices and conditions for the solution offered by a startup.

4 **Meaning of the factor for maintaining or enhancing customer satisfaction** – a failure to appreciate this aspect may potentially serve as a predictor of not achieving success in cooperation.

The purpose of maintaining or enhancing customer satisfaction is important for corporations for several reasons, and a failure to appreciate that may serve as a predictor of a startup's failure in its cooperation with a corporation. First, satisfied clients are more inclined to continue being loyal clients of a corporation. The long-term relationship with a client translates into revenue stability and value growth for a corporation. If a startup is not capable of delivering products or services that satisfy the expectations of a corporation's clients and if they do not contribute to enhancing customer satisfaction, then a corporation may begin to look for other partners, which may lead to the severance of cooperation with a startup.

Additionally, satisfied clients are more inclined to share their positive experiences and recommendations for a solution they use, or a technology. This behavior is termed in the literature as *co-creation* of innovation. Positive opinions and recommendations from current clients are a valuable source of not just retaining clients but also acquiring new ones.

Client satisfaction is also of crucial significance for the competitiveness of a corporation on the market. In today's dynamic business environment, the loyalty of clients frequently diminishes, while minor shortcomings on the part of a corporation may lead to them departing to go to the competition. Satisfied clients are more inclined to continue being attached to the brand and products of a given corporation, which attenuates the risk of losing clients to the competition. If a startup is not capable of delivering a solution that contributes to enhancing a corporation's client satisfaction, this may lead to a large company losing its competitive edge on the market. Accordingly, startups should deliver solutions that create real value for clients. Metrics such as NPS (Net Promoter Score meaning the level of the net recommendation) that measure how probable it is that clients will recommend an entity, its products, services and technologies to their friends and associates, Customer Satisfaction (indicating the level of client satisfaction), the Churn Rate (indicating the percentage of customers resigning from using a firm's services among the total number of buyers) and CLTV (*Customer Lifetime Value* illustrating the projected net profit on a relationship with a client) are important when evaluating the justification for engaging in long-term cooperation with a startup.

5 **Number of founding members** – a small number of founders may be a potential predictor of not achieving cooperation.

This result may be linked to the nature of the projects conducted by startups in inter-organizational cooperation with corporations. These projects are usually complicated and frequently require diverse skills, competences and resources. Having a larger number of founders may contribute to greater diversity in terms of knowledge, experience and market relationships which shareholders contribute to the company. Thanks to that the startup team has greater chances of having the indispensable competences to run a project with a corporation and deliver the expected results in accordance with the established schedule. In the case of a small founding team, these resources are restricted to a greater extent, which may lead to inefficiencies and a lack of progress in the preparations for POC or in executing the implementation in a corporation. This may also affect the ability of a startup to solve problems as part of the cooperation established with a large organization and decision-making. For instance, a larger number of founders may signify a broader array of technical, technological, business, marketing and sales skills in the company. Frequently, a person with expert knowledge (e.g., in the field of technology, UX) is designated to a specific topic on the part of the corporation. If a startup does not have the appropriate experts in the founding team, then the talks may not be on equivalent footing because there are disproportions in the level of knowledge. Then, the expert on the side of the corporation will perceive the startup through the prism of the lacking competences and thereby the very solution offered by a new company will be backtracked. Additionally, in the event of an illness or the resignation of one of the members of the founding team, a small startup team may have difficulties with continuing its business activity, which may affect the achievement of the intended goals of cooperation.

6 **Work in public administration by the main founder of the startup** may be a potential predictor of not achieving the assumed cooperation.

This may follow from the distinct nature of work in public administration and the skills obtained and the experience of founding members. Work in administration frequently entails the formation of skills and competences differing from work in the private sector, especially in the dynamic environment of startups. Skills such as flexibility, the ability to conduct negotiations, quick decision-making and the ability to work in evolving, frequently uncertain conditions are important for the development of a startup. People with experience in government administration may have less experience in doing business and also probably do not have the skills that are important from the vantage point of the operation of startups. On the other hand, work in public administration may have some value since in some aspects it is reminiscent of a corporation, especially in terms of procedures, bureaucracy, lengthy decision-making processes. It is worth recalling that people working in administration frequently become accustomed to a lengthy period of operation. They accept the reality surrounding them and may have diminished motivation to optimize processes and seek effectiveness. Organizational culture may also play a major role. Government administration and the startup sector are greatly different from one another in terms of their organizational culture, rules of operation and approach to innovation. Startups are poised for rapid and scalable development, experimenting and risk taking while government administration frequently acts slowly in accordance with established procedures and decision-making structures. Accordingly, persons with experience in administration may encounter difficulties in adapting to the flexible and dynamic organizational culture of startups. It is also worth remembering that work in government administration frequently involves a different type of contact network and access to resources in comparison to the private sector. Persons with experience in work in government administration may have limited access to investors and mentors. This may adversely affect the inter-organizational cooperation of businesses in which establishing and skillfully running and utilizing business relationships are vital when it comes to the success of working jointly with a corporation.

7 **Number of years of operation on the market** – a short period of operation may be a potential predictor of failure in inter-organizational cooperation.

Corporations customarily seek out startups that have robust foundations and a long-term operating perspective. Startups with a shorter history of operating on the market are perceived as more risky due to having less experience in relationships with large organizations, limited financial, technological and staff-related resources, and because their business model is frequently untested on the market, or their solution has not been fully tested. These factors may substantially impede the execution of complicated projects as part of cooperation with corporations.

A longer history of operation on the market in principle allows a startup to compile the requisite knowledge and appreciation for technologies, trends, the distinct traits of the market and the needs and preferences of clients. Having this type of knowledge makes it possible to match products, services and technologies better to the expectations of a corporation and its clients, which enhances the chances for achieving success in inter-organizational cooperation. Moreover, a longer period of operation on the market gives a startup potentially the ability to establish and develop a larger number of relationships with other businesses, suppliers, research institutions and industrial experts. These relationships may prove to be valuable at the stage of executing the POC in a corporation. They may supply additional resources and the support needed to test and the future implementation of the startup's product or service. Corporations ordinarily prefer cooperation with startups that have documented successes in cooperation with other large organizations, that have references and that have a good market reputation. Companies with a longer history of operation on the market and a finished and tested solution are perceived to a greater extent as reliable partners. With respect to them, cooperation may come about fairly quickly in accordance with the plug-and-play approach.

8 **Not using European Union funds at the stage of creation and at the current stage of operation of a startup** may be a predictor of not fully achieving cooperation.

It is worth noting that public funds, especially European Union funds frequently constitute a significant source of funding for startups, especially in countries in Central and Eastern Europe. Their availability on the market makes it possible to invest in research and development and infrastructure and develop innovative potential. The startups that do not avail themselves of this support may periodically encounter difficulties on account of limited financial resources, which may contribute to difficulties in executing projects in cooperation with corporations.

Moreover, using European Union programs entails a certain level of project selection and evaluation. These funds are frequently targeted to undertakings with a high innovative level. Startups that utilize these types of support may have greater chances of developing and implementing innovative solutions. Moreover, on account of the formal requirements associated with managing and squaring accounts for the awarded grants with public institutions (as the entities extending these grants), such startups may be better prepared to fulfill the formal requirements of corporations.

It is worth observing that during the course of the analyses conducted, six predictors were also recorded at the level of a statistical trend that may also potentially exert an impact on success in the cooperation of the parties in acceleration programs. The following may be counted among them:

1 **No history of previous cooperation with a corporation** may be a potential predictor of not achieving cooperation

Startups that could historically demonstrate cooperation with corporations are potentially better prepared for cooperation with technology clients (experience gleaned from cooperation) and thereby they may have greater chances of achieving success in cooperation. This may stem ordinarily from greater knowledge about how a corporation operates, its requirements, procedures and decision-making processes. This information is critical at the stage of performing tests in a large organization. A startup must adapt its solution and approach to the needs, processes, protocols and expectations of a corporation and also align itself to its organizational culture and prevailing procedures. The lack of this knowledge may lead to an improper appreciation for a corporation's requirements and an unsuitable preparation of the product, service or technology for the purposes of tests and future business cooperation. Corporations frequently have unique requirements, while their decision-making processes are time-consuming and complex. A lack of knowledge concerning these processes of the lack of skill of adjusting to them may potentially adversely affect the tests of the startup's products, services or technologies. It also seems that a lack of history of cooperation may be a signal for decision makers in a corporation that the startup does not yet have the appropriately refined standards of working with large business partners and refined systems of quality assurance, which are material in the effective cooperation with a corporation. Corporations frequently require appropriate standards of quality and control, while the absence of such systems may lead to failure in the tests run and as a consequence to the termination of inter-organizational cooperation. The lack of prior cooperation hinders the building of trust and may cause a corporation to be more cautious at the stage of tests or unwilling to continue cooperation with a startup following the completed acceleration program.

2 **Having foreign clients** may potentially serve as a predictor of achieving cooperation.

A startup having foreign clients may be a predictor of successful cooperation because it means that the new business is also capable of attracting clients outside the local market, which enhances its growth and scalability potential. This also is evidence of the value of the product or service offered by the company. If a startup gains the trust of foreign clients, this may evidence the attractiveness and competitiveness of its offering on the global market, the sustainability of its business model and the new company's capability of implementing solutions in varying cultural and businesses environments. These arguments may potentially persuade corporations to establish inter-organizational cooperation.

3 **Growing profitability and cost effectiveness** – appreciating this aspect may potentially be a predictor of achieving cooperation.

In principle, corporations endeavor to grow their profitability and improve their cost effectiveness to maximize profits and achieve a competitive edge on the market. Growing profitability indicators is one of the crucial elements of a corporation's long-term strategy as it drives its market value. Profitability also constitutes a major financial ratio for an organization that determines its ability to reinvest in development, innovations and market expansion. It is also for that reason that a startup that is capable of making a contribution to improving profitability or reducing a corporation's costs gains in attractiveness as a business partner. Moreover, a startup's ability to supply solutions that directly contribute to improving a corporation's financial results builds trust and strengthens the position of a new company as a partner in long-term cooperation. Theoretically, such a partnership may be analyzed in light of the Resource-Based View, which emphasizes the importance of having unique resources and competences as a source of competitive edge. Startups that offer unique, valuable and hard-to-copy solutions may in this manner gain a sustainable spot in business relations with corporations. Partnerships based on genuine and measurable financial benefits may lead to a corporation making further investments, joint ventures or long-term contracts that in turn may contribute to the startup's growth and expansion onto new markets. As a result, such cooperation not only augments a corporation's competitiveness, but it also facilitates a startup's dynamic development, by creating favorable conditions for further cooperation.

4 **Securing a technology, product from the competition** – appreciating this factor may be a potential predictor contributing to the success of cooperation.

Securing a technology, product from the competition is an important aspect of cooperation with corporations and should be a priority for startups at the stage of establishing cooperation. Corporations frequently invest substantial financial means and resources in developing innovative technologies and products. They strive to maintain a competitive edge on the market by holding unique solutions that are hard to copy by other entities competing on the market. From the time when a corporation elects to cooperate with a startup it expects that any and all information concerning technologies and products that is furnished as part of cooperation will be duly secured and will not make its way into the hands of the competition. A startup should take steps with suitable lead time to secure its intellectual property. This may involve securing a patent, registering trademarks, gaining copyright protection or implementing internal data protection policies. These types of safeguards form an important part of building trust in business relationships with corporations. A startup will elevate its attractiveness as a business partner and simultaneously strengthen a corporation's position on the market because a large organization may be aware that its potential investments in the development and commercialization of new technologies will not be in jeopardy due to the actions of competitors.

5 **Having a finished product/MVP** may be a predictor potentially contributing to inter-organizational cooperation.

A startup having a finished product or MVP gives it the ability to prove to the corporation during the running of tests that the offered solution is valuable and functional. Corporations that have access to specific data and complete knowledge about a product may make decisions with less risk concerning the continuation of cooperation. Additionally, having a fully operating product or MVP enables the startup to present clearly to the corporation the benefits its solution may accrue. Having a finished product is more persuasive than a solution that is just at the phase of development, including tests. For that reason, the lack of a finished product may delay the cooperation process. Moreover, the ability to run tests on a finished product, as well as compile opinions and feedback from a corporation and users in the form of a completed solution is invaluable. Thanks to that a startup may more efficiently adapt its solution to the corporation's needs and expectations and augment its chances for success in inter-organizational cooperation. One should remember that the essence of acceleration programs is to enable corporations to test solutions in their environment. Therefore, running tests requires having a finished solution. Information is frequently stated in the rules and regulations of acceleration programs that in terms of cooperation, consideration is given in the selection procedure to those startups whose solution has made it at least to the level of MVP.

6 **Number of employees hired – the small number of employees in a startup team** may be a predictor potentially affecting the success of cooperation

A higher number of employees customarily signifies differentiation in the competences and skills present in a startup team. Differentiation and skills may constitute a measure of a startup's operating capabilities. If a startup has various talents and experience this may help it face the broad spectrum of needs and challenges related to the process of testing solutions and technologies in the corporate environment. Such teams can more easily cope with varying challenges, including technical or operational tasks that may emerge suddenly in the course of cooperation.

Additionally, a greater number of people in a team prospectively augments the chances for ensuring the continuity of cooperation with the different business units in a corporation. Interactions between team members may lead to the emergence of synergies and to the generation of actions required to pursue proof-of-concept. Thanks to their diverse experience and competences employees of not just a startup but also a corporation can supplement one another thereby forging more structured and effective relations.

Conclusion

According to the analysis done in the databases called Web of Science and Scopus, the scientific works regarding inter-organizational cooperation between corporations and startups are fragmentary and contain multiple theoretical and empirical research gaps. The substantial shortage of research in this area is visible, especially on the Polish research front. This explicit research gap served as the primary inspiration and motivation for investigating more precisely the paradigm for open innovations in the operation of startup accelerators and their acceleration programs involving corporations. The author embarked on a theoretical analysis of this issue along with empirical research having the purpose of gleaning a meticulous understanding and investigating the impact exerted by the functioning of acceleration programs on inter-organizational cooperation. The purpose of this approach was to fill the existing gap in scientific knowledge and contribute to the development of research into inter-organizational cooperation between corporations and new innovative companies.

Comparing open and closed innovation with an eye to their approach, innovation processes (inbound, outbound and coupled) and application in businesses facilitated the formulation of a theoretical foundation. This served as the basis for further discussion and analysis into inter-organizational cooperation between corporations and startups in acceleration programs. The motives organizations have to undertake cooperation with external partners were identified, and a proprietary approach to defining the term "cooperation" was presented. It means a method of acting that leads to the joint attainment of goals that are mutually not at odds with one another as part of a temporary agreement.

Clarifying the potential obstacles to inter-organizational cooperation between corporations and startups in the open innovation model is crucial to be able to understand the challenges and possibilities of developing innovative products, services and technologies and implementing them in the structures of large organizations. The network perspective was investigated in terms of inter-organizational cooperation in which the network describes the interactions between different entities. This approach is characterized

DOI: 10.4324/9781003540366-8

by the constant search for innovations as part of cooperation with market partners and integrating external sources of innovations with an organization's in-house resources. It was observed that the paradigm of open innovations has become a source of competitive advantage where the value network model supersedes the traditional value chain. In turn, the value generated in the cooperation process stems from the usage of an organization's in-house resources and external sources and network relationships. In this context startup accelerators and their acceleration programs play a major role as liaisons and integrators of innovations in the structures of large businesses.

Analysis of the potential of startups and corporations in the open innovation model was also conducted, including the cooperation strategies of large organizations. The key components of a corporate strategy for cooperating with startups were defined. It should contain, among other things: (a) an identification of the goals and benefits, (b) a constant analysis of the startup ecosystem, (c) an incorporation of the various models for cooperation with startups, (d) a selection of those startups that dovetail to the greatest degree with the goals of a corporation and may deliver added value to an organization and produce, if possible, mutual benefits to the parties and (e) actions associated with monitoring the progress of inter-organizational cooperation.

The various models for cooperation between corporations and startups were characterized as part of these actions giving consideration to goals, rules, characteristics and financial needs. The detailed analysis encompassed models such as competitions, hackathons, internet platforms, venture building, strategic partnerships, cooperation with research and development (R&D) departments, corporate incubators, corporate accelerators, corporate venture capital funds and acquisitions of startups.

Additionally, it was determined that the identified models for attracting startups may be used effectively by adjusting them to the strategies and needs of corporations and the development phases of startups, such as the idea/Minimum Viable Product (MVP) stage, growth stage and scale-up stage. Each one of these three growth stages is characterized by its distinct goals, actions, challenges and financial capabilities. To gain a better grasp of these aspects, a tabular list has been drafted to incorporate the key attributes, goals and challenges characteristic of each one of the development phases in a young firm. Thanks to this, it was possible to subordinate the models for attracting startups most frequently employed by corporations to the appropriate stages of their development. Moreover, in order to investigate the effectiveness of these models more precisely, innovation processes were analyzed and they were assigned to the various models while performing a detailed analysis thereof.

An important element in the research conducted was the analysis done on the frameworks of startup accelerators, starting with cooperation between a corporation and an independent external accelerator through the model of setting up a startup accelerator within a corporation to the cooperation model between a corporate accelerator and an external startup accelerator independent of a corporation. This analysis was conducted with an eye to traits, advantages, disadvantages/challenges and resources. The major models for the startup accelerators on the market such as (a) equity accelerator, (b) equity-free accelerator, (c) accelerator based on an effectiveness model and (d) accelerator operating in a hybrid model. This analysis was conducted with an eye to the operating rules, advantages, disadvantages and how these models are perceived by corporations. The three dominant types of acceleration programs were also portrayed: (a) general acceleration program, (b) industrial acceleration program and (c) program with topical paths. Each one of these programs differs in terms of the approach to inter-organizational cooperation and alignment to a corporation's distinct needs. Just as in the case of the accelerator models, these programs were characterized, their pros and cons were flagged and a discussion was held on how they are perceived by corporations. Additionally, the three major procedures for organizing acceleration programs were subjected to analysis: (a) on-site program, (b) virtual program and (c) mixed program for the purposes of identifying the unique advantages, disadvantages and implications for each one of them.

Having in mind the foregoing analyses, it should be highlighted that appreciating the differences within the context of the startup accelerator frameworks, the operating models of accelerators, the types of acceleration programs and their funding sources is crucial for corporations planning cooperation with innovative companies. Such an approach will make it possible to make a more conscious choice of a suitable model and acceleration program that will best fit the needs and goals of large organizations. This will also make it possible to utilize effectively the acceleration programs that support open innovations.

An important part of the work undertaken was the proprietary detailed elaboration of the stages of an acceleration program encompassing the program planning process, startup recruitment, preparatory work for tests and the solution testing stage in the corporate environment, frequently wrapped up with a demo day-type event or a pitch to a corporation's management. In this approach the focus was on appreciating the key elements and challenges associated with each one of these stages.

It is also worth emphasizing the aspect of inter-organizational cooperation following the formal completion of acceleration, that is, post-acceleration. The possibilities of continuing cooperation were analyzed. They may assume the following forms: (a) capital investment by the corporation in the startup; (b) R&D cooperation; (c) business partnership, licensing technology; and (d) actions to enhance the culture of innovativeness in large organizations. The author's in-depth analysis of the forms of a business partnership covered the four major cooperation models that take into account the flow of financial means between the parties. These models encompass the following: (a) the solutions created by startups are distributed by a corporation under its own brand name; (b) creation of a joint product or service offering; (c) intermediation in the distribution of the startups' solutions to a corporation's partners and clients; and (d) acquisition or some other form of investment done by the corporation or an entity acting under a mandate from it (e.g., a corporate venture capital fund) in a startup.

In that manner the considerations set forth in the first part of this book accomplish the intended research goal as they systematize knowledge regarding inter-organizational cooperation between corporations and startups in acceleration programs in light of open innovation theory.

The systematic literature review conducted using PRISMA methodology in the following databases: Web of Science, Scopus and the review of the database BazEkon and the database of projects in the National Science Center in Cracow made it possible to gain a profound appreciation for the current state of knowledge and research context. This stage of the research made it possible not just to identify the research gap but also to designate the directions of further research in the field of inter-organizational cooperation between corporations and startups. The research findings obtained on the perception of acceleration programs managed by startup accelerators and their impact on cooperation between startups and corporations allowed the author to formulate the following conclusions:

1 Establishing cooperation with corporations is important to startups; however, this constitutes a challenge for most of them.
2 Cooperating with startups is important to corporations; however, their representatives are of the opinion that the very process of establishing this cooperation is complicated.
3 Acceleration programs play a major role in bringing together startups and corporations and contribute to the commencement of cooperation between them.
4 Startups affirmed that participation in acceleration programs involving corporations facilitates faster commercialization of their products or services. Moreover, the respondents confirmed that participation in an acceleration program increases the chances of implementing innovation and entering into commercial agreements to sell products and services to corporations in the future.
5 Cooperation produces benefits for corporations and startups alike while the benefits themselves surpass the expenditures incurred by both parties.

In turn, the findings of empirical research pertaining to inter-organizational cooperation in acceleration programs make it possible to formulate the following conclusions:

1 Large organizations and startups largely strive to realize divergent goals in terms of their cooperation with one another. For corporations the priority is to create innovative solutions, minimize costs, optimize processes and maintain a high level of customer satisfaction. In turn, startups concentrate their efforts on product development, checking their market fit, gaining references and testing their solutions in a corporate environment.

2 Large organizations and startups alike encounter major challenges in establishing cooperation. For corporations the major difficulties stem from the difference in the pace of decision-making, bureaucratic procedures and startups' overly excessive expectations, which may lead to tension and problems in the cooperation process. In turn, for startups, the major challenge is the lengthy decision-making process in corporations, bureaucracy and corporations' excessive conservatism. The lengthy time of waiting for corporate decisions may lead to delays in the execution of startups' projects and unexpected downtime in inter-organizational cooperation. The complexity of cooperation procedures and unclear operating rules may cause difficulties for startups to understand them in respect of a corporation's operating rules and requirements.
3 The results of the conducted analyses regarding the difficulties associated with establishing cooperation between corporations and startups have made it possible to identify the following challenges for both parties. In the case of corporations, the largest challenges pertain to agreeing on a suitable sales cycle for a business agreement after a successful test of a solution on a large organization's infrastructure. Additionally, a challenge is represented by establishing clear rules of cooperation within a company and devising an implementation plan that would contain the key performance indicators for a project. In turn, for startups, the key challenge is reaching the decision makers in a corporation who are responsible for making the decision on the prospective cooperation. Also the necessity of agreeing on the proper sales cycle for a commercial agreement and establishing unambiguous cooperation rules with a corporation constitute a significant challenge.
4 The results of the analysis of the achieved goals in terms of cooperation between corporations and startups have demonstrated that the two parties evaluate their execution at different levels. Corporations rated the execution of goals related to creating innovative technologies, products and services the highest, followed by those related to optimizing internal processes and building the image of a modern company. What is important is that the general evaluations given by the representatives of corporations pertaining to the achievement of these goals are moderate. In turn, startups indicated that they achieve the highest degree of achieving their goals. Particularly positive results were recorded on product or MVP testing, product/service development and verification of the product fit with the market. These results suggest that cooperation between the parties may accrue mutual benefits; however, there still are areas requiring further optimization and improvement in the process of inter-organizational cooperation.

The last topic touched upon, as part of the research conducted, was identifying the key attributes of startups that as predictors may potentially enhance the chances for successful inter-organizational cooperation between the parties in acceleration programs. Selecting the right companies for cooperation by an accelerator and a corporation is key for startups and large organizations alike to enter into the target business agreement. Identifying the predictors that may potentially affect the effectiveness of cooperation is important because it makes it possible to align startups to acceleration programs involving corporations better. As a result, the chances for the parties to achieve the intended goals of cooperation are augmented.

The research and analyses conducted provided the grounds for identifying eight predictors from among the 66 attributes that may potentially contribute to enhancing the effectiveness of cooperation. The following number among them:

1 Establishing cooperation with mid-sized businesses before starting cooperation with corporations potentially augments a startup's chance of achieving success in inter-organizational cooperation.
2 Establishing cooperation with a corporation at too early a stage of activity by a startup is a potential predictor of failure in inter-organizational cooperation.
3 Appreciation by the managers of a startup that revenue growth is a priority in the activities of large organizations is a potential predictor of success in cooperation.
4 Startups taking into account that corporations attach enormous importance to enhancing customer satisfaction is a potential predictor of success in cooperation.
5 A higher number of founding members in a startup fosters greater diversity of knowledge, experience and market contact network, which is beneficial for inter-organizational cooperation.
6 Avoiding a situation in which the main founder is a person with working experience in public administration since the skills and competences required in the private sector may differ substantially from the ones gained in public administration.
7 Market experience gleaned at an earlier stage (prior to joining an acceleration program) allows a startup to collect the requisite knowledge and skills, which may translate into a better fit between the products, services and technologies and the expectations of the corporation and its clients.
8 Taking advantage of European Union funds at the stage of setting up a startup and during its further development may contribute to better preparation for satisfying a corporation's requirements.

During the research six predictors were also identified at the level of a statistical trend, which may potentially affect the efficiency of inter-organizational cooperation. The following number among the predictors:

1 Lack of prior history of cooperation with a corporation may be a predictor of a startup not achieving effective cooperation with a large organization.
2 A startup having foreign clients may constitute a predictor of achieving inter-organizational cooperation.

3 The appreciation by the management of a startup that growing the profitability and cost effectiveness of a corporation may constitute a predictor of achieving cooperation between the parties.
4 Devising a joint approach that encompasses securing technology or a product from the competition posed by other corporations may constitute a predictor of achieving effective cooperation.
5 A startup having a finished product or MVP at the stage of joining an acceleration program may substantially contribute to enhancing the chances of success in cooperation between the parties.
6 A small number of employees employed in startups may constitute a predictor of not achieving success in inter-organizational cooperation.

Research limitations

Just like most empirical research, this research also has its limitations. The first limitation was the reach of the research conducted. It spanned the territory of Poland, instead of a broader area spanning other European countries. However, as demonstrated in the monograph, despite the possibilities of regional differences appearing, acceleration programs in the Central and Eastern European region have elements in common with the ones in Western Europe and the United States through the international nature of the corporations that participate in them. Corporations get involved in programs across the world, which leads to similarities in their structure and cooperation with new companies. These corporations seek innovative solutions that may be implemented globally regardless of the distinct nature of local markets.

Another possible limitation was the relatively small number of 25 corporations that took part in the research. This followed from the limited number of corporations in Poland that elected to cooperate with startups in acceleration programs. However, the author deemed it to be crucial for the full and comprehensive appreciation of the phenomenon under investigation to gain the perspectives of both parties involved in inter-organizational cooperation, which justified the adoption of this research sample. Even though a larger number of participating corporations could theoretically augment the ability to generalize the findings, the author, however, would like to emphasize that such a number does not make it possible to conduct an analysis, nor does it preclude the accurate interpretation of the results obtained.

Directions of research

The future research emerging from the conclusions in this book will concentrate on two areas:

1 Conducting an analysis on which one of the factors of trust and managerial practices may have a potential influence on the achievement of cooperation between corporations and startups. Trust at an organizational and

interpersonal level alike plays a fundamental role in forging sustainable relationships between the participants of acceleration programs. This research should encompass not only the model for attracting innovations from outside in the form of an acceleration program but it should also pertain to a comparison with other models, that is, a corporate incubator and startups' cooperation with the R&D departments of corporations. In particular, research is planned to make an attempt at evaluating how different cooperation models affect the building of trust, the effectiveness of the innovation process and risk and resource management. Juxtaposing acceleration programs with other models such as corporate incubators, which ordinarily offer more long-term support to startups and cooperation with R&D departments, which are frequently more integrated with corporations' internal processes, may provide valuable information about the differences in effectiveness, the degree of innovativeness and the level of engagement of the parties.

2 The second area of research will pertain to analyzing inter-organizational cooperation in terms of one of the models discussed in the first chapter, namely the corporate venture capital fund. The key issue in this respect will be to investigate the possible relationships that transpire between a Corporate Venture Capital fund (CVC) and a corporate accelerator. These relationships will be researched in the categories of cooperation and potential competition. According to the author, it would be desirable to appreciate how these two structures, which function as part of a single corporation can cooperate or compete at different levels, for example, in resource allocation, investment strategies or priorities related to developing innovative projects. From a scientific point of view, it would be particularly important to identify the potentially negative outcomes stemming from such cooperation, ones such as, for example, conflicts of interest, rivalry for projects or recognizing the limitations ensuing from the internal organizational structure. Such an analysis would contribute to deepening and enriching existing knowledge on cooperation between corporate accelerators and venture capital funds. This would provide new perspectives on the efficacy of these models and their impact on the innovativeness of corporations. This research could also flag the desirable directions for collaboration that would aim at mitigating potential conflicts and maximizing the benefits stemming from the operating synergy of these two mechanisms for attracting innovations to corporations.

Implications for corporate management

Analyzing the frameworks for the operating models of accelerators, their programs and the findings of empirical research delivers significant implications to a corporation's management. Samples of these implications are as follows:

1 Management should analyze precisely the available models for the functioning of accelerators and select the one that best fits the organization's

goals and business strategy. It is important for corporations to adjust their goals and strategies to the distinct nature of the selected accelerator model. The management should take into account in this case, insofar as it is possible, the needs and goals of the startups participating in the program.

2 Corporations should invest time and resources in building sustainable relationships with the participating startups after the completion of the acceleration program. They may achieve this through, among other things, supporting startups in their further development, making capital investments, long-term R&D cooperation and business partnerships.
3 Corporations should monitor and evaluate the effectiveness of the acceleration programs in which they participate. Thanks to that they can align their actions and strategies on an ongoing basis to evolving needs and market conditions. What is crucial is regularly monitoring the effectiveness of cooperation with startups to evaluate whether the intended goals are being achieved and whether this cooperation is producing the intended benefits. This type of evaluation not only contributes to streamlining processes but it also makes it possible to identify areas for improvement and more effective utilization of resources.
4 Corporations should identify on a timely basis the key difficulties to establishing cooperation with startups and introduce corrective measures with sufficient lead time. It is important for the management to adjust its approach to the selected model for the operation of the accelerator and its program.
5 Corporations should pay attention to those predictors of startups that may potentially contribute to the chances of achieving success in the cooperation between the parties. Thanks to that they will avoid squandering time and resources on projects with a low potential for future inter-organizational cooperation.
6 Corporations should actively utilize acceleration programs as a tool to promote the culture of innovativeness in an organization. These programs may form the foundation for building openness to new projects and supporting an entrepreneurial mode of thinking among staff. A key component in this process is enhancing awareness on acceleration programs and actively engaging in-house teams in these initiatives. By engaging employees at different levels in the organization – not just those staff members from R&D departments but also from operations, sales and the management in an acceleration program – it will be possible to support startups' projects in an organization. Corporations may to this end hold workshops, training sessions and internal presentations showcasing the startups' projects. In this manner they create a conducive environment in which innovations are perceived as an important part of an organization's development. Moreover, advancing innovativeness inside a corporation not only enhances employee engagement but also integrates the staff with their external partners. This type of approach may also contribute

to creating in-house teams playing the role of mentors and experts for startups, which will be conducive to mutual development and forging long-term inter-organizational relationships.

Implications for the team managing a startup

Analyzing the conclusions and findings of research also points to a multitude of implications for startups. They may help new companies prepare better for cooperation with corporations and effectively tap into the opportunities offered by accelerators and their programs. Samples of these implications encompass the following:

1. Prior to joining an acceleration program, startups should analyze precisely the available programs and select the one that best fits their needs and intended goals. Since every accelerator's model has its own unique traits such as, for instance, the offered resources, engagement of management, forms of funding, the managers of startups should tweak their operating strategies to the selected accelerator model and the distinct nature of the program to be realized.
2. Acceleration programs play a key role in the integration of startups with corporations. Participating in these programs is particularly important for startups since this makes it possible to test and improve the offered products, services and technologies. Additionally, these programs support the process of commercializing innovations and foster the establishment of sustainable relationships with large organizations, which may contribute to the long-term development of startups.
3. Startups may treat the results presented in this research work as a valuable source of hints that will enable them to engage in more effective cooperation with corporations. Utilizing the results may help them mitigate potential losses such as squandering time for ineffective processes that do not produce the expected outcomes, or excessive utilization of limited financial and technological resources. That is also why the application of the research conclusions will enable startups to be more aware of how they manage their resources, human and tangible alike.
4. Corporations and startups have divergent goals and priorities in terms of the established cooperation. That is why it is important for startups to be aware of these differences and to be flexible in adjusting their solutions to the needs of large organizations. Appreciating these differences is an important part of building long-term and effective cooperation between startups and corporations. Startups should carry out a preliminary analysis of the corporate business goals. Properly identifying these goals will enable startups to align their offering and value proposition better, which may augment their chances for successful cooperation with corporations. It is worth noting that the alignment of startups to the expectations of corporations does not signify abandoning their own innovative solutions but

rather evidences their flexible approach, which may lead to the effective integration of the offered solutions with corporate structures. Startups should demonstrate their ability to adapt and their flexibility in adjusting their product, technology and business model in response to corporations' evolving needs. This approach not only enhances the chances for prosperous cooperation but also enables startups to develop in terms of the more complicated and demanding corporate environments. This is crucial in terms of the desire to scale up a startup's activity to enter foreign markets.

5 The managers of startups should be aware of the prospective difficulties and challenges associated with cooperation with large organizations. Diligent preparation for the cooperation process, for example, business or technology-wise, may contribute to more effective cooperation. That is why managers, based on their knowledge of prospective difficulties, should mitigate the risk of their materialization with sufficient lead time. The managers of startups should devise specific procedures and tools that will enable them to respond flexibly to the changing conditions of cooperation and avoid delays or misunderstandings in inter-organizational cooperation.
6 Managers should concentrate on forging sustainable relationships with corporations not only during the course of an acceleration program but also after its formal conclusion (post-acceleration). Managers should be aware that continuing cooperation after the completion of an acceleration program may lead to the startup's more profound integration with the corporation's internal processes, which may lead to elevating the strategic value of both entities. Long-term partnership build trust and tighten the relationships between startups and corporations.

Implications for the management of startup accelerators

One may also indicate the significant implications for the management of startup accelerators based on the conclusions of findings of the research. These implications may substantially contribute to improving management and the more effective utilization of the potential offered by accelerators in terms of inter-organizational cooperation. Samples of these implications encompass the following:

1 The management of accelerators should be aware that corporations and startups have divergent goals and priorities in terms of their cooperation. Accordingly, it is critical to adjust acceleration programs so that the needs and expectations of both parties have a better fit. The key task for the management of accelerators is to create that type of cooperation environment that will allow corporations to achieve their strategic goals while simultaneously supporting the development of startups in the areas that are vital for them. Acceleration programs should be designed in such a way so that on one hand they satisfy the needs of corporations when it

comes to seeking for innovative solutions that may be implemented in their structures or with their partners and so that on the other hand they enable startups to test and develop flexibly their products in a corporate environment.

2 The managers of accelerators should concentrate on delivering added value to startups and corporations. The effectiveness of an acceleration program should be evaluated not only on the basis of the number of companies participating in it, but above all with an eye to the actual benefits both parties gain as a result of their cooperation.
3 Cooperation between corporations and startups, despite the numerous benefits thereof, has many inherent challenges that can affect the effectiveness of the realized acceleration programs. The management of accelerators should actively support the corporations and the startups alike in solving the encountered problems such as the following: bureaucracy, differences in the pace of decision-making, excessive conservatism on the part of corporations.
4 Having in mind the divergent frameworks for acceleration programs, the management of accelerators should give consideration to different operating models so as to adjust them to expectations in the best possible way. It is worth remembering that each one of these models offers distinct benefits and challenges. That is why the management of accelerators should diligently adjust the decision on model selection to a corporation's individual needs and goals in cooperation with the corporation's management team. It is crucial for this process to be based on a profound analysis of the strategic goals of the large organization, its approach to innovations and the expected outcomes from launching an acceleration program for startups. When it comes to the distinct nature of corporations the managers of accelerators should take into account whether a given organization's priority is the rapid implementation of new solutions, long-term engagement of startups in the development of breakthrough technologies or more flexible testing of the submitted projects in the corporation's environment.
5 Management should regularly monitor and evaluate the effectiveness of the startup acceleration programs under management. Systematic evaluation of acceleration programs may be critical for their long-term success and ensuring that they comport with the dynamically changing needs of the market and the expectations of the participating parties. Regularly monitoring results makes it possible to identify areas for improvement. Management should devise a set of indicators that are key for the success of the program and that take into account the perspective of startups (e.g., pace of development, commercialization of products, sourcing capital) and of corporations (e.g., implementing innovations, enhancing operational efficiency, expanding the portfolio of innovative projects). Moreover, introducing systematic mechanisms for evaluation will make it possible to manage risk better and respond more quickly to emerging difficulties.

6 Management should also actively promote acceleration programs involving corporations as an effective tool for establishing inter-organizational cooperation and implementing innovations in large organizations. Managers of accelerators should promote acceleration programs that not only accelerate the development of startups but above all generate benefits for corporations if only by shortening the time to implement innovations and reduce R&D costs. Examples of successful cooperation between corporations and startups may act as a marketing tool to demonstrate the genuine results of such programs and encourage other large organizations to take part in future editions.

Implications for the startup ecosystem

Effective cooperation between corporations and startups in acceleration programs substantiated by real-life business examples associated with marketing innovation not only contributes to the success of both parties but also exerts a substantial impact on the startup ecosystem. The implications for the startup ecosystem stemming from an analysis of the findings of this research and the discussed frameworks for startup accelerators and their programs and from the author's own experience may encompass the following aspects:

1 A higher number of acceleration programs run with the participation of corporations may substantially augment the developmental possibilities for startups and give large organizations more facile access to innovations hailing from outside their bounds. Effective acceleration programs attract new startups, investors and specialists from various industries who want to take part in these programs as participants or associates. As a result, the startup ecosystem is more open to cooperation. This is conducive to the development and diffusion of innovation which contributes to greater competitiveness. This in turn supports the region's economic and technological growth.
2 If corporations and startups succeed in inter-organizational cooperation, then the acceleration programs can attract more new companies into the startup ecosystem. This creates a positive strengthening effect as it incentivizes more corporations to open up to cooperation with young innovative firms and join the programs managed by external accelerators or for large organizations to set up their own business units responsible for scouting and running accelerator activities for startups.
3 Cooperation between startups and corporations may contribute to the creation of integrated ecosystems that bring together different industries and sectors (ranging from finance to technology to heavy industry). This may lead to the creation of innovative solutions and technologies at the crossroads of different fields such as, for instance, the combination of financial technologies (fintech) with artificial intelligence (AI) or block-chain solutions. What is important is that integrated ecosystems

stimulate the transfer of knowledge and technology among different entities. For instance, the merger of data from the health protection, AI and mobile technology sectors may lead to the creation of new solutions in personalized medicine.

4 The development of a startup ecosystem is something that makes a considerable mark on how the region is perceived and augments its attractiveness in the eyes of prospective investors and commercial undertakings. This may contribute to extensive economic, educational and market benefits. A dynamic startup ecosystem fosters the creation of innovative technological and business solutions that in turn attract domestic and foreign investment capital. A region that becomes more competitive and recognizable may attract larger corporations that, when they see potential, decide to open branches or R&D centers, which lends itself to the further development of the startup ecosystem. The growth in the recognition of the local startup ecosystem on the international arena may also lead to tightening cooperation with other more developed ecosystems such as Silicon Valley or the startup ecosystems functioning in Western Europe. This cooperation not only expands the global reach of local companies but also facilitates their access to new markets, capital and technologies. In this manner the development of the startup ecosystem contributes to the creation of conducive conditions for positive feedback. Feedback supports ongoing innovations, economic development and strengthening the position of the region on the map of global innovation centers.

Summary

To recap the results of this monograph one may assert that the scientific goal of this book has been attained in full. The conducted research supplied original and valuable knowledge regarding inter-organizational cooperation between corporations and startups as part of acceleration programs from the vantage point of open innovation theory. The research findings provide practical guidance that may help the parties make better decisions, especially with respect to the selection of startups for acceleration and enhancing cooperation processes. These results also provide a new perspective on scientific literature, thereby contributing to deepening our knowledge about the effective management of inter-organizational cooperation. It is worth emphasizing that the importance of the presented findings extends beyond cooperation between corporations and startups. They also span other key entities in the innovative ecosystem such as venture capital funds that can plan their investments better and public administrative entities responsible for shaping the policy on innovation and entrepreneurship.

The empirical research conducted and the systematized knowledge regarding acceleration programs involving corporations constitute an original contribution in the development of open innovation theory. The conclusions set forth in this monograph form a robust basis for further research and scientific discussions concerning inter-organizational cooperation.

References

Adamczewski, P. (2013). Funkcjonalne determinanty ICT przedsiębiorstw sieciowych. *Zeszyty Naukowe WSB w Poznaniu*, *49*(4), 121.

Adamik, A. (2008). Kumulowanie wiedzy organizacyjnej poprzez związki współpracy. In A. Glińska-Neweś (Ed.), *Zarządzanie organizacjami w gospodarce opartej na wiedzy. Zasobowe podstawy rozwoju organizacji* (pp. 17–35), Toruń: TNOiK, https://katalogi.bn.org.pl/discovery/fulldisplay?docid=alma9912135179705606&context=L&vid=48OMNIS_NLOP:48OMNIS_NLOP&lang=pl&search_scope=NLOP_IZ_NZ&adaptor=Local%20Search%20Engine&isFrbr=true&tab=LibraryCatalog&query=any,exact,Glinska-Neweś,%20Aldona&offset=0.

Adamik, A. (2012). Partnerzy, formy i obszary współpracy małych i średnich przedsiębiorstw w regionie i ich efektywność. In A. Adamik (Ed.), *Współpraca małych i średnich przedsiębiorstw w regionie. Budowanie konkurencyjności firm i regionu* (p. 252), Warszawa: Difin, https://ksiegarnia.difin.pl/wspolpraca-malych-i-srednich-przedsiebiorstw-w-regionie-budowanie-konkurencyjnosci-firm-i-regionu.

Almeida, P., & Kogut, B. (1999). Localization of knowledge and the mobility of engineers in regional networks. *Management Science*, *45*(7), 905–917.

Arreola, F., Favre-Bonte, V., & Tran, S. (2022). The corporate accelerator: A new kind of strategic factor market to access strategic resources. *M@n@gement*, *24*(1), 56–71.

Autio, E., Kenney, M., Mustar, P., Siegel, D., & Wright, M. (2014). Entrepreneurial innovation: The importance of context. *Research Policy*, *43*(7), 1097–1108.

Baloh, P., Jha, S., & Awazu, Y. (2008). Building strategic partnerships for managing innovation outsourcing. *Strategic Outsourcing: An International Journal*, *1*(2), 100–121.

Bannerjee, S., Bielli, S., & Haley, C. (2016). *Scaling together: Overcoming barriers in corporate-startup collaboration*. London: Nesta, Startup Europe, The Scale-Up Institute.

Bańka, M. S., Kukurba, M., Miklaszewicz, S., Trzebiński, A. A., Waszkiewicz, A., & Boulangé, P. (2022). *Crowdfunding: Research & practice* (p. 136), Warszawa: Difin.

Bańka, M., Salwin, M., Kukurba, M., Rychlik, S., Kłos, J., & Sychowicz, M. (2022). Start-up accelerators and their impact on sustainability: Literature analysis and case studies from the energy sector. *Sustainability*, *14*(20), 13397.

Bańka, M., Salwin, M., Waszkiewicz, A. E., Rychlik, S., & Kukurba, M. (2022). Startup accelerators. *International Journal of Management and Economics*, *58*(1), 80–118.

Barczak, B. J. (2012). Źródła efektów synergicznych w sieciach organizacyjnych. In R. Borowiecki & T. Rojek (Ed.), *Współpraca międzyorganizacyjna w działalności przedsiębiorstw: klastry, alianse, sieci* (pp. 1–187), Kraków: Wydawnictwo UE.

Becker, B., & Gassmann, O. (2006). Corporate incubators: Industrial R&D and what universities can learn from them. *The Journal of Technology Transfer*, *31*, 469–483.

Berchicci, L., & Tucci, C. L. (2008). *Entrepreneurship, technology and Schumpeterian innovation: Entrants and incumbents* (pp. 332–351). Oxford: Oxford University Press.

Bidault, F., & Castello, A. (2010). Why too much trust is death to innovation. *MIT Sloan Management Review*, *51*(4), 33.

Blank, S. (2020). *The four steps to the epiphany: Successful strategies for products that win*. New Jersey: John Wiley & Sons.

Blomqvist, K., & Levy, J. (2006). Collaboration capability – A focal concept in knowledge creation and collaborative innovation in networks. *International Journal of Management Concepts and Philosophy*, *2*(1), 31–48.

Brito, C., & Costa e Silva, S. (2009). When trust becomes the fourth. *The Marketing Review*, *9*(4), 289–299.

Bugdol, M. (2010). *Wymiary i problemy zarządzania organizacją opartą na zaufaniu* (p. 7). Kraków: Wydawnictwo Uniwersytetu Jagiellońskiego.

Cegielska, E., & Zawadzka, D. (2017). Źródła finansowania startupów w Polsce. *Annales Universitatis Mariae Curie-Skłodowska, sectio H–Oeconomia*, 51(6), 53–61.

Chesbrough, H. W. (2002). Making sense of corporate venture capital. *Harvard Business Review*, *80*(3), 90–99.

Chesbrough, H. W. (2003). *Open innovation: The new imperative for creating and profiting from technology*. Harvard Business School Publishing Corporation, XXVI.

Chesbrough, H. W. (2003). *Open innovation: The new imperative for creating and profiting from technology*. Brighton, Massachusetts: Harvard Business Press. https://books.google.pl/books/about/Open_Innovation.html?id=4hTRWStFhVgC&redir_esc=y

Chesbrough, H.W. (2006). *Open business models: How to thrive in the new innovation landscape*. Harvard Business Press.

Chesbrough, H. W. (2010). Business model innovation: Opportunities and barriers. *Long Range Planning*, *43*(2–3), 354–363.

Chesbrough, H. W., & Appleyard, M. M. (2007). Open innovation and strategy. *California Management Review*, *50*(1), 57–76.

Christenson, C. (1997). *The innovator's dilemma*. Cambridge, MA: Harvard Business School Press.

Clarysse, B., Wright, M., & Van Hove, J. (2015). *A look inside accelerators*. London: Nesta.

Clarysse, B., & Yusubova, A. (2014). Success factors of business accelerators. In *Technology business incubation mechanisms and sustainable regional development, Proceedings. presented at the technology business incubation mechanisms and sustainable regional development*, Toulouse, France: Toulouse Business School. https://biblio.ugent.be/publication/6842877

Clayton, P., Feldman, M., & Lowe, N. (2018). Behind the scenes: Intermediary organizations that facilitate science commercialization through entrepreneurship. *Academy of Management Perspectives*, *32*(1), 104–124.

Cohen, S. (2013). What do accelerators do? Insights from incubators and angels. *Innovations: Technology, Governance, Globalization*, *8*(3), 19–25.

Crişan, E. L., Salanţă, I. I., Beleiu, I. N., Bordean, O. N., & Bunduchi, R. (2021). A systematic literature review on accelerators. *The Journal of Technology Transfer*, *46*, 62–89.

Czakon, W. (2005). Istota relacji sieciowych przedsiębiorstwa. *Przegląd Organizacji*, *9*, 10–13.

Czakon, W. (2007). Dynamika więzi międzyorganizacyjnych przedsiębiorstwa. *Prace Naukowe. Akademia Ekonomiczna w Katowicach*, *35*, 1–259. https://www.ibuk.pl/fiszka/2309/dynamika-wiezi-miedzyorganizacyjnych-przedsiebiorstwa.html?srsltid=AfmBOoqKy8GqqqRUhE20wMbLDMA1i0fbUKytvN-3lZwCtFfUI5C9R104

Czakon, W. (2011). Metodyka systematycznego przeglądu literatury. *Przegląd Organizacji*, *3*, 57–61.

Czakon, W. (2014). Zarządzanie międzyorganizacyjne jako kompetencja przedsiębiorstwa. In A. K. Koźmiński & D. Latusek-Jurczak (Ed.), *Relacje międzyorganizacyjne w naukach o zarządzaniu* (pp. 186–217), Warszawa: Wolters Kluwer. https://static.profinfo.pl/file/core_products/2017/4/19/f1d8d0d2f0ff4edd016d8b77c9e344bd/pdf40424797_4.pdf?view

Czakon, W. (2016). W kierunku rozwoju badań ilościowych w naukach o zarządzaniu. *Organizacja i Kierowanie*, *173*(3), 41–52.

Dahl, M. S., & Pedersen, C. Ø. (2004). Knowledge flows through informal contacts in industrial clusters: Myth or reality? *Research Policy*, *33*(10), 1673–1686.

Dahlander, L., & Gann, D. M. (2010). How open is innovation? *Research Policy*, *39*(6), 699–709.

Danik, L. (2009). Zaufanie na rynku instytucjonalnym. In H. Brdulak, E. Duliniec, & T. Gołębiowski (red.), *Partnerstwo przedsiębiorstw jako czynnik ograniczania ryzyka działalności gospodarczej* (pp. 25–36). Warszawa: Oficyna Wydawnicza SGH.

Danik, L., & Żukowska, J. (2011). Czynniki wpływające na sukces kooperacji polskich przedsiębiorstw w innowacjach (w przekroju branżowym). *Prace Naukowe Uniwersytetu Ekonomicznego we Wrocławiu. Problemy regionalizmu i globalizacji*, *221*, 123–136.

De Wit, B. (2007). *Meyer r. Synteza strategii*. Warszawa: PWE.

Deakins, D., & Freel, M. (1998). Entrepreneurial learning and the growth process in SMEs. *The Learning Organization*, *5*(3), 144–155.

Donaldson, B., & O'toole, T. (2007). *Strategic market relationships: From strategy to implementation*. New Jersey: John Wiley & Sons.

Dougherty, D., & Hardy, C. (1996). Sustained product innovation in large, mature organizations: Overcoming innovation-to-organization problems. *Academy of Management Journal*, *39*(5), 1120–1153.

Drover, W., Busenitz, L., Matusik, S., Townsend, D., Anglin, A., & Dushnitsky, G. (2017). A review and road map of entrepreneurial equity financing research: Venture capital, corporate venture capital, angel investment, crowdfunding, and accelerators. *Journal of Management*, *43*(6), 1820–1853.

Duczkowska-Piasecka, M. (2012). *Model biznesu w zarządzaniu przedsiębiorstwem*. Warszawa: Oficyna Wydawnicza Szkoła Główna Handlowa w Warszawie.

Dudzik, T., Gołębiowski, T., Lewandowska, M., & Witek-Hajduk, M. (2008). *Modele biznesu polskich przedsiębiorstw* (p. 57). Warszawa: Oficyna Wydawnicza Szkoła Główna Handlowa w Warszawie.

Duysters, G., & Vanhaverbeke, W. (1996). Strategic interactions in DRAM and RISC technology: A network approach. *Scandinavian Journal of Management*, *12*(4), 437–461.
Dyduch, W., & Bratnicki, M. (2015). Tworzenie i przechwytywanie wartości w organizacjach współdziałających w sieci. *Prace Naukowe Wałbrzyskiej Wyższej Szkoły Zarządzania i Przedsiębiorczości*, *32*, 77–93.
Dyduch, W. (2019). Entrepreneurial strategy stimulating value creation: Conceptual findings and some empirical tests. *Entrepreneurial Business and Economics Review*, *7*(3), 65–82.
Dyduch, W. (2021). Tworzenie i przechwytywanie wartości w przedsiębiorstwach w Polsce: ocena podejmowanych działań, identyfikacja kluczowych zmiennych oraz ich wpływ na efektywność. *Przegląd Organizacji*, *6*, 7–16.
Dziewit, W. (2023). *Polskie startupy 2023*. Warszawa: Fundacja Startup Poland. https://startuppoland.org/report/luki-w-ekosystemie-startupowym/
Ekiz, E. H., & Bavik, A. (2008). Scale development process: Service quality in car rental services. *Electronic Journal of Business Research Methods*, *6*(2), 161–174.
Euchner, J. (2016). Emerging models for corporate innovation: Insights from the IRI 2015 strategy forum. *Research-Technology Management*, *59*(1), 56–60.
Fajczak-Kowalska, A. (2012). Wpływ współpracy partnerskiej firm na funkcjonowanie łańcucha dostaw. *Studia Ekonomiczne Regionu Łódzkiego*, *1*, 113.
Fasnacht, D. (2009). Open innovation: The new business paradigm. In *Open innovation in the financial services* (pp. 87–102). Berlin, Heidelberg: Springer. https://link.springer.com/book/10.1007/978-3-540-88231-2#affiliations
Fosfuri, A. (2006). The licensing dilemma: Understanding the determinants of the rate of technology licensing. *Strategic Management Journal*, *27*(12), 1141–1158.
Gambetta, D. (2000). Can we trust trust. *Trust: Making and Breaking Cooperative Relations*, *13*(2000), 213–237.
Ganesan, S., & Hess, R. (1997). Dimensions and levels of trust: Implications for commitment to a relationship. *Marketing Letters*, *8*(4), 439–448.
Gassman, O., & Enkel, E. (2004, July). Towards a theory of open innovation: Three core process archetypes. In *Proceedings of the R&D management conference* (pp. 6–9), Lissabon. https://www.alexandria.unisg.ch/entities/publication/40dcc448-44fa-4f12-b09b-cd614797467d
Gassmann, O., & Enkel, E. (2005). Open innovation Forschung. In M. Weissenberger-Eib (Ed.), *Gestaltung von Innovationssystemen* (pp. 289–308). Kassel: Cactus Group Verlag.
George, D., & Mallery, P. (2019). *IBM SPSS statistics 26 step by step: A simple guide and reference*. New York: Routledge.
Gianiodis, P. T., Ellis, S. C., & Secchi, E. (2010). Advancing a typology of open innovation. *International Journal of Innovation Management*, *14*(4), 531–572.
Gierszewska, G., & Romanowska, M. (2003). *Analiza strategiczna przedsiębiorstwa* (p. 169) Warszawa: PWE.
Gołębiowski, T., & Lewandowska, M. (2010). Kooperacja a sprawność marketingowa przedsiębiorstw na przykładzie polskich przedsiębiorstw przemysłu elektromaszynowego. Zeszyty Naukowe/Szkoła Główna Handlowa. *Kolegium Gospodarki Światowej*, *27*, 202–224.
Gulati, R. (1998). Alliances and networks. *Strategic Management Journal*, *19*(4), 293–317.

Gulati, R. (1999). Network location and learning: The influence of network resources and firm capabilities on alliance formation. *Strategic Management Journal*, *20*(5), 397–420.

Gutmann, T., Kanbach, D., & Seltman, S. (2019). Exploring the benefits of corporate accelerators: Investigating the SAP Industry 4.0 Startup Program. *Problems and Perspectives in Management*, *17*(3), 218.

Gutmann, T., Maas, C., Kanbach, D., & Stubner, S. (2020). Startups in a corporate accelerator: What is satisfying, what is relevant and what can corporates improve? *International Journal of Entrepreneurship and Innovation Management*, *24*(6), 413–442.

Gwarda-Gruszczyńska, E. (2013). *Modele procesu komercjalizacji nowych technologii w przedsiębiorstwach. Uwarunkowania wyboru-kluczowe obszary decyzji* (pp. 10–11). Łódź: Wydawnictwo Uniwersytetu Łódzkiego.

Hagedoorn, J. (1993). Understanding the rationale of strategic technology partnering: Interorganizational modes of cooperation and sectoral differences. *Strategic Management Journal*, *14*(5), 371–385.

Hair, J. F., Black, W. C., Babin, B. J., & Anderson, R. E. (2014). *Multivariate data analysis: Pearson new international edition* (Vol. 1, No. 2). Essex: Pearson Education Limited.

Hallen, B. L., Bingham, C. B., & Cohen, S. (2014). Do accelerators accelerate? A study of venture accelerators as a path to success? In *Academy of management proceedings* (Vol. 2014, No. 1, p. 12955). Briarcliff Manor, NY: Academy of Management. https://doi.org/10.5465/ambpp.2014.185

Harrison, J. S., Hitt, M. A., Hoskisson, R. E., & Ireland, R. D. (2001). Resource complementarity in business combinations: Extending the logic to organizational alliances. *Journal of Management*, *27*(6), 679–690.

Hausberg, J. P., & Korreck, S. (2020). Business incubators and accelerators: A co-citation analysis-based, systematic literature review. *The Journal of Technology Transfer*, *45*, 151–176.

Heinzelmann, N., Selig, C. J., & Baltes, G. H. (2020, June). Critical actions of and synergies between corporate entrepreneurship programs. *In 2020 IEEE international conference on engineering, technology and innovation (ICE/ITMC)* (pp. 1–9). IEEE.

Hill, C. W., Jones, G. R., & Schilling, M. A. (2014). *Strategic management: Theory & cases: An integrated approach*. Boston: Cengage Learning.

Hinkin, T. R., Tracey, J. B., & Enz, C. A. (1997). Scale construction: Developing reliable and valid measurement instruments. *Journal of Hospitality & Tourism Research*, *21*(1), 100–120.

Hirt, M., & Willmott, P. (2014). Strategic principles for competing in the digital age. *McKinsey Quarterly*, *5*(1), 1–13.

Hochberg, Y. V. (2016). Accelerating entrepreneurs and ecosystems: The seed accelerator model. *Innovation Policy and the Economy*, *16*(1), 25–51.

Hochberg, Y. V., & Fehder, D. C. (2015). Accelerators and ecosystems. *Science*, *348*(6240), 1202–1203.

https://www.parp.gov.pl/storage/grants/documents/21/Lista_projektow_wybranych_do_dofinansowania.pdf

https://www.prisma-statement.org/

Hutter, K., Gfrerer, A., & Lindner, B. (2021). From popular to profitable: Incumbents experiences and challenges with external corporate accelerators. *International Journal of Innovation Management*, *25*(3), 2150035.

Jackson, P., & Richter, N. (2017). Situational logic: An analysis of open innovation using corporate accelerators. *International Journal of Innovation Management*, *21*(7), 1750062.

Jap, S. D. (2001). "Pie sharing" in complex collaboration contexts. *Journal of Marketing Research*, *38*(1), 86–99.

Jelonek, A., & Moczała, D. (2020). *Metody I techniki projektowania innowacji*. Warszawa: Polskie Wydawnictwo Ekonomiczne.

Jung, S. (2018). Cooperating with start-ups as a strategy: Towards corporate entrepreneurship and innovation. In D. Jelonek & A. Moczała (Eds.), *Technology entrepreneurship: Insights in new technology-based firms, research spin-offs and corporate environments* (pp. 283–298) Warszawa: Polskie Wydawnictwo Ekonomiczne.

Kale, P., Dyer, J. H., & Singh, H. (2002). Alliance capability, stock market response, and long-term alliance success: The role of the alliance function. *Strategic Management Journal*, *23*(8), 747–767.

Kanbach, D. K., & Stubner, S. (2016). Corporate accelerators as recent form of startup engagement: The what, the why, and the how. *Journal of Applied Business Research (JABR)*, *32*(6), 1761–1776.

Kanter, R. M. (2006). Innovation: The classic traps. *Harvard Business Review*, *84*(11), 72.

Katz, M. L. (1986). An analysis of cooperative research and development. *The RAND Journal of Economics*, *17*(4), 527–543.

Katz, M. L. (1995). Joint ventures as a means of assembling complementary inputs. In Kalyan Chatterjee & Barbara Gray (Eds.), *International joint ventures: Economic and organizational perspectives* (pp. 5–22). Dordrecht: Springer. https://link.springer.com/chapter/10.1007/978-94-017-1944-5_2

Katz, R., & Allen, T. J. (1985). Organizational issues in the introduction of new technologies. In Paul R. Kleindorfer (Ed.), *The management of productivity and technology in manufacturing* (pp. 275–300). Boston, MA: Springer. https://link.springer.com/chapter/10.1007/978-1-4613-2507-9_12

Kaufmann, L., & Astou Saw, A. (2014). Using a multiple-informant approach in SCM research. *International Journal of Physical Distribution & Logistics Management*, *44*(6), 511–527.

Kelly, M. J., Schaan, J. L., & Joncas, H. (2002). Managing alliance relationships: Key challenges in the early stages of collaboration. *R&D Management*, *32*(1), 11–22.

Khanna, T., Gulati, R., & Nohria, N. (1998). The dynamics of learning alliances: Competition, cooperation, and relative scope. *Strategic Management Journal*, *19*(3), 193–210.

Klimas, P. (2012). Operacjonalizacja bliskości organizacyjnej. *Prace Naukowe Uniwersytetu Ekonomicznego we Wrocławiu*, *260*, 195–205.

Klimas, P. (2014). *Sieci innowacji: implikacje bliskości organizacyjnej*. Katowice: Prace Naukowe/Uniwersytet Ekonomiczny w Katowicach.

Kohler, T. (2016). Corporate accelerators: Building bridges between corporations and startups. *Business Horizons*, *59*(3), 347–357.

Komssi, M., Pichlis, D., Raatikainen, M., Kindström, K., & Järvinen, J. (2014). What are hackathons for? *IEEE Software*, *32*(5), 60–67.

Koźmiński, A. K., & Latusek-Jurczak, D. (2014). *Relacje międzyorganizacyjne w naukach o zarządzaniu*, Warszawa: Wolters Kluwer.

Krzakiewicz, K., & Cyfert, S. (2019). Strategic orientations of the organization-entrepreneurial, market and organizational learning. *Management*, *23*(1), 7–19.

Krzakiewicz, K., & Cyfert, S. (2020). *Podstawy zarządzania organizacjami*. Poznań: Wydawnictwo UEP, https://wydawnictwo.ue.poznan.pl/book.html?isbn=978-83-8211-034-0.

Kupp, M., Marval, M., & Borchers, P. (2017). Corporate accelerators: Fostering innovation while bringing together startups and large firms. *Journal of Business Strategy*, *38*(6), 47–53.

Latusek-Jurczak, D. (2014). Sieci międzyorganizacyjne jako struktury współpracy – podstawowe pojęcia analityczne. In A. K. Koźmiński & D. Latusek-Jurczak (Ed.), *Relacje międzyorganizacyjne w naukach o zarządzaniu, wyd. Relacje międzyorganizacyjne w naukach o zarządzaniu* (pp. 23–45), Warszawa: Difin, https://repozytorium.kozminski.edu.pl/pl/system/files/Relacje%20 miedzyorganizacyjne_0.pdf.

Levy, Y., & Ellis, T. J. (2006). A systems approach to conduct an effective literature review in support of information systems research. *Informing Science*, *9*, 181–212, http://www.inform.nu/Articles/Vol9/V9p181-212Levy99.pdf.

Lewandowska, M. S. (2018). *Koncepcja otwartych innowacji: perspektywa polskich przedsiębiorstw przemysłowych* (p. 116). Warszawa: Oficyna Wydawnicza SGH.

Liberati, A., Altman, D. G., Tetzlaff, J., Mulrow, C., Gøtzsche, P. C., Ioannidis, J. P., ... Moher, D. (2009). The PRISMA statement for reporting systematic reviews and meta-analyses of studies that evaluate health care interventions: Explanation and elaboration. *Annals of Internal Medicine*, *151*(4), W–65.

Liebeskind, J. P., Oliver, A. L., Zucker, L., & Brewer, M. (1996). Social networks, learning, and flexibility: Sourcing scientific knowledge in new biotechnology firms. *Organization Science*, *7*(4), 428–443.

Lyytinen, K., Yoo, Y., & Boland Jr, R. J. (2016). Digital product innovation within four classes of innovation networks. *Information Systems Journal*, *26*(1), 47–75.

Madjar, N., Greenberg, E., & Chen, Z. (2011) Factors for radical creativity, incremental creativity, and routine, noncreative performance. *Journal of Applied Psychology*, *96*, 730–743.

Mahmoud-Jouini, S. B., Duvert, C., & Esquirol, M. (2018). Key factors in building a corporate accelerator capability: Developing an effective corporate accelerator requires close attention to the relationships between startups and the sponsoring company. *Research-Technology Management*, *61*(4), 26–34.

Markides, C. (2006). Disruptive innovation: In need of better theory. *Journal of Product Innovation Management*, *23*(1), 19–25.

Mayer, R. C., Davis, J. H., & Schoorman, F. D. (1995). An integrative model of organizational trust. *Academy of Management Review*, *20*(3), 709–734.

Mishigragchaa, B. (2017). Accelerators as a tool to support startup ventures: Assessing their performance and success factors. *Literature Review. Studia i Prace WNEiZ US*, *48*(1), 9–19.

Mocker, V., Bielli, S., & Haley, C. (2015). *Winning Together: A guide to successful corporate-startup collaborations*. London: Nesta.

Moschner, S. L., Fink, A. A., Kurpjuweit, S., Wagner, S. M., & Herstatt, C. (2019). Toward a better understanding of corporate accelerator models. *Business Horizons*, *62*(5), 637–647.

Nandi, A., & Mandernach, M. (2016, February). Hackathons as an informal learning platform. In *Proceedings of the 47th ACM technical symposium on computing science education* (pp. 346–351), Memphis Tennessee, https://dl.acm.org/doi/proceedings/10.1145/2839509.

Ng, S. T., Rose, T. M., Mak, M., & Chen, S. E. (2002). Problematic issues associated with project partnering—The contractor perspective. *International Journal of Project Management*, *20*(6), 437–449.
Niemczyk, J. (2009). chciałbyś coś odkryć? *Przegląd Organizacji*, *10*, 3–5.
Niemczyk, J. (2016). Formułowanie i wartościowanie problemów naukowych. In W. Czakon (Ed.), *Podstawy metodologii badań w naukach o zarządzaniu* (pp. 103–118), Warszawa: Wydawnictwo Nieoczywiste.
Nooteboom, B. (1999). Innovation and inter-firm linkages: New implications for policy. *Research Policy*, *28*(8), 793–805.
Nowak, D. (2010). Bariery rozwoju powiązań kooperacyjnych w ocenie polskich przedsiębiorstw. *Zeszyty Naukowe Uniwersytetu Szczecińskiego. Finanse, Rynki Finansowe, Ubezpieczenia* (34 Uwarunkowania wzrostu wartości przedsiębiorstw w warunkach konkurencji), *34*, 289–302, http://bazekon.icm.edu.pl/bazekon/element/bwmeta1.element.ekon-element-000171289685.
Nowak, D. (2012). *Zarządzanie międzyorganizacyjnymi relacjami kooperacyjnymi w przedsiębiorstwach przemysłowych*. Poznań: Wydawnictwo Uniwersytetu Ekonomicznego w Poznaniu.
Pachura, A. (2015). Kultura organizacyjna a potencjał kreatywności przedsiębiorstwa. *Zeszyty Naukowe Wyższej Szkoły Humanitas. Zarządzanie*, *3*, 87–97.
Pauwels, C., Clarysse, B., Wright, M., & Van Hove, J. (2016). Understanding a new generation incubation model: The accelerator. *Technovation*, *50*, 13–24.
Peters, C., Blohm, I., & Leimeister, J. M. (2015). Anatomy of successful business models for complex services: Insights from the telemedicine field. *Journal of Management Information Systems*, *32*(3), 75–104.
Podręcznik Oslo (2020). *Zalecenia dotyczące pozyskiwania, prezentowania i wykorzystywania danych z zakresu innowacji. Pomiar działalności naukowo-technicznej i innowacyjnej* (p. 50). Warszawa, Szczecin: GUS.
Porter, M. E. (2006). *Przewaga konkurencyjna: Osiąganie i utrzymywanie lepszych wyników*. Gliwice: Helion.
Post, J. E., & Altma, B. W. (1994). Managing the environmental change process: Barriers and opportunities. *Journal of Organizational Change Management*, *7*, 64–81, https://www.semanticscholar.org/paper/Managing-the-Environmental-Change-Process%3A-Barriers-Post-Altma/f3f5bd9a19f29ea67eafbb51aa37c98bfc5d21eb.
Powell, W. W. (1987). Hybrid organizational arrangements: New form or transitional development? *California Management Review*, *30*(1), 67–87.
Poznańska, K. (2014). Sieci współpracy a innowacyjność przedsiębiorstw. In A. Sopińska & S. Gregorczyk (Ed.), *Granice strukturalnej złożoności organizacji* (pp. 151–160). Warszawa: Oficyna Wydawnicza SGH.
Prexl, K. M., Hubert, M., Beck, S., Heiden, C., & Prügl, R. (2019). Identifying and analysing the drivers of heterogeneity among ecosystem builder accelerators. *R&D Management*, *49*(4), 624–638.
Reimsbach, D., & Hauschild, B. (2012). Corporate venturing: An extended typology. *Journal of Management Control*, *23*, 71–80.
Rethlefsen, M. L., Kirtley, S., Waffenschmidt, S., Ayala, A. P., Moher, D., Page, M. J., & Koffel, J. B. (2021). PRISMA-S: An extension to the PRISMA statement for reporting literature searches in systematic reviews. *Systematic Reviews*, *10*, 1–19.
Richter, N., Jackson, P., & Schildhauer, T. (2018). Outsourcing creativity: An abductive study of open innovation using corporate accelerators. *Creativity and Innovation Management*, *27*(1), 69–78.

Ries, E. (2011). *The lean startup: How today's entrepreneurs use continuous innovation to create radically successful businesses*. Currency.
Rigg, C., & O'Dwyer, B. (2012). Becoming an entrepreneur: Researching the role of mentors in identity construction. *Education+ Training*, *54*(4), 319–329.
Roszkowska-Menkes, M. (2015). *Otwarte innowacje: w poszukiwaniu równowagi* (p. 125), Warszawa: Oficyna Wydawnicza Szkoły Głównej Handlowej w Warszawie.
Rutkowski, I. P. (2007). *Rozwój nowego produktu: metody i uwarunkowania*. Warszawa: Polskie Wydawnictwo Ekonomiczne.
Saebi, T., & Foss, N. J. (2015). Business models for open innovation: Matching heterogeneous open innovation strategies with business model dimensions. *European Management Journal*, *33*(3), 201–213.
Sakakibara, M. (1997). Heterogeneity of firm capabilities and cooperative research and development: An empirical examination of motives. *Strategic Management Journal*, *18*(S1), 143–164.
Selig, C. J., Gasser, T., & Baltes, G. H. (2018, June). How corporate accelerators foster organizational transformation: An internal perspective. In *2018 IEEE international conference on engineering, technology and innovation (ICE/ITMC)* (pp. 1–9). Stuttgart: IEEE.
Serwatka, A. (2018). Accelerators for startups in Europe. *Copernican Journal of Finance & Accounting*, *7*(1), 67–81.
Shankar, R. K., & Shepherd, D. A. (2019). Accelerating strategic fit or venture emergence: Different paths adopted by corporate accelerators. *Journal of Business Venturing*, *34*(5), 105886.
Shetty, S., Sundaram, R., & Achuthan, K. (2020). Assessing and comparing top accelerators in Brazil, India, and the USA: Through the lens of new ventures' performance. *Entrepreneurial Business and Economics Review*, *8*(2), 153–177.
Skala, A. (2018). *Startupy. Wyzwanie dla zarządzania i edukacji przedsiębiorczości*. Kraków: Wydawnictwo edu-Libri.
Skrzypek, A., & Sagan, S. (2018). Open innovation in business models. *Annales Universitatis Mariae Curie-Skłodowska. Sectio H. Oeconomia*, *52*(6), 97–109.
Skrzypek, E., & Skrzypek, A. (2019). Uwarunkowania i konsekwencje innowacyjności organizacji w gospodarce współdzielenia. In M. Cisek (Ed.), *Innowacje i cyfryzacja gospodarki* (pp. 25–44), Siedlce: Uniwersytet Przyrodniczo-Humanistyczny w Siedlcach.
Sopińska, A., & Dziurski, P. (2018). *Otwarte innowacje: perspektywa współpracy i zarządzania wiedzą*. Oficyna Wydawnicza SGH.
Sopińska, A., & Mierzejewska, W. (2017). *Otwarte innowacje produktowe realizowane przez przedsiębiorstwa działające w Polsce: podejście zasobowe* (p. 37), Warszawa: Oficyna Wydawnicza SGH.
Stępień, B. (2011). *Międzynarodowa kooperacja gospodarcza z polskiej perspektywy* (p. 15). Warszawa: Polskie Wydawnictwo Ekonomiczne.
St-Jean, E. (2012). Mentoring as professional development for novice entrepreneurs: Maximizing the learning 1. *International Journal of Training and Development*, *16*(3), 200–216.
Strzyżewska, M. (2011). *Współpraca między przedsiębiorstwami-odniesienie do polskiej praktyki*. Warszawa: Oficyna Wydawnicza SGH.
Svensson, G. (2004). Vulnerability in business relationships: The gap between dependence and trust. *Journal of Business & Industrial Marketing*, *19*(7), 469–483.

Świeszczak, K. (2017). Akceleratory przedsiębiorczości tworzone przez banki jako instytucjonalna forma wsparcia sektora FinTech. *Finanse*, *1*, 239–250, https://cejsh.icm.edu.pl/cejsh/element/bwmeta1.element.oai-journals-pan-pl-102469/c/oai-journals-pan-pl-102469_full-text_Fin._201_10_-17_2014-K.Swieszczak.pdf.

Szewc, A., Zioło, K., & Grzesiczak, M. (2011). *Umowy jako prawne narzędzie transferu innowacji*. Warszawa: Polska Agencja Rozwoju Przedsiębiorczości.

Tether, B. S., & Tajar, A. (2008). The organisational-cooperation mode of innovation and its prominence amongst European service firms. *Research Policy*, *37*(4), 720–739.

Thiel, P., & Masters, B. (2014). *Zero to one: Notes on startups, or how to build the future*. Currency. New York: Crown Currency Publishing Group.

Thorelli, H. B. (1986). Networks: Between markets and hierarchies. *Strategic Management Journal*, *7*(1), 37–51.

Tidström, A. (2006). Conflicts when competitors cooperate: Exploring elements of conflicts from a business network perspective. *Svenska handelshögskolan*, *13*, 1–236, https://harisportal.hanken.fi/en/publications/conflicts-when-competitors-cooperate-exploring-elements-of-confli.

Trotter, A. (2013). Six Lessons for corporations building innovation accelerators. *Strategy & Innovation*, *11*. https://www.innosight.com/insight/six-lessons-for-corporations-building-innovation-accelerators/

Tuusjärvi, E., & Möller, K. (2009). Multiplicity of norms in inter-company cooperation. *Journal of Business & Industrial Marketing*, *24*(7), 519–528.

Urbaniec, M., & Żur, A. (2021). Business model innovation in corporate entrepreneurship: Exploratory insights from corporate accelerators. *International Entrepreneurship and Management Journal*, *17*(2), 865–888.

Van Beers, C., & Zand, F. (2014). R&D cooperation, partner diversity, and innovation performance: An empirical analysis. *Journal of Product Innovation Management*, *31*(2), 292–312.

Veit, P., Kramer, A., Kanbach, D., & Stubner, S. (2021). Revising the taxonomy of corporate accelerators: Moving towards an evolutionary perspective. *International Journal of Entrepreneurial Venturing*, *13*(6), 568–599.

Venkatraman, N., & Grant, J. H. (1986). Construct measurement in organizational strategy research: A critique and proposal. *Academy of Management Review*, *11*(1), 71–87.

Von Hippel, E. (2005). Democratizing innovation: The evolving phenomenon of user innovation. *Journal für Betriebswirtschaft*, *55*, 63–78.

Weiblen, T., & Chesbrough, H. W. (2015). Engaging with startups to enhance corporate innovation. *California Management Review*, *57*(2), 66–90.

Wilding, R., & Humphries, A. S. (2006). Understanding collaborative supply chain relationships through the application of the Williamson organisational failure framework. *International Journal of Physical Distribution & Logistics Management*, *36*(4), 308–329.

Wojcik, P., Obłój, K., Wąsowska, A., & Wierciński, S. (2020). Corporate acceleration process: A systems psychodynamics perspective. *Journal of Organizational Change Management*, *33*(6), 1163–1180.

Yuan, F., & Woodman, R. W. (2010). Innovative behavior in the workplace: The role of performance and image outcome expectations. *Academy of Management Journal*, *53*(2), 323–342.

Zakrzewska-Bielawska, A. (2016). Tworzenie i apropriacja wartości jako cel strategii relacyjnej przedsiębiorstwa. *Prace Naukowe Uniwersytetu Ekonomicznego we Wrocławiu*, *444*, 609–622.

Zakrzewska-Bielawska, A., & Adamik, A. (2013). Organizacja w sieciach współpracy – od prostych do złożonych form współpracy międzyorganizacyjnej. In A. Adamik (Ed.), *Nauka o organizacji. Ujęcie dynamiczne*. Warszawa: Oficyna Wolters Kluwer Business, 440–473. http://zakrzewskabielawska.pl/wp-content/uploads/2021/03/publikacja_PODR_6.pdf.

Zastempowski, M., & Cyfert, S. (2023). A new angle on SMEs' competitiveness. How do agility capabilities affect a firm's competitive position? *Journal of Organizational Change Management*, *36*(4), 635–662.

Zedtwitz, M. V. (2003). Classification and management of incubators: Aligning strategic objectives and competitive scope for new business facilitation. *International Journal of Entrepreneurship and Innovation Management*, *3*(1–2), 176–196.

Zott, C., & Amit, R. (2010). Business model design: An activity system perspective. *Long Range Planning*, *43*(2–3), 216–226.

For Product Safety Concerns and Information please contact our EU
representative GPSR@taylorandfrancis.com
Taylor & Francis Verlag GmbH, Kaufingerstraße 24, 80331 München, Germany

www.ingramcontent.com/pod-product-compliance
Ingram Content Group UK Ltd.
Pitfield, Milton Keynes, MK11 3LW, UK
UKHW020150200926
475702UK00016B/2645
9781032889221